MW01038673

THE RIDDLES OF JESUS
IN JOHN

THE SOCIETY OF BIBLICAL LITERATURE
MONOGRAPH SERIES

Number 53
THE RIDDLES OF JESUS
IN JOHN
A Study in Tradition and Folklore
by
Tom Thatcher

THE RIDDLES OF JESUS
IN JOHN
A Study in Tradition and Folklore

Tom Thatcher

Society of Biblical Literature
Atlanta, Georgia

THE RIDDLES OF JESUS
IN JOHN
A Study in Tradition and Folklore

by
Tom Thatcher

Library of Congress Cataloging-in-Publication Data

Thatcher, Tom, 1967–
    The riddles of Jesus in John : a study in tradition and folklore / Tom Thatcher.
        p. cm.—(Monograph series / The Society of Biblical Literature ; no. 53)
    Includes bibliographical references and index.
    ISBN 0-88414-018-0 (hardcover : alk. paper)
    1. Bible. N.T. John—Criticism, interpretation, etc. 2. Folklore in the Bible.
    3. Riddles. I. Title. II. Monograph series (Society of Biblical Literature) ; no. 53.

    BS 2615.2.T46 2000
    226.5'066—dc21   00-027169

08 07 06 05 04 03 02 01 00   5 4 3 2 1

Printed in the United States of America
on acid-free paper

to

Becky,

my partner in everything

CONTENTS

ABBREVIATIONS

This study will utilize all standard abbreviations defined in the 1994 *Society of Biblical Literature Membership Directory and Handbook* (Decatur, GA: Society of Biblical Literature, 1995). The following abbreviations, which are not included in that handbook, will also be used. For complete citations, see the Bibliography.

BLD   Roger D. Abrahams, *Between the Living and the Dead: Riddles Which Tell Stories*

FE   The Fourth Evangelist, author of the Gospel of John

FFC   Folklore Fellows Communications Series

FG   The Fourth Gospel, or Gospel of John

FGIP   Robert T. Fortna, *The Fourth Gospel and Its Predecessor: From Narrative Source to Present Gospel*

FOW   Fernando F. Segovia, *The Farewell of the Word: The Johannine Call to Abide*

FTTG   Martin Dibelius, *From Tradition to Gospel*

GBSNTS   Guides to Biblical Scholarship New Testament Series (Fortress)

GID   Tzvetan Todorov, *Genres in Discourse*

HST   Rudolf Bultmann, *The History of the Synoptic Tradition*

HTFG   C. H. Dodd, *Historical Tradition in the Fourth Gospel*

JAF   *Journal of American Folklore*

LOR   W. J. Pepicello and Thomas A. Green, *The Language of Riddles: New Perspectives*

LRJT   Fernando F. Segovia, *Love Relationships in the Johannine Tradition:* Agapē/Agapan *in I John and the Fourth Gospel*

S&I   Tzvetan Todorov, *Symbolism and Interpretation*

SG   Robert Fortna's "Signs Gospel," a narrative source of the Gospel of John
SSG   Rudolf Bultmann, *The Study of the Synoptic Gospels*
TGOS   Robert T. Fortna, *The Gospel of Signs*
WF   *Western Folklore*, formerly *California Folklore Quarterly*

Multi–volume works are cited by volume and page number, separated by the decimal point. For example, Raymond Brown's two–volume Anchor Bible commentary on John is cited as

Brown, AB 1.25–26

indicating that the reference is to volume 1, pages 25–26.

All reprinted works include the original publication date after the title, followed by the publication information for the reprint:

Roman Jakobson, "Implications of Language Universals for Linguistics" (1961; rpt. in *On Language*, ed. Linda R. Waugh and Monique Monville–Burston [Cambridge, MA: Harvard University Press, 1990]) 110.

This citation indicates that Jakobson's paper was written in 1961 but cited here from the 1990 reprint.

Chapter 1
The Other Consensus

This study will suggest that the Fourth Gospel (FG) includes a large number of verses which may be categorized as "riddles." These riddles are scattered throughout the dialogues of Jesus in FG, many of which are structured as "riddling sessions." The presence of these riddles and riddling sessions is significant both to the exegesis of the passages in which they occur and to broader issues relating to the unity and composition–history of FG. In fact, the implications of this study, which are developed in Chapters 5–8, are sweeping, and challenge many of the standard approaches and conclusions of Johannine studies.

In light of these broad claims, it will be necessary to begin by explaining why Johannine scholars have failed to recognize these riddles and riddling sessions up to this point in time. Chapters 1–3 will provide this explanation. As will be seen, conventional approaches to the tradition–history of FG have utilized tools which are inherently incapable of identifying folk forms such as the riddle in written texts. Biblical Form Criticism has depended heavily on the comparative analysis of written documents, and has emphasized form over function. This approach makes it impossible to identify folk genres which are defined by function more than form, and which therefore do not often generate close "parallels." Along with this general deficiency in Form Criticism, Johannine scholars have been particularly reticent to look for specific folk genres in FG under the premise that the speeches of FG do not contain a substantial amount of Jesus tradition. It has therefore been deemed unnecessary to explore the possibility that portions of FG's discourses might be patterned after oral genres such as the riddle.

1

The remainder of Chapter 1 will attempt to document this bias against the Johannine speeches in the last century. Chapters 2 and 3 will then define a new approach to oral forms which is more suitable to the identification of riddles and similar speech genres in written texts.

D. Moody Smith's 1992 *John Among the Gospels* suggests that "the twentieth century has, in fact, more than once witnessed the dissolution of a consensus on the relationship of John to the Synoptic Gospels." Since a decision about FG's relationship to the Synoptics is prerequisite to any discussion of sources, Smith's analysis makes it possible to divide recent discussion of FG's sources into three eras. Early in this century, the Fourth Evangelist's (FE's) "positive use" of the Synoptics "was widely, if not universally, granted." This may be referred to as the "Bacon Era," since B. W. Bacon is perhaps the best known representative of this position. But gradually "the early consensus crumbled and was replaced by a consensus that represented almost the opposite point of view."[1] FG's possible dependence on the Synoptics was now questioned, and other sources, both oral and written, were sought. This new consensus so dominated Johannine scholarship in the mid–twentieth century that "in the past three decades [1960–1990] there has been no major new commentary . . . in which the fourth evangelist's knowledge of the Synoptics has been presupposed."[2] Because this shift was largely initiated by P. Gardner–Smith's *St. John and the Synoptic Gospels*, it is appropriate to refer to this consensus as the "Gardner–Smith Era."[3]

But Smith notes that "there is no question that the Gardner–Smith consensus is now significantly eroded." A number of scholars, particularly those associated with the "Leuven School" led by Franz Neirynck, have returned to the earlier position that FE knew the Synoptics and used them as a primary source. This approach does not concern itself with non–Synoptic sources, generally holding that "insofar as John departs from the Synoptics his

---

[1] D. Moody Smith, *John Among the Gospels: The Relationship in Twentieth–Century Research* (Minneapolis, MN: Augsburg–Fortress, 1992), both quotations 10.

[2] D. Smith, *John Among* 69, 189, quotation 69.

[3] P. Gardner–Smith, *St. John and the Synoptic Gospels* (Cambridge: Cambridge University Press, 1938). D. Smith notes that this book was almost unknown in Europe until after the Second World War (*John Among* 47–48).

redaction is original, his own composition, and serves a theological rather than historical purpose."[4] This period may be referred to as the "Neirynck Era." The Neirynck Era is notable not for the dominance of any particular consensus, but for the lack of one. At present the question of FG's sources is generating a number of conflicting views from numerous methodological approaches.

But another consensus, which Smith does not discuss, runs as an undercurrent through all three eras. The debate over FG's relationship to the Synoptics, or to other unknown sources, has been conducted exclusively in the arena of John's *narratives*. Many scholars in this century have, indeed, argued that FG's discourses are based on older traditional material, and that the present text occasionally opens a window to this earlier layer of tradition. But at some point in the compositional history, and particularly in the development of FG's discourses, this window was closed by an appropriation process which Francis J. Moloney has referred to as "johannisation."[5] This "other consensus," *that FG's discourses are primarily "Johannine" compositions,* has not dissolved at any point, and continues to provide a common ground for discussion. As a result, the great interest shown this century in the sources and traditions behind FG has not produced a sustained argument that large units of FG's discourses may be patterned after oral speech genres such as the riddle.

To demonstrate this Other Consensus, it will be necessary to review representative efforts to define the sources of FG in all three eras described above. This survey will also indicate the necessary course of the present study.

JOHN'S DISCOURSES IN THE BACON ERA

The Bacon Era saw a continuation of the traditional view that FG's primary sources were the Synoptics. Similarities between FG and the Synoptics were highlighted, and differences were attributed to FE's unique theological perspective. The discourse sections of FG, which vary

---

[4]D. Smith, *John Among,* first quotation 139, second quotation 181.

[5]See Francis J. Moloney, *The Johannine Son of Man* (Biblioteca Di Scienze Religiose 14; Rome: Libreria Ateneo Salesiano, 1976) 214; also J. Coppens, "Les logia johanniques du fils de l'homme," *L'Évangile de Jean: Sources, Rédaction, Théologie* (ed. Marinus de Jonge; BETL 44; Leuven: Leuven University Press, 1977) 314.

considerably from the Synoptics in style and content, were generally explained as FE's free compositions or creative expansions of Synoptic material. It was therefore deemed unnecessary to search for speech genres in FG which did not find immediate parallels in the Synoptics.

Early in the twentieth century, B. W. Bacon suggested that FG was written "to remedy (from doctrinal, not historical–critical motives) those 'defects' of Mark" which made Mark incompatible with FE's second–century environment.[6] Bacon believes that all of FG can be explained as FE's creative adaptation of the Synoptics to the needs of a later day. In FE's method, Matthew is largely ignored, "Mark is made the basis," and "supplements and changes are made by using Luke," or by further developing Mark along the lines set by Luke's precedent. Although the recasting is at times drastic, nothing is left out: "the fourth evangelist really employs every available shred of Mark in his own way; nor has he even added, except from Luke."[7]

Bacon's view that FG is a recasting of Synoptic episodes and themes rules out any independent "traditional" element. This is especially true of the discourses, which Bacon portrays as johannised versions of Synoptic speeches and sayings. The dialogue between Jesus and the Jews after the Bethesda healing at John 5:1–47 illustrates FE's "free combination of Mark and the Discourses, in a manner to 'bring out' the doctrinal values" by using the methods of "haggadah and midrash" with "truly Pauline freedom."[8] John 10:1–16 and 15:1–6 are Christological allegories spun out of parables from Mark and Luke. The Johannine Farewell reformulates and combines Mark's two eschatological discourses and Luke's two missions of the disciples along three major themes: "the disciples' work (Jn. 15:1–16)"; "their conflict with

---

[6]Benjamin Wisner Bacon, *The Fourth Gospel in Research and Debate* (New York, NY: Moffatt and Yard, 1910) 365, 371. Bacon dates FG between 110–120 CE.

[7]Bacon, *Research and Debate*, first quotation 367–368, second quotation 381. Bacon's method allows him to conclude that even FG's prologue is a revision of Mark 1:1–13. The changes, though "indeed profound," have "a completely adequate key in the basic postulates of Johannine (and Pauline) christology, to [explain] all the transformations effected" (374). Although Bacon believes that FE had been to Jerusalem on pilgrimage and could therefore occasionally add "a minute trace of much distorted historic tradition," he concludes that FE's qualifications and motives were spiritual rather than historical (383).

[8]Bacon, *Research and Debate* 380.

the world (15:17–16:4)"; and, "the promise of the Spirit (16:5–33; 13:36–14:31)."[9] Since all of FG's discourses could be explained as mutations of Synoptic material, Bacon did not need to explore the possibility that FG's discourses might follow non–Synoptic patterns and motifs.

B. H. Streeter's *The Four Gospels* introduced the influential Four Source Theory of Synoptic relationships. Streeter maintains the traditional view that FG must be included in considerations of the "Synoptic problem." Although contacts between FG and Matthew are "extremely slight," Streeter holds that "John is dependent on Luke as well as on Mark," using Mark and Luke in a way similar to Luke's use of Mark and Q. Aside from Mark and Luke, FE utilized no other written sources.[10] Mark, Luke, and John therefore form a series, "Luke being dependent on Mark, and John on both the others," and reveal a theological evolution from Jewish apocalyptic to universal Gentile mission.[11]

Unlike Bacon, however, Streeter feels that FE's manner of appropriating the Synoptics makes it all but impossible to trace specific transformations. John, like Paul, was a "personal mystic," and his use of Synoptic materials was influenced by extensive meditation. In fact, some episodes and details of FG may have been "visionary" in origin.[12] This combination of tradition, vision, and meditation was allegorized in FE's mind before FG was composed. FE's literary methods further complicate source analysis. In using the Synoptics, FE specifies vague references to persons and places and tends to enhance details from the perspective of his "mind's eye." Streeter therefore concludes that FG "belongs to the Library of Devotion."[13]

Streeter's analysis of FG's discourses is, consequently, not especially hopeful. Desiring to supplement Mark, FE reflected on Jesus' sayings and

---

[9]Bacon, *Research and Debate* 369.

[10]B. H. Streeter, *The Four Gospels: A Study of Origins* (1924; rev. ed.; London: MacMillan, 1964) 396, 417. Because verbatim agreement is less than 20% in the John–Mark parallels, Streeter suggests that FE did not write with a copy of Mark before him (397).

[11]Streeter, *Four Gospels* 424–425.

[12]Streeter, *Four Gospels* 366–367, 390–391.

[13]Streeter, *Four Gospels* 384–385, 403, 405, quotation 365. Thus, although "John recorded nothing that he did not believe to be historical . . . it does not follow that his belief was always justified" (388).

Paul's teachings, then produced discourses which merged source material with "all the fullness of meaning which years of meditation" had revealed. For example, the sayings about the Door and the Good Shepherd at John 10, and the Vine at John 15, are "interpretive transformations of what were originally parables of the Synoptic type. Epigrammatic logia will have been modified in a similar way."[14] At the same time, FE wrote in the historiographical tradition of Thucydides to satisfy his cultivated Ephesian audience. To Streeter's mind, this suggests that the discourses of FG were "organically related to what Christment taught in such a way as to be the doctrine which Christ would have taught had he been dealing explicitly with the problems confronting the church" of FE's day. FG's discourses therefore represent a "systematic summary of Christian teaching" rather than traditional words.[15] This being the case, there is no need to search for non–Synoptic discourse forms in FG.

Streeter represents the continuing expression of the traditional view in the early part of the twentieth–century: FE used the Synoptics as sources, freely adapting them and loosely basing the discourses of Jesus on Synoptic themes and forms. At the same time, however, *The Four Gospels* hinted at the shift in consensus that was soon to occur. Streeter opens his discussion by noting that the once "axiomatic" assumption that John knew all the Synoptics "of late . . . has been questioned."[16] Indeed, the questioning process was only beginning, and an entirely new consensus was soon to emerge.

JOHN'S DISCOURSES IN THE GARDNER–SMITH ERA

P. Gardner–Smith's 1938 *John and the Synoptic Gospels* had a monumental impact on Johannine studies in the English–speaking world. The

---

[14]Streeter, *Four Gospels* 372. Because this procedure was justified by FE's Paraclete doctrine, Streeter holds that FG should be studied parallel to the OT prophetic writings (374).

[15]Streeter, *Four Gospels*, both quotations 371.

[16]Streeter, *Four Gospels* 395. Streeter thinks it possible that FE was also acquainted with oral traditions and possibly used these to "correct" aspects of Mark (418–421). He also hints that some episodes, such as the Cana miracle and the raising of Lazarus, were derived "from an authority which . . . he [FE] regarded as no less authentic" than Mark (389). Attempts to reconstruct this tradition, however, would be "chimerical" in light of the freedom with which FE has transformed his sources (392).

traditional approach focused on the few agreements between FG and the Synoptics as evidence of dependence and then attempted to explain differences in terms of FE's theological or literary tendencies. Gardner–Smith proposes to examine a number of "parallel" passages to see if this method fit the evidence. He concludes that the disagreements so outweigh the agreements that it is "difficult to believe that the author of the Fourth Gospel was familiar with those [Synoptic] Gospels." What of the occasional verbatim agreements, then? Such "prove no more than that all the evangelists drew upon the common store of Christian tradition."[17] In Gardner–Smith's view, discrepancies between FG and the Synoptics do not represent intentional variations, but independent expressions of oral tradition. He asserts that his findings make a new case for "regarding the Fourth Gospel as an independent authority for the life of Jesus, or at least for the traditions current in the Christian Church in the second half of the first century."[18]

Less than twenty years after the release of Gardner–Smith's book, John A. T. Robinson sensed that a "new look" had emerged in Johannine studies in the form of a "widespread tendency" to regard Synoptic dependence as "unproven and indeed quite improbable." FE was no longer viewed as a recycler of Synoptic material but an editor of independent traditions. The "new look" was thus "new" in its evaluation that FG might possess "a real continuity, not merely in the memory of one old man, but in the life of an ongoing community, with the earliest days of Christianity."[19] Robinson's intuition proved correct, and the New Look developed into "an increasing consensus that by the end of the 1960's was quite striking."[20]

In the Bacon Era, when FG was thought to rely on the Synoptics as its primary source, it was technically unnecessary to speak of anything beyond

---

[17]Gardner–Smith, *St. John*, first quotation 88, second quotation 91. Gardner–Smith holds that even the Gospel genre was formalized in oral tradition before FG was written, which explains the basic similarities in outline between FG and Mark (89–90).

[18]Gardner–Smith, *St. John* 96. Gardner–Smith's chronological chart of the development of the Gospels puts John after Mark but before Luke and Matthew (98).

[19]John A. T. Robinson, "The New Look on the Fourth Gospel," 1957, rpt. in *Twelve New Testament Studies* (London: SCM, 1962) 96–106, first quotation 96, second quotation 106.

[20]D. Smith, *John Among* 63.

FE's mutation of Synoptic material, free composition, or indiscernible "special traditions" to explain FG's composition–history. The New Look approach of the Gardner–Smith Era, however, generated massive scholarly effort to describe an alternate traditional base. This reconstructed base sometimes consisted of oral traditions, sometimes written sources, sometimes eyewitness testimony, and sometimes all three. The base was sometimes considered to be more, sometimes equally, and sometimes less primitive than the Synoptic sources. Depending on the methodology utilized, varying degrees of specificity were achieved in source reconstruction. Further, once the various traditional strata had been separated, these could be used redaction–critically to track the development of FE's theology and community history. The scholarly output of the Gardner–Smith era was, consequently, extremely diverse in its approaches and conclusions.

These diverse approaches were united by two common presuppositions. The first was Gardner–Smith's rule that the Synoptic Gospels are not to be seen as the primary source of FG, even if FE knew them. The second was the implicit Other Consensus, continuing from the Bacon Era, that the discourses of FG have been johannised and are therefore not "traditional," at least not in the sense that the narratives are "traditional." Consequently, although New Look researchers might have considered the possibility that FG includes non–Synoptic speech genres, no such studies were generated. In general, the assumption prevailed that, while the sources behind FG did not include the Synoptics, they would nevertheless substantially resemble the Synoptics or their sources.

To demonstrate these presuppositions, two major New Look approaches to the sources of FG will be surveyed: the oral tradition/eyewitness approach, represented here by C. H. Dodd, Raymond Brown, Barnabas Lindars, Peder Borgen, and Oscar Cullmann; and, the source–critical approach, represented by Rudolf Bultmann, Robert Fortna, D. Moody Smith, and Urban von Wahlde.

PANNING FOR GOLD: SCATTERED SAYINGS

Several New Look scholars have been associated with the view that FG is based on oral tradition and/or eyewitness testimony. These scholars argue that the words of Jesus in FG may have real traditional, and sometimes even historical, value. Closer inspection, however, reveals that the oral tradition/eyewitness approach generally leads its proponents to discard the vast majority of FG's speech material, as well as the overall architecture of the discourses, in order to save a very few embedded logia which go back to a pre–Johannine stage of the tradition. These logia generally bear a striking resemblance to Synoptic texts, forms, or themes. Studies which follow this line therefore resemble attempts at panning for gold, sifting and separating the traditional nuggets from the mass of Johannine dirt in which they are encased.

Premiere among such studies is C. H. Dodd's 1963 *Historical Tradition in the Fourth Gospel*. Dodd's approach to sayings "common" to FG and the Synoptics is positive. A number of traditional aphorisms may be distilled from the Johannine discourses by comparison with the Synoptics.[21] Variations in these parallel sayings may represent FE's independent shaping of the same tradition, the use of independent traditions, or even alternate translations of an Aramaic original.[22] Dodd evidences a similar regard for FG's "parabolic forms."[23] John 10:1–5, for example, is a fusion of two traditional parables, 10:1–3a and 10:3b–5. The current combination is referred to as a παροιμία at 10:6, which Dodd thinks is synonymous with the Synoptic παραβολή as an alternate translation of the Aramaic מתלה. Such evidence leads him to conclude that FE "sometimes reaches back to the primitive Aramaic tradition by way of a different translation."[24] Dodd even suggests that in some of these "parables" FE "has preserved valuable elements in that tradition which the Synoptic evangelists have neglected."[25]

Dodd's opinion of the "predictions" in FG is higher still. The predictions of persecution in the Farewell are from a traditional nucleus also utilized by the Synoptics.[26] The motif of Jesus' "journey and return" at John

---

[21]C. H. Dodd, *Historical Tradition in the Fourth Gospel* (Cambridge: Cambridge University Press, 1963) 335. Note that "common" passages are those "in which form and content alike are identical, or closely similar, while differing verbally."

[22]Dodd, *HTFG* 343.

[23]Dodd insists that narrative is not an essential feature of the parable and redefined the genre in broader terms: an analogy suggested by a single scene; the use of primary tenses; the suggestion of typical experience via ὅταν or εἴ (*HTFG* 366).

[24]Dodd, *HTFG* 382–383.

[25]Dodd, *HTFG* 387.

[26]Dodd, *HTFG* 408.

13–14 parallels several Synoptic "return" parables. The original of all such sayings was "some oracular utterance of Jesus conveying . . . the assurance that his death meant a separation and was only temporary."[27] This saying was interpreted in the Synoptic branch of tradition in reference to the parousia; in another, FE's branch, it was interpreted as a reference to resurrection. But the very vague John 16:17 suggests neither tendency, so that here FG is more primitive than the Synoptics and the words "have good claim to represent authentically, in substance if not verbally, what Jesus actually said."[28]

Dodd thus evidences a generally high regard for FG's sayings material, arguing that a number of units are traditional, some show Aramaic originals, and a few may even go back to Jesus. But he hesitates to generalize about their current value because "so much of the teaching [of Jesus in FG] is embedded in literary forms which are an original creation of the evangelist." The "literary forms" Dodd has in mind remain unspecified, and he seems to mean simply that many portions of FG which do not derive from the Synoptics are FE's own compositions. John 10:1–5, noted above, illustrates the problem. Although 10:1–5 is a creative merger of two traditional units, "in what follows, x.7–18, the [fourth] evangelist has exploited it [allegorically] for his own purposes."[29] That is, FE composed the discourse to interpret the tradition.

Dodd highlights John 5:19–30 as another case of Johannine expansion. This section opens with a traditional parable, "the Son as Apprentice," and concludes with an aphorism, both well known Synoptic genres. "But in verses 20b–29 we have a typical piece of Johannine exposition, in which the terms of the parable are treated allegorically." The discourse in these verses was thus composed by FE to communicate a distinctly Johannine theological conception. Although a few predictive sayings in the Farewell are based on tradition, "in the farewell discourses our author's power of dramatic composition is at a peculiarly high level of accomplishment."[30] Many features

---

[27]Dodd, *HTFG* 418.

[28]Dodd, *HTFG* 420, 430, quotation 420. Dodd believes FE's tradition included both "detached units" and "rudimentary sequences" of sayings (388–389).

[29]Dodd, *HTFG*, first quotation 430, second quotation 385.

[30]C. H. Dodd, "The Portrait of Jesus in John and the Synoptics," *Christian History and Interpretation: Studies Presented to John Knox* (ed. W. R. Farmer, C. F. D. Moule, and R. R. Niebuhr; Cambridge: Cambridge University Press, 1967) 186, 198, quotation 198.

of the Farewell are so close to FE's theology that even if "traditional" in origin they are "Johannine" in their present form.[31]

As to the architecture of FG's speech materials, Dodd is suspicious of the dialogue format. Close resemblances between FG's dialogues and the Hermetic dialogues suggest that FE "has moulded his material in forms based upon current Hellenistic models of philosophical and religious teaching." Consequently, "the typical Johannine dialogue must be accepted as an original literary creation owing . . . little or nothing to primitive Christian tradition."[32] The same is true of the self–revelatory remarks of Jesus, where FE "is simply following a convention of other Greek writers, in making his hero the mouthpiece of statements which he himself believes to be true."[33] Notably, then, even in cases where FG betrays non–Synoptic speech forms, Dodd seeks a solution in literary parallels rather than considering the possibility that FE utilized other oral speech genres.

Dodd was unquestionably a champion of FG's traditional base, and urged that FG's discourses are not simply wholesale compositions of the evangelist. At the same time, his desire to extract a few traditional nuggets from the larger discourses allowed him to abandon the vast majority of FG's sayings material and the entire architecture in which the traditional units are situated. His analysis consistently gives priority to the Synoptic Gospels and their speech forms in the attempt to uncover a Johannine tradition.

Raymond Brown's magisterial contribution to the *Anchor Bible Commentary* appeared three years after *HTFG*. Brown's exegesis relies on the five–stage compositional theory he introduces to explain a number of literary problems in the present text of FG. Stage 1 of FG's tradition was a body of "material pertaining to the words and works of Jesus," similar to but independent of the Synoptic tradition. In Stage 2 this traditional material was developed into "Johannine patterns" by the preaching and teaching of FE or his "school" over a period of "perhaps several decades." This preaching produced

---

[31]Dodd, *HTFG* 408–409.

[32]Dodd, *HTFG*, both quotations 321.

[33]Dodd, "Portrait" 185. A similar view has been expressed more recently by Helmut Koester, *Ancient Christian Gospels: Their History and Development* (Philadelphia, PA: Trinity Press, 1990) 256–266.

"the individual stories and discourses that became part of the Fourth Gospel," which were gradually committed to writing. In Stage 3, the written material produced in Stage 2 was organized into a primitive Gospel, the first edition of FG. The editor of this document was the Fourth Evangelist, the "master preacher and theologian" primarily responsible for the shaping of the tradition. Stage 4 represents FE's publication of a revised edition of FG in order to meet new community needs after conflict with the synagogue. Stage 5 represents a final editing by "a close friend and disciple" of FE, who wanted to preserve other Stage 2 material not included in FG. He inserted these materials into FG at various points and made a number of rearrangements to accommodate them. The Redactor's finished product represents the version of FG known today.[34]

Obviously, then, Brown feels that FG is founded on old and independent traditions. Some of the sayings material, such as that underlying John 6:16–21, was certainly more primitive than the Synoptic sources. FE also may have known and utilized some of the Synoptic sources independently, even Q. But in the course of FE's preaching, "the [traditional] sayings of Jesus were woven into lengthy discourses of a solemn and poetic character, much like the discourses of personified Wisdom in the OT." These developing discourses were intertwined with narrative episodes to facilitate "the needs of preaching" and "the needs of incipient liturgy," both of which demanded "longer explanation and a more unified arrangement."[35] By the time the first edition of FG was compiled in Stage 3, FE "had probably phrased the tradition of Jesus' words in different ways at different times," creating a number of different versions of the discourses. Some of these duplicate versions, such as John 3:31–36, 12:44–50, and 16–17, were later picked up by the Redactor and added to the end of existing scenes.[36] The work of FE and the Redactor has thus almost completely obscured any traces of Stage 1 in the current speech materials, as the "formation of the sayings of Jesus into the Johannine discourses represented a profound theological synthesis."[37] This conclusion

[34]Raymond Brown, *The Gospel According to John* (AB; New York, NY: Doubleday, 1966) 1.xxxiv–xxxvii.
[35]Brown, AB 1.xxxv, xlviii, lv.
[36]Brown, AB 1.xxxvi.
[37]Brown, AB 1.xlix.

discourages any attempt to identify oral forms in the present text of FG, under the assumption that FE's base oral tradition has been heavily adapted and modified to comply with the narrative portions of FG. Brown does not consider whether FE's own compositional process may have utilized oral speech genres such as the riddle.

The next representative of the oral tradition/eyewitness approach to be considered here is Barnabas Lindars. Lindars also holds a very high view of FG's traditional base. FE had access to "excellent sources" which included narratives, sayings, and a passion.[38] These traditions had the same historical value, and underwent the same "preliterary stages of development," as the Synoptic sources, and at least some arose from "the primitive catechetical tradition" contemporary with Q.[39] Specifically, FG's discourses "contain traditional material in the form of sayings of Jesus, which are just as much comparable to the Synoptic traditions as the signs."[40] Lindars agrees with Dodd that some of FG's sayings are condensed versions of traditional parables, such as the Parable of "the Slave and the Son" at John 8:35. The case for FG's ἀμήν sayings is particularly strong, as this formulaic introduction "is a recurring sign that John is making use of a saying of Jesus from his stock of traditional material."[41] Initially, then, Lindars appears hopeful of utilizing FG as a real source for earlier traditions about Jesus, with the understanding that these traditions will likely resemble the Synoptic sources.

But Lindars' reconstruction of FG's composition–history illustrates the problem of johannisation particularly well. The solid traditions noted above were not, in fact, the building blocks of FG. Rather, the immediate sources "were homilies which he [FE] gave to the Christian assembly, possibly at the

---

[38]Barnabas Lindars, *The Gospel of John* (NCBC; Grand Rapids, MI: Eerdmans, 1972) 34; "Traditions Behind the Fourth Gospel," *L'Èvangile de Jean: Sources, Rédaction, Théologie* (ed. Marinus de Jonge; BETL 44; Leuven: Leuven University Press, 1977) 123.

[39]Lindars, "Traditions" 110–112. Lindars is adamant that these sources were in no way inferior to the Synoptic sources (*Behind the Fourth Gospel* [London: SPCK, 1971] 13, 16). At times, in fact, FE "uses sources used also by Luke, who indeed perhaps wrote later than John" (NCBC 48).

[40]Lindars, *Behind FG* 23.

[41]Lindars, *Behind FG* 44, quotation here; NCBC 48. In some cases, however, such as John 8:58, the ἀμήν formula is used "for the sake of [rhetorical] effect" (*Behind FG* 46).

eucharist" during a period of "close contact with Judaism and a lively debate between Church and Synagogue."[42] A number of these self–contained sermons and some new materials "more likely to have been composed especially for the Gospel" were eventually compiled in "response to the request of his [FE's] audience that he should put his homilies into some permanent form."[43] FE later revised and "very considerably enlarged" this preliminary Gospel several times, adding the Prologue, chapter 6, the Lazarus episode, and chapters 15–17.[44] Later redactors produced further "post–Johannine editions," adding 7:53–8:11, "all or part of 19:35," and chapter 21.[45] This extensive johannisation process has eclipsed FG's traditional base. The present text of FG "is dominated by his [FE's] theological purpose; he may have access to excellent traditions, but he recasts them radically to suit his interpretation of the meaning of Christ."[46]

This is particularly the case with FG's sayings material. The present discourses and dialogues are FE's homiletic compositions. Some expound traditional sayings or OT passages "along the lines of targumic exegesis," while others are based on traditional narratives, "built up from themes discovered in them by the evangelist."[47] Each discourse is a sermon "addressed

---

[42]Lindars, NCBC 51; *Behind FG* 60. The preaching context explains FE's tendency to narrate traditional miracles "in the manner of an epiphany, in order to lead into the crisis of decision," and "to build up his material to a climax which makes a powerful emotional impact" (*Behind FG* 39, 43, quotation here; "Traditions Behind" 109).

[43]Lindars, NCBC 46, 51, quotation 51; *Behind FG* 60. FE sometimes held over material from one homily and used it as the nucleus for the next section to increase continuity, a technique which represents "not what John does as a preacher, but it is one of his methods as a writer" (NCBC 51). In general, Lindars makes a sharp distinction between the compositional tendencies of preaching and writing.

[44]Lindars, NCBC 50.

[45]Lindars, NCBC 51. Note that Lindars thinks John 21:1–23 was composed by FE but omitted from earlier editions. These subsequent revisions are responsible for the "abrupt transitions and apparent dislocations" in the present text, "which is more coherent when they are dropped" (NCBC 46, quotation here; *Behind FG* 60).

[46]Lindars, NCBC 54.

[47]Lindars, "Traditions Behind" 115; *Behind FG* 48–49; NCBC 47. In the latter case, the narratives are introductions to FE's remarks, by which "John secures the interest of his hearers by telling a story of Jesus" (NCBC 50).

to Christians in order to deepen and strengthen their faith in a situation where Jewish objections to Christianity are a matter of vital concern," now cast "in the form of a speech by Jesus himself."[48] Consequently, even though FE knew "a number of sayings and parables of Jesus," "the discourses in which these are found are John's own compositions, in which he has used the sayings as the basis for very far–reaching creative developments."[49] These "creative developments" did not, however, fall very far afield of the Synoptic model. Just as FG's older traditional units may be identified by analogy with the Synoptic "sayings and parables," Lindars does not speculate on the possibility that FE's unique preaching style incorporated speech genres which the Synoptics do not highlight.

A similar approach to FG's composition history has been taken by Peder Borgen. Borgen suggests that Paul's letters might reveal traces of "pre–Synoptic usage of gospel materials," which could subsequently illuminate FE's appropriation of tradition. To determine Paul's method, Borgen analyzes the eucharist tradition at 1 Cor. 11:23–34. Paul quotes a traditional saying at 11:23b–25, then at 11:27–34 "gives a paraphrasing commentary on the quoted unit of tradition." This shows that "in the middle of the fifties the Jesus–tradition was so fixed that it was quoted and used as basis for added exposition."[50] FE, as Lindars argues, used traditional material in the same way. John 5:1–9, for example, is "a unit of tradition which has been handed down and received." At some point in the transmission process terminology from the story was borrowed and woven into "a halakhic debate"

---

[48]Lindars, *Behind FG* 47; NCBC 53. Perhaps "some may feel that John is morally wrong to do this, but it is to be explained simply as his homiletic method" (NCBC 53).

[49]Lindars, *Behind FG* 41, quotation here; NCBC 53. This explains why the present discourses of FG evidence a number of dramatic homiletic techniques. One such technique is "the trick of literal misunderstanding." Here FE portrays Jesus' audience as misunderstanding some aspect of his figurative discourse, which allows him to elaborate another implication of the traditional "text" being expounded *(Behind FG* 45–47; "Traditions Behind" 114).

[50]Peder Borgen, "John and the Synoptics: Can Paul Offer Help?," *Tradition and Interpretation in the New Testament: Essays in Honor of E. Earle Ellis for his 60th Birthday* (ed. Gerald F. Hawthorne and Otto Betz; Grand Rapids, MI: Eerdmans, 1987), first quotation 80, second and third quotations 83. Borgen is adamant that "John draws on oral traditions and is independent of the Synoptics" (85)

which developed the Sabbath question.[51] FE picked up this traditional unit and then "elaborated upon the Christological theme of 5:1–18 in the discourse of 5:19–47," which he himself composed.[52] Like Lindars, Borgen retains a traditional core but concedes that the majority of FG's discourses are later Johannine compositions.[53] Also like Lindars, he does not speculate on the significance of the present form of the Johannine material, except in cases where it seems to resemble the Synoptic tradition.

The presumption that FE independently utilized materials from oral tradition, then, is not necessarily followed by an attempt to situate the form and function of these materials apart from Synoptic parallels. Nor does the presumption that FE was an eyewitness to events of Jesus' life, as demonstrated by Oscar Cullmann's *The Johannine Circle*.

Cullmann believes that FE utilized three types of sources. The first was "a tradition *common* to *all* branches of early Christianity and made familiar to us through the Synoptic gospels." The second was "a *separate tradition* . . . which came down to him in the *particular circle* to which he belonged," some of which might have been in written form. The third source was FE himself, who is the "Beloved Disciple," a follower of both John the Baptist and Jesus

---

[51]Peder Borgen, "John and the Synoptics: A Reply [to Frans Neirynck]," *The Interrelations of the Gospels* (ed. David L. Dungan; BETL 95; Leuven: Leuven University Press, 1990), first quotation 456, second quotation 454. The composite followed the traditional form of stories "which state a case followed by a judicial exchange," such as Matt. 12:1–8 and Luke 13:10–17 ("Can Paul Help?" 88).

[52]Other examples of this transmission–exposition format appear at John 2:13–22; 6:51b–58; 9:1–41; 12:44–50 (Borgen, "Can Paul Help?" 88).

[53]James D. G. Dunn has also suggested that a number of FG's sayings may be regarded as "traditional." In FE's composition of the discourses, "these elements of the common tradition have provided the basis on which the passages . . . were developed, the core round which these larger treatises were woven" ("John and Oral Gospel Tradition," *Jesus and the Oral Gospel Tradition* [ed. Henry Wansbrough; JSNTSup 64; Sheffield: JSOT Press, 1991] 375). "[I]t would seem that the Johannine re–use and retelling of earlier tradition worked by elaborating earlier, briefer units of tradition into a richer tapestry of teaching where the nuances of the earlier forms were explored and drawn out," typically via the device of "misunderstanding" (376). FG's discourses "therefore have to be attributed almost entirely to the evangelist rather than to his tradition" (352).

and an eyewitness of some of the things he reports.[54] At least a portion of FE's source material is therefore not traditional at all, but in fact eyewitness testimony.

But Cullmann's conclusions on the discourses demonstrate that even eyewitness testimony does not protect against johannisation. FE realized the "historical" value of his sources and memories but also believed that the Paraclete is inspiring him "to reveal the deeper meaning and significance of these facts."[55] This belief has had a profound impact on FE's presentation of Jesus' words. "On the grounds of this conviction . . . the evangelist can allow himself to develop the discourses beyond what the incarnate Jesus said." Traditional sayings of Jesus bleed into the words of the risen Lord "without indicating the transition," in service of "the purpose followed by the author" in addressing his community's situation. Several literary features of the discourses are FE's own development, such as "the incomprehension of those to whom Jesus speaks, their inability to move from one sense of a word or expression to another, and in other cases their individual doubt, which ends in faith."[56] Overall, FE's personal experience of Jesus does not suggest that he has attempted to reproduce anything Jesus said, nor does it suggest to Cullmann that FE may have developed unique ways of preserving and communicating Jesus' teaching.

The New Look studies from the oral tradition/eyewitness perspective generally concluded that FG's discourses have been so johannised that they are no longer "traditional" in any real sense.[57] Consequently, these scholars, while

---

[54]Oscar Cullmann, *The Johannine Circle* (trans. John Bowden; Philadelphia, PA: Westminster, 1975) 7, 78–88, quotation 7, all emphasis original. Cullmann does not exclude the possibility that the non–Synoptic features of Jesus' discourse in FG might represent "a more intimate teaching given by Jesus to the Twelve" or Jesus' style in addressing disciples from heterodox branches of Judaism (quotation 24, see also 92–94). This independent branch of tradition should be taken seriously, and at some points where FG and the Synoptics conflict, "very serious arguments in favour of a number of historical elements in the [Fourth] Gospel" can be supported by exegesis (23). Some of this material, however, "may have undergone lengthy development" (80).

[55]Cullmann, *Johannine Circle* 8.

[56]Cullmann, *Johannine Circle* 18, 24, 28.

[57]John A. T. Robinson's *The Priority of John* (ed. J. F. Coakley; Oak Park, IL: Meyer–Stone, 1985) is no exception. Robinson asserts that FE, as the Beloved Disciple and

praising the traditional value of FG's narratives and occasionally preferring these over the Synoptics, were hesitant to authorize the discourses as representations of pre–Johannine tradition about Jesus' words. Those few verses of FG which may represent real tradition are those which most closely parallel the Synoptic Gospels in content or form. Non–Synoptic speech forms such as the riddle are automatically excluded from consideration.

TEARING THE SEAMLESS ROBE: FG'S WRITTEN PREDECESSORS

The New Look saw a vigorous renewal of Johannine Source Criticism. Although lacking the kind of parallels that facilitate source investigation in Synoptic studies, these scholars sought for traces of FE's editing and redaction of earlier written documents. Despite extremely diverse conclusions, several concerns unified the New Look's source–critical studies: how are sources to be detected? what are the number and nature of FG's sources? and, how did FE treat these sources in using them? The present study will examine four major representatives of this view, focusing on their conclusions about possible discourse sources and the way in which FE has appropriated these.

Rudolf Bultmann's influential commentary, which lacks a methodological introduction, is based on a notoriously complex source analysis.[58] His reconstruction develops in service of exegesis, and discussion

---

cousin of Jesus, was "internal to the tradition," so that FG "could take us as far back to source [Jesus] as any other [Gospel]" (21–22, 96, 105–122, 145). He therefore concludes that "there is no necessary absurdity or contradiction in asserting that the Johannine presentation could be *both* the most mature *and* the most faithful to the original truth about Jesus" (342, emphasis original). But the words "most mature" betray Robinson's true opinion of the discourses. When telling *stories* about Jesus, FE "tells it comparatively straight" (22), whereas in presenting the *words* of Jesus "he does not simply set them down straight, and then comment upon them. . . . Rather, it is worked up; the interpretation is thoroughly assimilated and integrated"; i.e., the sayings material is johannised (298).

[58]Rudolf Bultmann, *The Gospel of John: A Commentary* (trans. G. R. Beasley–Murray, Rupert W. N. Hoare, and John K. Riches; Oxford: Basil Blackwell, 1971). The introduction to the English version, which is a translation of the 1966 German edition, was written by Walter Schmithals. D. Moody Smith's doctoral dissertation, now *The Composition and Order of the Fourth Gospel: Bultmann's Literary Theory* (New Haven, CT: Yale University Press, 1965), offers a comprehensive discussion of Bultmann's method, and provides a reconstructed text and analysis of each proposed source.

of method is almost entirely relegated to footnotes.[59] Nevertheless, specific criteria for detecting literary strata are evident. Bultmann believes that FE, the later Redactor who produced the present text of FG, and each individual source manifest a distinct style. "Style" includes linguistic features such as vocabulary, grammar, and poetic rhythm, as well as larger literary devices such as dialogue or misunderstanding.[60] Narrative inconsistencies may also reveal strained appropriation of an earlier source.[61] Apart from these literary issues, FE, the Redactor, and some of the sources display distinct theological concepts and motifs.[62] Using such criteria, Bultmann posits a number of written sources,

---

[59]Note his remark, "*It goes without saying that the exegesis must expound the complete text*, and the critical analysis is the servant of this exposition" (Bultmann, *John* 17, emphasis original).

[60]In discussing John 2:1–12, for example, Bultmann asserts that the σημεῖα–source "in its style is clearly distinguishable from the language of the Evangelist or of the discourse–source" (Bultmann, *John* 113). The discourse–source evidences a peculiar vocabulary (161 n. 1). On grammar, at 15:9–17 FE's "own style is unmistakable in vv. 11–13 and can also be seen in vv. 14–17" (540 n. 1); on the other hand, John 17:17 is from a source because "the second half is characteristically different from the [style of the] Evangelist's definitions" (508 n. 4). Several features of FE's personal style are discussed on page 294, note 4. Bultmann frequently appeals to Semitisms as evidence of literary strata, apparently because FE's Greek does not evidence Semitisms but several of the sources do. The σημεῖα–source and passion–source, for example, use a "Semitising Greek," although the former is apparently not a direct translation of an Aramaic source (211 n. 1, 395 n. 2, 635–636). Poetic rhythm, including "antithetical style" and balanced lines, is characteristic of the discourse–source (161 n.1, 166 n. 2, 532 n. 3). FE has a tendency to add material at the end of this source's lines, creating an unbalanced structure (see, for example, 504 n. 2). On the dialogue structure, see 586 n. 2, 595 n. 5; on the use of double–entendre and subsequent misunderstanding, see 175.

[61]Most explicit in Bultmann's analysis of the trial–denial scene at John 18:12–19. The source named Annas as the priest who questioned Jesus. FE, in attempting to correct this to Caiaphas, did not rework the source sufficiently, causing the oft–noted confusion over which of the two is actually conducting the investigation (Bultmann, *John* 643). Bultmann also believes that FE's work had suffered massive dislocation before the Redactor received it, and the present order is apparently among those "glosses of a secondary redactor" which exegesis is not obligated to expound (17, see also n. 2 there). This justifies Bultmann's corrective rearrangement, upon which his exposition is based.

[62]The σημεῖα–source promotes a "divine man" Christology (Bultmann, *John* 179–180). The discourse–source is conspicuous for its gnostic mythology. Hence John

including a narrative σημεîα–source, a passion–source, and the *Offenbarungsreden*, a series of "revelation–discourses." The present study will focus on the nature of the *Offenbarungsreden* and FE's appropriation of that source in composing the discourses of FG.[63]

Bultmann first mentions the *Offenbarungsreden* in his discussion of FG's Prologue. This section stems

> from a collection of 'Revelation–discourses' which are to be thought of similar to the Od. Sal. [*Odes of Solomon*], and which the Evangelist has made the basis of the Jesus discourses in the Gospel.

The discourse source was written in Aramaic and originated with John the Baptist's community, to which "the Evangelist once belonged." A number of FG's most characteristic features derive from this source, including the

---

14:1–4 "mainly stems" from the discourse–source because the character of these verses was "originally mythological," as indicated by "Mandean parallels" (598 n. 6; for other Mandean features, see 623 n. 4). By contrast, John 17:18 "can hardly have come from the [discourse–]source" because "the sending out of the elect into the world by the Redeemer has no parallel in the [gnostic] myth" (509 n. 5, quotation here; 421, 433 n. 6, 446 n. 1). For specific discussion of the discourse–source's Gnosticism, see D. Smith, *Composition and Order* 16–18. The later redactor is notable for a more developed Christology and for ecclesial and sacramental interests (225 n. 1, 677–678, 706).

[63]Bultmann does not attempt a complete reconstruction of any of FG's literary sources and occasionally expresses doubt that such is possible. His remarks on John 15:18–16:11, from the discourse–source, are typical: "The text of the source, which the Evangelist has frequently expanded with his own comments, cannot always be recognized with complete certainty, but is clearly visible in outline" (Bultmann, *John* 548; also 179, 324 n. 1, 348 n. 2, 500 n. 4, 501 n. 1). Bultmann also believes that both FE and a later Redactor were aware of local oral traditions, some of which may have been related to Synoptic traditions. In deciding that John 10:40–42 is not derived from the σημεîα–source, Bultmann agrees with Kundsin that "here, as in 11.54–57, the fact comes to light that in these places 'in the time of the Evangelist a Christian community existed with its own local, though meagre, tradition'" (393 n. 2). John 12:24–26 is an embellishment of the discourse–source with "material taken from the Synoptic tradition," which explains the appearance of the Synoptic dominical saying at 12:25 (quotation 420, see also 424–425). As for the Redactor, John 1:27, 32 were both "an insertion from the Synoptic tradition" (85). At the same time, Bultmann adamantly denies FE's use of the written Synoptics (595 n. 2, 122 and n. 2 there, 125 n. 1, 635).

Prologue, the "I Am" sayings, the "lifted up" sayings, the Farewell, the Final Prayer, the Paraclete sayings, the "Son of Man" sayings, and the "abide" sayings.[64] Bultmann's approach would seem to suggest that these features of FG's discourses throw light on an old, possibly Palestinian, sayings tradition. But in appropriating these materials FE was faced with a problem, and his means of resolving it resulted in a thorough johannisation of any tradition which the discourse–source might have contained. Since the *Offenbarungsreden* was from a Baptist milieu, Bultmann likens it to the texts of a later Baptist sect, the Mandaeans, and concludes that it espoused a gnostic mythology. FE therefore "'historicizes' the revelation–discourses by working them into his portrait of the life of Jesus," making whatever theological adjustments were necessary to conform the source to the Christian orthodoxy of his day.[65] At times this was achieved simply by quoting the source but recontextualizing the content. For example, in the source John 7:17 took a "positive formulation and promissory future" which "strikes a note of invitation," so that "it is only in the context here [in FG] that it gains its polemical character."[66] The Jesus of the source probably used the self–designation "Son of Man" in the sense of the "archetypal man" of Gnosticism, but in FG it refers to Jesus as "a divine messenger wandering on the earth."[67] In such cases, FE has presumably left the source largely intact.

---

[64]Bultmann, *John*, block quotation 17 n. 5, second quotation 18. On the Prologue, see Bultmann, *John* 16 n. 3, 17 nn. 3 and 5, 132; on the "I Am" sayings, 344 n. 2, 360, 363 n. 4, 537 n. 1; on the "lifted up" sayings, 307; on the Farewell, 489; on the Paraclete sayings, 552 n. 2; on the "Son of Man" sayings, 149 n. 4, 422 n. 1; on the "abide" sayings, 266 n. 4.

[65]Parallel to the historicizing of independent logia by Matthew, Mark and Luke (Bultmann, *John* 132).

[66]Bultmann, *John* 274 n. 1. This recontextualization was sometimes achieved by juxtaposition with other traditional material. Jesus' discourse in John 3 is taken from the source, where it discussed heavenly birth in terms of gnostic "pre–existent origin" concepts. FE inserted the traditional logion at 3:3, 5 to canonize this "birth from above" as Christian conversion (135 n. 4).

[67]Bultmann, *John* 149 n. 4. Similarly, the "son of perdition" statement at John 17:12 was indefinite in the source, suggesting that "if a member of the community is lost, then he never was a true member." FE, however, has historicized it as a reference to Judas, although perhaps still regarding Judas as a paradigm for wayward community members (504 n. 2).

In many cases, however, FE's appropriation of the discourse–source called for more drastic measures, such as rearrangement, paraphrase and expansion. At John 3:12ff, for example, the source material has been so elaborated by FE "that the source provides, as it were, the text for the Evangelist's sermon."[68] In constructing John 5:1–47, FE combined a narrative from the σημεῖα–source with an edited discourse from the *Offenbarungsreden* and composed 5:28–ff "to harmonize Jesus' bold words with traditional [orthodox] eschatology."[69] The Vine parable at 15:1–17 is taken from the source but "the Evangelist has commented on it and expanded it with his own additions."[70] Other sections of FG's discourses, such as John 16:25–33, have no traditional base at all and "are probably almost entirely the work of the Evangelist." The dialogue format in which many of the discourse materials are now situated is also FE's literary creation.[71] Bultmann's source–critical conclusions thus support his earlier claim that "the Gospel of John cannot be taken into account at all as a source for the teaching of Jesus."[72] Apparently, this conclusion, plus Bultmann's preference for literary precursors, makes the identification of oral genres in FG unnecessary.

It would be difficult to overestimate the influence of Bultmann's commentary on subsequent Johannine Source Criticism. This has been particularly true of the σημεῖα–source. Aside from a large number of articles and monographs in the last three decades, the credibility of a signs source was enhanced by the adoption of this model in Rudolf Schnackenburg's exhaustive

---

[68]Bultmann, *John* 132. In this connection, the Prologue is a community hymn from the *Offenbarungsreden* with a number of interpretive additions. Such interpolations were used because "the ancient world has no knowledge of notes placed under the text" (16–17). FG's audience, however, would be aware of the interpolations because "in oral recitation the [evangelist's] 'comments' would be distinguishable by the tone of the speaker" (16 n. 3).

[69]Bultmann, *John* 237–238.

[70]Bultmann, *John* 529 n. 1. Here the source "spoke of ἀγάπη in the sense of myth, as the love of God received by the Son and mediated through him. That this love forms the basis of the command of love, is the Evangelist's [historicizing] conception" (540 n. 1).

[71]Bultmann, *John* 586 n. 2, 595 n. 2. Bultmann's view is typified in his comment that John 17:21 could be from the discourse–source, "but it has been so severely edited by the Evangelist that it can hardly be reconstructed" (512 n. 4).

[72]Rudolf Bultmann, *Jesus and the Word* (1934; trans. Louise Pettibone Smith and Erminie Huntress Lantero; New York, NY: Charles Scribner's Sons, 1958) 12.

commentary. But Schnackenburg also expressed what would become a rule of thumb in Johannine Source Criticism: "while the *sēmeia*-source [hypothesis] may be allowed some probability, a logia or discourse source must be rejected."[73] D. A. Carson's 1978 survey of "the most significant literary source theories" revealed that, while much effort had been expended to delineate a signs source for FG's narrative sections, the *Offenbarungsreden* had all but disappeared from discussion.[74] The disappearance of the discourse–source from that branch of Johannine scholarship which should be most interested in its recovery warrants explanation. As the following survey of Fortna, Smith, and von Wahlde will reveal, the primary causes of this trend have been methodological.

As a prelude to this investigation, it will be helpful to note that all recent source–critical studies have appealed to FG's "aporias" for determining literary strata. This term, coined by Eduard Schwartz in 1907, refers to "the conspicuous seams and style differences" which many detect in the surface texture of FG. These include interruptions, doublets, "passages with dense or

---

[73]Rudolf Schnackenburg, *The Gospel According to St. John* (trans. Kevin Smith; HTKNT; New York, NY: Herder and Herder New York, 1968) 1.167. Schnackenburg's version of the signs source is "a source which gave straightforward miracle–stories with no pretensions to deep theological significance, and certainly more numerous than the seven recounted in John" (discussion 1.64–74, quotation 1.66).

[74]D. A. Carson, "Current Source Criticism of the Fourth Gospel: Some Methodological Questions," *JBL* 97 (1978) 414–418. The broad rejection of Bultmann's sayings source was supported by the studies of Eduard Schweizer (1939) and E. Ruckstuhl (1951), which demonstrated a uniform style throughout FG (E. Schweizer, *Ego Eimi, die religionsgeschichtliche Herkunft und theologische Bedeutung der johanneischen Bildreden, zugleich ein Beitrag zur Quellenfrage des vierten Evangeliums* [ed. Rudolf Bultmann; FRLANT 56; Göttingen: Vanderhoeck and Ruprecht, 1939]; E. Ruckstuhl, *Die literarische Einheit des Johannesevangeliums, der gegenwärtige Stand der einschlägigen Erforschung* [Studia Friburgensia n. s. 3; Freiburg: Paulus–Verlag, 1958]). A notable exception to the rejection of a sayings source is Sydney Temple's 1975 monograph *The Core of the Fourth Gospel* (London: Mowbrays), which argues that FG is based on "a narrative–discourse source, in which in every case the discourse arises from the event which is narrated" (36). See also his earlier "A Key to the Composition of the Fourth Gospel," *JBL* 80 (1961), which suggests that the direct discourse of Jesus in the "Core" tradition was "straightforward, simple, and terse" (232). Temple's hypothesis has not won support.

overloaded wording," "inconsistencies, disjunctures and hard connections," "repetitive resumptions," sequence problems, terminological shifts, and theological inconsistencies.[75] Less controversial examples include the confusing presence of the Baptist in the Prologue, the correction of John 3:22 at 4:2, the geographical discrepancy of chapters 5 and 6, the continuation of the Farewell after 14:31, and the presence of John 21 after the closing statement at 20:31.[76] Such difficulties are taken to indicate the merger of disparate sources. The kind and number of aporias which a particular source analysis utilizes will determine the scope and nature of its source reconstruction.

Robert Fortna's 1970 *The Gospel of Signs* inaugurated a new era in Johannine Source Criticism. Desiring to utilize Redaction Criticism in the study of FG, Fortna proposes two stages in FG's composition history, "*basic document* and *redaction*," with FE as redactor of an earlier source.[77] After elaborating his criteria for source separation, Fortna notes that the two Cana miracles (John 2:1–11; 4:46–54) are numbered as "signs," suggesting a connection in the source. Since the other miracle stories of FG "are of an apparently similar type," Fortna proceeds to analyze these narratives "primarily on the basis of contextual evidence [literary aporias] but also with the help of Synoptic comparison where that is possible."[78] This exposes a primitive "Signs Gospel" (SG) beneath the text of FG, which presented a series of miracles followed by Jesus' death and resurrection but lacked any significant sayings material. A complete Greek text of SG appears in an appendix.[79] *TGOS* was

---

[75]First quotation W. Nichol, *The Sēmeia in the Fourth Gospel: Tradition and Redaction* (NovTSup 32; Leiden: Brill, 1972) 4; second quotation Robert T. Fortna, *The Fourth Gospel and Its Predecessor: From Narrative Source to Present Gospel* (Philadelphia, PA: Fortress, 1988) 4; third quotation Robert Fortna, *The Gospel of Signs: A Reconstruction of the Narrative Source Underlying the Fourth Gospel* (SNTSMS 11; Cambridge: Cambridge University Press, 1970) 2; fourth quotation Urban C. von Wahlde, "A Redactional Technique in the Fourth Gospel," *CBQ* 38 (1973) 520. See also von Wahlde's *The Earliest Version of John's Gospel: Recovering the Gospel of Signs* (Wilmington, DE: Michael Glazier, 1989) 17–20.

[76]All cited by Schnackenburg, HTKNT 1.44–48.

[77]Fortna, *TGOS* 2–3, 7–8, quotation 4, emphasis original.

[78]Fortna, *TGOS* 25.

[79]Fortna, *TGOS* 221, 235–245. SG was produced in a Jewish Christian milieu as "a missionary tract with a single end, to show . . . that Jesus is the Messiah" of Jewish

followed by a series of redaction–critical studies, and by 1978 Carson could state that Fortna "enjoys the premier sphere in influence among those involved in Johannine Source Criticism."[80]

In the early stages of his research, Fortna also seemed open to the possibility of a discourse source:

> An obvious literary distinction to be made in John is that between narrative and discourse, but it will be of no use here as a starting point. *Such a crude differentiation can hardly be the basis for separating Johannine and non–Johannine* [= pre–Johannine] *parts of the gospel*, for both classes of material [narrative and discourse] are probably composite.[81]

The SG itself may have contained "a few independent logia," and other sayings in the narrative sections of FG "very likely came to the evangelist directly from free oral tradition."[82] Why, then, is *TGOS* dedicated entirely to narrative sources? Fortna explains in a footnote,

> This limitation has been made *arbitrarily* in the sense that it recognizes that the source analysis of the discourses is an exceedingly difficult, not to say impossible, task. . . . [I]n any case, it is *only a working limitation* that is made.[83]

---

expectation (225, see also 228–229). While offering the complete text of a hypothetical source extracted from a later document solely on the basis of internal criteria might seem a bold move, Fortna justifies his reconstruction in terms of FE's redactional method. FE "regards SG, then, as gospel, and treats its language more conservatively than Matthew and Luke treat Mark," quoting the text verbatim and often adding to, but never subtracting from, its contents ("Christology in the Fourth Gospel: Redaction–Critical Perspectives," *NTS* 21 [1974–1975] 504). Consequently, FE's Christological development of SG does not indicate disrespect but is "simply [FE's] exegesis on the source's basic concept of sign" ("Source and Redaction in the Fourth Gospel's Portrayal of Jesus' Signs," *JBL* 89 [1970] 155). The main outline of Fortna's SG is defended on stylistic grounds by Edwin D. Freed and R. B. Hunt in "Fortna's Signs–Source in John," *JBL* 94 (1975) 563–573.

[80]Carson, "Current Source Criticism" 420.

[81]Fortna, *TGOS* 22, emphasis added.

[82]Fortna, *TGOS* 200. Fortna mentions John 1:51, 2:4, and 4:48 as possible oral traditions. Those embedded in SG are "notably only the sayings to Peter (1:42) and Nathaniel (1:47)" (200 n. 1).

[83]Fortna, *TGOS* 22 n. 3, emphasis added.

Further reflection, however, led Fortna to conclude that the distinction between FG's narratives and discourses was not as "crude" as he had initially assumed. Traces of this shift appear in his 1975 article "Christology in the Fourth Gospel: Redaction–Critical Perspectives." Fortna there reiterates that "redaction criticism of the discourse material is not now possible in any precise sense." But he also detects that SG's narrative "seems to have provided the basis for organizing the discourse materials," and that FE sometimes makes a sign "only an occasion for the revelatory discourse that he attaches to it."[84] Fortna now also observes that FE has inserted the Farewell (John 13–17) between SG's signs and passion to reinterpret the Christology of both by portraying the earthly Jesus as the exalted Lord. Indeed, "wherever John has inserted discourses into the pre–Johannine narrative we hear in effect not the earthly Jesus at all but the risen Lord speaking."[85] The discourses should therefore be associated primarily with FE's theological agenda.

Fortna's perspective on the origin of FG's discourses is stated most explicitly in his magnum opus, *The Fourth Gospel and Its Predecessor* (1988). *FGIP* opens with the warning that the exegetical challenge of FG "centers in the very nearly contradictory modes of Jesus' activity—his narrated deeds and the words of his discourses." FG's miracle stories are "vivid, brief, and earthy," "the type of narrative about Jesus familiar from the Synoptic Gospels." The discourses, on the other hand, offer "the more familiar portrait of the Jesus of universal Christianity."[86] Obviously, "the narratives and discourses stem from radically different origins . . . and they reflect distinct periods in the development of 4G[=FG]." "The narratives almost certainly represent the older, more traditional—clearly 'pre–Johannine'—layer"; "the discourses by

---

[84]Fortna, "Christology" 490–491.

[85]Fortna, "Christology in FG" 503. Here and elsewhere, Fortna's analysis gives the impression that FE used the discourses to add a symbolic component to the narratives, contra Bultmann's suggestion that FE used the narratives to historicize the discourses.

[86]Fortna, *FGIP*, first quotation 3, second and third quotations 1–2. Fortna notes that the Synoptic discourses are, by contrast, "concrete, timebound, usually secular" (2). Compare here Bultmann's remark that the Synoptic discourses "reflect in their form and content the actual conversations of the world in which Jesus, the Rabbis and the primitive Church moved. In John['s discourses] one feels that one has been transported into the world of C. Herm 13 and the Λόγος τέλειος" (Bultmann, *John* 132).

analogy can be attributed to the later author [FE], amplifying the earlier document(s)."[87]

In Fortna's view, then, FG's discourses are largely Johannine compositions.[88] This conclusion, combined with Fortna's opinion that portions of the discourses may have emerged from oral Jesus tradition, might have led him to speculate on the nature and origin of specific sayings or speeches in FG. But no such analysis appears anywhere in Fortna's work, and it is fair to say that this neglect is due mainly to his disinterest in the subject. Having reopened discussion of the sources of FG's narrative, Fortna has been content to leave the discourses unexplained.

Fortna's conclusions on the Signs Gospel have been significantly developed in a series of studies by D. Moody Smith.[89] Smith believes that SG is based on an independent collection of miracles. This collection opened with

---

[87]Fortna, *FGIP* 3, 7.

[88]Fortna's conclusion on the discourses is a necessary byproduct of his attempt to apply Redaction Criticism to FG. As with Mark, redaction–critical analysis of FG cannot proceed until one has reconstructed a hypothetical *Vorlage* with which to compare the current text. Fortna responds to this problem by insisting that FE's "redaction has been carried out so carefully that *the text of the source survives on the whole intact within the present Gospel* and can therefore be reconstructed with some facility and confidence, often simply by lifting off the patently redactional material" (Fortna, *FGIP* 7, quotation here, emphasis original; *TGOS* 223). But in the absence of the sort of clear parallels which facilitate Redaction Criticism of Matthew and Luke, how does one identify the "patently redactional material" within FG's narratives? By treating the discourses as theological commentary, Fortna could use these to determine peculiarities of FE's style and theology. Elements of the narratives which reflected these peculiarities could then be "lifted off" as glosses, leaving the original, unadulterated SG. This provides Fortna with the necessary *Grundschrift* for redaction–critical analysis, but at the expense of a possible sayings source.

[89]Smith's work on FG's sources has generally presupposed "widely acknowledged arguments and evidence on the side of a single (or major) collection of miracle stories" (D. Moody Smith, "The Setting and Shape of a Johannine Narrative Source" [1976; rpt. in *Johannine Christianity: Essays on Its Setting, Sources, and Theology* (Columbia, SC: University of South Carolina Press, 1984)] 81–82). Consequently, he has not offered an original reconstruction of any source. Smith does insist that SG and its sources were "independent of the Synoptics" ("Johannine Christianity: Some Reflections on Its Character and Delineation" [1974–175; rpt. in *Johannine Christianity: Essays on Its Setting, Sources, and Theology* (Columbia, SC: University of South Carolina Press, 1984)] 11).

an account of John the Baptist "in which he denied that he was the miracle–working eschatological prophet" and culminated "with the statement that John did no sign." Between these, Jesus was portrayed as a wonder–worker, which "confirmed his prophetic role, over against John." The presentation of Jesus in this pre–SG source "may have ultimately descended from the historical Jesus himself," perhaps via "Jesus' own disciples." Such a document probably arose "as a mission tract directed to members of the Baptist sect," confirming Bultmann's suspicion that FG had some connection with that group.[90] When FE's community began to evangelize the synagogue, this miracle tradition was combined with a passion tradition to provide an apologetic explanation of Jesus' death. John 12:37–40 was composed as a transition, and SG appeared as a "primitive gospel."[91]

Smith discusses the discourses of FG in his 1976 article "Johannine Christianity: Some Reflections on Its Character and Delineation." After opening with the assertion that FG's narratives "doubtless had a traditional history," Smith further suggests that a separate tradition of "dominical sayings or similar materials" is also "a real and significant possibility." But "the greater part of the discourse or sayings material in John has a distinctly Johannine ring." Smith attributes this to FE's belief that the Spirit will recall and expand what Jesus taught (John 14:25–26; 16:12–15). The discourses are "obviously spoken from the standpoint of a spirit–inspired post–resurrection community," and are therefore "to be regarded as the fulfillment of the promise of the Paraclete rather than the words of the historical Jesus." Thus, FG's distinct sayings tradition "grew up alongside the signs, partly on the basis of Jesus tradition analogous to the Synoptic, but very largely out of words uttered

---

[90]D. Smith, "Milieu of Miracle," all quotations 75-77. Elsewhere, "the Johannine literature is related to sectarian, perhaps gnosticizing, Judaism" ("Johannine Christianity" 28).

[91]D. Smith, "Setting and Shape" 88–90, 93. At the time of this article (1976), Smith's contention that "one may be justified in regarding [John] 12:37–40(41) in toto as a part of John's larger source" because of its function as a "primitive transition from signs to passion" (92) was offered as a correction of Fortna's reconstruction in *TGOS* and that of W. Nichol in *Sēmeia*. Fortna was apparently persuaded, as *FGIP* says of 12:37–40, "This passage, then, originally formed the bridge between signs and passion [in SG]" (131).

by early Christian prophets."[92] Much of this prophetic activity was conducted during a period of conflict with the synagogue. FE was composed during this conflict period, and "the miracle narratives seem to have become the foundation for the organization of the discourse materials."[93] As a result of this johannisation process, "such tradition of his [Jesus'] logia as has existed has been subjected to thoroughgoing reinterpretation . . . so that it has become all but unrecognizable."[94]

What led Smith to reject the possibility of discovering a discourse source? The primary reason lies in his source–critical method, which is very much concerned with factors outside the text of FG.

> The separation of strata or the identification of materials on the basis of criteria obtained from outside the [Fourth] Gospel itself . . . seems, however, to be more easily controllable and less subject to the danger of arbitrariness in objectifying one's own standards of consistency and coherence.[95]

For this reason, comparisons with the Synoptic Gospels are particularly important to Smith's analysis. Smith holds that FG's narratives are related to, and have possibly been influenced by, the Synoptics at some stage in their tradition history. Consequently, much of the narrative material can be analyzed comparatively to discover a traditional base.[96] Similarly, the few independent logia Smith hypothesizes are identified on the basis of Synoptic

---

[92]D. Smith, "Johannine Christianity," first two quotations 12, second, third, and fourth quotations 15, fifth quotation 34; see also "Setting and Shape" 93 n. 34.

[93]"The shape of the discourses is, of course, determined internally not only by the signs, but by the opposition of the Jews" contemporary with FE (D. Smith, "Johannine Christianity" 33). Jesus' words "are calculated not so much to answer the Jews' questions and arguments as to fulfill all their worst fears" (34).

[94]D. Moody Smith, "John and the Synoptics: Some Dimensions of the Problem," (1980; rpt. in *Johannine Christianity: Essays on Its Sources, Setting, and Theology* [Columbia, SC: University of South Carolina Press, 1984]) 170.

[95]D. Smith, "Johannine Christianity" 15.

[96]D. Smith, "Johannine Christianity" 11–12; "Milieu of Miracle" 78. Specifically, the Synoptics were known to members of FE's community but were not "fully appropriated into its traditions." Because FG did not develop in complete isolation, Synoptic parallels can sometimes illuminate FE's redaction ("John and the Synoptics" 170).

Parallels, and he tellingly cites the "Johannine thunderbolt" at Matthew 11:27 to prove the existence of such a tradition.[97] "But many of the narratives and most of the discourses in John are . . . obviously quite different from anything in Matthew, Mark, and Luke."[98] On the other hand, FG's discourses are similar in some respects to the Johannine Epistles, and at many points parallel the form or content of other Hellenistic or heterodox literature of the period.[99] Consequently, comparative analysis of FG and other texts suggest to Smith that the discourses were late, Johannine compositions.

Once again, however, one might suspect that Smith's belief that FG's sayings are at least related to traditional Jesus materials would lead him to explore the possibility that FE has utilized oral speech forms in composing the discourses. But such is not the case. As noted, Smith's analysis does not begin with actual source reconstruction but with scholarly consensus, and "few scholars have accepted the discourse source."[100] Since Fortna and others had also failed to speculate on the nature of the discourses in the current text of FG, Smith apparently deemed it unnecessary to do so. Further, since Smith's approach highlights analogies between FG and the Synoptics, it seems unlikely that any such exploration would have identified oral forms which are not prevalent in Mark or Q.

Urban von Wahlde's *The Earliest Version of John's Gospel* attempts to rectify the general neglect of the discourses in Johannine Source Criticism. Von Wahlde posits three stages in FG's compositional history, a primitive source, FE's redaction of that source, and the current version of FG.[101] To

[97]This tradition included those sayings of the Baptist which have Synoptic parallels; the "traditional words" at John 12:24–26; the "apparently traditional sayings in 4:35–38"; "scattered parabolic forms" which Smith does not identify; and, the love command at 13:34; 15:12 (D. Smith, "Johannine Christianity" 12).

[98]D. Moody Smith, "John 12:12ff and the Question of John's Use of the Synoptics," 1965; rpt. in *Johannine Christianity: Essays on Its Setting, Sources, and Theology* (Columbia, SC: University of South Carolina Press, 1984) 98.

[99]D. Smith, "Johannine Christianity" 15, 26–36.

[100]D. Smith, "Setting and Shape" 80.

[101]The first edition of FG was written before 90 C.E. and discussed Jesus' ministry from baptism to resurrection, focusing on the signs. FE revised this document around 90 in response to developing conflict with the synagogue. Division over the proper interpretation of this second edition led to the production of the present FG (*Earliest Version* 13–15).

identify material from the earliest stage, von Wahlde identifies two categories of aporias. "Contextual aporias, that is, sudden changes in thought, chronology, theology, or other forms of narrative sequence," are helpful in identifying seams "where the changes in authorship occur." Once these blocks have been separated, "various shifts in vocabulary, 'ideology,' and in theology . . . enable us to identify material as belonging to a given edition" of FG.[102]

Premiere among von Wahlde's ideological aporias are "terms for religious authorities" in FG. FE sometimes identifies religious authorities specifically as "Pharisees," "Chief Priests," "Rulers," or some combination of these terms, and sometimes more generally as "Jews." Since these two types of designation never appear in the same passage, "there can be no doubt that these two sets of terms for religious authorities stem from separate authors."[103] Further, whenever the authorities are called "Pharisees, Chief Priests, or Rulers," Jesus' miracles are referred to as "signs"; when the designation "Jews" is used, Jesus does "works."[104] Von Wahlde suggests that the terms "Jews" and "works" were used by FE, while the other terms are characteristic of the source.[105] After describing 20 additional criteria for source separation, von Wahlde boasts that his study, unlike Fortna's, will not be limited to FG's narratives but would "see where they [the source criteria] occur throughout the *entire* gospel."[106]

---

[102]von Wahlde, *Earliest Version* 27, 30. A number of contextual aporias are discussed on pages 17–28.

[103]von Wahlde, *Earliest Version*, 31–35, quotation 35. Whenever these sets of terms are juxtaposed, contextual aporias are present to suggest editing (34). See also his earlier study, "The Terms for Religious Authorities in the Fourth Gospel: A Key to Literary Strata," *JBL* 98 (1979) 233–242. Note von Wahlde's logic concerning the two sets of terms: "we would expect them to be [mingled] if they were the work of one writer" ("Terms" 242). Why these four terms represent two separate authors rather than four is not explained.

[104]von Wahlde, *Earliest Version* 36, 39.

[105]von Wahlde, *Earliest Version* 40, esp. n. 34. After delineating all 22 aporias, von Wahlde notes that "the discovery of all these features began with a first sorting of material on the basis of the appearance of either of the two sets of terms for religious authorities. All of the subsequent features have been found to be associated consistently and exclusively with one or the other sets of terms for authorities throughout the gospel" (63).

[106]von Wahlde, *Earliest Version* 65, emphasis original.

In light of this promising proposal, one is somewhat surprised to discover that von Wahlde's analysis, which claims to recover "well over ninety percent of the [source] material actually present" in FG, produces something quite similar to Fortna's signs source. Von Wahlde's "earliest version" *excludes* John 5:10–47; 6:27–58; all but the narrative verses of John 7; all but vv. 12–13 of John 8; all of John 10 save vv. 19–21 and 40–42; and all of John 13–17 because "there is no evidence of signs material associated with the Last Supper."[107] To explain this total exclusion of discourse material from the "earliest version" of FG, it will be helpful to consider two of von Wahlde's earlier articles on the subject.

Von Wahlde's basic argument concerning "terms for religious authorities" first appeared in a 1979 contribution to *JBL*. There, after assigning each set of terms to a different literary stratum, von Wahlde notes that his analysis will necessarily be limited to passages where the terms appear. He then presents a table of his findings, which excludes almost all of FG's discourse material from the source.[108] On this table, however, the only time Jesus uses either set of terms for the authorities is at John 13:33, where he reminds the disciples of something he said earlier to the "Jews." In general, it is the narrator who makes reference to the authorities, and the narrator naturally disappears during Jesus' long discourses. Von Wahlde's primary criterion for source analysis is inherently unable to detect traditional material in FG's discourses, because "terms for religious authorities" rarely occur there.

A different source–critical criterion, however, was utilized in the second study to be mentioned, a 1983 contribution to *Biblica* on John 6:51–58. Von Wahlde there appeals to a source–critical marker popularized by Frans Neirynck and M. E. Boismard, the *Wiederaufnahme* or "repetitive resumptive": "after an editor interrupted the sequence of a text in order to add material, he repeated a part of the original material in order to reestablish the original

---

[107]von Wahlde, *Earliest Version* 134 n. 136, see also 190–191.

[108]"The analysis of those parts of the gospel which do not contain the terms [for authorities] themselves must be done on the basis of content and style criteria, which are much less certain" (von Wahlde, "Terms" 240; the table mentioned above appears on 241). Von Wahlde later rejected style criteria altogether as a means of source separation (*Earliest Version*, 29 n. 8).

sequence of the passage."[109] Because this contextual aporia is found specifically in the discourse sections of FG, von Wahlde believes it might illuminate John 6. After specifying four literary criteria for identifying a "repetitive resumptive," he concludes that "application of these criteria . . . suggest strongly that vv. 51–58 are a redactional addition."[110] Does this mean that FE has inserted these verses into an older sayings tradition? Von Wahlde thinks not; rather, they represent an interpolation into FE's "second edition" by the later Redactor.[111] Von Wahlde's aporias could thus distinguish level 2 material from level 3 material in the discourses, but could not find sayings material in the earliest version. He could therefore presuppose in *Earliest Version* that "the discourse material was not a source but a second edition of the gospel."[112] Indeed, the criteria he utilized for source separation almost demanded this conclusion.

In summary, it may be observed that the major source–critical approaches have failed to identify oral genres in the discourses of FG for several reasons. Source Criticism is, by nature, concerned with written

---

[109]Urban von Wahlde, "*Wiederaufnahme* as a Marker of Redaction in Jn 6,51–58," *Bib* 64 (1983) 545. Neirynck's discussion appeared in "L'Epanalepsis et la critique littéraire. À propos de l'Èvangile de Jean," *ETL* 56 (1980). Boismard explains that this occurs because "when a redactor wishes to insert a gloss of average length into an already existing text, he is often compelled to resume . . . expressions used before the gloss in the primitive story, in order to be able to renew the thread of the story" ("Un procédé rédactionnel dans le quatrième évangile: la Wiederaufnahme," *L'Èvangile de Jean: Sources, Rédaction, Théologie* [ed. Marinus de Jonge; BETL 44; Leuven: Leuven University Press, 1987] 235, translation mine).

[110]The four criteria are "awkward repetition"; "phrases which have no other function than to resume or which are awkward"; aporias in the intervening material; finally, "the primitive sequence attained by the excision of the supposed addition must make reasonable sense" (von Wahlde, "*Wiederaufnahme*" 545–546). Boismard also argues that the *Wiederaufnahme* criterion can be applied specifically to FG's discourses to distinguish literary strata ("Un procédé" 235, 240).

[111]von Wahlde, "*Wiederaufnahme*" 549.

[112]von Wahlde, *Earliest Version* 57 n. 66. In this connection, von Wahlde's remark, "most scholars would agree that the miracles in the [fourth] gospel belong to the earliest 'stratum,' and that at least some of the material in the discourses reflect a second stage" (25), must mean that some of the discourses reflect the second (FE's) stage and some reflect the third (Redactor's) stage, but none the earliest version.

predecessors to the Gospels, and therefore gives little attention to forms and patterns which might reflect a distinctly oral milieu. Johannine Source Critics in particular have utilized tools which inherently prefer the narratives of FG over the discourses, either out of methodological necessity or simple neglect. As a result, while advocates of this approach have made great strides toward identifying the sources of FG's narratives, they have failed to recognize the presence and role of riddles in FG's discourses.

JOHN'S DISCOURSES IN THE NEIRYNCK ERA

In 1975, Frans Neirynck presented a paper to the 26th Colloquium Biblicum Louvaniense which signaled the end of the Gardner–Smith Era. Neirynck opened his remarks by observing that "the prevailing view in Johannine scholarship is undeniably that of John's independence" from the Synoptics.[113] He then proposed to analyze John 20:1–18, but with a critical *caveat*: if FG is found to be parallel with Matthew and Luke's "editorial compositions," "we should have to conclude to the dependence [of FG] on the Synoptic Gospels themselves."[114] Following this rule, Neirynck proceeded to argue that Luke 24:12 is "Luke's editorial composition" and that John 20:3–10 has been built up out of this verse. Here, at least, "the Johannine *Vorlage* is not a pre–Lukan form but the Lukan verse." This case study allowed Neirynck to assert a general rule: "the Synoptic Gospels themselves are the sources of the Fourth Evangelist."[115]

---

[113]Frans Neirynck, "John and the Synoptics," *L'Évangile de Jean: Sources, Rédaction, Théologie* (ed. Marinus de Jonge; BETL 44; Leuven: Leuven University Press, 1977) 73–77, quotation 73.

[114]"Themselves" means the Synoptics as they exist today, not their sources or prototypes (Neirynck, "John and Synoptics" 96). Note also Neirynck's later remark, "the problem of John and the Synoptics cannot be discussed without a more thoroughgoing examination of the Synoptic parallels [themselves]" ("John and the Synoptics: Response to Peder Borgen," *The Interrelations of the Gospels* [ed. David L. Dungan; BETL 95; Leuven: Leuven University Press, 1990] 443).

[115]Neirynck, "John and Synoptics," first quotation 99, second quotation 103, third quotation 106. In a later and more detailed study of the same passage, Neirynck charges that New Look source reconstructions "are so Synoptic–like, so similar to the Synoptics, that Johannine dependence upon the Synoptic Gospels is just one step further," and reiterates that

Neirynck's paper, and his further studies on the subject, sparked a chain reaction in Johannine studies. At the same Colloquium, Maurits Sabbe concisely stated the creed of this new school: "In questions of literary [source] criticism, one ought to give priority to the hypothesis explaining the literary data without claiming the existence of unknown sources."[116] The traditional view of Synoptic dependence had survived as an undercurrent throughout the Gardner–Smith Era, and Neirynck's work became an outlet for its reemergence, now with the moniker, "The Leuven School." The Leuven movement was supported in the English world with the translation of Werner Georg Kümmel's *Introduction to the New Testament* in 1975. Kümmel insists that "Jn's knowledge of Mk and Lk can be asserted with . . . probability, and knowledge of the Synoptics as a genre can be presupposed."[117] Then in 1978, C. K. Barrett, who had remained a staunch representative of the dependence theory throughout the Gardner–Smith Era, released the second edition of his commentary, which unashamedly reiterates, "I have to acknowledge . . . that I do not share in this [Gardner–Smith] consensus." FE surely used sources, but the present unity of style and "theological purpose" in FG "means that the only sources we can with any probability isolate are those which have a known independent existence."[118] Indeed, dissatisfaction with the variety of hypothetical source reconstructions produced by the New Look was a driving force in the reemergence of the dependence theory. By the 39th Colloquium

---

"the Johannine writer who depends on the Synoptics is not a secondary redactor but none other than the Fourth Evangelist" ("John and the Synoptics: The Empty Tomb Stories," *NTS* 30 [1984], first quotation 165, second quotation 179).

[116]Maurits Sabbe, "The Arrest of Jesus in Jn 18,1–11 and Its Relation to the Synoptic Gospels: A Critical Evaluation of A. Dauer's Hypothesis," *L'Èvangile de Jean: Sources, Rédaction, Théologie* (ed. Marinus de Jonge; BETL 44; Leuven: Leuven University Press, 1977) 234.

[117]Werner Georg Kümmel, *Introduction to the New Testament* (1973; trans. Howard Clark Kee; Nashville: Abingdon, 1975) 204. Note here also Norman Perrin's popular Introduction, which argued that "the gospel of John shows knowledge of the gospel of Mark, and perhaps also of the gospel of Luke" (Norman Perrin and Dennis C. Duling, *The New Testament, An Introduction: Proclamation and Parenesis, Myth and History* [2nd ed.; New York, NY: Harcourt, Brace, Jovanovich, 1982] 335).

[118]C. K. Barrett, *The Gospel According to St. John* (2nd ed.; Philadelphia: Westminster, 1978) 15.

Biblicum Louvaniense in 1990, Neirynck could assert that

> Johannine dependence on the Synoptics is not an idiosyncracy of Leuven. Those
> who call it the thesis of the 'Leuven school' should realize that this 'school' has its
> ramifications in Heidelberg, Mainz, Göttingen, Erlangen, Tübingen, and
> elsewhere.[119]

It is presently impossible to speak of a "consensus" on the question of
FG's relation to the Synoptics. But the Other Consensus remains firmly
entrenched more than two decades into the Neirynck Era. FG's discourses are
still typically treated as Johannine, whether FE had access to sources other than
the Synoptics or not. Indeed, if Neirynck and Barrett are correct, it is either
impossible or unnecessary to posit a discourse tradition: impossible because
there are not enough Synoptic parallels to conduct an investigation, or because
any independent sources are unrecoverable; unnecessary because FG's
discourses can, as in the Bacon Era, be explained as transformations of
Synoptic material.[120] This being the case, it is clearly unnecessary to search FG
for oral forms such as the riddle which do not appear prominently in the
Synoptics. Two Neirynck Era scholars who advocate the dependence theory

---

[119]Frans Neirynck, "John and the Synoptics: 1975–1990," *John and the Synoptics*
(ed. Adelbert Denaux; BETL 101; Leuven: Leuven University Press, 1992) 8–9.

[120]In 1990, Neirynck responded to charges by Peder Borgen by insisting, "I am not
aware that I ever gave such an exclusiveness to the Synoptic Gospels as to exclude John's
use of oral–tradition or source material," and cited his earlier statement that "direct
dependence on the Synoptic Gospels does not preclude the possibility of supplementary
information" ("1975–1990" 14; see "John and the Synoptics" 94). At the same time,
Neirynck's prevailing interest in the narrative portions of FG makes it unclear whether these
"supplementary" traditions included sayings material. At one point Neirynck refers to
Lindars' view as an "attractive theory" and says "I am on his [Lindars'] side when he writes
that . . . 'sayings from the tradition occur at strategic points in the discourses,'" but seems to
feel that "the tradition" in question here is the Synoptics themselves ("1975–1990" 29). In
analyzing Dunn's position, Neirynck says, "We can agree that Jn 3,5 'is certainly plausible
as a variant of Mt. 18.3, particularly as it is the *only* passage in which John echoes the normal
kingdom language of the Synoptics,' but it remains an unprovable suggestion that this
variation of the saying is one of 'the fixed points of the earlier tradition'" ("1975–1990" 57;
see Dunn, "John and Oral Gospel" 375). This seems to mean that Neirynck thinks John 3:3,
5 is to be understood as a direct transformation of Synoptic material.

will be examined to demonstrate the persistence of the Other Consensus, C. K. Barrett and Thomas Brodie.

Barrett suggests that "there crops up repeatedly in John evidence that the evangelist knew a body of traditional material that either was Mark, or was something much like Mark." Since the latter cannot be shown to exist, the former conclusion is more attractive. This explains the "Johannine logia with Synoptic parallels" which are occasionally to be found embedded in FG's discourses.[121] Barrett can thus, like Dodd and Lindars, find earlier traditional units in FG's discourses, but unlike them he prefers to see these as appropriations of Synoptic material. In Barrett's view, FE did not utilize the Synoptics with "slavish imitation," but freely and from memory to meet the needs of preaching. "Much of the discourse material in the [fourth] gospel can be readily understood as having been originally delivered in [FE's] sermons." In his preaching, FE "worked over the Synoptic sayings, illustrating them by symbolic narratives, expanding them into discourses, and condensing them into new aphorisms."[122] The Bread from Heaven discourse, for example, is based on, but never quotes, Mark 14:22. Similarly, most of the Farewell can be explained as a transformation of Synoptic material: the "new commandment" parallels Mark 12:31; the world's hatred Matthew 5:11ff; the "sending" motif Matthew 10:24. In the course of this preaching, FG's discourses were "thematically attached" to the miracles as interpretations of the events.[123] This produced a series of homilies which were ultimately compiled into a gospel.[124] Although Barrett begins from a different traditional base, his use of a compositional model similar to that of Lindars leads him to Lindars' conclusion: most of FG's discourse material is not traditional in any sense.

Thomas Brodie's 1993 *The Quest for the Origin of John's Gospel* represents a complete return to Bacon's position. Brodie seeks to demonstrate

---

[121]C. K. Barrett, "John and the Synoptic Gospels," *ExpTim* 85 (1973–1974), first quotation 232, second quotation 231; *St. John* 15–16. Barrett lists as examples John 1:42, 51; 3:3, 5; 4:44; 5:8; 12:13, 25.

[122]Barrett, *St. John* 17.

[123]Barrett, *St. John* 15–20. Barrett's insistence that "there is no sufficient evidence for the view that John freely created narrative material for allegorical purposes" must not apply to the discourses (141).

[124]Barrett, *St. John* 26.

that FE "used a diverse range of sources—some non–canonical material, the OT, at least one epistle [Ephesians], and, above all, the Synoptics, especially Mark."[125] Specifically, "Mark supplied the fundamental ingredients of John's *narrative framework*, and Matthew the fundamental ingredient of his *discourses*."[126] Matthew thereby takes the place of Bultmann's *Offenbarungsreden*, and Brodie proceeds to explain FG's discourses as a "dense synthesis" of material from Matthean sermons.[127] John 7–8, for example, is derived from the Sermon on the Mount, with the addition of most of Matthew 23:13–24:28 and "some of Mark." The Beatitudes have disappeared, and FE has turned the "salt and light" sayings at Matthew 5:13–16 into Jesus' "light of the world" saying at 8:12. This illustrates FE's technique "of turning something parabolic or parablelike into an 'I am . . .' saying." In John 7 the antitheses of Matthew 5–7 are supplemented with Mark 7:1–23 and reworked. Then at 8:31–59, FE combines Matthew 6:1–18, 23:13–36, and 3:7–9, "probably because of their inherent connectedness," and uses them to attack "superficial Jewish believers" of his own day. In general, FE tends to specify the "broad exhortations" of the Sermon on the Mount as specific events or qualities acted out by Jesus.[128]

Brodie's analysis makes explicit what is assumed by others who assert FE's reliance on the Synoptics: if FE builds on the written Synoptics, there is

---

[125]Thomas L. Brodie, *The Quest for the Origin of John's Gospel: A Source–Oriented Approach* (New York, NY: Oxford University Press, 1993) 30. Brodie does not nominate specific non–canonical sources, but insists on their existence because FE "was in dialogue with the Hellenistic world" (31). FE's Moses Christology borrows a number of motifs from the Pentateuch (33). The Final Prayer at John 17 is based on themes from Ephesians (33). FE also knows Acts, as John 3:1–21 has been built up from the figure of Gamaliel (32).

[126]Brodie, *Quest* 31. Compare here Bacon's remark on the arrest and passion: "In this section, detailed comparison would again prove the [fourth] evangelist's loyalty to the two essential elements of Synoptic story, Petrine [Markan] narrative and Matthean discourse, subject always to his formative principle of the 'spiritual' gospel of Paul" (*Research and Debate* 383).

[127]Brodie, *Quest*, quotation 32, 106, quotation 106.

[128]Brodie, *Quest*, quotations 103, 106, 107, 107, 109. On the last point, the motifs involving sheep at Matt. 9:35–11:1 have been "concentrated into an image of Jesus" at John 10 (110). Also, the footwashing in John 13 may be a historicizing illustration of the "down–to–earth human kindness" called for at Matthew 25:31–46 (115).

little methodological need for a sayings tradition, especially when it is held that other unknown sources cannot be reconstructed. This conclusion inherently predisposes the researcher to avoid a thorough search for non–Synoptic speech forms in FG. Consequently, the Neirynck Era has not seen the dissolution of the persistent Other Consensus, and has not produced a single study which highlights the role of riddles in FG.

THE NEED FOR ANOTHER "NEW LOOK"

At the end of his exhaustive study of FG's tradition, C. H. Dodd confessed,

> I do not at present see any way of identifying further traditional material in the Fourth Gospel, where comparison with the other gospels fails us, without giving undue weight to subjective impressions.[129]

Similarly, D. A. Carson closed his review of Johannine Source Criticism with the gloomy prospect that current approaches "do not encourage the conclusion that they will produce any more satisfying information regarding *literary sources*."[130] Fortna's observation is as relevant today as it was in 1988: "so far a precise way to explain the discourses' provenance and development has not been found."[131] It is therefore clear that the present study, which will assert that the Johannine discourses are based on a previously undetected oral form, the riddle, will require a fresh approach to the formation of FG's sayings tradition. In turn, a fresh approach to FG's sayings tradition will require the development of a new method. The above survey has indicated the basic course this new method must take, and certain obstacles which it must avoid.

Recent history has shown that the form–critical approach to FG's sayings tends to produce more positive results than the source–critical approach. Robert Kysar concluded his 1975 survey of approaches with this diagnosis: "What is needed . . . is a more highly developed method of Johannine Form Criticism; and until such methodology can be developed, our

---

[129]Dodd, *HTFG* 431.
[130]Carson, "Current Source Criticism" 429, emphasis original.
[131]Fortna, *FGIP* 3.

efforts in this regard may satisfy little more than the fancy."[132] D. Moody
Smith has also suggested that a form–critical approach might offer more
specific controls by providing external criteria for identifying traditional
units.[133] At the same time, current form–critical models have been able to
salvage only a very few embedded logia from FG's larger discourse units. To
move beyond the Other Consensus and locate riddles in FG, certain aspects of
conventional Form Criticism will require modification.

    First and primarily, the new Form Criticism must account for the fact
that FG bears few formal parallels with the Synoptics. Conventional Form
Criticism begins by comparing Synoptic parallels to determine traditional
forms, then attempts to verify these forms from non–canonical literature. Dunn
therefore observes that "our methodology [in Johannine Source Criticism]
inevitably depends on Synoptic–like parallels."[134] But true parallels between
FG and the Synoptics are few and far between, especially in the discourse
sections. Johannine scholars have attempted to compensate for this paucity of
parallels with two strategies, neither of which has been especially fruitful.
Some, like Dodd and Lindars, have imposed Synoptic categories onto
incompatible data from FG, forcing a redefinition of the forms themselves
and/or the conclusion that most of FG's discourse materials are not traditional.
The second alternative, taken by Fortna, Smith and others, has been to simply
ignore the discourses all together, usually under the premise that these
represent FE's own theological reflections. Neither alternative is satisfactory,
for even if the discourses originated entirely with FE it is probable that they
were generated in an oral environment and therefore may have absorbed oral
forms and patterns. The recognition of these oral forms and patterns is
therefore critical to the exegesis and composition–history of the passages in
which they appear. Since clear and specific parallels between FG's discourses
and the Synoptics are rare, the new Form Criticism cannot depend on them as
the basis of its investigation.

[132]Robert Kysar, *The Fourth Evangelist and His Gospel: An Examination of
Contempoary Scholarship* (Minneapolis, MN: Augsburg, 1975) 66.
    [133]D. Smith, "Johannine Christianity" 11–12; "Milieu of Miracle" 78.
    [134]Dunn, "John and the Oral Gospel" 377.

Second, this new Form Criticism cannot use criteria for determining traditional materials which exclude the possibility that certain sections of FG are traditional. There is no warrant for the adoption of methods which inherently prefer the Johannine narratives over the discourses, especially if this preference is based on analogies with the Synoptics. The unique circumstances of FE and the Johannine community make it highly probable that certain forms and patterns which are rare in, or absent from, the Synoptics would become essential to Johannine preaching. As will be seen, the riddle is one such form.

Finally, this new Form Criticism must avoid a persistent terminological difficulty. The reader of the preceding survey may have noticed that, up to this point, the words "historical," "traditional," and "Johannine" have been used indistinctly. This imprecision reflects the current state of Johannine scholarship, where these three terms and their relationships are understood differently by different researchers but rarely defined. The doctrine of johannisation, however, has produced a general agreement that the terms "traditional" and "Johannine" are somehow mutually exclusive. It will therefore be necessary to understand "traditional" in such a way that "traditional" and "Johannine" are not inherently opposed terms. It will also be especially important to clarify that the terms "traditional" and "authentic" are not synonyms. Sayings units in FG may be "traditional" in the broad sense that they are based on common oral speech patterns even if FE composed them whole cloth. As such, the present study will not be immediately concerned with whether or not Jesus himself used the riddles in the present text of FG, nor will it speculate on the origin of these units.

Chapter 2
Form Criticism and Folkloristics

Chapter 1 revealed that the most fruitful inquiries into the traditions underlying FG's discourses have utilized Form Criticism. In his introduction to this discipline for the *Guides to Biblical Scholarship* series, Edgar V. McKnight notes that NT Form Criticism examines the pre–literary oral tradition about Jesus as "individual sayings and narratives joined together in the Gospels by the work of the editors [Evangelists]." Craig Blomberg has more recently described the objectives of Form Criticism this way:

> It [Form Criticism] identifies the different 'forms' or subgenres which appear [in the gospels], and it attempts to describe the ways in which these forms developed during the period of time in which they were passed along by word of mouth prior to the writing of the Gospels themselves.[1]

Both definitions address the two–fold interest of this discipline, which is indicated by the two terms of its German name. First, *Formgeschichte* is concerned with "form," the genres of the oral units which preceded the written Gospels. This aspect of the discipline seeks to determine what circumstances and conditions led to the fixing of oral materials in particular modes of expression. It includes speculation about the conditions under which these units came into existence and about what methodological criteria are necessary to establish and describe them. McKnight refers to this aspect of Form

---

[1]Edgar V. McKnight, *What Is Form Criticism?* (GBSNTS; Philadelphia, PA: Fortress, 1969) 18; Craig L. Blomberg, "Form Criticism," *Dictionary of Jesus and the Gospels* (ed. Joel B. Green, Scot McKnight, and I. Howard Marshall; Downers Grove, IL: IVP, 1992) 243.

Criticism when he mentions the existence of "individual sayings and narratives," and Blomberg refers to it in his mention of "different 'forms' or subgenres."

Second, Form Criticism is concerned with the "history" of the transmission of these fixed formal units. This aspect of the discipline seeks to discover the methods by which these pre formed materials were appropriated, and the effect of this appropriation on the evolution of the tradition. The impact of this evolution on the "historicity" of the tradition is often considered. Of particular interest here are ways in which the Evangelists utilized preformed materials to compose the canonical gospels. McKnight refers to this aspect of Form Criticism when he speaks of the Evangelists "joining together" the individual preformed units, and Blomberg refers to it in his mention of the development of the tradition over the period of time in which the forms were "passed along by word of mouth."

These two aspects of Form Criticism are closely related, and both are relevant to the present study of FG's discourses. Both will also require certain methodological modifications to meet the criteria stated at the end of Chapter 1. Specifically, it will be necessary to identify the development and appropriations of oral forms in FG without recourse to Synoptic parallels. An alternative approach is offered by interdisciplinary research in speech genre and oral composition theory. This chapter and the next will reconsider the constituent elements of an oral "form," and will describe a prevalent oral form in the discourses of FG, the "riddle." These chapters will also address the "history" of the appropriation of such units in oral composition by appealing to the "Oral Formulaic" theory and to Ward Parks' discussion of synchrony and diachrony in oral traditions.[2]

---

[2]This approach to speech genres and to the "riddle" as a speech genre will distinguish the present study from Herbert LeRoy's monograph, *Rätsel und Missverständnis: Ein Beitrage zur "Form Criticism" des Johannesevangeliums* (BBB 30; Bonn: Peter Hanstein, 1968). LeRoy's understanding of the riddle is based on J. B. Friedreich's historical survey *Geschichte des Rätsels*, already a century old when LeRoy conducted his research (1860; rpt. Wiesbaden, 1969). Archer Taylor, who revived interest in riddles in the twentieth century, has referred to Friedreich's study as "a dilettante work which contains much useful information about such literary forms allied to the riddle as charades, logogriphs, anagrams, retrograde verses, and the like. The remarks on the traditional riddle are inadequate" (*A*

Before attempting modifications, however, it will be necessary to explore the roots of NT Form Criticism. This survey will provide a matrix for applying the interdisciplinary theories, and will allow continuity with the positive aspects of conventional form–critical approaches.

THE ROOTS OF NEW TESTAMENT FORM CRITICISM

Two major studies provided international impetus for the use of Form Criticism in the study of the Gospels, Martin Dibelius' *From Tradition to Gospel* (1919) and Rudolf Bultmann's *History of the Synoptic Tradition* (1921).[3] Aside from their influence, these works illustrate two similar but distinct approaches to the problems of form development and transmission history. They therefore provide a convenient starting point for the present study.

MARTIN DIBELIUS: FROM TRADITION TO GOSPELS

Martin Dibelius' *From Tradition to Gospel* does not explicitly formulate a theory of genre, and never strictly defines the constituent elements of a "form." Contemporary NT Genre Criticism generally follows the "form[/structure/style]–content–function" approach to genre popularized by scholars such as David Hellholm and David Aune.[4] Within this matrix, Dibelius' approach to form/genre theory is striking for its absolute dependence on function. Dibelius specifically devalues "content" as a criterion for

---

Bibliography of Riddles [FFC 126; Helsinki: Suomalainen Tiedeakatemia Academia Scientiarum Fenniga, 1939] 9). Taking Friedreich's descriptive historical approach to the genre, LeRoy identifies the following units in FG as "riddles": John 2:19–22; 3:3–5; 4:10–15, 31–34; 6:32–35, 41ff, 51–53; 7:33–36; 8:31–33, 51–53, 56–58.

[3]These studies were preceded chronologically by Karl Ludwig Schmidt's *Der Rahmen der Geschichte Jesu* (Berlin: Trowitzsch, 1919), which dealt the death blow to the traditional reliance on the framework of Mark.

[4]See David Hellholm, "The Problem of Apocalyptic Genre and the Apocalypse of John," *SBLSP 1982* (ed. Kent Harold Richards; Chico, CA: Scholars Press, 1982); David E. Aune, *The New Testament in Its Literary Environment* (Library of Early Christianity; Philadelphia, PA: Westminster, 1987). In the present study, "form" refers to genre, both specific genres and genre as a theoretical concept. Literary form as a constituent element of genres is referred to here as "style" or "structure."

categorization, refusing, for example, to regard "miracle story" as a distinct form because this category groups pericopae by their action contents.[5] The structural/stylistic aspect of form is also secondary in his analysis, under the premise that style is a byproduct of function.[6] An oral form's function is, in turn, a byproduct of the social setting in which the form developed. Life–settings call forth certain stylistic features, such as word choice and sentence construction, as the oral composer attempts to fit the material to the audience's situation.[7] The style and structure of each form is thus entirely a byproduct of the way situations compelled composers to shape their material. Dibelius therefore describes the stylistic features of each form only *after* determining a corresponding rhetorical function and life–setting through which the early Christians directed the oral material.

Because forms were forged in the life of the Church, Dibelius is particularly concerned to identify the typical settings of early Christian preaching. Dibelius defines "preaching" broadly as "all possible forms of Christian propaganda . . . mission preaching, preaching during worship, and catechumen instruction."[8] All three forms of preaching proclaimed salvation and utilized the "tradition," by which Dibelius meant the recollections of Jesus' disciples, to add "objectivity" to this proclamation. Dibelius thus postulates three typical situations in which Jesus tradition was utilized and shaped, each with a corresponding audience and unique rhetorical function. These situations are diagrammed on the following table.

---

[5]Martin Dibelius, *From Tradition to Gospel* (1933; trans. Bertram Lee Wolf; Greenwood, SC: Attic Press, 1971) 54. Also on content categories, Dibelius contends that "the fact of a dispute is not characteristic for a [form] category" (68).

[6]Admitting that the forms "Tale" and "Paradigm" share stylistic features, Dibelius asserts that, since the purpose of Form Criticism is to explain the formation of the tradition and not to make categories, the overlap of particular features within various forms is not determinative (Dibelius, *FTTG* 58–59).

[7]Dibelius, *FTTG* 6. "The style which it is our part to observe is 'a sociological result'" (7). Because the early Christians who shaped the preliterary material of the NT "desired to win men, and further to convince and to confirm those whom they had won," all early Christian oral forms evidence a style which "could be called edificatory" (37–38).

[8]Dibelius, *FTTG* 15. "What they narrated was secondary to this proclamation, was intended to confirm it and to found it." The tradition thus "explained, expanded, and, in accordance therewith, was either introduced into the preaching, or related at its close" (15).

Jesus
↓
"oral tradition" (disciples' memories)
↓ ↓ ↓

Tradition User	Evangelist	Teacher	Preacher
Function	↓ Conversion ↓	↓ Catechism ↓	↓ Exhortation ↓
Audience	Jews/Pagans/ Proselytes	Recent Converts	Christian Worshipers

The unique "Laws of Form–Construction" which operated in each situation caused aspects of the tradition to become fixed in their "outer and inner structure," creating a distinct "form."[9]

Turning to content, Dibelius suggests that three categories of Jesus material "stood in immediate connection with Christian preaching," passion stories, narratives, and sayings. Each genus, and the species within them, resulted from the particular set of laws operating in the preaching situation where the tradition was utilized. The Passion story was "fixed" as an independent formal unit very early because the Church was quickly forced to provide an apologetic for the cross in its evangelistic preaching, and later to demonstrate the theological significance of the cross in teaching and catechism. But "the description of the deeds of Jesus was not governed by the same interests in the course of preaching" as the Passion, because stories about Jesus' deeds were not immediately relevant to the proclamation of salvation.[10] In preaching, the deeds functioned as illustrations of "the salvation effected

---

[9]Dibelius, *FTTG*, first quotation 4, second quotation 10. Dibelius believes that these three preaching situations, with their corresponding functions, were transcultural. Universal forms developed in parallel fashion in different churches according to the "laws of development" of each typical situation, with individual variations representing particular local applications (21, 38).

[10]Dibelius, *FTTG* 22–24, quotation 24.

through Jesus Christ," so that these "could only be introduced as *examples* in support of the message" to "support its edifying tendencies."[11] Other narrative forms, such as "Tales" and "Legends," are similarly explained in terms of the various functions the tradition performed in the life of the Church.[12]

"We must presuppose the operation of still another law for the handing down of the sayings of Jesus."[13] This presupposition is once again necessitated by the fact that sayings were used in different settings to perform different functions from narratives. Dibelius suggests that the early tradition included a number of "isolated sayings, especially proverbs, metaphors, and commandments" which were "the common property of Christendom."[14] These sayings were used by "those *teachers* who are often mentioned in primitive Christian literature" for ethical instruction in catechetical contexts "within the framework of a Christian Halakha."[15] Sayings forms were shaped by their appropriation to the rhetorical needs of teaching in such contexts.

The priority that Dibelius gives to situation and function clarifies his form–critical method. Source criticism alone is insufficient because

> an analytical method which starts from the texts and goes back to the sources and isolated elements of the tradition is not satisfactory. Rather one requires a constructive method which attempts to include the conditions and activities of life of the first Christian Churches.[16]

---

[11]Dibelius, *FTTG* 26, emphasis original. Because the earliest narratives functioned as illustrations or models, Dibelius gave them the ancient rhetorical label "Paradigms." The unique preaching function of the Paradigm generated four distinct stylistic features: "brevity, edificatory style, emphasis upon the words of Jesus[,] . . . *the narrative should end in a thought useful for preaching purposes*" (48–58, quotation 58, emphasis original).

[12]"For the further development of evangelical tradition the *story–teller* and the *teacher* appear to have been of special significance" (Dibelius, *FTTG* 70). Features of the "Tale," a dramatized elaboration of the Paradigm (99), are delineated on pp. 70–71; those of the "Legend," which is rare in the Synoptics, are discussed on pp. 104–106.

[13]Dibelius, *FTTG* 27.

[14]Dibelius, *FTTG*, first quotation 27, second quotation 239. "*[T]he tradition of narrative and the tradition of words are not subject to the same law*" (28, emphasis original).

[15]Dibelius, *FTTG*, first quotation 240, emphasis original, second quotation 28.

[16]Dibelius, *FTTG* 10.

For each form, Dibelius begins by reconstructing a typical situation in the life of the early Church, and then suggests appropriate speakers, functions, and audiences for that situation. Appeal to the "laws of development" which operate in each social situation generates hypothetical oral forms, which Dibelius then tests by examining the present texts of the Synoptics, Acts, and Paul's letters. For example, to support the early fixing of the passion story and its elements, Dibelius appeals to the speeches of Acts and the primitive outline of the "Gospel" at 1 Cor. 15:1–7.[17] After discussing the early preaching contexts which produced the "Paradigm," he urges that "we must [now] turn our attention to the tradition which we have received [the Synoptics]," where he discovers eight "pure" paradigms and ten other stories which bear a close resemblance to this hypothetical form.[18] Overall, Dibelius' method moves from situation to function to oral form to literary text.

Because Gospel forms developed anonymously according to situational needs, Dibelius does not include ideological issues in his theory of form. In fact, the earliest forms developed *in spite of* the Christian preachers' sense of "'pneumatic' inspiration and apocalyptic excitement." Dibelius believes this pneumatic–apocalyptic ideology would make any fixed preservation of the Jesus tradition unlikely outside "the regulated activity of teaching and learning." "The primitive Christian Churches were prepared for the disappearance of this world and not for life in it," and therefore lacked any conscious intention of preserving and shaping the tradition.[19]

In summary, Dibelius' concept of "form" relies heavily on *functional* aspects of genre. These rhetorical functions operated in typical preaching situations and established "laws" of form construction, which forced the early

---

[17]Dibelius, *FTTG* 15–23.

[18]Dibelius, *FTTG* 40–43, quotation 40.

[19]Dibelius, *FTTG*, first quotation 10, second quotation 11, third quotation 240. The Paradigm, for example, "is the only form in which the tradition of Jesus could be preserved at a time when a yearning for the end and a consciousness of estrangement from the world would still entirely prevent concern for a historical tradition or the development of a literature" (69). Note that the term "ideology" is preferred over "theology" throughout this study as more relevant to genre theory. "Ideology" here includes theological and cosmological creeds, ethics and values, sociopolitical doctrines, and literary tendencies such as "biographical interest."

Christian preachers to shape the witness about Jesus into specific fixed patterns. These patterns became the vehicles for the individual units of Jesus tradition which were appropriated by Mark, Matthew and Luke. This leads to Dibelius' approach to the second concern of Form Criticism, the history of the transmission and appropriation of these fixed oral units "from tradition [reminiscence of Jesus] to [written] gospel."

Just as individual forms arose in specific life settings of the early Church, Dibelius believes the overall history of the tradition could not be described apart from the Church's history. "The fortune of primitive Christianity is reflected in the history of the Gospel form." In this formative period the Church moved through three developmental stages: conscious alienation from the world and self–limitation; the rise of distinct religious interests of the Church as institution; an eventual accommodation to the world and the world's relationships. The four major narrative forms, Passion, Paradigm, Tale, and Legend, arose in response to these historical developments.[20] New preaching situations also gradually altered the sayings tradition, a tendency which Dibelius refers to as "parenetic transformation."[21] One means of transformation was the development of primitive sayings collections, such as Q.[22] Dibelius believes that in many cases isolated sayings were brought together with "a hortatory interest" "to convey to Christendom a 'teaching' of Jesus on important questions of Church life."[23] These collected teachings were regarded as authoritative parenetic instruction and "were given to the missionaries orally or fixed in writing" "to give the Churches advice, help, and commandment by means of the master's words" in preaching and catechism.[24]

The effects of the laws of parenetic transformation were not, however, limited to compilation. Even Q shows evidence that the older forms were

[20]Dibelius, *FTTG* 287.
[21]Dibelius, *FTTG* 257, 259.
[22]Dibelius believes that Q's framework is too uncertain for reconstruction: "The present position of research into the source Q warrants our speaking rather of a stratum than of a document" (*FTTG* 235). Primitive narrative cycles also developed over time.
[23]Dibelius, *FTTG*, first quotation 241, second quotation 222.
[24]Dibelius, *FTTG*, first quotation 242, second quotation 246. Teachers cited these collections with formalized introductions which indicated their traditional status (242–243).

edited and developed to meet new situations. While much of Jesus' own teaching was delivered in hortatory forms, the Church tended to magnify and expand the parenetic value of his words. This included the moralizing use of some forms which must not have served that purpose in Jesus' ministry, such as metaphors, beatitudes, and parables.[25] As the functional use of the sayings material changed, "we must reckon that the tendency of the churches to derive *as much exhortation as possible from the words of Jesus* must have effected the handing down."[26] In this way, the developing forms were shifted from one function to another.

Alongside the functional alterations of parenetic transformation, the Jesus tradition underwent a process that may be called "epiphanization."[27] Here Dibelius explicitly brings ideological factors into consideration. Although fixed Aramaic forms may have developed early on, "it is the pre–Pauline *Hellenistic Christianity* which at least handed on the tradition and, to the extent that the formulation is Greek, also formed it."[28] Since these

---

[25]Dibelius, *FTTG* 244–249.

[26]Dibelius, *FTTG* 257, emphasis original. Especially in the case of parables, which were often applied to new situations with "complete misunderstanding," "the parenetic value set upon the words of Jesus has occasionally altered their content." Consequently, "we must reckon with the fact that we do not know the original references of numerous parables" (Dibelius, *FTTG* 255, 249). Since many of Jesus' parables borrow stock Jewish metaphors, Christian teachers might have interpreted them in their typical Jewish sense, and perhaps even accidentally attributed some Jewish parables to Jesus for their preaching value. In other cases incidental references in Jesus' parables may have been allegorically extended to suit the needs of preaching (Dibelius, *FTTG* 255–257).

[27]"We may say that the idea of epiphany guaranteed to the entire biographical material of Christ the meaning for the Church, and to this extent effected its preservation" (Dibelius, *FTTG* 299).

[28]Dibelius, *FTTG* 29, emphasis original. This conclusion is based on the assumption that Paul was instructed in such a tradition in Damascus. The earliest stage of form construction was "the Palestinian Circle of Jesus," whose preaching was Aramaic (28). These Aramaic units were translated at various points under various conditions; since the Hellenistic preachers were probably bilingual, they may have translated them spontaneously in preaching contexts. Hence the shift from Aramaic to Greek forms could "admit various possibilities from verbal translation (especially of the words of Jesus) to complete new formation (especially of narratives)" (34). Dibelius does not, however, believe that such Aramaic forms can be reconstructed, and they are not significant to his analysis (32–33).

Hellenistic churches were Jewish in outlook, they conceived of Jesus' activity "from the standpoint that a long–expected salvation had now been realized in particular events amongst the Jewish people."[29] At this stage the tradition about Jesus was distinct from the proclamation of salvation, and was used in support of that proclamation in the various settings described above. But over time, as Jesus' words became ethical guidelines and the Church began to see "salvation" not in the eschatological future but in Jesus' past activity, the Risen Lord of the proclamation became the subject of the tradition, "and the union . . . of the life of Jesus with Christology was completed."[30]

As the Church's ideology moved away from Jewish Messianism toward an epiphanized incarnational Christology, older forms were recast to portray the historical Jesus as God on earth. Thus, "a tradition of an unliterary nature, consisting of short narratives and striking sayings, which was repeated for practical purposes," evolved by stages into a stylized epiphanic mythology, from a Jewish to a distinctly Christian ideology.[31] Dibelius believes that the *formgeschichtliche Methode* can chronicle this progression: "from the forms it [Form Criticism] can deduce the leading interests of the tradition," because each stage of form development was dominated by the particular ideological conception of the Church at that time.[32] Ideology, then, does not define form, but form can reveal ideology. The degree of epiphanization which a pericope evidences, the extent to which the tradition is no longer distinct from and dependent upon the proclamation, reveals its position on the ideological and historical spectrums.

Dibelius understands the term "Gospel" to refer to a seamless combination of formed tradition and distinctly Christian ideology. Mark, for example, succeeded in keeping the tradition separate from his own proclamation. Since "the word 'Evangel' is the name given to the preaching of salvation," Mark is therefore not a true "gospel." Matthew, however, is

---

[29]Dibelius, *FTTG* 30. "In such Churches, therefore, worship, preaching, and teaching were of a Jewish kind although conducted in Greek. It is in this place that we must look for the real home of a tradition which was passed on to missionaries, preachers, and teachers" (30–31).

[30]Dibelius, *FTTG* 289, 298, quotation 298.

[31]Dibelius, *FTTG* 287.

[32]Dibelius, *FTTG* 295.

closer to "gospel," in that the tradition has not been kept separate from the proclamation but has been incorporated into it "with a systematic pedagogic arrangement and cast." Such self–conscious attribution of specifically Christian material to the historical Jesus shows that Matthew is at a more advanced stage of epiphanization than Mark.[33] For Dibelius, FG represents the climax of the tradition's ideological evolution, as Jesus' human life becomes an eschatological epiphany and "the decisive revelation of God."[34]

RUDOLF BULTMANN: FROM GOSPELS TO TRADITION

Rudolf Bultmann's form–critical method differed from that of Dibelius, but was very much in harmony with the interests of early 20th century scholarship. First, his method explicitly presupposes that all form–critical inquiry must begin with the literary gospels understood within the Two–Source Theory. Indeed, "even the distinction between tradition and redaction could not be made without literary analysis."[35] Dibelius' approach, which moves from community needs to oral forms to written gospels, was misguided. "I hold it wrong to proceed one–sidedly and simply deduce the forms of the tradition from the needs of the community."[36] Second, Bultmann clearly believes that his *formgeschichtliche Methode* can address pressing

---

[33]Dibelius, *FTTG*, both quotations 264.

[34]Dibelius, *FTTG* 300.

[35]Rudolf Bultmann, *The History of the Synoptic Tradition* (rev. ed.; trans. John Marsh; New York: Harper & Row, 1963) 3. Bultmann's "The Study of the Synoptic Gospels" opens with an overview of the Two Source model, outlining specific dates and lines of dependence. Matthew and Luke utilized Ur–Mark and "Q," where Q was a sayings collection which may have circulated in several different versions. Q, and possibly Ur–Mark also, was originally Aramaic (1933; rpt. in *Form Criticism: Two Essays on New Testament Research* [ed. and trans. Frederick C. Grant; New York, NY: Harper & Brothers, 1962] 11–15; see also *HST* 328). Bultmann believes that Matthew and Luke had written sources other than Mark and Q, but is less certain of Streeter's Four Source Theory ("SSG" 14; *HST* 321). Mark is dated post–70, Matthew and Luke "nearer 100" ("SSG" 15). The translation of *HST* cited here is based on the 3rd German edition of 1931.

[36]Bultmann, *HST* 5, 11. In this connection, Bultmann's claim that his form category label "Apophthegm" is "least question–begging" is apparently directed to Dibelius' more functional name, "Paradigm" (11). At the same time, however, he agrees with Dibelius that "the biographical apophthegms are best thought of as edifying paradigms for sermons" (61).

historical–critical issues. This concern is evident in the very format of his *Study of the Synoptic Gospels*, which opens with several questions about Jesus' life and mission, then surveys Form Criticism as a discipline, and then returns to answer the historical concerns in the conclusion, setting a historical frame around the method itself.[37] Bultmann regards Form Criticism as a natural extension of Source Criticism, useful for answering a number of questions which require speculation about the pre–Markan phases of the Gospel.[38]

To address such issues, Bultmann proposes an evolutionary model of form development which is, on the surface, similar in many respects to that of Dibelius. Like Dibelius, Bultmann believes that form evolution followed specific laws, which provided "a certain orderliness in change by which a body of tradition is always controlled in its growth."[39] These laws operated in "quite definite conditions and wants of life from which grows up a quite definite style and quite specific forms and categories." *Sitz im Leben* is not "an individual historical event, but a typical situation or occupation in the life of the community." Consequently, "form" is "a sociological concept and not an aesthetic one."[40] Universal forms developed under parallel conditions in different churches to perform typical functions, leaving individual preachers anonymous. The embedded forms which appear in the NT are products of these developmental laws.

But Bultmann differs sharply from Dibelius on the basic methodological question of how this developmental process should be reconstructed. Dibelius' functional theory of genre led him to begin with speculation about the typical

---

[37]"SSG" addresses three issues: the tension in Jesus' teaching between ethical prescription and eschatological urgency; Jesus' messianic self–consciousness; and, the motive behind Jesus' execution (23–24, 71–73). Bultmann's discussion of Form Criticism begins on page 25 with the statement, "Where is the way leading out of such perplexities?" Also revealing of his historical interests, he states that "one can only emphasize the uncertainty of our knowledge of the person and work of the historical Jesus" *before* opening his discussion of the method (20).

[38]The distinctions made in this study between "form" and "*Geschichte*," and between the literary and ideological motives governing the *Geschichte*, are more precise than Bultmann recognizes. The following discussion will seek to demonstrate that theoretical imprecision was an inevitable consequence of Bultmann's form–critical method.

[39]Bultmann, "SSG" 29.

[40]All three quotations Bultmann, *HST* 4.

situations in which forms developed, then suggest hypothetical forms, and then verify these forms from the NT texts. Bultmann takes the opposite approach, *beginning* with the written gospels and working backward through form to situation. This approach forged the tools of Form Criticism which underlie Butlmann's exhaustive *History of the Synoptic Tradition*.

The first "tool" of Bultmann's form–critical method is the Two–Source Theory. Observation and comparison reveal "a certain regularity in the way Matthew and Luke used Mark" and the "laws which governed the development of materials from Q." One may confirm these preliminary data by comparing Matthew and Luke with the later apocryphal gospels and, to a lesser extent, FG.[41] Further along the developmental trajectory, one may consider "the history of the text," noting tendencies in scribal emendation.[42] These comparisons will allow speculation about the laws of development for Jesus traditions within the early Church.

To verify these tendencies outside the Christian sphere, one may appeal to another form–critical tool, the findings of folkloristics on "the general laws governing popular narrative and tradition, such as stories and anecdotes." Here one might research the form development of "proverbs, anecdotes, and folk–tales," fairy tales, folksongs, and comparative texts such as "the Jataka collection of the Buddhist canon." Another helpful tool for verifying tendencies in the Christian tradition is comparison with other ancient documents, such as Jewish literature, the Rabbinic corpus, and "Hellenistic stories."[43] Ancient literatures and folklore models thus provide analogies

---

[41]Bultmann, *HST* 4–6; "SSG" 26, 29–30. On sayings forms specifically, "It is clear that we cannot confine our observations simply to those occasions where we can make a comparison with a source, but that we must push our considerations back even behind our earliest sources, Q and Mark, and in this way gain a glimpse into the growth of the tradition" (*HST* 93).

[42]Bultmann, *HST* 185–186, 344–345.

[43]Bultmann, "SSG," all quotations 30; *HST* 6–7. Bultmann's actual appeals to folklore "parallels" generally do not consider the possibility that modern folk forms which have arisen in contact with Christianity may have been directly influenced by the Gospels, making them the later stages of an evolution rather than interdisciplinary parallels. For example, Bultmann responds to the observation that Synoptic Wisdom Sayings often parallel OT forms by remarking, "so far as I can see, the proverbial literatures of all peoples exhibit more or less the same forms" (*HST* 46, 70, 97, 183–184, quotation 70). This assumes that

which allow further refinement of the developmental tendencies deduced from the Christian materials. This approach permits Bultmann to speculate with probability about the laws of form development.

Bultmann's tools, however, are powered by a key methodological assumption: "If we are able to detect any such laws [of form development], we may assume that they were operative on the traditional material even before it was given its form in Mark and Q."[44] Bultmann thus proposes to use observable literary sources to define the later stages of Gospel form development, check his conclusions against available ancient parallels and folklore models, then project these tendencies backward onto the earlier, oral period. Once these oral forms are established, the typical situations that produced them can be reconstructed. It is important to note that the logic of *HST* always follows this sequence, even though the presentation, which is notoriously complex, tends to analyze specific units in each form category *before* discussing the category itself.

Bultmann's form–critical method gives the appearance of greater objectivity than that of Dibelius because it takes the visible (written) stages of the Gospel tradition as a starting point, This impression, however, masks a serious flaw. Because his method focuses on the comparison of written texts, primarily the Synoptics under the Two Source model, Bultmann's various "forms" are apparently deduced entirely by observation, *without the benefit of any consistent theory of "form."* As a consequence, the parameters of the form categories suggested in *HST* are not consistent, and several of the suggested forms overlap. This is especially true of Bultmann's sayings forms, which will be the focus of this discussion. In each category and subcategory of sayings,

---

OT, Synoptic, and folk Wisdom Sayings represent parallel developments rather than an evolutionary spectrum. A particularly striking case of Bultmann's uncritical use of folklore "parallels" appears in his discussion of similitudes, where he attempts to verify the tendency to add an application in the form of a logion by citing a Russian fairy tale with explicitly Christian features (*HST* 186–187). Do such cases represent a "tendency" of all oral traditions, or the conscious imitation of biblical forms in secular folk texts?

[44]Bultmann, *HST* 6. "If we are able to deduce a certain regularity in this procedure, then we may certainly assume that the same laws held good even earlier, and we may draw conclusions as to the state of the tradition prior to Mark and Q" ("SSG" 29).

it is clear that Bultmann's taxonomy is guided primarily by his observation of Synoptic parallels rather than a careful analytical model.

To illustrate the imprecision of Bultmann's method, this study will focus on his discussion of "Dominical Sayings," those sayings "which have, or could have[,] been independent elements of the tradition." Bultmann subdivides dominical sayings into five categories. Three of these group units "according to their actual contents, though formal differences are involved as well": "Logia" or "Wisdom sayings"; "Prophetic and Apocalyptic sayings"; and, "Laws and community regulations." Two other categories group sayings primarily on the basis of style, "I–sayings" and "parables and related material."[45] All five categories are apparently developed on the basis of Bultmann's observation, analysis, and grouping of Synoptic pericopae.[46]

To subdivide units within the larger category Logia, "it is necessary to distinguish between *constitutive and ornamental motifs*," as the latter are presumably not determinative in form–critical considerations. "Constitutive" motifs are those integral to "the logical form of the sentence." Hence, *style* is the dominant generic criterion for delineating Bultmann's three forms of Logia: "Principles," declarative sentences; "Exhortations," imperative sentences; and, "Questions." But Bultmann's further subdivision of "Principles" is based on *content*: "Material Formulations," with a thing as subject; "Personal Formulations," with a person as subject; "Blessings"; and, arguments from major to minor. Without specifying the differences between these categories, Bultmann lists a number of OT examples to verify his taxonomy.[47] Here, a category, "Logia," is defined on the basis of *contents*; the first level of subcategories is based on *style*; and specific forms within the subcategories are again based on *contents*.

---

[45]Bultmann, *HST* 69.

[46]The same is true of Bultmann's narrative forms. The "Apophthegm," for example, is recognizable by a distinct *style* characteristic: "sayings of Jesus set in a brief context" (*HST* 11). Subforms within this category are based on *content*: "Controversy Dialogues and Scholastic Dialogues" (12) and "Biographical Apophthegms" (27). The dialogues may be further subdivided on the basis of the action *contents* which motivate Jesus' pithy saying: a healing (12); the conduct of Jesus or his disciples (16); Jesus is questioned by his disciples or others (21); Jesus is questioned by opponents (26).

[47]Bultmann, *HST* 70–76.

Bultmann's shifting conception of "form" is particularly evident in the subcategories of "Prophetic and Apocalyptic sayings." Four forms are included under this *content* category: the "Preaching of Salvation," which groups sayings on the basis of *content*; "Minatory Sayings," or woes, which groups sayings on the basis of *style*; "Admonitions," a *content* category which encompasses a variety of styles, including some parables; and, "Apocalyptic Predictions," which share common motifs and style features.[48] This content–based category ("Prophetic and Apocalyptic Sayings") thus includes two forms based primarily on *content* criteria and two forms based primarily on *style* criteria.

Bultmann's concept of "form" becomes only more obscure when one turns to "Legal Sayings and Church Rules." His discussion opens with the admission that eight sayings which deal with "the Law or Jewish piety" have already been treated as "Logia," so that these categories overlap. The "Legal Sayings," aside from their contents, sometimes evidence a particular "legal style, i.e. they are sentences whose first clause contains a condition . . . and whose second part is an imperative or an assertion . . . and which has the sense of legal prescription." Without elaborating what a "sense of legal prescription" might be, Bultmann immediately warns that this form may actually evidence a variety of styles, so that sometimes it is recognizable only by its "general effect."[49] Here, then, it seems that *rhetorical effect* is considered an aspect of form. After noting some specific stylistic variations, Bultmann indicates that "Legal Sayings" would also include "those which, by means of a proverb or an appeal to Scripture, justify or base the new outlook over against the old."[50] "Outlook" would seem to be an ideological feature of texts, so that Bultmann here regards *ideology* as an aspect of form. It is particularly apparent with this category that Bultmann can postulate connections between several Synoptic sayings for any number of reasons. Once a connection is made, these sayings could be grouped and analyzed to determine common style or contents. The results of this second analysis are treated as forms, even though the members of his categories manifest different features and functions.

---

[48]Bultmann, *HST* 109–120.
[49]Bultmann, *HST* 130–132, quotations 132.
[50]Bultmann, *HST* 136.

Bultmann's last two sayings forms, "I–Sayings" and "Similitudes and Similar Forms," clearly overlap with the other three categories. Closer inspection reveals that these are actually not "forms" at all, but rather sets of topoi and literary motifs which can appear in a variety of contexts. An "I–Saying" is any saying which involves a self–"reference to the person of Jesus," including those embedded in apophthegms. Subcategories of I–Sayings are based on the type of reference involved. For example, Jesus often speaks about himself in terms of his "coming"; in other cases, "the *risen Lord speaks of his person*" in various ways.[51] The former subgroup is based on a particular topos, the latter on the character who delivers the utterance. "Similitudes and Similar Forms" are a collection of literary devices which may appear in any of the other forms. These include "figures," metaphors ("shortened comparisons lacking the comparative word"), similes, similitudes (expanded and detailed figures), parables (similitudes cast in the form of a concrete story rather than general experience), and "exemplary stories" (developed parables which lack a symbolic component and offer models for behavior).[52] Each of these stylistic devices can interact with a number of content types. None, however, represents a distinct form.

In summary, it is evident that Bultmann's form categories are the product of an attempt to create a taxonomy of Synoptic texts without any explicit conception of the parameters of the categories themselves. A "form" in *HST* may be any group of texts with similar style, contents, literary/rhetorical motifs and devices, ideological peculiarities, or any combination of these. This imprecision, however, is acceptable to Bultmann because it serves his ultimate form–critical objective. In discussing the occasional difficulty of distinguishing similitudes and parables, Bultmann makes an important methodological concession:

> conceptual differentiation [of forms] is necessary for understanding the motive which determines the form; but no intelligent person would expect any particular instance to give pure expression to any particular form.[53]

---

[51]Bultmann, *HST*, first quotation 150, second quotation 157.
[52]Bultmann, *HST* 167–179.
[53]Bultmann, *HST* 174–175.

Indeed, Bultmann is much less interested in the "conceptual differentiation" of traditional forms than in the "motives" which governed their development and appropriation. Questions of form often cannot be differentiated from the developmental history of the tradition in his form–critical analysis. This observation leads to the next topic, Bultmann's perspective on the *Geschichte* of the tradition.

Bultmann conceives of the history of the Synoptic tradition as a series of alterations and expansions of oral forms. He attributes some of these developments to literary motives, as the Church utilized existing forms to confront new situations. Other developments, however, were the result of ideological readjustments, which kept the tradition compatible with the Church's developing belief system. This ideological development generally did not involve "a conscious introduction of particular dogmas, but something which is for the most part an unconscious tincture of Christian ideas."[54] Since the written gospels are products of these literary and ideological trends, their authenticity is subject to question. The "history" and the "historicity" of the Synoptic tradition are therefore intertwined in Bultmann's analysis.

Primary among the literary trends of the tradition–history was a tendency to intensify units by making them more precise, either in application or in detail. Because the earliest material "was made up almost entirely of brief units (sayings or short narratives)," this process included the "*expansion of an original saying by addition.*"[55] Early Logia, for example, were often "enlarged with an illustration" in transmission. Pre–existing Logia might be brought together, or new sayings or phrases added to an existing Logia, in the spirit of Hebrew parallelism to emphasize a point.[56] Similitudes were especially vulnerable to this sort of literary development. Applications were frequently attached to the end of similitudes and parables with an οὕτως ("thusly") or λέγω ὑμῖν ("I tell you") clause. These applications might be preexisting sayings or new compositions. Like Logia, the similitudes were grouped in transmission, and sometimes new units were produced to create a series. Such

---

[54]Bultmann, *HST* 93.

[55]Bultmann, first quotation "SSG" 25, second quotation *HST* 89, emphasis original.

[56]Bultmann, *HST* 81–87, quotation 81. "I–Sayings" in particular proliferated in the later stages of the tradition (162–163).

expansions and combinations might require stylistic changes to accommodate formulaic introductions or transitions, particularly in the literary stages of transmission.[57] These literary alterations sharpened the point of the sayings and made them more useful to Christian proclamation.

Recontextualization was another means of making Dominical Sayings more precise. For example, "apophthegms developed in the tradition when independent sayings were joined to an already existing [narrative] situation." Here the narrative increased the drama of a saying by associating it with a concrete episode in Jesus' life. This device was so effective that it took on a "generating power," so that ideal narrative settings were created for existing sayings in cases where a traditional story could not be found.[58] An example here is the *productive power of the controversy dialogue.*[59] This species of apophthegm encases a dominical saying in an ideal situation which involves "some action or attitude [of Jesus or his disciples] which is seized upon by the opponent and used in an attack by accusation or by question." When situated in such frameworks, "dominical sayings . . . were given vividness by being set in a concrete scene."[60]

Along with recontextualization, another literary tendency of the tradition was increased narrative detail. The earliest apophthegms were simple narratives, with concise sayings and economy of detail about time, place, or characters other than Jesus.[61] But the Synoptics reveal that "as soon as the apophthegm is affected by an interest in history or developed story telling we meet with more precise statements."[62] Thus, Jesus begins to initiate situations

---

[57]Bultmann, *HST* 130, 184–187, 194–195. In more extreme cases, traditional units were shifted from one form to another to facilitate combination ("SSG" 51–52).

[58]Bultmann, *HST,* first quotation 61, second quotation 62. Although Bultmann is uncertain whether sayings forms were fixed before narrative forms (11), his treatment of the apophthegms would suggest that the sayings were more significant to the earliest Church.

[59]Bultmann, *HST* 51, emphasis original.

[60]Bultmann, *HST* 39, 47, 55, first quotation 39, second quotation 47. In general, "the sayings have commonly generated the situation, not vice–versa" (47), but in some cases the style of a saying was altered to correspond with the new context (94–95).

[61]Bultmann, *HST* 62–64. "The interest of the apophthegms is entirely confined to the *sayings of Jesus*" (62, emphasis original).

[62]Bultmann, *HST* 67.

rather than simply responding to them; "the [later] narrator prefers to give in direct discourse what his source gave indirectly"; anonymous persons in stories tend be named; "there is an active tendency seeking always *to present the opponents of Jesus as scribes and Pharisees.*"[63] Such changes represent an increasing literary interest in the narrative for its own sake, and the development of dramatic elements with little historical interest.

Alongside and beneath these literary developments, and of much greater interest to Bultmann, the oral gospel forms evolved along a specific ideological trajectory. The effort to trace this evolution precisely and to situate Synoptic pericopae within it is perhaps the most characteristic feature of Bultmann's form–critical method. Bultmann believes three distinct ideologies are relevant to form–critical inquiry—those of first–century Judaism, Jesus, and the early Church. It will be helpful here to briefly review Bultmann's understanding of each of these ideologies and the affect each had on the developing Jesus tradition.

The "Judaism" of *HST* is a monolithic religion, characterized by non–eschatological legalism and represented by the rabbinic documents.[64] Bultmann uses this Judaism as a backdrop, against which Jesus' "characteristically individual spirit" was set in bold relief. Jesus' teaching and religion always "contain something characteristic, new, reaching out beyond popular wisdom and piety and yet in no sense scribal or rabbinic nor yet Jewish apocalyptic."[65] If not apocalyptic, Jesus' message was certainly eschatological, so that Bultmann characterizes him as "the preacher of repentance and the coming kingdom."[66] Jesus' message was "an energetic summons to

---

[63]Bultmann, first quotation "SSG" 34, second quotation *HST* 57, emphasis original; see also *HST* 53, 66, 333.

[64]In "SSG," Bultmann notes that primitive mystic Gnosticism may have influenced Palestinian Judaism, appearing in such forms as the Baptist sect. But because he believes the Church emerged from normative Judaism, Bultmann's comparative research focuses entirely on this sector and the rabbinic corpus which it produced (18–19).

[65]Bultmann, *HST*, first quotation 128, second quotation 105.

[66]Bultmann, *HST* 101. This kingdom was not conceived "as an human community" either by Jesus or by the earliest Church, and he never spoke of its "growth" (200). For form–critical analysis, Bultmann portrays Jesus primarily as an eschatological prophet who believed God's kingdom was at work in his proclamation, and stresses that "it seems too

repentance" which demanded "a new disposition of mind" in "flaming opposition to legalistic [Jewish] piety."[67]

The Church's ideology became increasingly distinct from that of Jesus and Judaism as it developed from a small sect of Palestinian Judaism into an independent Hellenistic institution. In the course of this development, the Jesus tradition was continually transfused with the Church's ideology, particularly its views of Christ and its own community life. The early Palestinian Church framed its Jesus tradition within Jewish expectations of a Messiah who would return as Son of Man. The later Hellenistic Church knew Jesus only as the Risen Lord of faith, Spirit, and sacrament, and portrayed him as a Hellenistic redeemer figure.[68] The cultic Christ figure was gradually pushed back onto the tradition, so that Jesus' life and ministry became the deeds of a pre–existent, miraculously born, incarnate deity.[69]

Alongside this Christological development, the Church appropriated the tradition to forge its own identity as a group distinct within, and later from, Judaism. Traditional materials were recast as Jesus' definitive statements on Judaism and the Law.[70] Sayings were used parenetically to create institutional codes of conduct, in which "the church was conscious, not of its churchly duties but of its characteristic piety in distinction from that of Judaism." To validate its worship and sacraments, the Church reshaped the tradition "to trace the origin of the 'cultic' observance[s] in the fate of the cult–deity," Jesus Christ.[71] In this way the eschatological urgency of Jesus' message was smoothed out to fit the ethical needs of a Church which expected to live in the world for some time.

In service of these Christological and institutional concerns, traditional sayings were eventually gathered into primitive collections which authorized the Church's doctrine by producing a "teaching" of Jesus on a particular topic. The earliest collections were based on content or form, "though now and then

---

fantastic for me to suppose that Jesus believed that he would one day become the 'Son of Man'" (137).

[67]First two quotations Bultmann, *HST* 105, third quotation "SSG" 58.
[68]Bultmann, "SSG" 17; *HST* 369–370.
[69]Bultmann, "SSG" 68–69; *HST* 348–349.
[70]Bultmann, "SSG" 59–60.
[71]Bultmann, first quotation *HST* 146, second quotation "SSG" 67.

pure chance takes a hand." Because their motives were ideological rather than historical, the early compilers "collected without any reference to the place or time when they [the sayings] were spoken."[72] These editors adjusted the traditional material as necessary to make individual units compatible to the overall theme, and sometimes offered explicit commentary.[73] Apophthegms were brought together for "apologetic and polemic" interests, while sayings collections "grew out of the need for paraenesis and Church discipline." This *"collection of the material of the tradition began in the primitive Palestinian Church"* and climaxed in the written gospels.[74] The Synoptic Evangelists represent a high degree of editorial sophistication, producing narrative cycles and speeches which completely effaced the ideology of the earlier forms.[75]

With Dibelius, Bultmann believes that ideological factors can situate the written gospels as a unique genre arising within a particular period of the Church's life. Mark's editing consciously portrayed the deeds of Jesus as "secret epiphanies" to reflect the ideology of "the Hellenistic Churches of Paul's persuasion." This sustained attempt to merge traditional forms with the Hellenistic kerygma makes Mark the first "gospel," in which the sayings of Jesus are presented as the teachings of the Risen Lord who is present in the Church's faith and worship.[76] FG is the most sophisticated example of the genre "gospel." "In John, the original meaning of the gospel comes out in fullest clarity, in that the evangelist while making free use of the tradition creates the figure of Jesus entirely from faith," so that "the myth has

---

[72]First quotation Bultmann, *HST* 322, second quotation "SSG" 26. Specifically, early compilations might involve (a) topical or thematic organization; (b) "association by formal relationship"; (c) "association by catchword" (*HST* 325–326).

[73]Bultmann, *HST* 326–327.

[74]Bultmann, *HST* 368, emphasis original.

[75]Bultmann, *HST* 322.

[76]This unique ideology leads Bultmann to conclude that the gospels are *sui generis*, "an original creation of Christianity" (Bultmann, *HST* 347–348, 374). The gospel genre "was obviously far removed from the Palestinian Church," and *"the Gospels themselves are expanded cult legends"* (Bultmann, *HST*, first quotation 369, second quotation 371, emphasis original; "SSG" 64–65). The imminent eschatology of the Palestinian Church apparently suppressed interest in coherent historical presentation.

completely violated the historical tradition."[77] The speeches of the Synoptics, for example, are thematic compilations of independent materials which lack organic unity. When such integration is present, "as in the Fourth Gospel, it is no longer simply a question of the development of the older tradition, but something quite new."[78] Like the early Palestinian Church, although from a different ideological motive, FG propagates a picture of Jesus which does not distinguish between theology and history. The Synoptics represent a brief period in the Hellenistic Church between eschatological immanence and developed cultic mythology when a limited "historical" interest in Jesus existed.

The Synoptics are therefore a potential source for historical information about Jesus. But the literary and ideological trends described above warn against naive assumptions. Very early in *HST*, Bultmann specifies that

> in distinction from Dibelius I am indeed convinced that form–criticism, just because literary forms are related to the life and history of the primitive Church[,] not only *presupposes* judgements of facts alongside judgements of literary criticism, but *must also lead to* judgements about facts.[79]

Bultmann believes that the literary and ideological trends of the tradition revealed by comparative analysis can explain various features of the Synoptics. These trends thus supply criteria of authenticity for evaluating any particular pericope, and by this means the form–critical method could answer Bultmann's original questions about the historical Jesus.

ORAL WORDS ARE EVENTS

In moving toward a new perspective on oral forms and form–critical method, it will be helpful to highlight a prominent feature of both Dibelius'

---

[77]Bultmann, first quotation "SSG" 70, second quotation *HST* 371.

[78]Bultmann, *HST* 322. On narratives, FE adjusted the Apophthegm so that "all Jesus does springs from his own initiative" (66). The footwashing episode of John 13 "derives from Luke 22[27] (or some similar saying), although admittedly it no longer has the primitive style of the old apophthegm" (48).

[79]Bultmann, *HST* 5, emphasis added.

and Bultmann's Form Criticism. Although oral forms have individual oral utterances as their content and substance, neither of these scholars explicitly elaborate a theory of oral discourse. They doubtless judged such inquiry redundant, since *neither conceives of any theoretical difference between oral and written speech.* The assumption that oral and written discourse are of the same substance manifests itself in the form–critical method of each scholar in a variety of ways. At this point it will be helpful to trace some of the effects of this conceptual vagueness.

The technology of writing provides words with a physical existence separate from their utterance contexts. This allows words, as written texts, to evidence certain properties of physical objects. Both Bultmann and Dibelius impose the durability of written speech onto the Christian oral tradition, producing a static conception of oral utterances as "objects" which can be copied, borrowed, changed, and moved from place to place. This allows them to think of oral words in distinction from the interactive human contexts in which they were uttered.

The objectification of oral utterance is particularly explicit in Bultmann's analysis as an accident of his method. Bultmann begins with written documents as keys to trends in the tradition history and assumes that the oral tradition would have similar properties. Since written words are physical objects, Bultmann also thinks of oral utterances as physical objects and attributes qualities of physical objects to them. His discussion of the Apophthegm, for example, relies on two such object qualities: the ability of physical objects to retain identity while moving through time and space; and, the ability of physical objects to generate new objects.[80] Bultmann believes that many of the sayings in Synoptic apophthegms predate their frameworks: "the arguments were in many cases already there before the narratives themselves."[81] This statement presupposes that one part of the speech unit, the saying, can be separated from the other parts and thought of as an independent object which enjoyed a prior existence in some other place and context, from which it has been moved to the new context. Further, such sayings, as things,

---

[80]The latter property could perhaps be described as a "person property." For convenience, this discussion considers "persons" a subcategory of objects.

[81]Bultmann, *HST* 47.

possess within themselves "productive power," by which they can generate other things such as narrative frameworks.[82] Thus, "apophthegms developed in the tradition when independent sayings were joined to an already existing situation, whether this were unitarily conceived or compounded of elements."[83] The Synoptics may therefore be thought of as jigsaw puzzles, which the Evangelists put together and which Bultmann aspires to take apart.

Another analogy, the shopping basket, is helpful for analyzing Bultmann's discussion of oral sayings collections. The anonymous Christian preachers went, it seems, to market, and there purchased sayings which had been grown in other times and places, such as the life of Jesus or contemporary Judaism. Their baskets were the primitive collections, and their work involved "serializing the dominical sayings without reference to their context," arranging these objects carefully in a new pattern so they would fit into the basket better. Bultmann refers to the total contents of these baskets as "the treasury of Christian instruction,"[84] from which preachers could select items when necessary and replace them when finished, somewhat like a library with no checkout desk. Bultmann here assumes that oral utterances, like written words, can be thought of in distinction from the human contexts in which they occur, as things moving from one situation to another.

This model of borrowing and returning sayings assumes that oral units, like physical objects, are able to change while retaining identity. One might therefore observe the "*expansion of an original saying by addition*," or see a similitude "enlarged with an illustration."[85] "Original" in the former quotation implies distinct preexistence, while "addition" creates the visual image of a new component being attached to an older thing which also retains its individuality. Among such additions, the Evangelists frequently glued introductions and conclusions onto older utterances to fit them together like pipes, allowing for a tighter narrative plumbing.[86] Because he treats oral utterances as things, Bultmann can conceive of transformation and

---

[82]Bultmann, *HST* 51, 55, 61.

[83]Bultmann, *HST* 61.

[84]Bultmann, *HST*, first quotation 322, second quotation 145.

[85]Bultmann, *HST* 82, 182–185, first quotation 89, second quotation 87.

[86]Bultmann, *HST* 91, 130, 148, 180.

recontextualization as metamorphosis.[87] He can also speak of the need to determine whether or not the Evangelists have placed a saying in its "right setting," where "right" apparently means similar to the place it sat in the earlier days of its existence.[88] This objectification of oral utterance allows Bultmann to conceptualize an evolutionary model in which sayings can retain their identity even after radical linguistic or ideological alteration.

The objectification of oral speech is not a tangential aspect of Bultmann's Form Criticism, but a foundational working premise. The assumption that oral words may be treated as written texts is explicit in his discussion of the objectives of Form Criticism. Form Criticism seeks to distinguish "secondary additions and forms"; it "sets out to give an account of the history of the *individual units of the tradition*, and how the tradition passed from a fluid state to the fixed form in which it meets us in the gospels."[89] These statements are particularly revealing. First, Bultmann seems to think of individual oral units as objects with a distinct "history," where "history" implies movement and change through time without loss of identity. Second, part of this historical movement and change involved the growth of "secondary additions," which here seem to be distinct appendages which can be thought of as separate from the "original." These two considerations make it impossible to determine the conceptual difference between a "fluid state" of language and a "fixed form." "Fixed" here would obviously include the written Synoptics, but Bultmann ascribes the properties of written language to pre–Synoptic oral utterances systematically in *HST* in service of his evolutionary model. The following *caveat* was therefore foundational to Bultmann's method: "it is immaterial whether the oral or the literary tradition has been operative: there is no difference in principle."[90] As will be seen below, there is a difference in principle, and that difference is fundamental.

The objectification of oral utterance is also an underlying principle in Dibelius' thought, even though his method, which begins with analysis of

---

[87]Bultmann, *HST* 94–95, 148.

[88]Bultmann, *HST* 193–194.

[89]Bultmann, *HST*, first quotation 6, second quotation 3, emphasis original.

[90]Bultmann, *HST* 87, in the context of a discussion about the tendency of logia to generate new sayings.

situations and functions, does not require it. In the first paragraph of *FTTG*, Dibelius suggests that the transmitters of the Gospel tradition acted "not merely as vehicles, but also as creative forces by introducing changes or additions." The Synoptics are simply collections of this oral material, and the Evangelists "are principally collectors, vehicles of tradition, editors," whose work was "handing down, grouping, and working over."[91] The language of "change," "addition," "handing down," and "grouping" belongs to discussion of objects, uttered words as things which retain their identity across time and space. Where the Evangelists have "worked over" these objects, Dibelius uses the metaphor of "spoiling," so that paradigms which do not evidence editorial additions have an "unspoiled character."[92]

This "spoiling" of the tradition was not limited to paradigms, and did not begin with the Evangelists. Dibelius can also speak of the "*assembling and grouping*" of sayings, and early catechisms utilized "loosely connected sayings which had been handed down." The terms "assembled," "grouped, "connected," and "handed down" all suggest that individual oral sayings enjoyed a previous distinct existence in different times and contexts before being "collected." Dibelius' discussion of parables clearly imposes the object traits of written language onto oral units. As with Bultmann, some parables were borrowed from Judaism, some were allegorically extended, and "we do not know the original references of many parables."[93] Movement from one environment to another, extension and growth, and maintenance of identity from one context to another are all properties of physical objects. Not surprisingly, then, Dibelius insists that his suggestions are applicable whether the early materials were written or oral.[94] As with Bultmann, Dibelius makes no conceptual differentiation between oral and written speech in questions of form or tradition history.

Dibelius' objectification of oral utterance, attributing to it the properties of written texts, clarifies an apparent paradox in his method: personal

---

[91]Dibelius, *FTTG*, first quotation 1, second quotation 3.

[92]Dibelius, *FTTG* 44–46, 61, quotation 61.

[93]Dibelius, *FTTG* 249–255, first and third quotations 255, second quotation 27 quotation 255.

[94]Dibelius, *FTTG* 39.

situations are critical to Dibelius' concept of form development, but the actual persons involved in these situations are not. While insisting that forms developed in response to typical situations, Dibelius also stresses the anonymity of the Christian preachers who spoke in such situations. "[T]he personal peculiarities of the composer or narrator have little significance . . . the tradition is cast by practical necessities, by usage, or by origin," and "the individuality of an original writer played no part" in form development.[95] The key to this puzzle lies in Dibelius' treatment of oral utterances as things which exist apart from human contexts. This allows him to focus on abstract "developmental laws" and "typical" situations with complete disregard for the specific human contexts in which words were uttered. Further, since the early forms were the product of laws rather than persons, it is methodologically unnecessary for Dibelius to consider ideology as a possible constituent aspect of form. Individual persons and their beliefs play no significant role in the earliest NT Form Criticism.

The form–critical methods of Dibelius and Bultmann amply illustrate Walter Ong's discussion of the typical approach to "oral literature" early in the twentieth century.

> With their attention directed to texts, scholars often went on to assume, often without reflection, that oral verbalization was essentially the same as the written verbalization they normally dealt with, and that oral art forms were to all intents and purposes simply texts, except for the fact that they were not written down. The impression grew that . . . oral art forms were essentially unskillful and not worth serious study.

---

[95]Dibelius, *FTTG*, first quotation 1, second quotation 4. In this light, Dibelius's remark, "in the case of primitive Christian propaganda only . . . the hearers, can have caused any significant variation," must regard "the hearers" as synonymous with "the situation" (38). Dibelius even questions the rhetorical capacity of the early preachers, "lowly people" who "probably enjoyed insufficient elasticity of speech" to impact the shaping of the tradition, and who "had neither the capacity nor the inclination for the production of books" (first quotation 7, second quotation 38, third quotation 9). The last quotation is consistent with Dibelius' determination that oral forms, and the Synoptic Gospels which utilized them, were "unliterary," arising from "that lower stratum which accords no place to the artistic devices and literary tendencies of polished writing" (1). "Without a doubt these are unliterary writings. They should not and cannot be compared with 'literary' works" (2). "Literary" here means written with a conscious stylistic intention for broad publication.

As noted, Bultmann explicitly assumes that the oral Gospel "was essentially the same as the written" gospels, a text waiting to be written down, and Dibelius expresses a low view of the rhetorical skill of the primitive preachers. Almost as a commentary on early NT Form Criticism, Ong continues:

> Writing makes 'words' appear similar to things because we [literates] think of words as the visible marks signaling words to decoders: we can see and touch such inscribed 'words' in texts and books. Written words are residue. Oral tradition has no such residue or deposit. When an often–told oral story is not actually being told, all that exists of it is the potential in certain human beings to tell it.[96]

Written words are physical things which can be touched and manipulated. By contrast, oral words are *events*, interactions between persons in situations where the potential of uttering is realized. Ong thus warns against Bultmann's simple presupposition that the tendencies revealed by a model of literary dependence can be imposed onto the oral stages of the Gospel tradition. Indeed,

> [one] cannot without serious and disabling distortion describe a primary phenomenon [oral speech=oral Gospel forms] by starting with a subsequent secondary phenomenon [writing = Synoptics] and paring away the differences. Indeed, starting backwards in this way . . . you can never become aware of the real differences at all.[97]

TRANSMISSION, MEMORY, SYNCHRONY, DIACHRONY

Sensitivity to the event nature of oral speech calls for a revision of traditional views on oral "transmission." Even as Dibelius and Bultmann were formulating their conclusions on the tradition history of the Gospels, Milman Parry was initiating a revolution in classical studies that has significantly impacted a number of disciplines. Parry's research is dedicated to the "Homeric Question": how could one person ("Homer") orally produce such a massive, sophisticated, and sometimes self–contradictory corpus? And if

---

[96]Walter J. Ong, *Orality and Literacy: The Technologizing of the Word* (New York, NY: Routledge, 1982), first quotation 10, second quotation 11.

[97]Ong, *Orality and Literacy* 13.

Homer truly lived in the Greek dark ages, how could subsequent generations of oral bards faithfully transmit these materials by memory? One camp, the "Analysts," cited aporias, Homer's infamous "nods," in *Iliad* and *Odyssey* to support their conclusion that the Homeric texts are redactions of traditional works composed by a number of authors over an extended period of time. This perspective was opposed by the "Unitarys," who held to the traditional view of a single, unified authorship.[98] Parry demonstrates that both positions were flawed due to a popular misconception of oral "transmission." Through careful study of Homeric style, particularly noun–epithet formulae, Parry concludes that Homer was a "traditional poet." The present Homeric texts were not pieced together by a redactor, but nor were they slavishly memorized and transmitted by oral poets. Rather, the Homeric corpus was orally composed and recomposed many times over many generations under the influence of a traditional, fixed style, a tradition of telling.[99] The existing written versions of these stories are simply one such composition, captured in writing and subsequently canonized.

Parry sought to test his conclusions on classical literature by studying the methods of modern oral bards in (then) Yugoslavia. He was assisted by Albert Lord, who completed this field research after Parry's death. Lord's findings represent the first full expression of the "Oral Formulaic Theory" of transmission and composition. In his 1960 *Singer of Tales*, Lord concludes that "traditional" oral epics are not memorized or "transmitted" as fixed texts. Rather, bards learn techniques, motifs, and formulae which they use to compose and recompose epics spontaneously. Dismantling traditional views of "oral transmission," Lord stresses that "every [oral] performance is a separate song; for every performance is unique, and every performance bears the signature of its poet singer. . . . The singer of tales is at once the tradition

---

[98] John Miles Foley, *The Theory of Oral Composition: History and Methodology* (Bloomington, IN: Indiana University Press, 1988) 5.

[99] Milman Parry, *L'Épithète Traditionnelle dans Homère: Essai sur un Problème de Style Homérique* (1928; rpt. in *The Making of Homeric Verse* [ed. Adam Parry; New York, NY: Arno, 1980]) 6. Foley traces the development of Parry's thought in *Composition* 19–31.

and an individual creator."[100] The traditional composer therefore holds a view of "transmission" and "oral tradition" different from that of the literate analyst.

Whereas the [oral] singer thinks of his[/her] song in terms of a flexible plan of themes, some of which are essential and some of which are not, we [literates] think of it as a given text which undergoes change from one singing to another. . . . His[/her] idea of stability, to which [s/]he is deeply devoted, does not include the wording, which to him[/her] has never been fixed, nor the unessential parts of the story.[101]

Since the appearance of *Singer of Tales*, the Oral–Formulaic Theory has been successfully tested and refined by application to a number of cultural traditions and to ancient and Medieval oral–based texts.[102]

The oral–formulaic approach has consistently advocated the view that "traditional" texts are spontaneous compositions utilizing traditional elements, rather than fixed surface units "transmitted" by memorization from one generation to another. "Variations" are seen as the results of situational factors during a specific telling, particularly the posture of the audience.

Whether the performance takes place at home, in the coffee house, in the courtyard, or in the halls of a noble, the essential element of the occasion of singing [=composing] that influences the form of the poetry [oral text] is the variability and instability of the audience.[103]

---

[100]Albert B. Lord, *The Singer of Tales* (Cambridge, MA: Harvard University Press, 1960) 4.

[101]Lord, *Singer* 99.

[102]See Foley, *Oral Composition* 74–93. Foley's survey includes the influence of the Parry–Lord theory on biblical studies. The earliest application of the theory to the NT was Charles H. Lohr's "Oral Techniques in the Gospel of Matthew," *CBQ* 23 (1961). Lord himself has contributed to the dialogue with biblical scholars; see his "The Gospels as Oral–Traditional Literature," *The Relationships Among the Gospels: An Interdisciplinary Dialogue* (ed. William O. Walker, Jr.; San Antonio, TX: Trinity University Press, 1978). David Stern has also recently applied the Parry–Lord thesis to the rabbinic materials; see his *Parables in Midrash: Narrative and Exegesis in Rabbinic Literature* (Cambridge, MA: Harvard University Press, 1991) 34-35.

[103]Lord, *Singer* 13–17, quotation 16. Audience response particularly affects the length and ending of the composition.

More recently, Ruth Finnegan has insisted that audience must be considered in analyzing oral texts because the audience "is directly involved in the realization of the poem [oral text] as literature in the moment of its performance."[104] This involvement can range from vocal response to the influence of the silent presence of certain persons. Since oral composers must respond to them, "it is clear that audiences do often have an effect on the form and delivery of a poem."[105] Edwards and Sienkewicz note that "the oral artist's sensitivity to the audience . . . can affect both the length and the content of the performance."

> In oral cultures . . . performer and audience are part of a single performative dynamic. . . . Not only does the oral artist mould performance to accommodate audience reaction, but the division between audience and performer is much less clear–cut. Performance is viewed much more as interaction between artist and audience.[106]

Rather than attempting to reconstruct or canonize "original" texts, contemporary folklorists focus on the situational nature of oral discourse, the responsive, dialogic relationship between the composer and the audience, and the ideology of the parties involved. Surface features of the text and, to some degree, its contents or "themes" are treated as byproducts of these situational factors. In this respect, folkloristics has not upheld the view of Bultmann and Dibelius that the oral Gospel was shaped by "laws of form development" which superseded the anonymous carriers of the tradition. At every stage of "transmission," and every time a portion of the Gospel was performed, both the performer and the immediate audience played a critical role in the surface texture of the story on that particular occasion.

---

[104]Ruth Finnegan, *Oral Poetry: Its Nature, Significance, and Social Context* (Bloomington, IN: Indiana University Press, 1992) 214.

[105]Finnegan, *Oral Poetry* 231. Finnegan stresses that the "audience" which influences oral composition is not necessarily the society at large but the specific subculture with which the poet interacts (235).

[106]Viv Edwards and Thomas J. Sienkewicz, *Oral Cultures Past and Present: Rappin' and Homer* (Cambridge, MA: Basil Blackwell, 1990), first quotation 68, second quotation 65.

The oral–formulaic perspective also calls for a revision of literate views of textual "synchrony" and "diachrony." Bultmann and Dibelius hold the traditional view that "synchrony" involves a text's relationship to other texts of the same time period, while "diachrony" involves a text's relationship to other earlier texts, including earlier versions of the same text which may have "influenced" its present form. This model is inapplicable, however, to the pre–literate Gospel, because multiple oral "texts" cannot coexist in the same context, and because a single oral text cannot exist across time. The problems of oral synchrony and diachrony have been explored recently by Ward Parks. Parks' approach focuses on the fact that oral texts cannot exist independently of their human composers and audiences. As such, both the synchronic and diachronic axes of the oral text must be analyzed in terms of their human terminal points, the composer and the audience, and the transmission of data between them.[107]

In literary studies, "synchrony" refers to the relationship between written texts produced (or read) at approximately the same time. Such a relationship is highlighted, for example, in a written synopsis of the NT Gospels. As oral utterance, however, no two texts can exist together in the same place at the same time. Oral synchrony concerns the individual text as utterance, "the oral transmission of narrative matter from speaker through message to audience."[108] The synchronic dimension of the oral text is not a relationship between this message and other texts, but rather the sum of the extralinguistic components of the utterance context plus their relations. These situational components include the "physical performance setting, perhaps a common mood and sense of occasion, [and] an awareness of specific present individuals." The question, then, in analyzing oral texts synchronically is not how one text relates to

---

[107]Ward Parks, "The Textualization of Orality in Literacy Criticism," *Vox intexta: Orality and Textuality in the Middle Ages* (ed. A. N. Doane and Carol Braun Pasternack; Madison, WI: University of Wisconsin Press, 1991) 54. "I will assume that ultimately human beings stand at the beginning and end points of any dialogue."

[108]Ward Parks, "Orality and Poetics: Synchrony, Diachrony, and the Axes of Narrative Transmission," in *Comparative Research on Oral Traditions: A Memoriae for Milman Parry* (ed. John Miles Foley; Columbus, OH: Slavica, 1987) 512. Parks refers to synchronic transmission as "actual transmission" because it involves an interpersonal exchange "within the confines of a single communication act" (513).

another, but how the performer relates to the audience in the moment of text production.

The most important of the situational factors in oral text production is the spatial and temporal immediacy of the oral audience. Unlike literary texts, which manipulate the distance between author and audience for aesthetic purposes, "the consciousness of [oral] performer and [oral] audience has to be concentrated at virtually the same point of articulation at the same moment of time."[109] The oral text exists only at the moment of its creation and reception, and the rhetorical conventions and hermeneutical strategies of the oral composer and audience are adapted to this reality.[110] To facilitate composition and interpretation, composers and audiences must appeal to situational cues.

Since the oral text has no physical durability, it exists beyond the moment of composition only in the memories of the speaker and audience. Memory is therefore critical to any understanding of the "transmission" of an oral text across multiple performances. Remaining within the boundaries of the Oral–Formulaic Theory, Parks suggests that oral "repetition" is most properly "a dialogue with memory," the present performance recalling earlier performances.

> Oral tradition has thus a continuous life at the level of latent memory, which is brought into expression intermittently through specific performance acts. . . . Since tradition as such resides only in latent memory, at the moment of performance nothing except that performance exists.[111]

The diachronic "history" of an oral text represents not a series of variants but the total number of synchronic performances in which that text has been composed. It is only in the sense that two unique performances tap into a common mnemonic vein that one may speak of the "repetition" of an oral text.

In view of these realities, any form–critical method must also develop a means for describing textual continuity between oral performances. To signal that a performance is traditional and to facilitate recall of past

---

[109]Parks, "Textualization" 54, both quotations here; "Orality and Poetics" 518.

[110]Parks, "Orality and Poetics" 519; "Textualization" 54.

[111]Parks, "Orality and Poetics" 523, quotation here; "Textualization" 57. Parks therefore prefers the term "intermnemonic"over "intertextual."

performances, oral composers draw materials for their texts from an oral archive of motifs and formulaic structures. This oral archive does not contain the specific surface features of past performances, but rather the performer's memory of how the story in question is traditionally told.[112] In this sense, the oral composer's role differs greatly from that of the literary author. "The oral poet conceives of [her/]himself as [her/]his tradition's voice," and uses the oral archive as a tool for reviving the memory of that performance tradition. What such composers "transmit is not a text, reified, absolute, . . . but an art of telling that comes into manifestation only in synchronic performance."[113] In oral settings, there are no traditional texts, only traditions of telling. "Diachrony" is the composer's self–association with such a tradition.

To further explore the nature of "oral tradition" and "oral forms," it will be necessary to examine the specific elements of the synchronic contexts in which oral utterances are produced, and to explain in greater detail how these contexts can be related in a diachronic sequence. In so doing, it will become possible to describe a form–critical method which does not depend exclusively on the comparative analysis of parallel documents to identify traditional forms. These issues will be explored in Chapter Three.

---

[112]Note here Parks' assertion that "oral performances are characterized by a heavy incidence of diachronically–generated formulaic structures projected into the synchrony of the specific song–rendering" ("Orality and Poetics" 522–523).

[113]Parks, first quotation "Orality and Poetics" 524, second quotation "Textualization" 55.

Chapter 3:
The Nature of Oral Forms

Chapters 1 and 2 have demonstrated that conventional approaches to the speeches of FG have produced primarily negative results. These results are largely due to limitations in NT Form Criticism, specifically a heavy dependence on literary parallels. Since the riddles in FG bear few parallels to other extant texts, it will be necessary to describe a method of form–critical analysis which does not depend on literate models of genre and text production.

This chapter will appeal to a number of language theorists whose research explores the nature of oral forms. The theories of Roman Jakobson and M. M. Bakhtin will highlight the functional, situational, and dialogic nature of oral speech. Lloyd Bitzer's theory of rhetorical situations will clarify the elements of speech situations, and their impact on the discourses produced within them. Several themes raised by these three theorists come together in Tzvetan Todorov's theory of discourse genres. This situational approach to genre, which is particularly compatible with the event nature of oral speech, will necessitate theoretical clarification of the relationship between genre and ideology. Todorov will again be helpful here, as will Robert C. Post's theory of genre, which explicitly addresses the ideological dimension of genres. This investigation will produce a concise, yet theoretically comprehensive, delineation of the constituent elements of an oral form or "speech genre." Once conceptual clarity on the nature of oral forms has been achieved, it will be possible to describe a specific oral form, the riddle, and to identify this form in FG.

SITUATION AND FUNCTION

Any comprehensive theory of speech genres or oral traditions must begin with a clear conception of the nature of oral texts. The present study will build on the work of Roman Jakobson, perhaps the premier authority on oral language in the last century. Jakobson's theory of oral discourse is conveniently summarized in the 1956 article "Two Aspects of Language." He begins with the thesis that "speech implies a *selection* of certain linguistic entities and their *combination* into linguistic units of a high degree of complexity." The use of linguistic signs in discourse thus involves two modes of arrangement: "selection," discrimination between lexical options in the language code; and, "combination," relating each word to other words in the discourse.[1] These dual modes of arrangement give the utterance two contexts, both of which the audience must interpret. The *language context*, the abstract lexicon from which each word is selected, gives words a "general meaning" by similarity with and difference from other words. The "contextual meaning" of a word is determined by its specific relationship to other words in the *discourse context*. Words in discourse are thus defined at two levels: "it is the external relation of contiguity which unites the constituents of a [discourse] context, and the internal relation of similarity which underlies the [lexical] substitution set."[2]

Jakobson's approach to language thus acknowledges abstract categories but insists that discourse becomes "meaningful" in specific human contexts. The external relations of words used in situations generate a "contextual meaning" which cannot be separated from the total meaning of the utterance. While the language system provides a general meaning which unites the

---

[1]Roman Jakobson, "Two Aspects of Language and Two Types of Aphasic Disturbances" (1956; rpt. in *Language in Literature* [ed. Krystyna Pomorska and Stephen Rudy; Cambridge, MA: The Belknap Press of Harvard University Press, 1987]) 97, emphasis added. Jakobson's discussions are frequently directed toward problems of general semiotics. This study will apply his theory exclusively to the problems of verbal discourse, and, for clarity, will not discuss units of discourse smaller than the word or idiom.

[2]Jakobson, "Two Aspects" 99–100, quotation 104. Words are always defined by their relations to other words. Jakobson refers to the abstract lexical context as the "internal" mode of relation and the discourse context as the "external" mode of relation (100).

speaker and audience and makes communication possible, the contextual relations of words, generated by specific moments of language use, are also critical to understanding.

The problem of contextual relations introduces Jakobson's doctrine of "dominance." Every discourse will include a "mandatory and invaluable constituent" which regulates its "hierarchy of values." Jakobson calls this mandatory element "the dominant."

> The dominant may be defined as the focusing component of a work of art: it rules, determines, and transforms the remaining components. It is the dominant which guarantees the integrity of the structure.[3]

Jakobson discusses the dominant in terms of rhetorical function. In "poetic" writing, for example, the "aesthetic function" dominates the "referential function." The "referential function," dominant in scientific and other descriptive discourse, focuses attention on the object under discussion and shows little concern for ornament in the language used. Poetic language, by contrast, "is directed precisely toward the sign as such." The poetic function is dominant in all poetic language in every period and culture, although it expresses itself uniquely in each poetic canon. Within each canon, the dominant poetic function specifies what are "the indispensable, distinctive elements without which the work cannot be identified as poetic."[4] Varying hierarchies of these elements will produce the various subgenres of "poetry." Jakobson's doctrine of the dominant thus shifts generic classification from features of style to the level of semiotic functions. These functions, in turn, generate local styles appropriate to local linguistic and cultural expression. As with language in general, Jakobson conceptualizes poetic genres at two levels: a potential, functional level; and, a level of concrete stylistic expression realized in specific communication environments.

Jakobson offers a complete analysis of poetry from the perspective of functional dominance in his influential paper "Linguistics and Poetics." In

---

[3]Roman Jakobson, "The Dominant" (1935; rpt. in *Language in Literature* [trans. Herbert Eagle; ed. Krystyna Pomorska and Stephen Rudy; Cambridge, MA: The Belknap Press of Harvard University Press, 1987]) 41–42.

[4]Jakobson, "The Dominant," first quotation 44, second quotation 43.

order to isolate the poetic function, "language must be investigated in all the variety of its functions." He therefore presents a complete functional model of communication. Because function is intricately related to situations of language use, Jakobson first offers "a concise survey of the constitutive factors in any speech event."[5] These factors are six in number: the traditional triad, "addresser," "message," "addressee"; "context referred to," or referent, which the addressee must be able to comprehend; "code," the language being used, which again must be common to addresser and addressee; and, "contact," the "physical channel and psychological connection between the addresser and addressee," the conduit for communication.[6]

Each element of the discourse situation has a corresponding function. The "emotive/expressive" function "aims a direct expression of the speaker's attitude toward what [s/]he is speaking about." The "conative" function involves "orientation toward the addressee." "[A]n orientation toward the context," the referent of the message, characterizes the "referential" function. The "metalingual" function represents the speaker's attempts to ensure that she and the addressee are using the same code. The "phatic" function concerns the opening, maintenance, or closing of the contact channel. Finally, "the set (*Einstellung*) toward the message as such, focus on the message for its own sake, is the POETIC function of language."[7] Each individual act of communication is directed toward all six situational elements, so every

---

[5]Roman Jakobson, "Linguistics and Poetics" (1958; rpt. in *Language in Literature* [ed. Krystyna Pomorska and Stephen Rudy; Cambridge, MA: The Belknap Press of Harvard University Press, 1987]) 66. Jakobson's model was introduced to NT studies in Norman Petersen's *Literary Criticism for New Testament Critics* (GBSNTS; Philadelphia, PA: Fortress, 1978) 33–48.

[6]Jakobson, "Linguistics and Poetics" 66.

[7]Jakobson, "Linguistics and Poetics," first quotation 66, second quotation 67, third quotation 66, fourth quotation 69, emphasis original. The emotive function produces the impression of emotion on the part of the speaker. The purest verbal representation of this function is the interjection, while the conative function "finds its purest grammatical expression in the vocative and imperative" (67). Because the phatic function assumes the possibility that communication is not occurring, its formal expressions are often highly stylized or ritualized (68). The poetic function, "by promoting the palpability of signs, deepens the fundamental dichotomy of signs and objects" (69–70). It is thus the opposite of the referential function.

function is operative in every discourse.[8] In each discourse, however, one function will be dominant. The dominant function will characterize the individual discourse and create an internal hierarchy among the other functions. This hierarchy will, in turn, shape the surface structure of the discourse. "The verbal structure of a message depends primarily on the predominant function."[9] This provides a framework for delineating genres. Works of "poetry," the object of Jakobson's analysis, are those in which the poetic function is dominant. As to subgenres, "the particularities of diverse poetic genres imply a differently ranked participation of other verbal functions along with the dominant poetic function." All discourse where the poetic function dominates is in the genus poetry; species within this genus, individual genres of poetry, represent alternate combinations of the other five functions in varying hierarchies. These hierarchies produce "the empirical linguistic criterion," or unique stylistic features, of each genre of poetry.[10]

Jakobson's theory carries two related implications to the discussion of speech genres. First, his functional approach makes structure or "form" a product of language use in specific situations. The surface features of a given discourse are a byproduct of the functional hierarchy in the communicative act. Second, since all six situational elements and all six functions are relevant to every language event, the addresser and addressee influence the structure of every discourse. This leads to the second major principle of oral language to be discussed here, the "dialogic" nature of oral discourse. This doctrine has been forcefully advocated by Jakobson, but is more commonly associated with,

---

[8]This parallels Jakobson's more general contention that every individual element of a discourse is "meaningful" in some sense. "An important structural particularity of language is that at no stage of resolving higher units into their component parts does one encounter informationally pointless fragments" ("Parts and Wholes in Language" [1960; rpt. in *On Language* (ed. Linda R. Waugh and Monique Monville–Burston; Cambridge, MA: Harvard University Press, 1990)] 113).

[9]Jakobson, "Linguistics and Poetics" 66.

[10]Jakobson, "Linguistics and Poetics," first quotation 70, second quotation 71. In terms of his selection–combination axes, Jakobson says, "*The poetic function projects the principle of equivalence from the axis of selection into the axis of combination.*" Contiguity is replaced by similarity as the sequencing principle at the verbal level. Consequently, repetition is a universal feature of "poetic" discourse (71, emphasis original). Other surface features commonly generated by the poetic function are discussed on 73–78.

and expounded in greater detail by, M. M. Bahktin. The theories of both scholars on this subject will be surveyed here.

DIALOGIC DISCOURSE

Those acquainted with the work of Ferdinand de Saussure may have detected conceptual parallels between Jakobson's selection–combination axes and Saussure's *langue–parole* axes.[11] Jakobson was, in fact, directly influenced by Saussure, and his concept of "dialogic" discourse is concisely stated in a 1942 lecture on Saussure's theory. In Saussure's system, *langue* represents the abstract, potential dimension of language, language as it exists in dictionaries and grammars as the system of options from which speakers may choose. Because *langue* is abstract, Saussure thought of it as the social and collective, rather than individual, dimension of language. Jakobson refers to this dimension of language as "code." *Parole* represents language as used by actual individual speakers, specific discourses uttered in specific situations. As the concrete and situational aspect of language, Saussure felt that *parole* lacked a collective social dimension. Jakobson refers to this dimension of language as "message."[12]

Jakobson begins by affirming Saussure's categories:

> every communication, every conversation, every exchange of words[=every *parole*] presupposes the necessary existence of a [*langue*= a] repertory of linguistic resources that have an identical value for all participants.[13]

---

[11]See Ferdinand de Saussure, *Course in General Linguistics* (trans. Roy Harris; La Salle, IL: Open Court, 1986). This translation is based on the 5th French edition of 1955.

[12]Roman Jakobson, "Langue and Parole: Code and Message" (1942; in *On Language* [ed. Linda R. Waugh and Monique Monville–Burston; Cambridge, MA: Harvard University Press, 1990]) 89–91. On the terms "code" and "message" as parallels to *langue* and *parole*, see Jakobson, "Patterns in Linguistics (Contribution to Debates with Anthropologists)" (1952; rpt. in *Selected Writings* [The Hague: Mouton, 1971]) 2.224. The definitions of *langue* and *parole* offered here represent Jakobson's interpretation of Saussure. The specifics of Saussure's theory, and whether or not Jakobson's interpretation of it is accurate, are beyond the interests of this study.

[13]Jakobson, "Langue and Parole" 88.

But Jakobson disagrees with Saussure on a key point, arguing that *both langue* and *parole* have personal *and* collective dimensions. Although abstract norms and patterns exist collectively, they also exist personally: "the linguistic values approved by collective consent still need the personal consent of the speaker." Every language user has an "individual langue" which operates within the broader, collective *langue*.[14] Conversely, *parole*, although representing the actualization of a specific discourse by an individual speaker, also has a collective, social dimension. This collective aspect of *parole* leads Jakobson to elaborate "The Dialogic Nature of Language."

Jakobson first points out that *parole*, even by Saussure's definition, requires two persons, a sender and a receiver. Indeed, "sending implies receiving." The speaker is not fully autonomous in constructing a discourse. "One of these parts [speaker and audience] implies the other, one brings about the other, one adapts to the other."[15] This mutuality of speaker and audience in the discourse environment, this "reciprocity between the addresser and addressee," controls the production of *parole*. "The addresser and addressee necessarily presuppose each other, and parole contains within its structure the imprint of both parties."[16] For Jakobson, every utterance is shaped and structured in anticipation of the receiver's response. *Parole*, contra Saussure, is never entirely personal or private, but always "dialogic," presupposing a dialogue between the sender and receiver. Indeed, "the dialogic form of parole is fundamental,"[17] meaning that language is expressly designed to evoke a response.

The dialogic nature of utterance has been most thoroughly discussed by M. M. Bakhtin. Bakhtin's theory of oral discourse focuses on the conceptual

---

[14]Jakobson, "Langue and Parole" 90.

[15]Jakobson, "Langue and Parole," both quotations 92.

[16]Jakobson, "Langue and Parole," first quotation 96, second quotation 96–97.

[17]Jakobson, "Langue and Parole" 94. Jakobson therefore revises Saussure's doctrine: "Langue has an individual aspect in addition to its social aspect, and parole has a social aspect in addition to its individual aspect" (98–99). Jakobson contends that even monologue is dialogic. Although monologue does not anticipate verbal response, it is conditioned by the anticipated or actual nonverbal response of the audience. Absolute cases of monologue, such as theatrical asides, are found only in the arts as the result of conscious and highly stylized conventions (94–97).

distinction between language as abstract potential and language used in human situations. He produces a series of contrasts between the "sentence" and the "utterance" which develop into a sociological conception of speech genres. The "sentence" in Bakhtin's model represents the abstract, linguistic dimension of the utterance, "everything in the text [utterance] that is repeated and reproduced, everything repeatable and reproducible."[18] As language, a community product, the sentence can be reproduced an infinite number of times by different persons. It has no connection to specific human intention, and therefore no "meaning." But sentences can manifest themselves only as concrete, situational "utterances" delivered by individual speakers.[19] The utterance, unlike the sentence, "is individual, unique, and unrepeatable," because it emerges in a specific moment and context of human interaction. The utterance makes the common and repeatable (language) unique and individual.[20] Bakhtin concentrates on two aspects of the utterance's individuality, expressiveness and "addressivity." Both contribute to the style and surface structure of the utterance.

"Expressiveness" encompasses all aspects of the utterance which this study has referred to as "ideological." Words and sentences, as language units, belong to no one and therefore express no individual ideology or intention. By contrast, "there can be no such thing as an absolutely neutral utterance," because utterance implies human choice.[21] "[E]motion, evaluation, and

---

[18]Mikhail Mikhailovitch Bakhtin, "The Problem of the Text in Linguistics, Philology, and the Human Sciences: An Experiment in Philosophical Analysis" (1959–1961; in *Speech Genres and Other Late Essays* [trans. Vern W. McGee; ed. Caryl Emerson and Michael Holquist; Austin, TX: University of Texas Press, 1986]) 108. Bakhtin did not complete this essay; the current text is a series of his personal notes from 1959–1961, which were edited and published by V. Kozhinova as "Problema teksta: opyt filosofskogo analiza," *Voprosy literatury* 10 (1976) 122–151.

[19]Bakhtin, "Problem of Text" 71.

[20]Bakhtin, "Problem of Text," quotation 105, see also 119–120. Because it involves time and the total human context, the utterance cannot be repeated. "[T]he reproduction of the text by the subject [speaker] is a new, unrepeatable event in the life of the text" (106). Every utterance "is always a new utterance (even if it is a quotation)" (108). For this reason, the utterance aspect of language "can never be completely translated" (106).

[21]Mikhail Mikhailovitch Bakhtin, "The Problem of Speech Genres" (1952–1953; rpt. in *Speech Genres & Other Late Essays* [trans. Vern W. McGee; ed. Caryl Emerson and

expression are foreign to the world of language and are born only in the process of its live usage in a concrete utterance."[22] The speaker's individuality is thus expressed in the utterance and imprinted upon it. *Ideologically*, the author's imprint "makes a claim to justice, sincerity, beauty, and truthfulness (a model utterance), and so forth." *Structurally*,

> [T]he utterance, its style, and its composition are determined by its referentially semantic element (the theme) and its expressive aspect, that is, the speaker's attitude toward the referentially semantic element.[23]

In other words, the speaker's choice of theme and her attitude to that theme are primary factors in the stylistic and compositional development of the utterance. In this way, expressiveness shapes the utterance.

Bakhtin, however, resists those theories of discourse which assign a purely passive role to the audience.[24] As a language unit, the sentence belongs to no one and lacks the ideological individuality necessary to invite a response.[25] The utterance, by contrast, specifically invites the audience's response, and absorbs this response as a constituent element. Bakhtin refers to this trait of the utterance as "addressivity," "the quality of turning to

---

Michael Holquist; Austin, TX: University of Texas Press, 1986]) 84. "Words belong to nobody, and in themselves they evaluate nothing" (85).

[22]Bakhtin, "Speech Genres" 87. Words thus do not make utterances expressive; rather, words become expressive when used in an utterance (86–87).

[23]Bakhtin, first quotation "Problem of Text" 12, second quotation "Speech Genres" 90. This imprinting is accidental, a natural feature of the utterance itself. "To express oneself means to make oneself an object for another and for oneself" (110). As a result, "the author's [ideological] relation to what he depicts always enters into the image [utterance]. The author's relationship is a constitutive aspect of the image [utterance]" (115).

[24]Specifically, that of Saussure (Bakhtin, "Speech Genres" 68–70). "The text is not a thing, and therefore the second consciousness, the consciousness of the perceiver, can in no way be eliminated or neutralized" ("Problem of Text" 107).

[25]Bakhtin, "Speech Genres" 72–73, 83. The sentence finds its total context within language and is not connected to any extraverbal context or any utterance. It therefore cannot elicit the response of an extraverbal audience. For example, an abstract sentence may take the form of an assertion, but it becomes assertive only when used in a human context.

someone."[26]   Addressivity makes the utterance dialogic. Dialogue is most obvious when the audience responds directly and verbally, as in arguments, parodies, polemics, and commendations, but not all dialogic response is verbal. The very act of "understanding is always dialogic to some degree," even "silent responsive understanding."[27] This dialogue is double–pronged, as the audience evaluates both the theme of the utterance and the speaker herself. Evaluation of the speaker is an ideological act, as it engages the speaker's claims about truth and value which are encoded in the utterance.[28] Addressivity is critical to the structure of the utterance because *the speaker shapes the utterance in anticipation of the audience's response.* Calculating the audience's reaction, the speaker selects the genre and style which she thinks will most likely elicit a favorable reply.[29] Thus, Bakhtin gives both parties in the utterance context, the speaker and the audience, an active role in the production of oral discourse.

Bakhtin's sensitivity to the event nature of discourse tends to highlight the individuality of oral speech. If every utterance is indeed a unique and unrepeatable event in time, can there be enough continuity between speech events to speak of a "genre" of discourses? Having determined that every utterance is an island, is it possible to build a bridge between them which is anything but abstract? Bakhtin appeals here to the nature of the situations in which discourse in produced. His remarks on this subject will serve as an introduction to Lloyd Bitzer's theory of "rhetorical situations."

THE RHETORICAL SITUATION

In Bakhtin's system, genre facilitates the speaker–audience dialogue. In the production of the utterance, the speaker chooses, and the audience

---

[26]Bakhtin, "Speech Genres" 99.

[27]Bakhtin, "Problem of Text" 111, 121, 125, first quotation 111; second quotation "Speech Genres" 69. "[W]hen the listener perceives and understands the meaning (the language meaning) of speech, [s]he simultaneously takes an active, responsive attitude toward it" ("Speech Genres" 68).

[28]Bakhtin, "Problem of Text" 122–123, 125.

[29]Bakhtin, "Speech Genres" 69, 94–97. Note that a "favorable reply" is a response the speaker desires to provoke, whether positive or negative.

anticipates, a "speech genre" which provides guidelines for constructing the utterance. But again, how can Bakhtin posit the existence of uniform genres while insisting that each individual utterance is a unique and unrepeatable act? The answer lies in his conception of the nature of utterance contexts. Utterances are generated and delivered in the various arenas of human activity within a particular community. These arenas supply the social configurations which unite speaker and audience in the dialogic matrix. The "thematic content, style, and compositional structure" of each individual utterance "are equally determined by the specific nature of the particular [social] sphere of communication." Each individual utterance is thus shaped by its social arena. Within a group, *certain social arenas are typical*, recurring on a regular basis and consistently generating utterances which follow the same social rules. "Each separate utterance is individual, of course, but each [social] sphere in which language is used develops its own *relatively stable types* of these utterances. These we may call *speech genres*."[30] Parallel situations produce parallel utterances by creating similar human social situations in which dialogue can occur.

If situation represents the abstract dimension of Bakhtin's model, the empirical component of genre involves the thematic (content), compositional, and stylistic features of the utterance. Each genre also provides a typical conception of the audience.[31] The genre will also assist in word selection by specifying a local, generic meaning for certain terms in the language lexicon, a feature Bakhtin refers to as "generic specification."[32] Genre thus sets the

---

[30]Both quotations Bakhtin, "Speech Genres" 60, emphasis original. The number and diversity of speech genres within a given community will therefore reflect the number and diversity of its social interactions (60–61). Bakhtin separates speech genres into two broad categories, "primary (simple)" and "secondary (complex)." Primary genres are those which "have taken form in unmediated speech communion," common social discourse. Secondary genres are composite, absorbing and internally integrating primary genres to address highly organized cultural interactions. Secondary genres would thus include literature, drama, scientific discourse, and commentary (62).

[31]Bakhtin, "Speech Genres" 64, 95.

[32]"Genres correspond to typical situations of speech communication, typical themes, and, consequently, also to particular contacts between the *meanings* of words and actual concrete reality under certain typical circumstances" (Bakhtin, "Speech Genres" 87, emphasis original).

stylistic and dialogic boundaries of the utterance, and since every utterance is shaped according to some genre, there is no such thing as completely "free" style. "[A] speaker is given not only mandatory forms of the national language (lexical composition and grammatical structure), but also forms of utterances that are mandatory, that is, speech genres."[33] Once chosen, a genre will determine the number and type of sentences, and the compositional links between them, necessary to fulfill the speaker's intention. This mandatory aspect of the utterance assists the audience, who appeal to the genre to facilitate responsive understanding.[34] Genre is thus an essential feature of the dialogic creation and reception of utterances in social contexts.

The nature of these social contexts is the topic of Lloyd Bitzer's "The Rhetorical Situation," which opened the first volume of the journal *Philosophy and Rhetoric*.[35] A "rhetorical situation" is

---

[33]Bakhtin, "Speech Genres" 80. Thus both the sentence and utterance aspect of language follow certain guidelines. This would seem to contradict Bakhtin's assertion that individuality is a constituent element of the utterance. To avoid this problem, he states that individuality is tangential to genre: "in the vast majority of speech genres (except for literary–artistic ones), the individual style does not enter into the intent of the utterance, does not serve as its only goal, but is, as it were, an epiphenomenon of the utterance, one of its by–products" (63). Further, Bakhtin argues that genres, because they involve individual utterances, are more flexible than the lexical and grammatical rules of language. Different genres allow varying degrees of stylistic expression. "Artistic" genres take the expression of individual style as their goal (which allows Bakhtin to assert that even the most creative compositions follow the "rules" of a genre), whereas some genres are so standardized that the very choice of the particular genre indicates the speaker's purpose (63, 79–80).

[34]Bakhtin, "Speech Genres" 79–81.

[35]Lloyd F. Bitzer, "The Rhetorical Situation," *Philosophy and Rhetoric* 1 (1968). Bitzer seeks to delineate the constituent elements "of those contexts in which speakers or writers create rhetorical discourse" (1). In Bitzer's mind, traditional rhetorical criticism, which focused on oratorical methods and actual speeches, did not sufficiently consider the relationship between context and discourse. His attempt to make situation "a controlling and fundamental concern of rhetorical theory" offers a new perspective on both rhetorical criticism and the nature of discourse itself (2–3). George Kennedy introduced Bitzer's theory to NT studies in his *New Testament Interpretation Through Rhetorical Criticism* (Chapel Hill, NC: University of North Caroline Press, 1984), which made situation a critical aspect of rhetorical analysis. Kennedy notes that Bitzer's "rhetorical situation" "roughly corresponds to the *Sitz im Leben* of form criticism" (34).

a complex of persons, events, objects, and relations presenting an actual or potential exigence which can be completely or partially removed if discourse, introduced into the situation, can so constrain human decision or action as to bring about the significant modification of the exigence.[36]

Rhetorical situations may be analyzed in terms of three major components which exist "prior to the creation and presentation of discourse": a controlling exigence; an audience; and, constraints. The *"exigence* is an imperfection marked by urgency," an imbalance in the situation which calls for correction.[37] Each situation is likely to present a number of imperfections, but "there will be at least one controlling exigence which functions as the organizing principle."[38] Since rhetoric concerns speech which persuades and changes, "rhetorical" discourse requires an *audience* which can be moved to act. Hence, "a rhetorical audience consists only of those persons who are capable of being influenced by discourse and of being mediators of change." In addressing the audience with a view to correcting the exigence, the speaker must overcome various situational *constraints*, such as "beliefs, attitudes, documents, facts, traditions, images, interests, motives and the like," as well as her own character, proofs, and style.[39] Human situations involving speakers, audiences, exigencies, and constraints are the crucible in which all rhetorical discourse is forged.

Bitzer's analytic model allows a functional definition of "rhetorical discourse" as speech which responds to a rhetorical exigence. A *"rhetorical utterance"* is one which "participates naturally in the situation" and "by means of its participation with situation obtains its meaning and rhetorical character."

---

[36]Bitzer, "Rhetorical Situation" 6.

[37]Bitzer, "Rhetorical Situation," both quotations 6, emphasis original. "In the best of all possible worlds, there would be communication perhaps, but no rhetoric—since exigencies would not arise" (13).

[38]Bitzer, "Rhetorical Situation" 7. Bitzer conceives of "exigence" as an actual objective aspect of the situation. Consequently, the speaker and the audience may not realize the exigence, or may not regard it as significant, in any particular case.

[39]Bitzer, "Rhetorical Situation" 8. As an illustration of the first quotation, the rhetorical audience of a Mercedes–Benz advertisement consists only of those persons who could afford to purchase such an automobile, even though the actual audience may include many persons who cannot.

This makes form immaterial to "rhetoric": "neither the presence or absence of formal features in the discourse nor persuasive effect . . . can be regarded as reliable marks of rhetorical discourse."[40] "Rhetoric" is any discourse which functions in a rhetorical situation to alleviate an exigence. Bitzer can treat both the utterances of tribal fishermen and the works of Cicero as "rhetorical" because "the difference between oratory and primitive utterance . . . is not a difference in function."[41]

Bitzer's functional approach to rhetoric, however, allows him to go beyond classification. From the observation that situations temporally precede rhetorical discourse, it is only a short step to Bitzer's contention that "it is the situation which calls the discourse into existence."[42] Bitzer describes this generative power of situations with two metaphors, the "invitation" and the "prescription." The first metaphor seems to imply choice: "the situation which the rhetor perceives amounts to an invitation." But the invitation carries a dress code, requiring all who attend to wear a "*fitting* response, a response that fits the situation." In some cases the speaker is fitted in a lab coat, following Bitzer's second metaphor: "every situation *prescribes* its fitting response; the rhetor may or may not read the prescription accurately."[43] In many situations the prescription is quite detailed, establishing not only the function of discourse but also its form and content. A situation which has clear and important elements will dictate "the purpose, theme, matter, and style" of the utterance, and will even control the speaker's thought.[44] Each rhetorical utterance is ultimately a product of the human situation which produced it.

How, then, does Bitzer explain the existence of rhetorical types or genres? As with Bakhtin, since rhetorical units arise from rhetorical situations, *typical situations produce rhetorical types.* "Due to either the nature of things or convention, or both, some situations recur." Bitzer illustrates this principle with forensic genres. In the courtroom, "comparable situations occur, prompting comparable responses; hence rhetorical forms are born and a special

[40]Bitzer, "Rhetorical Situation," first quotation 5, second quotation 6.

[41]Bitzer, "Rhetorical Situation" 5.

[42]Bitzer, "Rhetorical Situation" 2.

[43]Bitzer, "Rhetorical Situation," first quotation 9, second quotation 10, emphasis original, third quotation 10, emphasis added.

[44]Bitzer, "Rhetorical Situation" 7, 10, quotation 10.

vocabulary, grammar, and style are established." Over time, past utterances begin to impact the situations themselves, so that "the tradition [of speaking] itself tends to function as a constraint upon any new response in the form." That certain situations become typical, consistently calling forth similar rhetorical responses, explains the existence of "*rhetorical* literature," speeches which demonstrate enduring persuasive power "precisely because they speak to situations which persist—which are in some measure universal [typical]."[45]

Two points of Bitzer's theory of rhetorical discourse will be highlighted here. First, Bitzer's theory makes it possible to conceive of rhetorical forms in cases where few literary artifacts of that form exist. If one can demonstrate the existence of typical rhetorical situations, one can speculate that appropriate forms might arise to address them. This will be more the case where the typical situations are heavily stereotyped or involve exigencies which are clear and important to the speaker.

The second point raised by Bitzer's theory relates particularly to the event nature of oral language. Since Bitzer insists that a rhetorical situation involves real persons, objects, places, and relations, all of which exist and persist as things in the world outside the text, he makes it is possible to speak of *genres of rhetorical situations* which produce typical forms of discourse. Consider his example of the courtroom. Although the oral words uttered in a courtroom are momentary events rather than things, the setting itself—the physical objects, persons who typically speak, and relations between these persons and objects—remains constant over time. Because of this, the courtroom situation will impose similar conventions and constraints upon each individual language event. Following Bitzer's theory, these common constraints will produce similar presentations, which may collectively be thought of as a generic style or "form." Thus the speeches of the judge, litigants, and attorneys will be similar from day to day and year to year, even though each individual discourse represents a specific situation and a specific moment. This rhetorical situation will thus eventually produce a discourse tradition, which may then dictate the conventions speakers in the courtroom are expected to follow. Here the situation creates certain typical rhetorical

---

[45]Bitzer, "Rhetorical Situation," all quotations 13.

functions, and these functions suggest a "form," even though this form may display considerable variations in style depending on the individual speaker.

POETICS AND SPEECH ACTS

Several of the themes explored thus far come together in the work of Tzvetan Todorov. Todorov's approach to genre is one aspect of his complex theory of the poetics of language. While much of his theory is outside the interests of the present study, it will be necessary to briefly review Todorov's conception of oral discourse before describing his position on oral genres.

Todorov's theory of discourse is concisely summarized in his *Symbolism and Interpretation*. Agreeing with Jakobson and Bakhtin, Todorov depicts "language" as an abstract collection of lexical choices and grammatical rules with "*sentences* as its output." "Discourse," on the other hand,

> is a concrete manifestation of language, and it is produced, necessarily, in a specific context that involves not only linguistic elements but also the circumstances of their production: the interlocutors, the time and place, the relations prevailing among these extralinguistic elements.[46]

A "discourse," then is a sentence, a unit of language, which is uttered in a specific human situation. Discourse is therefore "doubly determined": its total "meaning" is the general linguistic meaning of the sentence as specified by a specific contextual reference. Words in discourse thus "take on a more specific meaning, a precise situational meaning, than words in language."[47]

The dual nature of discourse as both sentence and utterance allows Todorov to posit two types of meaning which can coexist in discourse. In receiving a discourse as its audience, sometimes "the signifier of a single proposition leads us to knowledge of two signifieds, one *direct* and the other *indirect*." The "direct" meaning relates to the *sentence* nature of the discourse, the "natural" meaning or general meaning that the words and syntax themselves would imply as units of language. The "indirect" meaning relates

---

[46]Tzvetan Todorov, *Symbolism and Interpretation* (1978; trans. Catherine Porter; Ithaca, NY: Cornell University Press, 1982), both quotations 9.

[47]Todorov, *S&I* 10.

to the *utterance*, or contextual, nature of the discourse, the "situational" meaning which the audience infers in a particular context. Because the indirect meaning refers the audience to something outside the discourse unit, something not immediately present in the discourse as language, Todorov refers to the indirect aspect of discourse as "verbal symbolism." The two types of meaning, direct and symbolic, require the audience to undertake two mental operations: "the receiver *understands* discourses [as language units] but *interprets* [discourses as] symbols."[48]

For example, in a particular situation a speaker might utter the sentence, "the coffee is hot." The hearer would *understand* the *direct* meaning of this utterance to be an indication of the temperature of a particular beverage. But if, in the specific utterance context, the hearer is preparing to drink the coffee, the hearer will *interpret* the utterance to have a certain *indirect*, or *symbolic*, value: "be careful how you drink the coffee." Todorov asserts that the direct value always logically and temporally precedes the symbolic value of the utterance in the audience's perception, so that understanding always precedes interpretation. "The indirect [symbolic] meaning is grafted, by definition, onto the direct, it presupposes anteriority, thus temporality."[49] Todorov's approach should not, however, be confused with purely phenomenological approaches to audience response. The symbolic dimension of the utterance is an actual quality of the text itself, and both understanding and interpretation are guided by the text.[50]

---

[48]Todorov, *S&I* 11–18, first quotation 40, emphasis added, second quotation 18.

[49]Todorov, *S&I* 13. This does not imply that the symbolic meaning always displaces the direct meaning. When both the direct and indirect meanings can be retained at once, as in the example concerning the hot coffee above, the indirect meaning builds on the *proposition* expressed by the direct meaning. Todorov calls this "propositional symbolism." The direct proposition, "the coffee is hot," serves as the basis for the symbolic proposition, "be careful how you drink the coffee." Propositional symbolism thus brings together two independent "facts": "from the first proposition we deduce not a better description of the same fact but the description of a *second fact*" (49, emphasis original). In other cases, however, the symbolic meaning will replace the direct meaning as the sole meaning of the utterance. Todorov refers to this as "lexical symbolism" (41, 45).

[50]Todorov defends this claim by appeal to the universal experience of language: "I take the capacity to observe this difference [between direct and symbolic meaning] to be a characteristic feature of the human mind" (*S&I* 15).

The text guides symbolic interpretation through the presence of empirical indices. "[W]e [audiences] require that the text itself indicate to us its symbolic nature, that it possess a series of observable and undeniable properties through which it leads on to that peculiar form of reading which is 'interpretation.'"[51] These indices operate in conjunction with the "rule of pertinence": "if a discourse exists there must be a reason for it." The audience must be able to identify coherence in the discourse. If the direct meaning of the discourse seems to violate this rule, the audience must investigate "whether the discourse might not reveal its pertinence through some particular manipulation [interpretation]."[52]

Todorov refers to the impertinent text's invitation to interpret as "evocation." The audience will search for clues within the text, empirical indices, which evoke symbolic interpretations if the discourse does not meet the criteria of pertinence. Todorov organizes these indices under two categories. "Syntagmatic" indices "derive from the establishment of a relation between the given [language] segment and . . . other utterances belonging to the same *context*." "Paradigmatic" indices "derive from the establishment of a relation between the given [language] segment and . . . the shared knowledge of a community, with its *collective memory*."[53] Impertinence may thus represent discrepancies within the discourse or discrepancies *between the discourse and community ideology*. Once detected, these indices invite the reader to generate an indirect, symbolic meaning for the discourse.

In Todorov's view, then, discourse always has two levels of meaning, both of which bring together the speaker, the discourse, and the audience.[54]

---

[51]Todorov, *S&I* 19.

[52]Todorov, *S&I* 28.

[53]Todorov, *S&I* 30, emphasis original. Syntagmatic indices can be "based on lack," contradiction, or discontinuity within the language of the text, or "based on excess," tautology, repetition, or superfluity. Subcategories of paradigmatic indices are based on the kind of community knowledge or norms violated by the discourse. In these cases, interpretation seeks to make utterances intelligible, scientifically plausible, and culturally plausible (30–31).

[54]This is true even in the case of "literal discourse," "discourse that signifies without evoking anything. . . . [E]ven the most literal utterance inevitably evokes a group of other meanings" (Todorov, *S&I*, both quotations 53). Therefore, "literal discourse is not discourse

The direct meaning is the linguistic meaning of the utterance which the speaker and audience share via the common language code. Symbolic meaning is evoked by indices which the speaker inserts into the discourse and which invite the audience to construct a secondary meaning. The symbolic meaning of discourse in fact relies entirely on the audience's response to the utterance. "A text or discourse becomes symbolic at the point when, through an effort of interpretation, we discover in it an indirect meaning."[55] This invitation to interpret gives the "meaning" of discourse a dialogic dimension.

Todorov's concept of genre builds on his concept of discourse. His theory may be analyzed in three aspects: the poetics of genre; the genesis of historical genres; and, social and ideological aspects of genre.

In terms of the poetics of language, Todorov sees genre as a two–storied structure parallel to his conception of language and utterance. Todorov refers to the language, or abstract, dimension of genre as "type." "The type is defined as the conjunction of several properties of literary discourse, judged important for the works in which they are found."[56] Every analysis of genre begins with a doctrine of the nature of the work, "which involves on the one hand a certain number of abstract properties, on the other a certain number of laws governing the relation of these properties."[57] Type is not, however, simply a heuristic

---

from which any secondary meaning would be absent, but discourse in which secondary meanings are completely subordinate to the direct meaning" (54). Nor is it possible for discourse to be entirely evocative, having no direct meaning at all. Todorov refers to this type as "transparent discourse," which is evident "if when we perceive it [understand the utterance's direct meaning] we pay no attention to its literal meaning" (56).

[55]Todorov, S&I 19. Because symbolic meaning must be constructed by the audience, every evocation has a degree of indeterminacy, depending on how strongly the evocations are determined by the discourse. When the evocation is weak, "The result is not, as one might have imagined, a situation in which it is impossible to supplement the discursive relations with symbolic relations, but rather, on the contrary, an overabundance of symbolic associations, among which the absence of discursive underpinnings makes it impossible to choose" (both quotations 87, emphasis original).

[56]Tzvetan Todorov, *Introduction to Poetics* (1973; trans. Peter Brooks; Minneapolis, MN: University of Minnesota Press, 1981) 62.

[57]Tzvetan Todorov, *The Fantastic: A Structural Approach to a Literary Genre* (1970; trans. Richard Howard; Ithaca, NY: Cornell University Press, 1975) 15, 19, quotation 15. Todorov's view of the "work" is concisely summarized on pages 19–20 of *Fantastic*.

tool, but rather a poetic force which generates theoretical possibilities and realizations of those possibilities as historical genres.

> We [Todorov] have decided to consider all the immediately observable elements of the literary universe as the manifestation of an abstract and isolated structure, a mental construction, and to establish an organization on this level alone.[58]

At the type level, genre is capable of configuring and reconfiguring poetic channels and placing theoretical genres in relationships where they mutually define and redefine one another.[59] The pervasive influence of type provides continuity between works and genres of diverse regions and eras.[60]

The poetic dimension of genre leads Todorov to reject definitions which proceed from the surface features of discourse. Observation can, at best, produce "probabilities" in considerations of genre, because one "would have to say that a given work manifests a certain genre, not that this genre exists in the work."[61] If genre does not exist within the work itself, but operates as a governing principle, "there is no necessity that a work faithfully incarnate its genre, there is only a probability that it will do so." Indeed, one work might manifest multiple genres, or one genre might express itself in works with a variety of surface features.[62] Taxonomies of texts are therefore misguided.

This leads to Todorov's view of the origin of specific historical genres. Whereas "type" corresponds to the abstract, language dimension of discourse, genre corresponds to the social, utterance dimension of discourse. Language

---

[58]Todorov, *Fantastic* 20, quotation here; *Genres in Discourse* (trans. Catherine Porter; Cambridge: Cambridge University Press, 1990) 15.

[59]Note that "as a rule, moreover, a genre is always defined in relation to the genres adjacent to it" at the type level (Todorov, *Fantastic* 27).

[60]This is apparently why Todorov sees genre as an indispensable concept in literary analysis.   "Failing to recognize the existence of genres is equivalent to claiming that a literary work does not bear any relationship to already existing works. Genres are precisely those relay–points by which the [individual] work assumes a relation with the universe of literature" (*Fantastic* 8). There are no exceptions to this rule. Works which seem to violate generic regulations only demonstrate the existence of genres, since "transgression requires a law—precisely the one that is to be violated" (*GID* 15).

[61]Todorov, *Fantastic* 18–21, quotation 21.

[62]Todorov, *Fantastic* 22.

produces sentences from vocabulary and rules of grammar. "Sentences are [then] articulated among themselves and uttered in a given sociocultural context; they are transformed into utterances, and language is transformed into discourse." Genres operate in the social crucible where sentences are transformed into utterances. A genre is present *when the rules of utterance in a social context limit the choices offered by the language.* "Any verbal property, optional at the level of language, may be made obligatory in discourse; the choice a society makes among all the possible codifications of discourse [offered by its language] determines what is called its *system of genres.*"[63] In a given discourse situation, for example, the German language may offer the speaker one–hundred ways to express a particular thought, but the immediate social context of the utterance may eliminate ninety–seven of these possibilities. The empirical effect of this restriction reveals a historical discourse genre. As cultural institutions which set guidelines for social interaction, genres facilitate dialogic communication. In composing discourses, speakers and authors utilize (or violate) known genres, and audiences use generic regulations to understand, interpret, and respond.[64]

GENRE AND IDEOLOGY

The emphasis laid on the social nature of genre by Jakobson, Bakhtin, Bitzer, and Todorov raises again an issue that must now be considered in its own right: the relationship between ideology and genre. Todorov's views on this subject will serve as an introduction to the more comprehensive discussion of Robert C. Post.

Because Todorov makes genre a mechanism that transforms neutral language into social utterance, genre in his system absorbs the ideological components of discourse. All discourse, because situational and dialogic, is

---

[63]Todorov, *GID*, first quotation 9, second quotation 10. "[G]enres, indeed, are nothing but such choices among discursive possibilities, choices that a given society has made conventional" (10).

[64]Todorov, *GID* 18–19. "In a given society, certain discursive properties are institutionalized, and individual texts are produced and perceived in relation to the norm constituted by that codification. A genre, whether literary or not, is nothing other than the codification of discursive properties" (18).

saturated with the social and individual ideologies of the speaker and audience. "Every discourse bears traces of the personal and individual acts of its production."[65] As a corollary, genres "depend quite as much on a society's linguistic raw material as on its historically circumscribed ideology." Each genre, as a social institution, "stands in some relation to the dominant ideology" of the group.[66] Some genres, notably poetry and literature, are completely ideological and have no definite formal existence. "Poetry in general does not exist, but variable conceptions of poetry exist." The task of generic studies of poetry is to determine "whether there may . . . be some affinity among all the different reasons for which . . . a text has been labeled poetic."[67] For Todorov, ideology is a constituent element, and sometimes the only constituent element, of genre.

Todorov's implication becomes an explicit doctrine of genre in Robert C. Post's discussion of the nineteenth–century novel. Post suggests that historical trends in textual imitations of reality "may in fact be caused by a larger cultural evolution in the apprehension of reality itself."[68] Post refers to this cultural apprehension as the "moral reality" of the text, that "conception of manners, soul, and society" which the work presupposes.[69] These conceptions are drawn from the audience's ideology, to which the text must relate in some degree to be comprehended as aesthetically plausible. A text's moral reality is therefore "predicated upon specific and demonstrable [cultural] assumptions about the nature of the world, about the way in which individuals,

---

[65]Todorov, *Poetics* 25. In his 1980 preface to this work, Todorov clarifies the ideological input of the audience: "[E]very work is rewritten by its reader, who imposes upon it a new grid of interpretation for which [s]he is not generally responsible but which comes to him[/her] from his[/her] culture, from his[/her] time" (xxx).

[66]Todorov, *GID*, both quotations 19. The first quotation makes the significant, and unsupported, assumption that language, as an abstract concept, is not ideological. To support the second quotation, Todorov formulates the rule that only those speech acts which "correspond most closely to its [a group's] ideology" are developed into genres. For this reason, genres reveal "the constitutive [ideological] features of the society to which they belong," making them an interpretive key to the society's ideological topography (19).

[67]Todorov, *GID* 71.

[68]Robert C. Post, "A Theory of Genre: Romance, Realism, and Moral Reality," *American Quarterly* 33 (1981) 368.

[69]Post, "Theory of Genre" 370.

society, or the natural universe must exist in order for human meaning to be possible."[70] Because moral reality limits possible relations in natural and human affairs, making some relations "plausible" and some "implausible," it has a marked effect on the surface structure of the text, determining methods of characterization, portrayal of dialogue or events, "treatment of natural and social settings," and the logic of narrative organization. Texts "which share a common moral reality will therefore also share common aesthetic attributes. We classify these family resemblances as [historical] genres."[71] In making surface structure a product of moral reality, Post insists that ideology is a constituent element of genre. This approach, he feels, allows the structural features of the text "to be related in a coherent manner to the circumstances of cultural and intellectual history" from which it emerged.[72]

SUMMARY: THE NATURE OF SPEECH GENRES

The theories surveyed above lay the foundation for a concise theory of genre compatible with the event nature of oral speech. Oral speech is an interaction between persons in specific social contexts. Oral "genres" are an aspect of these social contexts, *the guidelines which regulate the production and reception of discourse*. The speaker's role in this exchange makes *function* a critical aspect of speech genres. The audience's role makes discourse *dialogic*, compelling the speaker to shape the utterance in anticipation of a response. The fact that speaker and audience are members of a social group with specific ideological norms which control their social

---

[70]Post, "Theory of Genre" 369. This is the case whether the author intends to affirm these norms or violate them. Even a "revolutionary" text must rebel against a specific ideological conception grasped by the audience in order to achieve its rhetorical effect.

[71]Post, "Theory of Genre" 370.

[72]Post, "Theory of Genre" 390. Post proceeds to analyze the genres "romance" and "realism" in terms of contrasting moral realities (379–390). The complex relationship between these opposing genres is easily defined at the ideological level: "Just as realism is not 'the objective representation' of social reality, but is instead a genre whose common aesthetic characteristics derive from a particular understanding of moral reality, so the romance can be defined with reference to a moral reality of precisely analogous logical properties and coherence" (372).

interaction makes genre *ideological*. Speech genres, like the oral utterances which they organize, are at once utterly personal and utterly social, utterly individual and utterly normative. The style and content of each genre is a byproduct of the means it utilizes to regulate verbal interaction.

It is now possible to define concisely the elements of a "speech genre." *A speech genre, or oral "form," is that set of parameters which governs the verbal interaction between composer and audience in a rhetorical situation.* There are thus genres of situations, not of oral texts. While this definition is not based on the surface structure of texts, it does not make genre a question of abstract poetics. Genre is a set of relations, but observable relations among empirical realities in the rhetorical situation, the configuration of "things" in the presence of which the utterance is produced. Since this verbal interaction always involves living persons who bring their own thoughts and values to the speech context, ideology is a constituent element of every genre, sometimes more and sometimes less explicit. When rhetorical situations become "typical," uniting similar discourse participants in similar contexts on multiple occasions, a certain uniformity of surface structure, or "style," may be observable across multiple performances. In this sense, "style" as a typical use of language in similar situations becomes an element, more specifically an accident, of genre, an empirical byproduct which reveals the presence of certain rules of verbal interaction.

This perspective allows a final critique of the fathers of NT Form Criticism. The situational theory of genre advocated here strongly prefers the approach of Dibelius to that of Bultmann. Bultmann's form–critical method was not undergirded by an explicit theory of genre, and his research produced a taxonomy of pericopae by comparing surface features of the written Gospels. But this approach is explicitly rejected by Todorov, who argues that descriptions of historical genres "must be subject to the explanation of a coherent theory" to avoid subjectivity.[73] Bakhtin agrees, insisting that taxonomies of texts based on stylistic features are doomed to be "inexhaustive and incompletely differentiated,"[74] a fitting critique of Bultmann's *History of the Synoptic Tradition*. The survey of Bultmann's method in the previous

---

[73]Todorov, *Fantastic* 21.
[74]Bakhtin, "Speech Genres" 65.

chapter confirms Bakhtin's suspicion by demonstrating that Bultmann's form–critical categories were, indeed, insufficiently differentiated and highly subjective. This imprecision was a byproduct of Bultmann's failure to adequately consider the functional, situational and dialogic dimensions of speech genres. Bultmann also failed to consider that ideology effects the *forms* as well as the *history* of an oral tradition. As a consequence, he falls under the scrutiny of Todorov's and Post's insistence that the ideology of the composer and the audience are crucial aspects of discourse, shaping the form and structure of texts.

Dibelius' method, by contrast, is largely affirmed by the approach taken here. Both Dibelius and Bitzer begin analysis with typical human situations and regard texts as products of the language functions which operate in these situations. This functional approach is affirmed by Jakobson. Dibelius' method was insufficient only inasmuch as it was incomplete. Concluding that oral forms were shaped in the human contexts of the early Church's life, Dibelius did not proceed to consider the dialogic and ideological dimension of these situations, and made form a product not of the situations themselves but of abstract laws. Human situations were, in Dibelius' mind, the arena in which these abstract laws of form development created the oral Gospel forms. This focus on laws led him to de–emphasize the individual and ideological aspect of speech genres. The approach taken here agrees with Dibelius that oral forms arose within typical situations in the life of the Church, but goes beyond him in suggesting that these forms *were byproducts of those situations*. This makes it possible to speak of forms or genres of oral speech while retaining the integrity of each speech event as a unique interactive moment, and while allowing each individual who uses the form to retain a distinct individuality and style.

This approach to speech genres is consistent with the conclusions of the Oral–Formulaic Theory. Synchronically, each telling of a "traditional" story is a product of the bard's telling tradition and personal ability and the audience's responsive reception. Diachronically, singers and audiences remember past performances and contexts and recall these during performances. Parallel situational elements in a succession of performances create a "traditional style," with certain stereotyped themes, motifs, and formulae. "Transmission" is therefore repetition, but not of a surface text;

rather, it represents a recomposition of a remembered oral performance in a new but generically similar context. Each oral performance is thus same and unique, new and old, at once.

ORAL FORMS AND JOHANNINE IDEOLOGY

The functional approach to genre advocated here offers a new method for form–critical research into FG. First, it agrees with Dibelius against Bultmann that literary analysis of the written Gospels must *follow* speculation about the community in which forms were shaped. Consequently, analysis must begin with the community, not the comparison of written texts. This is particularly helpful in the study of FG, which rarely evidences specific Synoptic parallels, making comparison almost impossible.

Second, since speech genres are byproducts of typical situations involving real persons, the possible existence of an oral form may be explored whenever (a) a particular typical situation in the life of FE's community may be clearly identified; or, (b) a particular ideological position is consistently advocated. This is the case because oral speech is shaped by individual persons in dialogic exchanges. When the material circumstances of this dialogue (the human participants and setting) or the ideological postures which regulate it can be nominated, it is possible to suggest a speech genre which might have arisen under such conditions. Here one may consult interdisciplinary studies to determine the formal features of speech genres which have emerged in similar situations. These genres may or may not appear in the Synoptics as well; in cases where FE's ideology or social situations were unique, the text of FG may evidence traditional forms which defy comparative analysis. The observable formal features of these genres may then be sought in the surface text of FG.

While the typical situations in which FG's tradition took shaped are presently unknown, the ideological posture of FE, evident in the current text of FG, has been thoroughly investigated. This posture is a clue to the possible existence of speech genres which might have arisen to express it. For the purposes of this study, it will be sufficient to summarize the conclusions of Johannine scholarship on FE's ideology.

The popularity of John 3:16–17 is, from an interpretive standpoint, unfortunate. The warm universalism of this passage, which assures that all people may accept the Gospel and that Jesus has come to save rather than judge, is uncharacteristic of FE's thought, an island of hope in a sea of despair. FE's Jesus has no need to judge only because all who do not believe in him have been judged already (3:18). In FG, rejection of Jesus is not a matter of opinion or of academic inquiry, but rather a revelation of one's true nature as a hater of light and lover of darkness, a doer of evil deeds whom Jesus, the "light," exposes (ἐλεγχθῇ) and condemns (3:19–20). There is, it would seem, no middle ground, no innocent bystander. All can be saved, but most are not.

Because most people are under judgement, FE is consistently suspicious of "the world." Of course, God loved the world, so much so that he gave his only–begotten (John 3:16), but it is everywhere apparent that this love is unrequited. At risk of contradicting himself, FE's Jesus later informs the blind man and the Pharisees (9:39), and then the Passover multitude (12:31), that he has, in fact, come to bring judgement to "this world" in the form of Himself. This is doubtless the reason the world will rejoice at Jesus' death (16:20), but this brief respite will be disturbed when the "other Paraclete" appears to continue the work of convicting and judging (16:8–11). As a logical corollary, the world rejects the followers of Jesus because they bear his word of judgement; true disciples, indeed, are not "of the world" (17:14–16). Categorically, the world hates (μισέω) Jesus (7:7) and will hate anyone who follows Jesus (15:18–19). The disciples have power to endure this hate only because Jesus has "overcome the world" (16:33). FE's feeling that non–Christians are generally hostile to believers is so strong that he states the relationship between the two groups in ontological, dualistic terms.

FE is particularly suspicious of one subgroup within the world, "the Jews." This designation is remarkable in that almost every major character in FG is Jewish. It is reasonable to suggest that in some cases FE uses "the Jews" as a title for the religious leaders of the Jewish people. In this sense, Nicodemus is a "ruler of the Jews" (John 3:1); "the Jews" question the man at Bethesda about his Sabbath healing (5:10); the parents of the heroic blind man of John 9 will not testify about their son because they "fear the Jews," who have conspired to expel Jesus' followers from the synagogue (9:22). At the very least, FE sees the Jewish leaders as enemies of Jesus, and Jesus' prediction at 16:2 suggests that the same situation will prevail in later generations.

But FE also uses the term "Jews" to refer to Jewish persons who are apparently not leaders of the people. After the feeding of 5000 and crossing of the sea, Jesus addresses the "multitude" (ὄχλος; John 6:2, 5, 22, 24). A hostile confrontation ensues, which ends with Jesus' claim to be "the bread of God" which gives eternal life to those who believe. When the multitude grows skeptical of Jesus' claims, FE suddenly identifies them as "Jews." John 8:31 stages a discussion between Jesus and an unusual group, "Jews who believed." As their dialogue with Jesus develops, however, it becomes apparent that they are more "Jews" than "believers." Jesus meets their claims to Abraham's lineage with challenges, and identifies them as children of the devil (8:44), who is a "murderer" and a "liar." After further remarks, the Jews conclude that Jesus is a Samaritan demoniac, and that he must be stoned for his blasphemous words (8:48–59). The Jews attempt another stoning at 10:24–39. Jesus later attributes these aborted efforts to the fulfillment of "their Law" (15:25). Overall, there is a strong distinction in FG between Jesus' true disciples and "Jews" which transcends national and social boundaries. Like the world, the posture of the Jews is uniformly hostile, both to Jesus and his people (16:2).

These data have received considerable attention in the last three decades. J. Louis Martyn opened a new round of dialogue on the issue with his *History and Theology in the Fourth Gospel*. Martyn argues that John 9, the story of the blind man, can be read at two levels: the life of Jesus and the experience of FE. At the level of FE, the passage reflects "experiences in the dramatic interaction between the synagogue and the Johannine church."[75] To explore this interaction, Martyn focuses on 9:22, the statement that the Jews had agreed to excommunicate anyone who confessed Jesus as Messiah. After investigating a number of historical possibilities, Martyn concludes that this verse indicates that "*the formal separation between church and synagogue has been accomplished in John's* milieu *by means closely related to the Jewish Benediction Against Heretics*," a ruling of the Jamnia Academy (ca. 85 CE). FE's community is therefore a messianic Jewish group banned from the

---

[75]J. Louis Martyn, *History and Theology in the Fourth Gospel* (2nd ed.; Nashville, TN: Abingdon, 1979) 37. The first edition was published in 1968.

synagogue: "What had been an inner–synagogue *group of Christian Jews* now became—against its will—a separated *community of Jewish Christians*."[76] According to Martyn, then, the traditions behind FG were shaped by a fringe group of the Jewish community, whose ties with the synagogue were severed sometime in the mid–80s.

The same conclusion has been reached by scholars who have approached FG from other methodological perspectives. Fortna contends that the Signs Gospel was a missionary tract produced by Christian Jews before the excommunication. In fact, SG "is probably the purest example we have of a document written within the context of Christians who were still part of Judaism," indeed, "an early and pure Christian Judaism."[77] In Fortna's model, then, even the written precursor of FG was produced by a fringe group within "orthodox" Judaism. Oscar Cullmann goes further, arguing that the "Johannine circle" originated with converts from heterodox Jewish groups, such as the Baptist sect.[78] Here again, FG is associated with a subculture within Judaism, possibly with persons who moved from one branch of heterodoxy to another upon confessing Jesus to be Messiah.

For purposes of this study, it is sufficient to note that contemporary Johannine scholarship often associates FG with a heterodox Jewish subculture which maintained a hostile posture toward mainline Judaism. This posture generates what Norman Petersen refers to as the "anti–language" of FG, the persistent use of terms and concepts taken from orthodox Judaism which have been "transformed in contrastive or antistructural ways."[79] Even the Christology of FG is, to a large degree, an "anti–christology," a portrait of Christ in terms of what he is "greater than."[80] In interdisciplinary terms, it may

---

[76]Martyn, *History and Theology* 50-62, first quotation 50, second quotation 66, emphasis original.

[77]Robert T. Fortna, *The Fourth Gospel and Its Predecessor: From Narrative Source to Present Gospel* (Philadelphia, PA: Fortress, 1988), first quotation 9–10, second quotation 214.

[78]Oscar Cullmann, *The Johannine Circle* (trans. John Bowden; Philadelphia, PA: Westminster, 1975) 89–94.

[79]Norman R. Petersen, *The Gospel of John and the Sociology of Light: Language and Characterization in the Fourth Gospel* (Valley Forge, PA: Trinity Press, 1993) 5.

[80]Petersen, *Sociology* 91–108, 127–132.

be said that *FE is a member of a subculture which is exploring beliefs and knowledge held to be "forbidden" by the group at large.* It is in the human contexts of such an environment that the Johannine Jesus tradition took shape, developing and absorbing forms in the dialogue among members of this heterodox, messianic Judaism.

Chapter 4:
The Riddle As A Speech Genre

Chapter 3 offered a new definition of oral forms and a new form–critical method for approaching the speeches of Jesus in FG. This method begins by identifying the situational or ideological contexts in which speech genres develop, then identifies forms which typically appear in such contexts, and finally tests possibilities through analysis of the surface text. Such an approach is particularly amenable to the speeches of FG, which receive little illumination from methods of analysis which depend on literary parallels. It was also observed in Chapter 3 that most Johannine scholars believe FG was produced by a fringe group which had been violently separated from its Jewish heritage. In response to this separation, the group defined itself against mainline Judaism, using an "anti–language" of Jewish terms and symbols.

What speech genres might arise in such a situation? One oral form which might find its way into FE's "anti–language" under these social conditions is the riddle. Jack and Phyllis Glazier define the "riddle" as a verbal challenge which creates purposeful ambiguity between description and referent. Riddles use conventional language, but while normal discourse reveals its referent, the riddle hides its referent through intentional confusion. To resolve this confusion and answer the riddle, the riddlee must organize possible answers "based on the taxonomic principles the riddle offers."[1] "Correct" answers will normally advocate those taxonomic boundaries and relationships which the group affirms. Elli Köngäs Maranda has therefore

---

[1] Jack Glazier and Phyllis Gorfain Glazier, "Ambiguity and Exchange: The Double Dimension of Mbeere Riddles," *JAF* 89 (1976) 211; Dan Ben–Amos, "Solutions to Riddles," *JAF* 89 (1976) 252, quotation here.

stated that "riddles play with boundaries, but ultimately to affirm them."[2] It seems reasonable to suggest that FE might utilize this traditional form to clarify the ideological boundaries between his group and orthodox Judaism.

To explore this possibility, it will be necessary to develop a precise definition of the riddle consistent with the model of speech genres established in Chapter 3. This task will require a survey of the major approaches to the riddle as a folk genre.

WHAT IS A "RIDDLE"?

This study will survey a number of recent folklorists whose research offers guidelines for the present investigation. The theorists to be discussed will be addressed in chronological order to show theoretical developments in folk research over the last century. Folkloristics, like every academic discipline, has followed a methodological continuum in which each new movement is related to previous trends, and the study of riddles is subject to that continuum. Careful analysis of the conclusions of these scholars will allow a precise definition of the riddle as a traditional oral form which can be applied to the text of FG.

TAYLOR: AESTHETICS AND GENRE

Archer Taylor's voluminous research on riddles and proverbs set the pace for a revival of modern interest in these folk forms. His vast knowledge of the field is evident in the historical and cross–cultural illustrations that pepper his work. Yet, despite the scope of his interest, Taylor's definition of the riddle is precise and intends to comprehend riddles in all times and places.

Typical of folkloristics in the early twentieth century, Taylor makes a sharp distinction between "popular and folk materials and literary, learned, or artistic materials."[3] "Popular" texts, which would include all oral forms, are generated by the "folk" spontaneously and are relatively unsophisticated in

---

[2]Elli Köngäs Maranda, "Riddles and Riddling: An Introduction," *JAF* 89 (1976) 131; also Glazier and Glazier, "Ambiguity and Exchange" 212–217.

[3]Archer Taylor, *The Literary Riddle Before 1600* (1948; rpt. Westport, CT: Greenwood Press, 1976) 1.

style and theme. "Literary" texts, by contrast, are produced with a conscious emphasis on style and abstract themes by more learned authors. Because this distinction involves judgements about the stylistic quality of the text, Taylor's approach to genre may be called "aesthetic."

Taylor distinguishes "true" or "descriptive" riddles from "false" riddles or *"Wissensfragen."* The "true" riddle is "descriptive" in that it relies on common knowledge and provides enough clues for the audience to determine its referent.[4] By comparing this referent to "another entirely different object," the riddle suggests "a false answer with its contradiction found in the solution."[5] In the standard descriptive riddle, the true referent is blurred within the structure of the text by the conflicting presence of "positive and negative descriptive elements." The "positive" description of the referent appears first and misleads the audience because it must be "understood figuratively rather than literally." The "negative" description that follows must be taken literally but, in juxtaposition with the positive description, "seems impossible."[6]

Taylor illustrates this principle with the well known English riddle "Humpty Dumpty":

Humpty Dumpty sat on a wall
Humpty Dumpty had a great fall
All the King's horses and all the King's men
Couldn't put Humpty together again.

Lines one and two of this rhyme are a positive, metaphorical description of the referent. The proper name and the actions sitting on a wall and experiencing

---

[4]Archer Taylor, "The Varieties of Riddles," *Philologica: The Malone Anniversary Studies* (ed. Thomas A. Kirby and Henry Bosley Wolf; Baltimore: Johns Hopkins Press, 1949) 3. In a "true" riddle, "the description [of the referent] must contain some discordant detail to put the hearer on [her/]his guard and suggest the correct answer" ("The Riddle," *California Folklore Quarterly [WF]* 2 [1943] 129).

[5]Taylor, first quotation "Riddle" 129; second quotation "Varieties" 3.

[6]Taylor, "Riddle" 130; "Varieties" 3. "[A] true riddle consists of two descriptions of an object, one figurative and one literal, and confuses the hearer who endeavors to identify an object described in conflicting ways" ("Riddle" 130). "The [positive] description in general terms is understood metaphorically; the [negative] description in specific terms is understood literally" ("Varieties" 3).

a fall are figurative descriptions that would normally apply to a person or animal. But how can it be that a fallen person or animal could not be "put together again" by agents of the King? The audience is compelled to seek another referent which might resolve this contradiction. The solution, that Humpty Dumpty is not a person but an egg, makes the negative description literal (one might attempt in vain to "put together" the pieces of a broken egg) and reveals that the positive element, the name, the wall, and the fall, were metaphorical, personifying the egg. The true answer, an egg, thus resolves the tension created within the riddle text by the apparent answer, a person.

Taylor's subgrouping of riddles is based on the type of metaphorical comparison which the riddle initiates. He explores five major types of comparison, "equating an object to a [hu]man [being], an animal, a plant, and another object," and comparison "to a scene or an event . . . with some impossible or contradictory quality."[7] Referential blurring in the use of these comparisons may be achieved through a variety of structural arrangements. Some riddles play on words which have different senses in different contexts. Others present metaphorical dialogues between unknown speakers, often objects or animals, whose identity must be guessed.[8] Some riddles enumerate contradictory elements of an object or scene, or use contradictory terms to describe a unified object or scene.[9] In every case, descriptive riddles defy normal patterns of language use by purposefully blurring the links between common signs and common referents.

_____

    [7]Taylor, "Riddle," first quotation 131, second quotation 133. The object is most frequently a house or something observable in the vicinity of a house, such as the stars, the sky, a ditch, or a churn. But "the extremely varied themes of the riddles employing these [object] comparisons apparently show no restrictions on their choice" (133).

    [8]Dialogue appears in the riddle in one of three forms: self–characterizing monologue ("I am," "I do," "I come from"); first person narrative ("when I was going to St. Ives"); and, dialogue between multiple characters ("the babbler said to the prowler") ("Riddles in Dialogue," _Proceedings of the American Philosophical Society_ 97 [1953] 61 62–65).

    [9]On object comparisons, "a few true riddles do not achieve a clear picture [of the referent], but merely enumerate the [seemingly contradictory] parts of an object," while others use contradictory terms (Taylor, "Riddle" 134). On scene comparisons, sometimes "the situation itself seems inexplicable" based on the definition, and sometimes the scene has internal contradictions which are reflected by the text ("Varieties" 6). Taylor thus allows that ambiguity may be located in the sign or the referent.

By contrast, *Wissensfragen*, "riddling questions or 'false' riddles," "require the possession of special information that is not supplied in the question." These puzzles, which lack the positive and negative descriptive elements of true riddles, rely upon the audience's specialized knowledge to link sign and referent.[10] Taylor describes five types of false riddles based on structural features. The "alternative" offers the audience two choices, "would you rather X or Y," where one choice is "apparently impossible or wholly objectionable. The correct choice is the one that is less attractive at first glance."[11] The "dialogue riddle" describes metaphorical subjects in a dialogue whose identity cannot be specified without prior information. The "message riddle" is embedded in a narrative and "consists of a dialogue communicating information in terms which the bystanders [in the story] cannot understand."[12] The "neck riddle" also occurs in narrative and requires special information about the biography of the riddler. Here "the speaker saves his neck by the riddle, for the judge or executioner has promised release in exchange for a riddle that cannot be guessed." The fifth type is the "wisdom question," a catechetical formula often used in teaching religion, mathematics, social norms, and laws.[13] Taylor thus divides riddles into two broad categories in terms of the relationship between question and answer. "True riddles" are those in which the answer is provided by the question itself. To answer "false riddles," the audience must already possess special knowledge which the question does not supply.

Taylor's aesthetic categories are superimposed on the "true/false" division. The "popular or folk riddle" is generally brief and uses "simple" rhetorical devices.[14] It utilizes typical folklore themes drawn from everyday experience, and is orally composed. "Literary" riddles, by contrast, are "composed by conscious literary intention." These "differ from oral true riddles in subject matter by admitting abstract themes and in form by

[10]Taylor, "Varieties" 3, 6, quotation 3; "Riddle" 145.
[11]Taylor, "Varieties" 18, quotation here; "Riddle" 145–146.
[12]Taylor, "Riddle" 146–147. It is unclear whether Taylor thinks all dialogue riddles are false riddles; as noted above, he elsewhere discusses this type with descriptive riddles.
[13]Taylor, "Varieties" 6; "Riddle" 145.
[14]Taylor, *Literary Riddle* 1–2.

employing the first person and elaborate antitheses."[15] The literary riddle's more sophisticated structure often involves "a long series of assertions and contradictions," sometimes in the form of a first person metaphorical monologue. This may lead to an excess of contradictory details of the referent, leaving the audience overwhelmed.[16] The themes of literary riddles are "obviously suited only to learned elaboration." Historically, these themes have included "classical mythology, and history," "Tiresias, Solomon, nobody (Nemo)"; exotic creatures like the "dragon, tiger, panther, chameleon, leopard, scorpion, chimera, and ostrich"; philosophical topics such as "God, necessity, nature, fate, and hope," "case (grammatical), . . . age, old age."[17] In general, "literary" riddles are similar to folk riddles in their referential structure, but differ in the complexity of their style and themes.

While Taylor's research offers many valuable insights, his approach to the riddle evidences a number of weaknesses typical of the folklore scholarship of his day. Several of these weaknesses involve his way of approaching the data. It is apparent that Taylor, like Bultmann, derived his theory of the riddle from extensive observations of written texts without a precise theoretical conception of speech genres. This has several noticeable effects on his analysis. First, he is guilty, like Bultmann, of utilizing imprecise categories. This is particularly obvious in his attempt to distinguish "folk" from "literary" riddles. To argue that "literary" riddles are "more complex" and "more abstract" than oral folk riddles is to invite subjectivity. Taylor further admits that this scheme often does not easily fit the data:

> Since the sharp separation of literature and folklore has come about only slowly, we often find little difference between the riddles of art and the riddles of the folk as we go backward in time.

---

[15]Taylor, "Riddle" 143; *Literary Riddle* 4. Since they utilize writing, literary riddles may involve "manipulations of the answers in which letters are added, omitted, or altered [from the name of the referent]. Such tricks have no trace of the folk in them," presumably because the "folk" compose orally (50).

[16]Taylor, *Literary Riddle* 3. The literary riddle thus often "confuses themes belonging to entirely different conceptions of the object [referent]" (36).

[17]Taylor, *Literary Riddle*, quotations selected from 59, 63, 74, 82.

Indeed, the earliest known examples of the form utterly defy this distinction.[18]
The "folk vs. literary" dichotomy is further complicated by the fact that "not
a few literary riddles give evidence of being a deliberate artistic elaboration of
the folk theme," while there are also "literary riddles that have degenerated in
the process of oral transmission."[19] If folk themes and styles can appear in
literary riddles and vice–versa, one must suspect that Taylor has imposed an
artificial aesthetic criterion. A further imprecision in categories concerns
Taylor's "true or false" model. It is uncertain, for example, whether Taylor
thinks "dialogue riddles" are true or false. At one point he speaks of "neck
riddles" as true riddles, but in the next paragraph uses them as an example of
Wissensfragen.[20]

Along with imprecise categories, Taylor shares Bultmann's tendency to
treat oral units as objects. While this might be appropriate to the discussion of
literary riddles, Taylor also treats oral riddles as things with object properties.
Despite his admission that it is difficult "to set up a hypothetical original" even
when one can trace the evolutionary process behind a group of texts, Taylor
continues to speak of the transformation of riddles by cultural adaptation. He
also argues that "the variations in detail which appear in the versions of a
riddle have arisen in the course of oral transmission" as if speaking of the
successive editions of a book.[21] Taylor shares Bultmann's insensitivity to the
situational, event nature of oral speech.

---

[18]Taylor, *Literary Riddle* 12.

[19]Taylor, *Literary Riddle*, first quotation 7, second quotation 9. For examples see
15–16, 22, 27, 42, 64–65; "Riddle" 143–145. The following statement is typical: "[this
riddle] may have a foundation in folklore, but shows the elaborations characteristic of the
literary artist" (*Literary Riddle* 27).

[20]Taylor, "Varieties" 6. Similarly, Taylor does not sufficiently elaborate the nature
of the "special" knowledge required to answer false riddles. If "special knowledge" means
knowledge acquired by initiation or education, then all literary riddles, which require literacy
and utilize "learned" themes, are "false" inasmuch as such learned knowledge is not
disseminated throughout the population.

[21]Taylor, "Riddle," first quotation 137, second quotation 138. For example, after
examining differences between similar traditional riddles in France and Germany, Taylor
concludes that "obviously, the French riddler dropped the element [in question] . . . or the
German riddler added it, but only a careful comparison of many [written] versions and the
citing of all relevant evidence can determine what happened" (138).

Further, also parallel Bultmann, Taylor's vast knowledge of written texts and his treatment of oral units as objects that exist and develop independently explains his silence on the sociological aspects of riddle composition and performance. It seems that riddles, in his system, emerge from a vacuum. Consequently, *after* examining and categorizing the various types of false riddle, Taylor asserts that one "may now inquire into their origin, distribution, history, and stylistic peculiarities," an inquiry he does not undertake.[22] Taylor thus relegates the situational factors of riddle composition to a secondary level of inquiry distinct from the problems of the genre itself. His theory suffers from general theoretical imprecision, which derives from his failure to explicitly define his analytic categories.

A second cluster of shortcomings relates to Taylor's aesthetic concerns. As noted above, the aesthetic categories "folk" and "literary" are imprecise. Beyond this, Taylor frequently passes personal judgements on the aesthetic value of individual texts. A particularly striking case appears in *Literary Riddle*, where, after citing a riddle from a historic Spanish collection, Taylor remarks that "some of the riddles in this collection are too obscene to reprint."[23] Still more unfortunate is Taylor's cultural prejudice. Discussing variations in riddling, Taylor claims that "the more sophisticated cultures have lost the quick readiness to perceive similarities in altogether unrelated objects."[24] It is difficult to determine how the loss of a mental capacity is consistent with the designation "more sophisticated." Taylor's theory labors under an overly sharp distinction between "the folk" and "the learned," and an insufficient distinction between oral and literary forms.

Despite these deficiencies, Taylor's work offers a number of helpful insights to the present study. First, his extensive knowledge of cross–cultural and historical literature supports the conclusion that "riddling is virtually universal."[25] Specifically, the riddle was a popular speech form in the Jewish

---

[22]Taylor, "Varieties" 8.

[23]Taylor, *Literary Riddle* 105. For further examples see 75, 81, 83, 96–97.

[24]Taylor, "Riddle" 139. Taylor speculates that this may be the case because "modern man" has a more complex experience of reality, and is therefore aware of too many potential referents to select the correct answer to the riddle.

[25]Taylor, "Riddle" 141.

community from the composition of the OT through the Middle Ages, making it reasonable to suggest that riddles might appear in FG.²⁶

A second and more important insight arises from Taylor's discussion of "false" riddles. Discussing "enumeration riddles," riddles which list the qualities of the referent and challenge the audience to name it, Taylor notes that often the audience must appeal to a cultural schematic about oppositions, time, or nature.²⁷ This principle applies to many types of riddle. The "Riddle of Sphinx," for example, appeals to a cultural schematic:

> What goes on four legs in the morning
> Two legs in the afternoon
> Three legs in the evening?

---

²⁶Taylor, *Literary Riddle* 31–37, and the bibliographic note on 31 n. 44. The riddle has been well documented in Judaism and the Greco–Roman world. On Jewish riddles, see Josephus, *AJ* 7.5.3 (parr. 1 Kings 5, 9; trans. H. St. J. Thackeray; LCL; Cambridge, MA: Harvard University Press, 1966) 646–649; V. Hamp, "חִידָה *chîdhāh*," *TDOT* (trans. David Green; ed. G. Johannes Botterweck and Helmer Ringgren; Grand Rapids, MI: Eerdmans, 1980) 4.320–323; Joseph Jacobs, "Riddle," *The Jewish Encyclopedia* (ed. Isidore Singer; New York, NY: Funk and Wagnalls, 1905) 10.408–409; Harry Torczyner, "The Riddle in the Bible," *HUCA* 1 (1924) 125–150; James L. Crenshaw, *Samson: A Secret Betrayed, A Vow Ignored* (Atlanta, GA: John Knox, 1978) 99–111; John M. Thompson, *The Form and Function of Proverbs in Ancient Israel* (The Hague: Mouton, 1974) 74–75, 92–93; Galit Hasan–Rock, "Riddle and Proverb: Their Relationship Exemplified by an Aramaic Proverb," *Proverbium* 24 (1974) 936–940; Solomon Schrecter, "The Riddles of Solomon in Rabbinic Literature," *Folklore* 1 (1890) 349–358. On Greco–Roman riddles, see Aristotle, *The Poetics* 22.1–7 (trans. W. Hamilton Fyfe; LCL; Cambridge, MA: Harvard University Press, 1982) 84–87; Athenaeus of Naucratis (170–230 C.E.), *The Deipnosophists* 10.448–459 (trans. Charles Burton Gulick; LCL; Cambridge, MA: Harvard University Press, 1927) 530–583; Friedrich Hauck, "Παροιμία," *TDNT* (ed. Gerhard Friedrich; trans. Geoffrey W. Bromiley; Grand Rapids, MI: Eerdmans, 1967) 5.854–855; Konrad Ohlert, *Rätsel und Rätselspiele der alten Griechen* (2nd ed.; 1912; rpt. New York, NY: Olms, 1979); Raymond Theodore Ohl, trans. and ed., *The Enigmas of Symphosius* (Philadelphia, PA: University of Pennsylvania, 1928). The studies by Friedreich (*Geschichte des Rätsels*), Mathilde Hain, (*Rätsel* [Stuttgart: J. B. Metzler, 1966]), and Mark Bryant (*Riddles Ancient and Modern* [New York, NY: Peter Bedrick, 1983]) each survey Jewish, Greco–Roman, and modern European riddles.

²⁷Taylor, "Riddle" 134.

To identify the correct referent, a human being, one must appeal to an ideological schematic of human life common in western culture: that life develops in stages; that the infant stage may be represented by morning and the elderly stage by twilight; that infants crawl and elderly persons walk with canes. None of this information is supplied by the riddle itself, but all may be supplied from the cultural schematic in order to arrive at the correct referent. This confirms Taylor's general observation that *Wissensfragen* often require the audience to possess special knowledge.

As Taylor observes, because all riddles build on group knowledge and experience, the genre can take a wide variety of surface forms. Although riddles can be traced to early Babylonian civilization, and although riddles have been a distinct field of western academic inquiry since the 17th century, Taylor can still complain that "the stylistic varieties of true riddles are virtually unknown [=uncatalogued]."[28] Riddles that require special knowledge are particularly variable in their form, and Taylor introduces them by noting the absence of the formal features characteristic of "true" riddles.[29] Because they utilize special group knowledge, riddles develop special group forms.

ABRAHAMS: THE STRUCTURE OF CONTEXT

Roger D. Abrahams' work, which includes several significant essays on the riddle, represents a shift toward context as the key interpretive factor in folkloristics. To situate his theory, it will be helpful to briefly summarize the state of riddle research, and of folkloristics in general, in the early 1960's. This may be done by comparing three studies, Georges and Dundes' "Toward a Structural Definition of the Riddle" (1963), Donn V. Hart's *Riddles in Filipino Folklore* (1964), and Charles T. Scott's *Persian and Arabic Riddles* (1965). The distinct emphases of these studies will illuminate Alan Dundes' call for a paradigm shift in folklore methodology. Abrahams' work, as will be seen, is a product of that shift.

Robert Georges and Alan Dundes' 1963 article represents a "structuralist" approach to folk texts. Arguing that Taylor's definition of the true/descriptive riddle was incomprehensive, they insist that cross–cultural

---

[28]Taylor, "Riddle" 139, quotation here; *Literary Riddle* Preface, 110.
[29]Taylor, "Riddle" 145.

genres must be delineated "in terms of morphological characteristics." Indeed, "the best way to arrive at a definition of the riddle is through structural analysis, since definitions based on content and style have proved to be inadequate."[30] This statement indicates the level at which "structural" analysis operates. Georges and Dundes seek to identify a universal riddle structure which operated *below* the localized language and content of specific texts. "Structure" in this sense does not relate to the form or grammar of specific linguistic units of the text but to a deeper arrangement and interaction of textual elements, a textual equation, which could express itself in a variety of styles and themes in different situations and cultures.

The structuralist approach first identifies "a minimum unit of analysis," which, again, is not equal to any specific linguistic unit in a surface text. Georges and Dundes identify the "descriptive element" as the riddle's minimum structural unit. Each descriptive element is composed of two essential subunits, a "topic" and a "comment." "The *topic* is the apparent referent; that is, it is the object or item which is allegedly described," the subject of the riddle question which stands for the answer. "The *comment* is an assertion about the topic," usually indicating "the form, function, or action of the topic."[31] In the example discussed earlier, the lines "Humpty Dumpty sat on a wall, Humpty Dumpty had a great fall," present two descriptive elements. The topic of the first element is "Humpty Dumpty," and the comment about that topic is "sat on a wall." The second element has the same topic but a different comment, "had a great fall." In both cases the topic, Humpty Dumpty, represents the actual referent of the riddle, an egg, and the comment describes something about both Humpty Dumpty and the egg.

Having identified the "minimal structural unit" of the riddle, Georges and Dundes can define the riddle in terms of the structural relations among such units in the riddle text: "A riddle is a traditional verbal expression which contains one or more descriptive elements, a pair of which may be in

---

[30]Robert A. Georges and Alan Dundes, "Toward a Structural Definition of the Riddle," *JAF* 76 (1963), first quotation 111, second quotation 113.

[31]Georges and Dundes, "Structural Definition" 113, all emphasis original. Jeffery L. Kallen extends this approach via the theme–rheme model of the Prague school in *Linguistics and Oral Tradition: The Structural Study of the Riddle* (Dublin: Trinity College, 1981).

opposition; the referent is to be guessed."[32] Riddles which contain conflicting descriptive elements are "oppositional riddles," while those with a single descriptive element or nonconflicting descriptive elements are "nonoppositional riddles."[33] Again, such "opposition" is present in or absent from the underlying structure of the text, not the actual words, grammar or content of the specific riddle. Whenever the structure, "topic(s) + comment(s) + referent must be guessed," underlies an utterance, that utterance may be considered a "riddle" regardless of specific local accouterments. Georges and Dundes' analysis therefore does not rely on specific samples. They also suggest that the contexts in which riddles are produced and exchanged could be explored only *after* the genre has been defined in structural terms.[34]

By contrast, Donn Hart's 1964 study of Filipino riddling represents a purely anthropological approach to folklore. Noting Taylor's three–fold emphasis on collection, description, and history in folklore studies, Hart complains that previous research on riddles "rarely included the functions or cultural milieu of riddling. As a result, far more is known about riddles than *riddling.*" Hart's study is concerned exclusively with riddling as a social phenomenon, under the assumption that riddle performance might provide a key "to societal values or political and religious content and functions."[35] He shows little interest in the structure of the actual riddle texts in his data pool.

---

[32]Georges and Dundes, "Structural Definition" 113, emphasis removed.

[33]The nonoppositional riddle can be "literal," meaning that the referent and the topic(s) are identical, or "metaphorical," meaning that the referent and the topic(s) are different and that the topic(s) represent the referent metaphorically (Georges and Dundes, "Structural Definition" 113–114). "Oppositional riddles are characterized by the occurrence of an opposition between at least one pair of descriptive elements" (114). This opposition may be achieved structurally in three ways. The "antithetical contradictive" structure makes the opposed descriptive elements mutually exclusive (114). The "privational contradictive" structure "results when the second of a pair of descriptive elements is a denial of a logical or natural attribute of the first" (115). The "causal contradictive" structure makes the second descriptive element deny or defy the anticipated consequence of an action stated in the first descriptive element; it therefore implies temporal sequence (115–116). While oppositional riddles may utilize literal topics, at least one topic is "almost always" metaphorical (116).

[34]Georges and Dundes, "Structural Definition" 111.

[35]Donn V. Hart, *Riddles in Filipino Folklore: An Anthropological Analysis* (Syracuse, NY: Syracuse University Press, 1964), both quotations 9, emphasis original.

After cursorily surveying a number of theoretical approaches to the riddle, Hart indicates that his study will accept Taylor's formal definition of the true/descriptive riddle without modification.

This interest in social usage over text is reflected in Hart's analytic method. His study focuses exclusively on the cultural items which are adopted as riddle *subjects*, irrespective of the ways in which those subjects are represented in the riddles themselves. He distributes these subjects across a taxonomy of twenty categories drawn from the "Human Relations Area Files scheme for classifying cultural data." Consistent with his interests, when a subject might fit into more than one category Hart places it "in the group most closely associated with its contemporary use in the Philippines." This table allows Hart to speculate about the relative importance of the various riddle subjects in Filipino folklife, under the assumption that "the sheer number of riddles about a subject ... probably reflects its importance in Christian Filipino society."[36]

Hart's taxonomy of riddle subjects creates a body of anthropological data, which he proceeds to analyze in search of clues to Filipino folklife. He focuses on the social distribution of riddle subjects and the social contexts in which riddles are delivered. As a general rule, "riddling does appear to be most attractive to certain age groups."[37] The occasions on which riddles are told varies from culture to culture, although in many cases "riddles are [at least] exchanged during wakes, courtship, and contests."[38] Riddles often perform latent social functions, such as relieving anxiety, offering sexual gratification by innuendo, and shaming.[39] Several of Hart's negative conclusions are also of anthropological interest. One might expect, for

---

[36]Hart, *Filipino Folklore* 10, 26, both quotations 26. Nineteen of Hart's categories are apparently based on the "Human Relations Area Files." The twentieth category, "Miscellaneous," represents those riddle subjects (about 5% of the total) which did not fit the standard categories. As an example of his criteria for categorizing answers, Hart places the riddle subjects "candle" and "lamp" under different headings because the social group under surveillance used lamps for domestic purposes and candles for religious purposes.

[37]Hart, *Filipino Folklore* 38.

[38]Hart, *Filipino Folklore* 48–60, quotation 60.

[39]Hart, *Filipino Folklore* 64. Despite these other functions, Hart concludes that "the entertaining aspect of riddling appears central" (69).

instance, that riddle subjects would be distributed across a social group by age and gender in conjunction with the sectors of the society most likely to use or contact them, but Hart did not find this to be the case.[40] Hart also suggests five criteria which explain why certain features of social experience become riddle subjects while others do not. Riddle subjects must be familiar rather than arcane or exotic; they generally must be observable objects or processes, not abstractions; "selection of riddle subjects is influenced by a people's value system," in that items with a "negative" value are generally avoided as riddle topics; some subjects offer "inherent riddle potentialities" by their very nature, in that they readily provide analogies or suggest anomalies; once riddle forms have become fixed, the form itself may prefer subjects more suitable to its mode of expression.[41]

Overall, Hart's study views riddles as manifestations of latent cultural tendencies and assumes that "expression of attitude toward natural phenomena, political institutions, and religious or social behavior could profitably be studied by thematic analysis of riddles."[42] He consequently disregards the actual text of the riddle in preference for its subject, and to focus on the social value of the subject rather than the structure or production of the text. In Hart's own words, "riddles are the means, not the goal, of such research."[43]

In the year following the release of Hart's study, Charles Scott published a book which represents a strictly linguistic approach to folklore (1965). While Hart's anthropological approach focused exclusively on cultural context to the detriment of the riddle text, Scott's linguistic approach focuses exclusively on the text to the detriment of cultural context. Before discussing Scott's remarks on the riddle, it will be necessary to survey two aspects of his complex approach to language, the nature of "style" and the "tagmemic" dimension of language, as well as his general approach to genres.

Scott argues that "style" in language involves relations between sentences or linguistic units larger than sentences.[44] Whereas linguistic units

---

[40]Hart, *Filipino Folklore* 40.
[41]Hart, *Filipino Folklore* 69–74, quotation 70.
[42]Hart, *Filipino Folklore* 10.
[43]Hart, *Filipino Folklore* 60.
[44]Charles T. Scott, *Persian and Arabic Riddles: A Language–Centered Approach to Genre Definition* (Bloomington, IN: Indiana University Press, 1965) 3. Relations between

are mutually defined by contrast, "style" involves attempts to create relations of identity. When a particular relation of identity between sentence units recurs systematically and intentionally, that relation may be described as a "stylistic device."[45] Concisely,

> stylistic structures are constituted of recurrent linguistic entities, which are related to each other in terms of the principle of identity, and which can be said to occur over spans wider than the limits of the sentence. The deployment of these linguistic entities must exhibit a conscious attempt at pattern or design.

Since these entities and patterns are observable features of texts, style analysis is "purely a taxonomic activity," which seeks to classify the stylistic devices "which are available to the artist in terms of permissible linguistic structures and the accepted conventions of the literary tradition."[46] "Style" in Scott's analysis is thus an observable feature of texts, a set of relations between sentences and larger linguistic units which express themselves in conventional devices observable on the surface of the text.

The second relevant aspect of Scott's theory of language is his focus on hierarchical relationships among linguistic units. Here he adopts Kenneth Pike's theory of the "tagmeme." "[T]he core of Pike's theory of language design is the application of the concept of classes of items distributed in significant positions and, forming with these positions, significant units of structure." In the hierarchy of language units, every level of structure is a combination of open positions and lower lever units which can fill these positions. Pike and Scott refer to these open positions as "'slot–class correlate' units," and to the sum of a slot–class correlate plus all the lower linguistic units which might fill that position as a "tagmeme."[47]

---

linguistic units *within* the sentence involve "grammar." Note that in Scott's system both grammar and "style" encompass phonological, morphological, and syntactical issues (3–5).

[45]Scott, *Language–Centered* 5. Note that "identity" can be established at the phonological, morphological, or syntactical levels. Rhyme, for example, may identify sentences at the phonological level whose lexical meanings are different; meter can make sentences syntactically equivalent.

[46]Scott, *Language–Centered*, first quotation 7, second quotation 5. Scott also insists that "conventional deviations from an accepted norm" are an aspect of "style" (3).

[47]Scott, *Language–Centered* 65-66, quotation 66..

For example, in the English sentence, "The X is hot," X represents a slot–class correlate. This open position in the sentence could be filled by any English word or phrase which can be modified with the definite article ("the") and the adjective "hot." This slot–class correlate plus all the possible English words which might complete the sentence "the X is hot" represent a tagmeme. At a higher linguistic level, in the sequence of sentences, "It's raining today. Y," Y represents a slot–class correlate which calls for a second sentence which can be juxtaposed with the statement "it's raining today." Y plus all the possible sentences which might fill that position compose, again, a tagmeme.

In this way, every linguistic unit can be explained in reference to the smaller units of which it is composed and the larger units in which it participates. Sentences are brought together to fill meaningful positions in the "utterance," a linguistic unit definable "in terms of shift of speaker." Utterances, in turn, are combined in "discourses."[48] Internally, the sentence is organized by observable rules of grammar; externally, sentences are brought together to create meaningful utterances, in which they may be held together by observable stylistic devices. Since language is one form of human behavior, all discourse, at the highest level, participates in some way in the total set of human behaviors.[49] The tagmemic approach is consistent with Scott's understanding of style, in that it focuses on the internal arrangement of sentences and on their external distribution and relationships within larger linguistic units.

Scott's hierarchical approach to language and style informs his theory of genre. Scott's genre analysis involves two steps, "definition" and

---

[48]Scott, *Language–Centered* 67. Scott's complete hierarchy is word (morpheme + affixes) → phrase → clause → sentence → utterance → discourse → hyperdiscourse → total social behaviors (68). Of course, in some cases a single word or phrase may function as a sentence and an utterance, and a single sentence may also be a complete discourses. In such cases, the linguistics unit should presumably be analyzed at each level of the hierarchy.

[49]Scott, *Language–Centered* 64–65. On the external distribution of riddles into non–verbal behaviors, note that Scott regards "all verbal art as a phenomenon which falls under that class of human behavior known as art" (2), and accepts Pike's contention that language is one form of social behavior which can be related to other social behaviors (64). Language is composed of emic units, "structurally relevant parts of a system," all of which may be defined in terms of their interaction with the total language structure (65).

"description." Definition begins by recognizing that a culture has institutionalized a certain sub–class of verbal behavior. Apparent members of this class may then be examined to determine what persistent stylistic features unite them. Defining traits may be extremely isolated or apparently trivial. In this step, "overt stylistic devices may be isolated and catalogued, and then put to use for typological purposes." Further classification requires detailed "description" of units bearing the defining feature(s). Description involves the delineation of every identifiable stylistic feature of the texts "in order of their [the features'] relative importance." Subgenres may be determined by further groupings on the basis of descriptive features.[50] Scott summarizes his position on genre analysis by asserting that "since literary utterances are presented through linguistic structure the distinctions between the types, genres, or categories [of utterances] can most probably be made in terms of linguistic–stylistic criteria."[51]

Scott's approach to language and genre places a number of explicit limitations on his analysis of riddles. First, since his approach to genre involves local stylistic peculiarities, Scott warns that his conclusions on Persian and Arabic riddles might not be applicable to texts from other cultures. Second, Scott's introduction notes that "the particular approach under examination here is one which grants highest priority to formal linguistic features." As a consequence, his analysis is limited to riddle texts and could not pursue the cultural role of riddles or contexts of riddle production. Third, his study is admittedly addressed to broader problems of "literary typology." In fact, "the real problem of this particular study is not to distinguish varieties of the riddle form, but to see if defining stylistic devices can be isolated in order to distinguish the riddle form from all other literary genres."[52]

With these *caveats*, Scott proceeds to define the riddle by two characteristics, "binary construction and [obscured] semantic fit." In terms of linguistic hierarchy, Scott notes that riddles evidence a binary construction, question and answer, which in turn involves two speakers, riddler and riddlee.

---

[50]Scott, *Language–Centered* 7–9, both quotations 8. Scott insists that any "formal literary taxonomy will depend greatly upon a taxonomy of stylistic devices" (7).
[51]Scott, *Language–Centered* 11.
[52]Scott, *Language–Centered*, 10–11, 71, first quotation v, second quotation 9.

This change in speakers makes the question and answer segments of the riddle two distinct "utterances." Since the riddle as a total unit brings together two utterances, "the riddles under investigation are in fact units of discourse whose internal composition is statable in terms of utterances." Scott expresses this internal composition of the riddle discourse with the equation "Ri = +Pr: U_p +Ans: U_a": "a riddle is a unit of discourse consisting of an obligatory proposition slot filled by an utterance p and an obligatory answer slot filled by an utterance a."[53] By Scott's criterion, the riddle is a language unit which unites two distinct utterances into one conversational discourse.

Binary construction, however, is common to a number of folk genres, so this feature must be accompanied by "partially obscured semantic fit" before a text can be identified as a riddle. Scott discusses semantic fit as an aspect of the problem of linguistic "meaning." The smallest unit of linguistic meaning is the "sememe." The sememe is a combination of smaller units called "allosemes." The interaction of the allosemes within the sememe produces a unit of linguistic meaning. Allosemes are "contextually conditioned variants": the same allosemes may produce a different sememe in a different context or, more importantly here, different combinations of allosemes may interact to create the same sememe in one text. In overly simplified terms, there is more than one way to say the same thing; there is more than one set of allosemes which can be utilized to produce the same sememe in a given context. In light of this, Scott states the following rule:

> partially obscured semantic fit between two utterances [combined into one riddle discourse] is attributable to an unusual or unexpected collocation of the allosemes of one utterance with the allosemes of the second utterance.

Considered together, the allosemes of the riddle question and riddle answer produce equivalent sememes, equivalent meanings. But the "semantic fit"

---

[53]Scott, *Language–Centered*, first quotation 72, second and third quotations 69. Note that in Scott's analysis the "answer" is a linguistic proposition, not the actual extra–linguistic referent. Scott specifies that in some cases the proposition slot is filled by an exchange of utterances rather than a single statement, which allows him to argue that "neck riddles" are like all other riddles in that they are embedded in larger discourses. While normal riddles are embedded in conversations, neck riddles are embedded in narratives (70–71).

between them is obscured because the particular sememe which can be expressed by the two sets of allosemes is not the most obvious sememe for the answer. Hence, "the partial obscurity of the [semantic] fit is necessarily due to the rare occurrence of a context which can be shared both by the set of allosemes of the proposition and by the alloseme(s) of the answer."[54]

The principle of obscured semantic fit may be illustrated by the English riddle "Humpty Dumpty." The words "Humpty Dumpty sat on a wall" represent a combination of allosemes that together create a meaningful unit, a sememe. A second sememe is created by the words "Humpty Dumpty had a great fall." Following Scott's view that the riddle text encompasses both question and answer, one can note that the words to the answer, "an egg fell off a wall," are also allosemes which create a meaningful unit. In the context of the riddle, the sememes of the proposition are identical to the sememe of the answer. But the set of allosemes that express this sememe in the proposition differ greatly from the allosemes that express it in the answer, so that it is not immediately clear what sort of meaningful unit can unite these descriptions. In this sense, the "semantic fit" of the proposition and answer, although exact, is "obscured."

Having addressed the problems of binary opposition and obscured semantic fit, Scott offers the following strictly linguistic definition of the riddle, which encompasses both internal arrangement of lower linguistic units and external distribution in larger units:

> The riddle is defined as a grammatical unit of discourse, externally distributed within a matrix of longer discourse or of nonverbal behavior, and internally composed of two obligatory utterance–level units, between which there obtains a partially obscured semantic fit.[55]

The theories of Georges and Dundes, Hart, and Scott illustrate a methodological tension between "text" and "context." Some studies in the

---

[54]Scott, *Language–Centered*, first quotation 73, second quotation 74.

[55]Scott, *Language–Centered* 74. Commenting on a number of other approaches to the riddle, Scott argues that "they are little more than descriptions of the major characteristics of the genre, and tell us nothing about how the riddle qua genre is formally distinct from other literary or folkloristic genres within cultures" (15).

1960's focused primarily on transcriptions of folk performances, while others highlighted the social setting of these performances. In many cases exclusive preference for text or context created analytical imbalance. Archer Taylor's text–based approach found new expression in the emerging structuralism of Georges and Dundes and in Scott's strictly linguistic analysis. The structuralist and linguistic approaches treated social function as a secondary issue, to be discussed *after* the riddle genre had been defined. This overemphasis on theories of language and literary structure to the exclusion of the actual production context created a number of methodological difficulties.

First, the structuralist and linguistic approaches were each internally inconsistent, as Scott explicitly acknowledged. The linguistic approach, by placing discourse in an overall hierarchy of human behavior, made cultural distribution a critical dimension of genre but lacked the tools necessary to address this distribution.[56] This same inconsistency is evident in Georges and Dundes' structural definition of the riddle as "a traditional verbal expression which contains one or more descriptive elements, a pair of which may be in opposition; the referent is to be guessed."[57] "To be guessed" is not an aspect of the structure of the text, but a statement about social use: it implies either the invitation of a speaker or the response of an audience or both, an invitation and response which structural analysis cannot comprehend. As a second problem, the scope of structural and linguistic studies was ill–defined. Here again, Scott admitted that his analysis was severely restricted: "the description of the [riddle] genre's external distribution is a necessary component of a definition, and it is this component in particular which restricts a complete definition to a specific linguistic community."[58] Georges and Dundes' conclusions, on the other hand, suffered from the over–generalization characteristic of structuralism. Their desire to create a cross–cultural model which could comprehend riddle texts of all times and places eliminated the local and situational aspects of specific riddles.

Hart's study aptly illustrates the shortcomings of the context–only approach, treating the riddle exclusively as a cultural artifact and ignoring the

---

[56]Scott, *Language–Centered* 74–75.
[57]Georges and Dundes, "Structural Definition" 113, emphasis removed.
[58]Scott, *Language–Centered* 74.

riddle text. Because his analysis explicitly utilized riddle texts in service of a cultural taxonomy, he cursorily adopted Taylor's model without consideration of the literary structure of his corpus. Each of these three approaches to the riddle, the structuralist, the linguistic, and the anthropological, focused too exclusively on one dimension of folklore and, losing valuable insights from the other perspectives, offered an imbalanced perspective on the riddle.

Dundes himself took steps toward building a methodological bridge between text and context. Noting the chasm between literary and anthropological approaches, Dundes insisted that folklore analysis must pass through two stages, "identification" and "interpretation." "Identification essentially consists of a search for similarities; interpretation depends on the delineation of differences." The folklorist must first attempt to identify similarities between texts, then differentiate groups of similar texts from other groups. Since differentiation is sometimes based only on social use, Dundes felt that the "text–without–context orientation" was incapable of producing a complete analysis.[59]

Dundes attempts to correct this methodological fallacy by dividing the folklore text into three components and associating a specific analytic task with each component. First, the "texture" of a folklore text "is the language, the specific phonemes and morphemes employed." This level of the text is approachable through linguistic analysis. Linguistic analysis alone, however, cannot complete the tasks of identification and interpretation because similar linguistic features may appear in more than one genre. Second, "the *text* of an item of folklore is essentially a version or a single telling of a tale, a recitation of a proverb, a singing of a folksong," in other words, a transcribed performance. This level of the text is approachable through structural analysis to define its "folkloristic structure." Third, "the *context* of an item of folklore is the specific social situation in which that particular item is actually employed." Context may be analyzed by examining the social settings in which a genre occurs. Again, exclusive focus on context is insufficient, because in a given society a number of different genres may operate in the same social setting. Dundes insists that the best definitions of any folk genre

---

[59]Alan Dundes, "The Study of Folklore in Literature and Culture: Identification and Interpretation" (1965; rpt. in *Analytic Essays in Folklore* [The Hague: Mouton, 1975]) 28.

will be those which address the text at all three levels through linguistic (texture), structural (text), and anthropological (context) analysis.[60]

Dundes returns to the riddle to illustrate the value of his new proposal. In some cases the structure of a riddle text provides an anthropological key to the social context in which it occurs, while in other cases the social context will help differentiate the riddle text from other structurally similar genres. In the first case, Dundes notes that oppositional riddles, those with apparently contradictory descriptive elements, are frequent fixtures of courtship and marriage rituals. He suggests that such riddles, which unite dissimilar entities through a common referent, may reveal social attitudes about the union of persons in marriage.[61] Sometimes, however, context differentiates textual structure. In many cases, for example, riddles and proverbs are structurally identical and can be generically distinguished only by their use. Riddles generally request a referent while proverbs take the situation itself as their referent.[62] Considering all three aspects of the riddle text thus decreases the possibility of overlooking a critical dimension of the riddle in a specific riddle corpus.

It is clear, however, that Dundes continued to understand "text" as an entity separate from, and methodologically prior to, context. After this entity is defined, one may consider how it shapes or is shaped by the context in which it is used. Dundes felt justified in maintaining the priority of text because "text is less variable than texture and context."[63] For example, in opening an analysis of an American Indian story, Dundes states, "In order to analyze this tale in terms of Potawatomi culture, one must first identify the tale not as an indigenous Indian story, but as a European tale–type." He concludes that the story in question "is a borrowing from a French version of Aarne–Thompson tale type 569," and proceeds to treat structural variations in the Potawatomi text as cultural keys. Here, Dundes begins with a structural analysis and then, having defined the text on the basis of structure, proceeds

---

[60]Alan Dundes, "Texture, Text, and Context" (1964; rpt. in *Interpreting Folklore* [Bloomington, IN: Indiana University Press, 1980]), first quotation 22, second and third quotations 23, emphasis added.

[61]Dundes, "Texture, Text, Context" 24–25.

[62]Dundes, "Texture, Text, Context" 29–30.

[63]Dundes, "Texture, Text, Context" 32.

to analyze its use in American Indian culture. Form remained the *primus inter pares* of his method.[64]

Building on Dundes, Roger D. Abrahams' approach to folklore, and his extensive writing on the riddle, represents a complete methodological merger of text and context. Abrahams notes that previous folklore studies had tended to focus exclusively on one aspect of the folk text, either the creative work of the performer, or the text itself, or the rhetorical effect of the text, or the role of the audience in text production.[65] To correct this imbalance, Abrahams offers a new, comprehensive definition of "folklore": "*folklore* is a collective term for those traditional items of knowledge that arise in recurring performances."[66] Folkloristics therefore requires an analytic model which merges literary and anthropological concerns and addresses "all aspects of the esthetic performance: performance, item [text], and audience." Such analysis would "look simultaneously at the performer, at the piece [s]he performs, and at the effect which this has on the audience." While Abrahams retained the structuralist model, his understanding of genre encompasses Dundes' "structure of context" as well.[67]

---

[64]Dundes, "Identification and Interpretation," first quotation 32, second quotation 33. The Aarne–Thompson index is a catalogue of folktale structures based on the narrative functions of features (plot, setting, characters) which manifest themselves in a number of collected folktales. Each structure is regarded as a "tale type," and each tale type is assigned a number. Tale type 569, to which Dundes refers, is "The Knapsack, the Hat, and the Horn." The following structural definition is offered: "The youngest of three brothers finds a magic object . . . , exchanges it for another, and by means of the second, secures the first one again . . . . Objects produce food, soldiers, etc. Makes war against the king" (Antti Aarne, *The Types of the Folktale: A Classification and Bibliography*, 2nd revision and translation by Stith Thompson, FFC 184 [Helsinki: Suomalainen Tiedeakatemia Academia Scientiarum Fenniga, 1961] 209).

[65]Roger D. Abrahams, "Introductory Remarks to a Rhetorical Theory of Folklore," *JAF* 81 (1968) 144.

[66]Roger D. Abrahams, "The Complex Relations of Simple Forms" (1969; rpt. in *Folklore Genres* [ed. Dan Ben–Amos; Austin, TX: University of Texas Press, 1976]) 195.

[67]Abrahams, "Rhetorical Theory," first quotation 144, second quotation 145; "Complex Relations" 195. Abrahams explicitly borrows the term "structure of context" from Dundes ("Rhetorical Theory" 146 and 157 n. 4; cf. Dundes, "Texture, Text, Context" 25).

Dundes had broadly equated the "structure of context" with the "social situation" of the folklore performance. Abrahams defines the term more narrowly as the specific relationship between composer and audience "as the relation is modified by time and place and occasion."[68] In Abrahams' analysis, this relation is not secondary to the text itself but is one of three parallel dimensions of textual organization. The *linguistic* organization of the text "involves the interrelationship among the building materials of folklore items—words, actions, tones." The text's "*dramatic organization*" involves "conflict between characters depicted and a resolution provided for this conflict." The "*structure of context*," the third dimension of the text's organization, "is the level of structure where the patterns of relationships between the participants in the aesthetic transaction are considered."[69] Unlike Dundes, Abrahams does not treat context as analytically secondary to text. In fact, although Abrahams' three dimensions of textual organization are theoretically equal, he tends to give methodological priority to context structure as the defining element of genre.

Abraham's methodological preference for context affects his theory of folklore in two ways. First, he sees all folklore as persuasive and therefore "rhetorical." "[E]ach item of expressive culture is an implement of argument, a tool of persuasion." Every folk text is based on an argument strategy which seeks the sympathy of the audience and which all three dimensions are organized to fulfill. Abraham's analysis is therefore less concerned with the composition of the audience than with "the effect which this [particular performance] has on the audience." The desired sympathetic reaction of the audience is encoded in the structure of the text but manifests itself only in the structure of context, where it acquires rhetorical power.[70]

---

[68]Dundes, "Texture, Text, Context" 25; Abrahams, "Rhetorical Theory" 146. While in some cases context may include the physical arrangement of the setting in which the text is produced, "the central focus of the structure of context is on performer–audience relations" ("Complex Relations" 198).

[69]Abrahams, "Complex Relations," first two quotations 198, third quotation 199. Because Abrahams' analysis is comprehensive, "folklore items" in the above quotation comprehends texts of varying media—voice, music, dance, drama, and visual arts.

[70]Abrahams, "Rhetorical Theory," first quotation 146, second quotation 145.

A second effect of the context approach is Abrahams' emphasis on the social value of folklore performance. Folklore portrays the conflicts which might threaten group solidarity and allows the audience, through sympathy, to explore these conflicts vicariously. The performance thus becomes a cultural playroom, where "play" refers to "the objectifying and impersonalizing of anxiety situations, allowing the free expending of energies without the threat of social consequence." "Recurrent social conflicts" are projected into a textual arena and then resolved, assuring the audience that group cohesion can be retained. Folklore thus promotes "accepted attitudes and modes of action" while providing a forum for the resolution of unacceptable feelings and behaviors. The artistic dimension of this rhetorical task involves the composer's ability to facilitate catharsis by manipulating psychic distance. The audience must be drawn close enough to the conflict and its resolution to experience catharsis, but must remain distant enough to perceive the problem as impersonal.

> The rhetorical approach [to folklore] therefore asks the observer to see the control of both the esthetic object [the text] and of the [performance] context to witness how the two interrelate in creating pleasure and proposing action.[71]

Abrahams' holistic, rhetorical approach is evident in a number of statements about the nature of genres and Genre Criticism. "Genre" is a useful analytic concept because genres "help us focus on *the relationship between performer and audience*" by giving "names to traditional attitudes and traditional strategies which may be *utilized by the performer in [her/]his attempt to communicate with and affect the audience.*" Situations call forth folk performances by determining appropriate rhetorical functions. Thus, a group's "conventions associate certain sets of problems with certain sets of expressive forms—a genre or genres." In this way, a genre's structure of context may determine its themes and structural characteristics. Formal features develop within each genre to provide the audience with interpretive

---

[71]Abrahams, "Rhetorical Theory," all quotations 149. This vicarious exploration can involve actual or potential conflict. Along with affirming group norms and boundaries, folklore may provide a controlled environment for violation of these boundaries and the expression of antisocial tendencies.

cues on their relationships with the performer and the text.[72] "Genre Criticism" therefore does not just categorize texts but "is concerned with making a taxonomy of *expressive habits and effects.*" While genres must be delineated by "patterns of form, content, and context," Abrahams, contra Dundes, makes context the *primus inter pares* of analysis.[73]

Having defined genre primarily by context, Abrahams distributes a number of common folk genres across a "structure of context" spectrum. This spectrum ranges from those genres which relate performer and audience in "the personal interactions of the conversation" to those which facilitate the "'removal' of performer from audience." Abrahams subdivides this generic spectrum into four quadrants, "conversational genres, play genres, fictive genres, and static genres." The table below represents Abrahams' spectrum and gives a typical example of each category.

direct personal interaction----------------------*removal from performer*			
concrete representation-------------------------*symbolic representation*			
focus on conflict--*focus on resolution*			
Conversational Genres: The Proverb	Play Genres: The Riddle	Fictive Genres: The Legend	Static Genres: Folk Art
smaller text--*larger text*			

---

[72] Abrahams, "Complex Relations," first two quotations 193, third quotation 196, all emphasis added. The structural features in question include "size or length of the performance item" and "the relationships between the component parts of the composition" (197). On the complex problems of differentiating European myths, legends, and folktales, Abrahams suggests that these genres are indistinct at the structural (tale type) level but can be isolated in terms of "the way in which the audience apprehends the tone of the performer and interprets [her/]his meaning" (199).

[73] Abrahams, "Complex Relations," first quotation 193, emphasis added, second quotation 196. Abrahams believes Genre Criticism can be used for two ends: to provide evidence of a group's social and rhetorical organization, an anthropological function; to create categories for cross–cultural literary analysis, a comparative function. On the latter, "genre analysis provides a common frame of reference by which such conventions of form and use may be compared and thus permits one genre or group of genres to cast light on others, either within one group or cross–culturally" (195).

In terms of the structure of context, "conversational genres" involve a "spontaneous communicative relationship in which opportunities to introduce traditional devices of persuasion commonly arise." In these "everyday discourse" genres speakers relate to one another "as themselves," real individuals referring to real world situations. By contrast, in "fictive genres" "all movements and motives are depicted figuratively." Here characters distinct from the performer and audience play symbolic roles which are experienced vicariously. Several prominent European folk forms fall under this heading, such as legends, myths, and tales. "Static genres" involve the complete removal of the performer from the audience, using physical media with highly symbolic representations.[74]

Abrahams classifies the riddle as a "play genre." As in conversational genres, play genres allow immediate dialogue between performer and audience. But while in conversational genres persons speak as themselves (as individuals in the real world), "play" genres assign traditional symbolic roles to performer and audience. These roles are "universalistic" in the sense that they bestow stereotypical identities, like "riddler" and "riddlee," which can be fulfilled by any number of persons. Further, "to make these roles significant and symbolic, . . . a stylized play world is created, which is very like the real world but psychologically (and often physically) removed from it in time and space." Since "play" offers a controlled illusion, these genres allow participants to safely engage in cathartic interactions without suffering the "real world" consequences of those actions. The controlled play environment in which

---

[74]Abrahams, "Complex Relations" 201, 205–207.Genres which involve greater personal interaction tend to involve texts which are smaller and more concrete, while those with less direct interaction tend to involve texts which are larger and more abstract (Abrahams, "Complex Relations" 200). Movement toward greater distance between audience and performer also affects the internal dramatic structure of the text. While all folklore articulates conflict, those genres which allow greater distance between performer and audience tend to treat conflict in formalized and symbolic ways and focus on resolution. "[T]he dramatic focus gradually changes from being almost solely upon conflict in the shorter genres to almost completely upon resolution in the fictive and static types." Conversational genres point to an actual conflict which is perceived to exist in the real world and propose a future resolution which they do not portray. For this reason, only the fictive genres truly evidence a projected "dramatic structure" which treats both conflict and its resolution within the text (208).

riddles are performed is the "riddling session, a special occasion for performance somewhat removed from casual conversation and in which an implicit set of rules and boundaries operates."[75]

Abrahams subdivides play genres into three categories. That subcategory which borders on the fictive genres includes play forms which portray complete cycles of conflict and resolution, such as rituals, dramas, traditional dramatic dances, and role playing. A second subcategory includes spectator sports, organized debates, "and contests like spelling bees," in which the audience observes conflict and resolution through actors playing traditional roles. That subcategory which borders on the conversational genres requires the audience to participate directly in the text by adopting a play role in the conflict–resolution cycle. These genres generally script only two roles, "the players are each others' audience, and the activity provides little interest for spectators." This subcategory of play genres includes riddles, jokes, "other traditional verbal contests," folk dances, and "most games." These genres are agonistic, stressing conflict over resolution and thereby providing catharsis of anxiety or anti–social impulses. The riddle, for example, presents a series of minor conflicts and resolutions as each question is posed and answered. Like the conversational genres, however, the riddle exchange does not provide an overall resolution.[76]

As a folk genre, the riddle's unique structure of context performs a specific rhetorical function. Here Abrahams treats the riddle as an interactive metaphor. In Abrahams' theory, metaphors are a social coping mechanism. The human mind attempts to order the natural and social worlds by assimilating new data into existing mental categories. These categories are culturally determined. Members of a group, "when confronted with the inchoate, the unnamed, will take already established orders from other domains and try them out in this new environment."[77] Metaphors facilitate this process of associating new data with established orders by placing unfamiliar items in a "this is that" matrix.

---

[75]Abrahams, "Complex Relations," both quotations 202.
[76]Abrahams, "Complex Relations" 203–208, quotation 208.
[77]Roger D. Abrahams, *Between the Living and the Dead: Riddles Which Tell Stories* (FFC 225; Helsinki: Academia Scientiarum Fenniga, 1980) 14.

Riddles are a type of metaphor in that they "conjoin elements from widely different domains."[78] Unlike other metaphors, however, riddles bring "the whole idea of classification under question," because they conjoin elements which are normally kept conceptually distinct. Rather than integrating categories, riddles confuse them, challenging "the very domains which we usually use as a means of asserting order." For example, conventional ideological patterns would not immediately place the concepts "Humpty Dumpty sat on a wall, Humpty Dumpty had a great fall," and "an egg fell off a wall" in the same category. Riddles thus provide a play environment "in which an exploration of the spaces between [ideological] domains can be opened up, admitted to, and explored" in a controlled setting.[79] The answer to the riddle resolves this confusion, affirming the validity of traditional categories.[80]

The social function of riddles explains a number of features in their structure and performance. First, confusion of ideological categories is generally accompanied by interior referential disruption between question and answer. Abrahams suggests that this disruption can be achieved in one of four ways: by suggesting opposition between the traits of the referent; by providing insufficient information to unite the traits of the referent; by including a distracting excess of inconsequential detail; or, "a false *Gestalt* is created; the traits [of the referent] seem to combine meaningfully with the description as given, but the apparent referent is not the same as the true referent."[81] Second, in some cultural contexts riddles are performed even when all members of the audience know the answer. In these cases, "the recitation of the riddle with its answer is a traditional demonstration of group solidarity."[82] Such performances affirm a common belief that conventional categories can

---

[78]Abrahams, *BLD*, first quotation 13, second quotation 15.

[79]Abrahams, *BLD*, first quotation 17, second quotation 16.

[80]Abrahams, "Rhetorical Theory" 152. For this reason, Abrahams insists that the riddle text includes both question and answer: "the riddle itself operates metaphorically then only when the referent or the joining term is provided in the answer" (*BLD* 13).

[81]Abrahams, "Rhetorical Theory" 151; Roger D. Abrahams and Alan Dundes, "Riddles," *Folklore and Folklife: An Introduction* (ed. Richard M. Dorson; Chicago, IL: University of Chicago Press, 1972) 131.

[82]Abrahams, "Rhetorical Theory" 152.

overcome incomprehension. Third, the agonistic tone of the riddle session is an aspect of its cultural value. Riddles performed in carefully scripted play sessions "take energies potentially destructive of the community and its values and channel them into harmless, indeed psychologically helpful, creative avenues of expression."[83] The riddle text is a product of these social functions.

Abrahams, contra Dundes, focuses on context rather than form in genre analysis because parallel forms may perform different functions in different social settings.[84] He therefore allows texts with a wide variety of structures to be categorized as riddles, so long as they share the same structure of context. The most common Western riddle is the "true riddle," an "enigmatic question in descriptive form." "True" riddles include "poetic, metaphoric riddles"; "riddles that describe objects or actions in literal terms by selecting salient traits"; description of a stationary object as actor or object of action; the "orthographic riddle," "whose referents are words and letters as orthographic rather than linguistic entities," and whose clues often describe the sound or shape of the letters of the answer, such as, "What's high in the middle and round on both ends? Ohio"; and visual riddles, which describe by gesture or sketch.[85] The "neck riddle" is an embedded form, often "framed by the story of the man who saved his neck by the exercise of his wit, by propounding a riddle his executioner could not answer." These riddles typically relate to the unique experience of the character propounding the riddle "and are therefore insoluble to anyone who has not witnessed the events described." The "puzzle" requires the riddlee to apply a logical process to answer a problem.[86] This list of formal categories of riddles could be extended indefinitely, because "the analysis of riddles must take into account the total range of items that arise in riddling sessions."[87] Social context identifies members of a genre, which can then be structurally analyzed.

Abrahams' theory of the riddle is helpful to this study at a number of points. First, his overall emphasis on context in considerations of genre

---

[83] Abrahams, "Rhetorical Theory" 150.

[84] Within a culture or cross–culturally; see Abrahams, "Complex Relations" 196.

[85] Abrahams and Dundes, "Riddles" 130–136.

[86] Abrahams and Dundes, "Riddles" 137–138, first quotation Abrahams and Dundes, "Riddles" 133; second quotation Abrahams, *BLD* 9.

[87] Abrahams and Dundes, "Riddles" 139.

supports the theory of speech genres developed in Chapter 3, particularly in his focus on the relationship between context and generic structure. As a corollary, his approach challenges theories of genre which rely exclusively on textual analysis. The "spectrum of genres" provides a matrix for defining the objectification of oral discourse more precisely. In Abrahams' terms, objectification occurs when the structure of context of static genres (written gospels), whose media (writing) allow complete separation of performer and audience, is imposed upon conversational, play, or fictive genres (oral forms). This methodological imposition facilitates the notion of oral "transmission" and blurs the boundaries between oral genres.

Second, Abrahams' research set an important precedent by suggesting that riddles can function to define or to violate ideological boundaries, to challenge conventional ways of thinking or to affirm them.[88] The riddle's relationship to group ideology is therefore somewhat unique among traditional genres, in that it creates a play world in which forbidden beliefs and practices can be safely explored. In this sense riddles define group boundaries negatively, in terms of what a group does not believe.

Abrahams also identifies two types of riddles which are particularly relevant to FG. The first is the "catch riddle." In the course of a riddling session, the riddler may offer a question whose answer is apparently obvious. This "obvious" referent, which is always incorrect, may be a social taboo or an obscenity. By enticing the riddlee to state the obvious answer, the riddler both demonstrates the riddlee's inferiority and opens the riddlee to ridicule for thinking of the taboo subject.[89] Catch riddles thus attempt to lure the riddlee into a compromising position by appearing to offer an obvious answer. This type of riddle would be particularly effective where the audience of the riddle session realizes that the riddlee has fallen into a trap.

---

[88]A similar view was promoted by Ian Hamnet's influential article, "Ambiguity, Classification and Change: The Function of Riddles," which suggests that the riddle can "mediate between [conceptual] sets that are not only different, but in many aspects opposed, and in this way it [the riddle] can form the basis for a differing system of classification, or allow contrasting classifications and conceptual frameworks to co–exist at the same time" (*Man,* n. s. 2 [1967] 382).

[89]Abrahams and Dundes, "Riddles" 140.

The second type of riddle Abrahams identifies is the "wisdom question," which corresponds with Taylor's "false riddle." "The wisdom question cannot be answered from the content of the question. The answers must be known already." These riddles are solvable only by "learned response," the question serving as a cue for the repetition of memorized answers. Abrahams notes that wisdom questions are often used in contexts of catechism, where they rehearse special group knowledge.[90] Riddling sessions in which the riddlee delivers memorized answers can function to verify membership in a group by demonstrating this special knowledge.

MARANDA: LOGIC, TRANSFORMATION, CLASSIFICATION

Elli Köngäs Maranda has applied the principles of logic and generative grammar to Finnish and Melanesian riddles. Aligning herself with "structural analysis," Maranda understands each text as a "surface structure," while "under every performance there is a process in which some materials . . . are transformed to fit the deep ('timeless') structures of the culture."[91] Every text thus expresses an underlying structure and a process of generative transformation. In the specific case of riddles, Maranda refers to the surface structure of the text as "riddles" and the performance aspect of textual production as "riddling."

Maranda treats questions of text/riddles and context/riddling as equally important but analytically distinct, leaving her approach to the riddle less integrated than that of Abrahams. This distinction provides a convenient outline for analyzing Maranda's theory. In discussing the "riddle," the textual

---

[90]Abrahams and Dundes, "Riddles" 137.

[91]Pierre Maranda and Elli Köngäs Maranda, "Introduction," *Structural Analysis of Oral Tradition* (Philadelphia, PA: University of Pennsylvania Press, 1971) ix. Because "all uses made of a language are creative acts" guided by cultural rules of text generation, Maranda refuses to speak of the "repetition" or "transmission" of folklore items. "I choose to maintain that folkloric utterances are created whenever they are made" (Elli Köngäs Maranda, "Theory and Practice of Riddle Analysis," *JAF* 84 [1971], first quotation 54, second quotation 60). Identical texts represent multiple uses of the same elements and same rules of composition ("Theory and Practice" 57; "A Tree Grows: Transformations of a Riddle Metaphor," *Structural Models in Folklore and Transformational Essays* [ed. Elli Köngäs Maranda and Pierre Maranda; The Hague: Mouton, 1971] 136).

unit, Maranda applies principles of logic and generative "transformation." In discussing "riddling," the social interaction, Maranda focuses on the ideological functions of riddle performance.

Maranda's approach to the logic structure of the riddle begins with a hierarchical theory of ideological sets. Each culture utilizes an ideological classification scheme which distributes data across categories and subcategories. Every subdivision of the hierarchy is binary, making the two sets which appear at each level of the classification scheme logical "opposites." For example, Maranda, a native Finn, notes that Finnish culture distributes all things into the equal but opposite sets "animate versus inanimate." "Animate" is further subdivided into the opposites "supernatural" and "natural." "Natural" divides into "human" and "animal," while "animal" breaks down into the sets "domestic" and "wild." Each higher set which includes two opposed sets is a "superset."[92] Thus, the superset "animal" includes the opposed sets "domestic" and "wild," while the superset "natural" includes the opposed sets "animal" and "human."

At the most basic level, the "riddle" is a language structure which unites opposed sets by demonstrating their common participation in a superset. The riddle may therefore be described as "a continuous reconciliation of opposites on the . . . cognitive level."[93] This reconciliation is achieved by identifying a function or element which the opposed sets share as co–members of the superset.[94] Within the text of the riddle, the first set is represented by the question or "riddle image" and the second set by the answer.[95] Because the riddle's question and answer directly equate opposed sets, Maranda offers this preliminary definition: "Riddles are *metaphors* which establish, on the basis of an initial insight . . . the equivalence of two sets."[96]

---

[92]Elli Köngäs Maranda, "The Logic of Riddles," *Structural Analysis of Oral Tradition* (ed. Pierre Maranda and Elli Köngäs Maranda; Philadelphia, PA: University of Pennsylvania Press, 1971) 215; "Tree Grows" 118.

[93]Maranda, "Logic" 192–193.

[94]Maranda, "Tree Grows" 138.

[95]Maranda, "Theory and Practice" 54. For this reason, Maranda stresses that question and answer must be considered together as one unit in structural analysis (54; "Logic" 191–192).

[96]Maranda, "Tree Grows" 138, emphasis added.

A more comprehensive definition of the riddle requires a fuller discussion of the "metaphor." Maranda's theory of metaphor accommodates her hierarchy of ideological sets. Each of the variables in the metaphor "A = C" has two components, a set and its members, "A" and "C" (=sets) and "a" and "c" (=members of sets A and C). This allows her to speak of every metaphor, even metaphors which equate individual items rather than sets ("a = b"), as "a sign consisting of *two sets*."[97] Maranda defines the "simple" riddle as a special type of metaphor in this way:

> since riddle metaphors bring the two 'opposed' sets into a position where they are shown to be only elements of one superset, then contiguity is established between them, and they are brought into a metonymic relation.[98]

The simple riddle shows that the opposed sets "A" and "B" share a common function or element which relates them to one another at a higher ideological level. Simple riddles differ from "normal" metaphors in that they are "conditional metaphors, and the riddle image [question] states the condition under which the metaphor holds true."[99] Normal metaphors have no such conditions.

---

[97]Maranda, "Logic" 193, emphasis added; "Tree Grows" 117–118. As the relations between each set and its items are explored, the metaphor develops into an "analogy." Maranda begins with Aristotle's definition of the "analogy" as a parallel relationship between one pair of terms and another pair, "A/B = C/D" (A is to B as C is to D). She then specifies this definition to fit her theory of sets. Because it involves direct equation, the analogy includes a metaphor, but whereas the metaphor equates items and sets the analogy equates *relationships* between items and sets. Whereas the metaphor may be represented by the equations "A = C" and "a = c," Maranda expresses the analogy as "a/A = c/C," which suggests that the relationship between item "a" and set "A" is equivalent to the relationship between item "c" and set "C." Ultimately, every metaphor is an analogy: "the analogy a/A = b/B underlies the equations, that is, the metaphors, a = b and A = B" ("Logic" 194). Maranda's understanding of the specific distinction between "analogy" and "metaphor" is unclear. The discussion here is based on her association of the simple riddle with the metaphor and the compound riddle with the analogy and utilizes her understanding of these types of riddles to clarify her understanding of the corresponding structural units.

[98]Maranda, "Tree Grows" 118.

[99]Maranda, "Logic" 196.

Maranda proceeds to identify five structural components of the simple "intellectual" riddle (cp. Taylor's "true riddle") and names each component from the language of logic. The metaphorical subject of the question is the "given term" and the answer is the "hidden term." The question includes a "true" or "constant" premise, which "holds true of the given term and the hidden term alike," and a "false" premise or "given variable" which "shows that the given term is not to be accepted" literally. Finally, the riddlee appeals to a "hidden variable," prerequisite knowledge which indicates that the false premise cannot apply to the given term.[100] When question and answer are considered separately, these five items create two truisms which intersect at the point of the constant premise. To answer the riddle, the riddlee must disentangle the truisms by considering all five elements in the following logic sequence: recognize the given term; understand the true/constant premise; apply the hidden variable to identify the incongruity between the given term and the false premise; compare the constant premise and the false premise to identify traits of the answer; reveal the hidden term.[101]

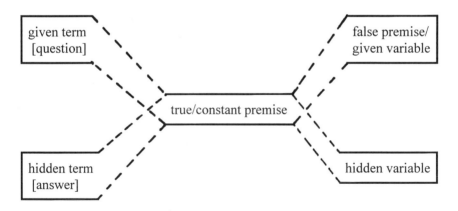

Maranda illustrates this principle by analyzing the simple Finnish riddle, "one pig, two snouts—a plough."

---

[100]Maranda, "Logic" 197, quotations here; "Tree Grows" 119–120.
[101]Maranda, "Logic" 198–199.

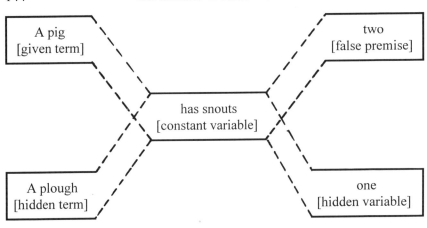

The "given term" of this riddle, which forms the base of the metaphorical image, is "pig." The hidden term, or answer, is "plough." The "true" or "constant" premise which accurately describes both terms is "has snouts." The false premise, which is true of the Finnish double–bladed "fork plough" but not of the pig, is "two." The hidden variable, which the riddlee must supply to determine an incongruity in the riddle image, is the fact that a pig has only one snout. These five elements represent two truisms, "a pig has a snout" and "a plough has two snouts [blades]." To answer the riddle, one must complete the following logic sequence: identify the item "pig"; understand what "has snouts" means; recognize that a pig does not have two snouts; recognize that the true referent must, in some sense, have two snouts; recognize that a plough's double blades can be thought of as two snouts.[102]

Riddle metaphors generate "analogies" through the process of "transformation." Whereas a simple riddle *establishes* a basic relationship between two sets, transformations *explore* this relationship. "Once the

---

[102]Maranda, "Logic" 198–199. This riddle is "simple" because it has only one given term, one true premise, one false premise, and one answer. "If any of the components is multiplied, we have a compound riddle" (Maranda, "Logic" 197; "Tree Grows" 119). More complex is the "string riddle," in which "the image consists of a list of terms and the answer another list of terms" (197). Maranda's examples indicate that the string riddle is a series of simple riddles whose questions/images are united by a poetic scheme. Each member of the string must be distinguished and answered separately as a simple riddle consisting of the five basic elements (219).

metaphor has been stated, it can be examined by a series of 'moves', *i.e.*, transformations which focus on more and more common elements between the two sets."[103] Transformation thus produces a series of "variants" on the theme of the basic metaphor, which Maranda calls the "kernel riddle."[104] Transformation of the kernel riddle is achieved in the variants by "transformers," new true/constant premises which relate the given and hidden terms in new ways. Transformers are logically verbal statements which explore functional relations between items and sets, creating analogies which "seem to explore the possibilities of the original riddle metaphor."[105]

For example, Maranda analyzes a cluster of Finnish riddles which compare a tree (given term) to a woman (hidden term). The basic metaphor, "what grows without roots?—a person," relies on the constant variable "grows": a tree grows with roots and a woman grows without roots. Having equated the sets, the transformers explore the relations between items relevant to trees and items relevant to a woman, fa/T = fb/W (item "a" functions to a tree as item "b" functions to a woman). This exploration utilizes the transformers "is decorated," "is fertilized," "reproduces," "feeds its dependent," and "dies." At each point the premises change to represent items which function similarly in reference to the given and hidden terms, a tree and a woman. Whereas a tree, for example, is decorated with leaves, a woman may be decorated in a wedding gown. In this way, "transformations of riddles come about by the expansion of the analogy, that is, by an examination of the correspondence of the elements of the two sets in question."[106]

Maranda mentions four basic categories of transformation, "reversal," "inversion," "particularization," and "generalization."[107] All are based on the

---

[103]Maranda, "Tree Grows" 125, quotation here; "Logic" 202.

[104]Maranda, "Tree Grows" 136. In this sense, transformation is a generative mechanism. "Transformation . . . is a PROCESS . . . and transform designates the end PRODUCT of the process, the riddle variant itself" (124, emphasis original).

[105]Maranda, "Logic" 204; "Theory and Practice" 54–55. Maranda stresses that the relationship between a kernel riddle and its variants is synchronic and logical rather than diachronic or developmental. The kernel of a series of variants may be assumed by the variants even if it never appears in the corpus.

[106]Maranda, "Tree Grows" 119–121; "Logic" 200, quotation here.

[107]Maranda, "Theory and Practice" 57.

types of variation achieved in a series of variants. "Reversal" switches the given and hidden terms. Within a corpus, "if A is like B, by a metaphoric 'jump,' this jump can be reversed, and a riddle will be found that illustrates that B is like A."[108] When each of the two sets equated in the basic metaphor have clear complements, "inversion" may occur. For example, if a series of riddles exists in which a woman is compared to a leafed tree, another series should appear in which a man is compared to an evergreen tree.[109] Although Maranda does not discuss particularization and generalization, these transformations apparently refer to series of variants which specify or generalize the functional similarities between the sets.

On the basis of her structuralist model, Maranda believes it possible to predict riddle texts. Patterns of transformation manifest the generative "rules" by which texts are produced. After deducing nine "rules of riddle production" from a particular transformation series, she asserts that "the generative power of the above rules is such that knowing the classifications of a culture one can predict all possible (acceptable) riddles." This is the case even where "a culture does not realize all the [textual] possibilities." Maranda therefore makes a distinction between "possible" and "realized" riddles. She insists that the absence of a possible riddle from an actual corpus in no way invalidates the generative model.[110]

Maranda's remarks on the context of riddle performance are limited exclusively to the riddle's social function. Irrespective of local uses, riddles have a universally cognitive function related to each group's hierarchy of values.[111] This function is subversive. Because they unite sets which are normally opposed in the ideological system, "riddles remind the speakers of the

---

[108]Maranda, "Logic," quotation 196, see also 205; "Tree Grows" 119, 126, 138. Regular metaphors are not normally reversible.

[109]Maranda, "Tree Grows" 130–139.

[110]Maranda, "Tree Grows" 136–139, both quotations 139. Once a kernel riddle can be identified or reconstructed, "expansions and reversals and expansions of the reversals are easy to predict and easy to build" (136). She admits, however, that "this is a hypothesis which is almost impossible to verify," due to the spontaneous nature of riddle production and the difficulties of collecting (139).

[111]Maranda, "Riddles and Riddling" 131.

language that these classifications are not unassailable."[112] The fact that opposed sets share certain characteristics threatens the distinctions between categories. The riddle, and particularly the transformation series, provides a mechanism for determining exactly how sets are the same and how they are different. To discover the answer to a riddle, the riddlee must follow "certain rules of the (thinking) game." The examination process, and the integration of the opposed sets in the superset, confirms the validity of conventional thought patterns. "Riddles play with boundaries, but ultimately to affirm them."[113]

The subversive rhetorical function of riddles makes them the "underdog's channel." Maranda's field work leads her to conclude that "this art form [the riddle] is utilized by those persons to whom other institutionalized expression is denied: women, commoners, unmarried men, and children." Perhaps this is why "'riddlers' are eager to 'break' any classifications that come their way."[114] This may also explain why riddles are often performed spontaneously in less formalized contexts than forms such as myth.[115] In this way riddles provide oppressed persons with a "safe" means of challenging the established social order.

Despite a number of valuable insights, Maranda's approach is weakened by her failure to clarify the relationship between general logic and local ideology, or between text and context. Her analysis would be strengthened by a more explicit emphasis on context and ideology as features of the riddle text. This is particularly the case in her understanding of the "hidden variable" and the process of "transformation." Both of these concepts are "logical" only within the ideological sphere of the group, and emphasizing this point clarifies several features of Maranda's discussion.

Closer inspection reveals that the "hidden variable" is not, as Maranda suggests, a component of the riddle text, but rather its ideological *prerequisite*.

---

[112]Maranda, "Theory and Practice" 54. "[R]iddles make a point of playing with conceptual boundaries and crossing them for the intellectual pleasure of showing that things are not quite as stable as they appear" (53).

[113]Maranda, first quotation "Tree Grows" 119, second quotation "Riddles and Riddling" 131.

[114]Maranda, first quotation "Theory and Practice" 58, second quotation "Tree Grows" 138.

[115]Maranda, "Theory and Practice" 53.

Maranda suggests that three of the riddle's five structural components—the given term, the true/constant premise, and the false premise—are provided by the riddler in the riddling session, and two of the elements—the hidden variable and the hidden term—are supplied by the riddlee. Discussing a particular sample, she specifies that the hidden variable "is not explicit in the wording of the riddle; I can only reiterate that it is an obvious fact."[116] This apparently means that the logic of riddle solution requires the riddlee to recognize an "obvious" discrepancy between the given term and the false premise. Since it represents a perceived discrepancy rather than an element of the riddle text, the hidden variable is not equal to the four structural components, but an indication of the *absence* of a component of the text. The riddler creates this absence, is aware of the information needed to fill it, and assumes that the riddlee also has access to this information. The "hidden variable" is therefore more accurately defined as *the shared knowledge upon which the riddle text is built.*

The "hidden variable," then, is not an aspect of the text, but a prerequisite item of group knowledge or belief. This knowledge is prerequisite not only to the solution of the riddle, but also to recognition of the genre. Appealing once again to Maranda's pig riddle, if the riddlee is unaware that a pig has only one snout, the phrase "one pig, two snouts" is not only insoluble, it cannot be identified as a riddle. Further, even when such knowledge is available, this particular text could easily function as a proverb; only the performance context in which it is uttered specifies its genre. Both the hidden variable's absence from the text and the mutual recognition of this absence by the riddler and riddlee are defining features of the genre.

This redefinition of the "hidden variable" calls for a reevaluation of the logic sequence underlying Maranda's "simple riddle." It will again be helpful to consider the riddle, "one pig, two snouts—a plough." Closer inspection reveals that this riddle is not as "simple" as Maranda suggests. She distributes the five components of the riddle through two truisms, "a pig has a snout" and "a plough has two snouts." But those familiar with snouts and a ploughs will recognize that the latter sentence is not a truism at all; literally, it is

---

[116]Maranda, "Logic" 199.

nonsense.[117] Hence, while the information in the false premise ("two") points the riddlee away from the pig, it does not, contra Maranda, point toward the plough, but rather toward the *metaphorical* constant variable, "has snouts." To unlock the metaphor "snout of a plough," the riddlee must refer to the hidden variable, prerequisite information about pigs and ploughs absent from the riddle text. This information includes the facts that a pig has only one snout, that a pig uses its snout to dig in the earth, and that a plough uses its two blades to dig in the earth. This "simple" riddle may be diagramed $f_x 1s/Pi = f_x 2b/Pl$, where one snout (1s) functions (f_x) to the pig (Pi) as two blades (2b) function (f_x) to the plough (Pl) in that both dig in the earth ($_x$). But Maranda suggests that this sort of exploration of the functional *relations* between items and sets (snouts to pigs and blades to ploughs) is characteristic of the transformation or "variant," not the kernel riddle metaphor. Rather than distinguishing "simple" from "complex" riddles, it would be more accurate to state that, in Maranda's terms, some riddles leave the metonymic aspect of their analogy implicit while others explicitly trace it on the surface text.

This reading of the "simple riddle" redefines the "kernel riddle" and the entire concept of "transformation." Maranda's own analysis clearly indicates that "transformation" is "logical" only within the canons of group ideology. In her major example of transformation, Maranda begins with the "kernel riddle" "a tree grows without roots—a person." She cites "variants" of this structure from her corpus which suggest the following transformation sequence: birth→marriage→pregnancy→ nursing→dying. Commenting on the underlying "logic" of this sequence, Maranda states, "[I]t seems necessary to consider the transformations a chain, for (ideally) a woman is not made pregnant before being wed, does not give birth before being pregnant, and cannot nurse without giving birth."[118] "Necessary" apparently implies logical necessity, but the word "ideally" indicates the degree to which this series is "logical" only within a local ideology. It seems universally obvious that a woman is born before she dies, but it is not universally obvious that death is logically preceded by marriage, pregnancy, and nursing. Further, while pregnancy universally precedes childbirth, marriage does not, and it does so

---

[117]Maranda, "Logic" 198.
[118]Maranda, "Tree Grows" 128.

"ideally" only according to local cultural values. As such, these "transformations" do not represent "logical" relations between these texts, but an ideological taxonomy of the texts generated from the values of Finnish culture. It is only from the perspective of these values that "transformation" is a viable concept. Overall, the "kernel" riddle in a series is only ideologically, not logically or structurally, prior to its "transformations."

This observation applies particularly to Maranda's two major categories of transformation, "reversal" and "inversion." For example, Maranda suggests that riddles which compare women to leafed trees (B = A) are "reversals" of riddles which compare leafed trees to women (A = B), and that riddles which compare evergreen trees to men are the "inverse" (-A = -B) of those which compare leafed trees to women.[119] It is unclear, in Maranda's presentation, how the term "trees" has logical priority over the term "women," and how the term "women" has logical priority over the term "men." It is reasonable, however, to suggest that certain terms may have *ideological* priority over others.

Further, Maranda does not explore the possibility that reversal and inversion may depend on the *situation* in which the riddle is generated. For example, if two men are walking in the forest and propose riddles, it seems likely that "tree" would appear in the riddle question, since the context makes it a "given" term, while "woman" would appear in the answer, since the absence of women from the context would "hide" this term. But if the same two men attend a wedding ceremony and propose riddles, it seems likely that the term given by that context, the bride, would appear in the question, while trees would appear in the answer. Reversal and inversion may thus be products of ideological and contextual factors, and in this way ideology and context can transform the surface text of the riddle. "Transformation" is not a move from creating relations between sets to exploring relations between sets, but a move from one situation or one ideological expression to another.

The revised approach to the hidden variable and transformation suggested here remains consistent with Maranda's observations on the riddle's "subversive" function. While the riddle challenges one piece of conventional knowledge, it can do so only on the basis of agreement about another piece of

---

[119]Maranda, "Tree Grows" 130–135.

conventional knowledge, the hidden variable. For example, to challenge the notion that pigs and ploughs belong in separate categories, the riddler and riddlee must first agree that pigs have snouts which dig in the earth and that ploughs have blades which dig in the earth. Challenging one aspect of the ideological taxonomy thus reenforces another. In fact, the riddle is a particularly powerful tool for ideological classification. The true premise, or constant variable, names a quality which is characteristic of members of a superset. The false premise, which is true only of the answer and not the given term, names a quality which makes one member of the superset different from another. By establishing equality, riddles categorize; by establishing difference, they subcategorize. The genius of the riddle text is that it performs both of these operations, categorization and subcategorization, at once. In this sense, riddles create a stronger sense of taxonomy than direct analogy or direct contradiction alone could facilitate.

One other minor point of Maranda's analysis, drawn from her observations of riddle performance among the Lau people of Melanesia, will be helpful to this study. The Lau utilize stereotyped opening formulae to introduce riddles because "Lau do not have a marked riddle style." These opening formulae include the Lau term for "riddle," so that "the Lau riddle poser announces simply his intention by naming the genre he is about to present."[120] This observation suggests that not every riddle corpus will evidence a distinct "style" which distinguishes the riddle from other genres. Each group will presumably develop its own means of indicating when a particular statement should be interpreted as a "riddle."

PEPICELLO AND GREEN: THE LANGUAGE OF AMBIGUITY
The most extensive recent contribution to riddle studies has resulted from the collaboration of W. J. Pepicello and Thomas A. Green. Pepicello and Green have consistently advocated the thesis that riddles, as one type of "linguistic play," are best understood against the background of "normal language" and other forms of verbal art.[121] "Our aim, then, is to examine

---

[120]Maranda, "Theory and Practice" 58.
[121]W. J. Pepicello and Thomas A. Green, "The Folk Riddle: A Redefinition of Terms," *WF* 38 (1979) 7. Severely criticizing previous theorists, particularly Maranda,

riddles as language and performance, focusing on the ways in which riddling exploits conventional patterns of discourse."[122] It will therefore be helpful to begin analysis of their work by examining their perception of the difference between "conventional" discourse and riddle performance.

Pepicello and Green feel that "conventional" interactions support social cohesion. Cohesion prefers resolution over conflict and supports the group's "normal power structures." Cohesion is facilitated by shared "paradigms of perception," common ways of thinking and speaking about cultural items and topics.[123] Conventional discourse, as a form of social interaction, supports order and group cohesion. For this reason, conventional discourse attempts to clarify rather than confuse. Questions are asked only of those persons believed capable of answering. Utterances are clearly related or, if figurative, can be clearly related to a specific context. "[U]tilitarian speech strives for clarity" by consciously avoiding possible overlap of referents.[124] "Redundancy" is an important issue in discussing linguistic clarity. In an ideal language system, every conceptual unit would be represented by a one unique phonetic unit. But natural languages are pressed to transmit more thoughts than their phonetic systems can bear, leaving many conceptual units phonetically similar or identical. This form of redundancy is known as "homophony," similarity in

---

Pepicello and Green insist that "we are obliged to subject these [riddle] constructions to proper analysis as language" before "speculation on the genre as phenomenology in a new key can be productive" (7).

[122]W. J. Pepicello and Thomas A. Green, "Wit in Riddling: A Linguistic Perspective," *Genre* 11 (1978) 3.

[123]W. J. Pepicello and Thomas A. Green, *The Language of Riddles: New Perspectives* (Columbus, OH: Ohio State University Press, 1984) 125, 128–129. Although Pepicello and Green consistently contrast riddle performance with conventional interactions, they do not specifically describe these conventional interactions and discourse patterns. The discussion here is based on the apparent logic of their presentation.

[124]Pepicello and Green, *LOR* 13, 124–125, quotation 13. This effort is observable at all three levels of language, phonemes, morphemes, and syntax. "Phonology" describes the sound units utilized by the language. "Morphology" addresses "the combination of distinctive units of sound (phonemes) into meaningful grammatical units, which we call morphemes." "Syntax" defines "the underlying , or conceptual, structure of an utterance and relat[es] this conceptual structure to the actual utterance," or "surface structure" (14–18, quotations 15).

sound. Homophony allows speakers to communicate the maximum amount of information through the minimum number of phonetic signs. In conventional discourse, audiences specify the meanings of redundant, homophonous signs by considering the utterance context.[125] This allows language users to communicate clearly with the limited number of phonetic signs offered by the language.

Conventional discourse, however, is subject to "accidents," unintentional errors in the use of the linguistic code.[126] Such accidents create "blocks" in the communication channel, or "ambiguity." "Ambiguity . . . refers to the situation which obtains in language when two or more underlying semantic structures may be represented by a single surface representation." While this situation obtains in all cases of redundancy, "ambiguous" utterances do not provide a sufficient context for the audience to discriminate among the possible intended meanings.[127] Pepicello and Green identify various types of ambiguity and situate these on a continuum between purely linguistic and purely cognitive/figurative errors.

"Linguistic ambiguity" occurs when the *literal* interpretation of an utterance could reasonably suggest more than one referent. Linguistic ambiguity can be generated at any of the three levels of language. *Phonological* ambiguity is an accident of homophony. Here one phonetic unit can represent a variety of lexical items, all the same part of speech, but the utterance context does not permit the audience to determine which item is intended. *Morphological* ambiguity also results from homophony, but here the homophonous lexical items represent different parts of speech, such as the irregular past tense of the verb "read" and the adjective "red." Again, context does not allow the audience to discriminate among the possible terms. *Syntactic* ambiguity arises when one utterance can reasonably represent more than one underlying proposition. Once again, context does not allow the

---

[125]Pepicello and Green, *LOR* 97–100. In normal language, the speaker must explicitly clarify the referent when it cannot be distinguished by the context.

[126]Discourse may also be disrupted by "noise," distortion of the message before it reaches the audience (Pepicello and Green, *LOR* 97).

[127]Pepicello and Green, *LOR* 13, quotation here; "Wit" 5.

audience to determine which of the underlying propositions is intended.[128] In this way, linguistic ambiguity violates the rules of conventional language by accidentally confusing the audience.

But speakers do not always intend that their words be understood literally. Some conventional discourse is figurative, using devices such as metaphor. Metaphors are inherently disposed toward ambiguity because they unite items and categories which are normally cognitively distinct, allowing a higher degree of subjectivity in interpretation than literal language.[129] For this reason, the use of metaphors in conventional discourse is carefully controlled. In a "pure metaphor," "the signifier–signified relation is straightforward, and the relationship is the basis of the paradigm [comparison]."[130] This "straightforwardness" is maintained by several social mechanisms: mutual cultural understanding of the "salient features" of the speech situation; "speaker–listener cooperation," whereby both parties agree that the metaphor is interpretable; finally, the underlying proposition of the metaphor must be analogous to its referent "in a recognizable way." Pepicello and Green

---

[128]Pepicello and Green, "Wit" 6; *LOR* 13, 22–23. Syntactic ambiguity can represent two types of relationships between underlying propositions. In "phrase structure ambiguity," multiple underlying propositions share the same constituent elements but arrange them in alternate configurations, where any of the arrangements could be expressed by the same utterance (*LOR* 24). For example, the English sentence, "John looked over the car," could represent the propositions "John's line of vision was higher than the car" or "John inspected the car," depending on the position of the term "over." The distinction between morphological and phrase structure ambiguity is obvious only in the deep structure of the text. For example, in the riddle, "How is a goose like an icicle? Both grow down," "down" is ambiguous because the same phonetic unit could represent an adverb or a noun. This is a case of phrase structure ambiguity because the alternate morphologies create two distinct phrases. The second type of syntactic ambiguity arises "when the application of transformations to two different underlying structures results in homophonous surface structures." In this case, two underlying propositions with different elements can be expressed by the same surface text through normal transformation sequences (*LOR* 48).

[129]Pepicello and Green, *LOR* 109. In this sense, "metaphor is an extension of the phenomenon of ambiguity in ordinary speech" (109). True metaphors must be figurative in current language use, irrespective of historical origin. English terms such as "*eye* of a needle" are therefore homophones for different lexical items rather than metaphors (106).

[130]Pepicello and Green, *LOR* 126.

therefore define the conventional metaphor as a figurative use of language which "involves a *shifting denotation* of an expression as *determined by context, within the limits of cultural convention.*"[131]

Sometimes, however, cultural conventions are accidentally violated, obscuring the analogy between the metaphor and the thing or situation it represents. The effect of such errors is "contextual ambiguity," which "depends upon more general associations or analogies between the literal and figurative elements concerned" than linguistic ambiguity.[132] Pepicello and Green refer to contextual ambiguity as "vagueness," where "*vagueness* refers to situations in which the degree of description provides an inadequate basis for solution." Whereas linguistic ambiguity creates an excess of possible referents, "vague" metaphors are not connected to their contexts strongly enough to suggest any referent.[133] This again causes the audience "confusion," disrupting communication.

Within each "ambiguous" or "vague" utterance it is possible to identify the specific textual element which disrupts normal communication. Pepicello and Green refer to this element as the "block." The block presents the audience with an "unsolvable opposition."[134] Blocks are carefully avoided in conventional discourse.

Following the thesis that riddles must be understood in comparison with normal language and verbal art, Pepicello and Green assert that the "verbal component of riddling must ultimately be considered within the larger contexts within which artful combination of words finds its proper home."[135] These larger contexts are "performances," interactive discourse situations in which the group's linguistic (grammatical) and aesthetic (symbolic) conventions are suspended. "Performance" is signaled to the discourse audience by "metamessages" which create an artistic "frame" around a particular behavior. This frame "transform[s] organizational patterns appropriate to serious behavior into ludic actions." In a performance context, "behavior that would

---

[131]Pepicello and Green, *LOR*, first quotation 138, second quotation 136, emphasis added.

[132]Pepicello and Green, *LOR* 109, quotation here; "Wit" 12.

[133]Pepicello and Green, *LOR* 111, emphasis original.

[134]Pepicello and Green, *LOR* 22.

[135]Pepicello and Green, "Wit" 10.

ordinarily be labeled inept or even overtly antisocial is frequently permitted
and, in fact, encouraged." "Artistic" interactions thus manipulate the group's
"preestablished cultural framework." As a type of artistic folk performance,
"riddles play upon a common cultural repertoire of traditional categories . . .
which are subject to playful manipulation, but never demolished, on riddling
occasions."[136]

As a performance genre, the riddle is characterized by *the intentional,
artful use of verbal ambiguity and vagueness.* "In riddles the system of
language employed by the folk group may be subverted in various ways
through *the intentional overlapping of frames of reference for purposes of
intentionally blocking communication.*" Whereas conventional discourse
carefully avoids "blocks" in communication, in riddle performance "the
blocking of direct transfer of information is the ideal." "Wit" is the ability to
artistically create linguistic ambiguity, or to resolve ambiguity.[137]

Pepicello and Green devote much of their work to describing the artistic
strategies which create intentional blocks in riddle performance. These
strategies manipulate the normal language code, metaphorical language, or
both at once, creating a continuum of riddle types based on the primary
blocking strategy.[138] For each type, they distinguish the "process" of riddle
production from the "act." The "process" of riddling concerns the means "by
which certain linguistic or cultural devices are in some way identified as

---

[136]Pepicello and Green, *LOR*, first quotation 8, second quotation 11, third and fourth
quotations 4. Pepicello and Green see "intentionality as the central criterion for separating
art from simple behavior" (12).

[137]Pepicello and Green, *LOR* 5, 12–13, 22, quotation 12–13; "Wit" 13. "These same
types of ambiguity, which are considered linguistic accidents in ordinary speech, may be
consciously manipulated in riddling" ("Wit" 7). "Thus, the basic strategy of the riddle is the
disorientation of the riddlee" ("Wit" 13; *LOR* 5). Pepicello and Green compare the riddle
to "slapstick, physical comedy," another performance genre which creatively manipulates
behaviors normally considered clumsy or embarrassing. Similarly, "in riddling we classify
our linguistic clumsiness and present it in a way which permits us to control it in a
performance context" (W. J. Pepicello, "Linguistic Strategies in Riddling," *WF* 39 [1980]
16; Pepicello and Green, *LOR* 58). The riddle's "exploitation of maladroitness as an art
form" is most obvious in those riddles which incorporate common "slips of the tongue,"
particularly the reversal of sounds or words (*LOR* 58–59).

[138]Pepicello and Green, *LOR* 112–118, quotation 112.

potential block elements and subsequently incorporated as such into the riddle form."[139] The "act" of riddling concerns the specific strategies by which these block elements are used artistically in a performance context.

The process of selecting *linguistic* blocks "is initiated at the level of surface structure, rather than at an underlying level."[140] Riddlers do not consciously explore potential linguistic accidents to create material for riddles. Rather, "grammatical blocks are derived from their occurrences as actual utterances." Linguistic blocks are thus appropriations of observed linguistic accidents, specifically those accidents which "amuse and entertain." "Thus it is the strikingness of a contradiction or confusion at the surface level that in some way identifies potential blocks, and it is at this point that the process of [linguistic] riddle creation begins."[141]

The act of linguistic riddling utilizes twelve blocking strategies. Pepicello and Green place these strategies on a sub–continuum with three major divisions: "riddles which are oral in nature, . . . those which function either in oral or visual form, . . . [and] those which are exclusively visual in nature."[142] "Oral" and "visual" here refer to the conceptual basis of the ambiguity, not the medium of distribution; all linguistic riddles are delivered orally. On this continuum, "oral" riddles "exploit each linguistically relevant level of language," utilizing the phonological, morphological, and syntactic "accidents" described above. "Visual" riddles are delivered orally but play on "formal or metatheoretical aspects [of orthography,] such as the names of graphemes and their shapes."[143] To solve a riddle, the riddlee must first determine which element of the text is ambiguous, and then whether that ambiguity is operative at the phonological, morphological, syntactic, or visual level.[144]

---

[139]W. J. Pepicello and Thomas A. Green, "The Riddle Process," *JAF* 97 (1984) 190.

[140]Pepicello and Green, "Riddle Process" 194.

[141]Pepicello and Green, "Riddle Process," all three quotations 198.

[142]W. J. Pepicello and Thomas A. Green, "Sight and Spelling Riddles," *JAF* 93 (1980) 29–30; *LOR* 68.

[143]Pepicello and Green, "Sight and Spelling" 24, 31, 32, first quotation 31, second quotation 32; "Riddle Process" 196–197.

[144]Or at multiple levels. Pepicello and Green, "Wit" 7; *LOR* 27.

Pepicello and Green identify four phonological strategies for generating linguistic ambiguity in the riddle text. *Lexical* ambiguity plays on the confusion which arises when multiple lexical items of the same morphological value can represented by the same phonetic unit.[145] *Word stress* alters the natural stress patterns of compound words, making them aurally indistinct from adjective–noun combinations. *Juncture*, or "pause phenomena," performs the same operation by inserting a pause between the components of a compound term.[146] The fourth phonological strategy exploits "*minimal pairs*," words which are aurally distinct in only one phoneme, such as the English terms "pet" and "bet." Here the basic phonetic similarity of two unrelated terms is used to compare incompatible referents. All four phonological strategies "depend upon oral transmission," as writing often eliminates the aural indistinctness on which they rely.[147]

Riddlers utilize three morphological strategies to create linguistic ambiguity. The first "plays on *homophony*." This strategy is identical to phonetic lexical ambiguity, but here the homophonous items have different morphological values, representing different parts of speech.[148] The second and third morphological strategies involve "the arbitrary division of words into their morphemes, and then the use of these morphemes as if they were independent lexical items." In some cases these are independent morphemes, but in others they are "pseudomorphemes." "Pseudomorphemes" are "sequences of phonemes that are homophonous with English morphemes but

---

[145]Pepicello and Green, "Wit" 7; *LOR* 27. Example: "What has an eye that never closes? A needle." Note that Pepicello and Green consider "eye" a homophone rather than a metaphor, due to the regularization of the term "eye of a needle" in contemporary usage.

[146]Pepicello, "Linguistic Strategies" 3–5; Pepicello and Green, *LOR* 30–33. Example of a word stress riddle: When is a black dog not a black dog? When it is a greyhound/gray hound. In both word stress and juncture riddles, "the 'answer' is the set of contrasting utterances, rather than just one of them" ("Linguistic Strategies" 6). The "answer" to this riddle is thus "greyhound/gray hound."

[147]Pepicello, "Linguistic Strategies" 6–7, quotation 6. Example: What is the difference between a baby and a coat? One you were and one you wear. In *LOR*, Pepicello and Green state that this strategy falls outside their definition of linguistic ambiguity (35).

[148]Pepicello and Green, "Wit" 8, quotation here, emphasis added; *LOR* 37–40; Pepicello, "Linguistic Strategies" 7. Example: What's black and white and red/read all over? A newspaper.

which themselves are devoid of semantic content." For example, in the riddle, "What room cannot be entered? A mushroom," the phonetic unit "room" is not an independent morpheme of the compound "mushroom," and is therefore not semantically equivalent to the independent lexical item "room" as the riddle suggests.[149] Because morphological strategies rely on homophony, they also depend on oral transmission.

Two strategies for generating linguistic ambiguity operate at the level of syntax. In both cases, the surface structure of the text can reasonably represent more than one underlying phrase structure. The "block" element must therefore be identified in the generative process and not the text itself. The first syntactic strategy, which exploits phrase structure ambiguity, is rare in English riddling.[150] The more common syntactic strategy exploits transformational ambiguity. Here, both the surface structure and the transformations are conventional; confusion arises because the riddlee cannot determine which of two different propositions actually underlies the surface text. One commonly exploited transformation is "deletion," the elimination of repetition in the underlying structure from the surface text. For example, the riddle, "Would you rather have an elephant kill you or a gorilla?" can be generated from the proposition, "Would you rather have an elephant kill you or a gorilla kill you?," or the proposition, "Would you rather have an elephant kill you or kill a gorilla?" Here the riddlee cannot determine whether the surface text has deleted the redundant "kill you" from the first proposition or the redundant "kill a" from the second proposition.[151] Another transformation strategy questions the constituent terms of an idiom as if the idiom were a literal syntactic unit. This strategy violates the rule that idioms cannot undergo interrogative transformations.[152] A third transformational strategy "is that in

---

[149]Pepicello and Green, *LOR*, first quotation 41, second quotation 43; "Wit" 8; Pepicello, "Linguistic Strategies" 7–10. In some cases the pseudomorpheme is generated by homophony and therefore relies on orality, as in the riddle, What kind of ears does a train have? Engineers.

[150]Pepicello and Green, *LOR* 43; "Wit" 7–9; Pepicello, "Linguistic Strategies" 11–12.

[151]Pepicello and Green, *LOR* 48–50. Correct answer: I'd rather have the elephant kill the gorilla.

[152]Pepicello and Green, *LOR* 53–55; Pepicello, "Linguistic Strategies" 11–12. Example: What goes most against a farmer's grain? A reaper. Here the term "grain" from

which a given syntactic construction is homophonous with a morphological construction." Here a series of transformations generates an utterance which is phonetically identical to another utterance which displays normal morphological processes.[153] Syntactic strategies rely on the absence of a context which would specify which underlying propositions are represented in the riddle. By exploiting the phonological, morphological and grammatical levels of language at once, they also demonstrate that "in all riddles a variety of strategies, linguistic or otherwise, are at work simultaneously."[154]

Pepicello and Green explore the fourth category of linguistic strategies, that employing orthography, in their 1980 article "Sight and Spelling Riddles." Riddles at the visual end of the strategy continuum "relate to the systems of the Roman alphabet and roman and arabic numerals," specifically the shapes and names of written letters and numbers. Although transmitted orally, these riddles cannot be answered without visual representation.[155] The orthographic system is exploited by manipulating the names of letters, the relationship between written letters and the sounds they represent, or the shapes of written letters or numerals. In the first strategy, the riddler may exploit the homophony between the name of a letter or a sequence of letters and an independent lexical item.[156] The second visual strategy exploits the dual nature of English words as semantic entities and assemblages of letters. These riddles treat a term as a group of graphemes rather than a total semantic unit.[157] Shape riddles exploit

---

the idiom "goes against her grain" (irritates her) is treated as an independent lexical item in the surface text.

[153]Pepicello and Green, *LOR* 56; "Wit" 9. Example: Why can't you starve to death in the desert? Because of the sand which/sandwich is there.

[154]Pepicello, "Linguistic Strategies" 13; Pepicello and Green, *LOR* 57.

[155]Pepicello and Green, "Sight and Spelling" 23–25, quotation 25. The visual representation of these riddles may or may not be reenforced by writing, but does not depend on that technology. "The sight on which the wit of such riddles depend is a type of envisionment, an imagination of their orthographic forms" (33).

[156]Pepicello and Green, "Sight and Spelling" 25. Example: Spell "enemy" in three letters? NME. Confusion is generated because the sequence NME is "semantically empty" (25).

[157]Pepicello and Green, "Sight and Spelling" 26–27. Example: What makes a road broad? The letter "B." This riddle also exploits syntax, since the surface text could represent two underlying phrase structures (28).

the appearance of written letters or numbers, sometimes combining homophony and orthography.[158] Sight and spelling strategies thus explore "questions about the written code itself, rather than about the message it carries." They can be effectively transmitted orally or in writing.[159]

Pepicello and Green situate all riddles which utilize linguistic ambiguity at some point on this continuum. Because they see the riddle as a primarily oral form, often dependent on the medium of oral speech, phonology is critical to their analysis. The three oral strategies they describe represent a hierarchy, as morphological ambiguity depends on phonological ambiguity, specifically the homophony of terms which represent different parts of speech, and syntactic ambiguity exploits the grammatical implications of morphological blurring. Many of the visual riddles they discuss also rely on the homophony of letter names and independent lexical items. Their analysis thus implies that phonological redundancy is critical to riddling.

As with linguistic riddles, metaphorical strategies are "surface oriented," in that an ambiguity in the surface text confuses underlying categories. In this case, however, the blurred categories are cognitive or cultural rather than linguistic.[160] Blocks are created "by providing an inadequate cognitive basis for solution." Most metaphorical riddles are linguistically unambiguous, but the absence of those contextual clues which regulate the use of metaphors in normal speech makes it impossible for the riddlee to complete the metaphorical comparison.[161] Metaphorical riddle strategies are thus primarily contextual rather than textual, manipulating the communicative environment in which metaphors are normally delivered. Pepicello and Green offer the following as an example of a concise, metaphorical riddle: "There is something with a heart in its head? A peach." This riddle evidences no linguistic ambiguity; its ambiguity arises from the violation of the cultural conception that items do not have "hearts" in their "heads." The revelation of the answer provides a linguistic context which clarifies the metaphorical terms of the question.[162]

---

[158]As in the riddle, What state is high in the middle and round on both ends? Ohio (Pepicello and Green, "Sight and Spelling" 30).

[159]Pepicello and Green, "Sight and Spelling" 28.

[160]Pepicello and Green, "Riddle Process" 200.

[161]Pepicello and Green, *LOR* 111.

[162]Pepicello and Green, "Folk Riddle" 12; *LOR* 114–116.

Although the *act* of metaphorical riddle performance is similar to the act of linguistic riddle performance, in that both manipulate the surface text to suggest multiple underlying categories, the *process* of choosing metaphorical blocks differs significantly. Unlike linguistic riddles, the ambiguities generated by metaphorical riddles are not based on observed accidents in language use, but on conscious manipulation of linguistic and cognitive categories. Metaphorical riddles are realized in surface utterances but originate in "underlying cultural categories," making it impossible to describe them in terms of the "rules of production" which govern the linguistic code. The process by which metaphorical blocks are selected as riddle metaphors is therefore undefinable.[163]

Pepicello and Green do not treat the social functions of the riddle in great detail. They suggest that the riddle genre performs two social functions, one metalinguistic, the other metacultural. As metalanguage, riddles "permit a rehearsal and reinforcement of grammatical norms." The signified of the riddle is not the "answer," but the "pliability of the grammar itself" and the possibility of manipulating it.[164] Because language reflects culture, "we may [also] regard riddling as a type of metacultural play." In the exploration of linguistic norms, "we rehearse our ability to perceive order by selectively disordering our interactions." The riddle's blocking of normal linguistic and cognitive patterns forces group members "to come to terms" with the traditional paradigms reinforced by other forms of folk art.[165]

The consistency and exhaustiveness of Pepicello and Green's analysis limits any critique to the scope of their work rather than its depth. The nature of their corpus raises questions about the general applicability of their conclusions. In *LOR* they indicate that their data pool was compiled from a

---

[163]Pepicello and Green, "Riddle Process" 200–202. "[W]e must conclude that riddles relying on figurative language for their wit originate at an underlying cognitive level rather than the surface level, and that it is at this [cognitive] level that the riddling process begins for such riddles" (200).

[164]First quotation Pepicello, "Linguistic Strategies" 16; second quotation Pepicello and Green, *LOR* 128. In this way, "riddling forces participants to come to terms with the mechanisms of expression" (144).

[165]Pepicello and Green, *LOR* 129, 144. First quotation Pepicello, "Linguistic Strategies" 13–14; second quotation Pepicello and Green, "Wit" 13.

variety of sources: published riddles; oral riddles collected from "colleagues and students" at the University of Delaware, Temple University, and Texas A&M University between 1976 and 1981; several riddles "recorded at a brief riddle session between two seven–year–old children"; and, riddles "provided by audience members who approached us after paper presentations at professional meetings."[166] This explains their earlier admission that their materials were collected in situations which "cannot be regarded as entirely spontaneous."[167] In an appendix to *LOR* they further test their conclusions on "three hundred [published] Spanish riddles from several riddling traditions."[168] While a comprehensive response to this manner of developing a corpus is beyond the scope of this study, it is important to note that Pepicello and Green's data are not diverse, the majority of their materials being collected from the most literate sector of contemporary American society. Their analysis of "riddles," therefore, is actually an analysis of *modern, literate American riddle performance.*

The narrow scope of this corpus limits, and at times confuses, Pepicello and Green's conclusions. Most modern Western, and almost all modern American, riddle performance occurs in contexts of "leisure–time riddling."

> The ostensible function of riddling in this situation is entertainment. While there may be secondary consequences of involvement in this type of riddling, the explicit intent is not to further or test knowledge, or to promote in a central way some ritual or expressive result.

In many cultural settings, however, riddles perform primarily educational or ritual functions which are fulfilled by other interactions in modern Western culture.[169] The exclusive use of the genre for entertainment in contemporary

---

[166]Pepicello and Green, *LOR* 153–155, quotations 155.

[167]Pepicello and Green, "Wit" 2.

[168]See Pepicello and Green, *LOR* 145ff. Pepicello and Green's method of manipulating their data makes it impossible to determine the breadth of their conclusions.

[169]Thomas A. Burns, "Riddling: Occasion to Act," *JAF* 89 (1976) 145. Burns describes five other cross–cultural contexts of the riddle: initiation and death rituals; courtship and weddings; "the educational encounter between teacher and student"; greetings; embedded in larger genres, "particularly narratives and songs" (143–144).

American society explains Pepicello and Green's observation that all twelve linguistic riddle strategies have immediate parallels in "jokes."[170] Not only is their corpus limited to one culture, it is limited to one culture which uses riddles almost exclusively for recreation, avoiding the more "serious" potential of the genre.

By limiting their analysis to leisure–time riddles, Pepicello and Green are led to contradict themselves in establishing criteria for identifying members of the genre. Their most comprehensive definition indicates that a text must follow a conceptually interrogative format, must be orally transmitted, and must be "included in the riddle category by informants" to be considered a "riddle."[171] The third criterion is essential to a culturally sensitive description of any folk genre: if the group uses a particular text as a member of a particular genre, that text should be considered a member of that genre for analytic purposes. Because their corpus reflects a culture which uses the riddle as an entertaining test of wits, it would be reasonable for Pepicello and Green to insist that *English* riddles are defined by ambiguity, wit, and the "criterion of solvability."[172] But their claim that *any* verbal challenge which involves "the recall of esoteric facts rather than the exercise of wit" is *not* a riddle is, at best, provincial. Using this criterion, Pepicello and Green state that the following are *not* riddles: catechetical or ritual questions, which "demand an automatic response rather than a thoughtful solution"; the Zen *koans*; "clever questions or wisdom questions"; neck riddles, both because these are unsolvable and because they appear in narratives rather than "in a socially defined riddling context"; and, the "joking question," whose referent is "so tenuously connected to the question" that it cannot be identified by wit.[173] Here they fail to consider that some cultures may use certain texts as riddles which do not satisfy the "criterion of solvability."

---

[170]Pepicello and Green, "Riddle Process" 196–197.

[171]Pepicello and Green, "Folk Riddle" 17.

[172]Pepicello and Green, "Wit" 1, 5, quotation 1 n. 1.

[173]Pepicello and Green, "Folk Riddle," first quotation 17, second and third quotations 18, fourth and fifth quotations 19. "Esoteric" knowledge "consists of familiarity with a body of information—religious, circumstantial, etc.—that cannot be obtained by virtue of the conventional experiences acquired by membership in the culture in which the riddle arises" (17 n. 48). "Circumstantial" knowledge apparently refers to neck riddles.

Using their own example, Charles Zug's study of the Zen *koans* suggests that these texts are "riddles" in both their historical development and contemporary use, making them educational or catechetical riddles. In direct response to Zug's conclusions, Pepicello and Green state that the *koan* "is unsolvable in the sense that solvability is used in this [our] study, and so is a non–riddle."[174] According to Pepicello and Green's conflicting criteria, the *koan* should be treated as riddles because of their local cultural application, but cannot be riddles because their resolution does not require wit. This contradiction, however, is unapparent to them because their corpus is limited to riddles whose cultural definition includes wit as a constituent element.

Further, Pepicello and Green's examples sometimes defy their own understanding of "wit." In their earlier articles, the riddle is defined as "a linguistically ambiguous question" and "wit" is defined as the ability to create or resolve such questions.[175] In many of their examples, however, the riddle question is unambiguous. For example, Pepicello and Green consider the text, "When is coffee like the soil? When it is ground," to be a morphological riddle which plays on the homophony of the noun "ground" and the past tense of the verb "grind." This wordplay, however, is evident only in the answer, not the question. The same is the case with their model syntactic riddle, "What goes most against a farmer's grain? A reaper."[176] The question here gives no indication of ambiguity; only the answer reveals that the idiom "goes against the grain" has been ruptured through a literal interpretation. In both examples, the riddlee is simply an audience for the performer's wit, which is not apparent until the answer is revealed. Pepicello and Green acknowledge this phenomenon in *LOR*, noting that in some cases "the answer . . . depends upon the *creation* of ambiguity rather than its resolution." This recognition leads them to redefine ambiguity in riddling: "it is the case that the wit of the riddle depends on the resolution of ambiguity somewhere in the riddle structure, which includes the answer as well as the question."[177] By this they apparently

---

[174]Charles G. Zug III, "The Nonrational Riddle: The Zen *Koan*," *JAF* 80 (1967) 81–85; Burns, "Occasion to Act" 144. Response in Pepicello and Green, "Folk Riddle" 18.

[175]Pepicello, "Linguistic Strategies" 1, quotation here; Pepicello and Green, "Wit" 5; "Folk Riddle" 14–15; *LOR* 22.

[176]Pepicello, "Linguistic Strategies" 2–3, 11.

[177]Pepicello and Green, *LOR*, both quotations 34.

mean that sometimes the question uses ambiguous language, while sometimes the answer uses ambiguous language. But in the latter case, while the riddlee may suspect ambiguity due to the performance context, she cannot locate it in the text and must wait for the riddler to provide an answer which generates it. The same situation prevails in "vague" metaphorical riddles, which are insufficiently contextualized for the riddlee to limit, or even establish, possible referents. This changes the role of the riddlee in the performance context from interactive participant to passive observer, similar to the audience of narrative folk genres. In these cases "wit" is a unidirectional phenomenon, and the riddlee's pleasure in the entertainment situation arises solely from the observation of the riddler's clever use of language.

Two further points of Pepicello and Green's analysis are relevant to the present study. The first concerns the format of the linguistic unit under investigation. Criticizing the "true riddle" approach of Taylor and Georges and Dundes, they insist that the "riddle" as a structural unit has two equal components, question and answer. The first component is always interrogative, even if not formally a question. "[A]n essential criterion for defining the riddle, then, is a traditionally conceptualized interrogative format, whether the interrogation is manifested on the surface level or not."[178] Image and response always function as question and answer, irrespective of local grammatical forms.

Second, by discussing riddles against the backdrop of "normal" language and other performance genres, Pepicello and Green characterize the riddle as a manipulation of linguistic and cultural norms. They insist, however, that this manipulation depends upon a "preestablished cultural framework" which is "never demolished" in riddle performance. This allows the riddle text to be both ambiguous and recognizable at once. Their approach places the riddle genre within Norman Petersen's definition of "anti–language." Petersen defines "anti–language" as a use of "everyday language . . . in a special way, a way that is both implicitly and explicitly contrasted with everyday usage."[179] This involves blurred referents, the synonymous use of terms which are not normally synonymous, and a heavy emphasis on definition by contrast, all

---

[178]Pepicello and Green, "Folk Riddle" 17. Also Maranda, "Theory and Practice" 54.
[179]Petersen, *Sociology of Light* 9–10, 22, 48, quotation 9.

characteristics of the riddle as Pepicello and Green describe it. The riddle is a form of anti–language, delivered in a performance environment that sanctions this type of verbal behavior.

CAMP AND FONTAINE: RIDDLES IN WRITTEN TEXTS

A number of recent studies have discussed folk forms in the Hebrew Bible, including the riddle.[180] Claudia V. Camp and Carole R. Fontaine's paper on "Samson's riddle" (Judges 14:12–14) for the 1988 "Conference on the Hebrew Bible and Folklore" is notable among these studies for two reasons. First, their work is truly "interdisciplinary," in that it both borrows from and contributes to folkloristics by proposing a model which could be applied to non–biblical riddles. Second, their treatment accommodates the special problems of riddle performance portrayed in narrative. Aligning themselves with the "ethnography of speaking" approach, Camp and Fontaine suggest that any study of the "rhetorical use of wisdom forms" can be assisted by "the literature on folklore performance in social contexts," particularly the work of Peter Seitel and Alan Dundes.[181] A review of this literature will situate their discussion of Judges 14.

In an influential 1962 paper, Dell Hymes called for greater sensitivity to the "ethnography of speaking" in anthropology and linguistics. While structural linguistics had made significant strides toward identifying patterns of contrast and substitution in language, linguists had overlooked the fact that "for much of the lexicon and most larger units of speech, the contextual frames

[180]Particularly "Samson's riddle" at Judges 14:12–14. See Hans Peter Müller, "Der Begriff 'Rätsel' in Alten Testament," *VT* 20 (1970) 465–489; Edward L. Greenstein, "The Riddle of Samson," *Prooftexts* 1 (1981) 237–260; Jürgen Kegler, "Simsson—Widerstandskampfer und Volksheld," *Communio Viatorum* 28 (1985) 97–117; Philip Nel, "The Riddle of Samson," *Bib* 66 (1985) 534–545; Othniel Margalith, "Samson's Riddle and Samson's Magic Locks," *VT* 36 (1986) 225–234. The most extensive contributor is James L. Crenshaw; see his "Wisdom," *Old Testament Form Criticism* (ed. John H. Hayes; San Antonio, TX: Trinity University Press, 1974); "Riddle," *The Interpreter's Dictionary of the Bible Supplemental Volume* (ed. Keith Crim; Nashville, TN: Abingdon, 1976); "Impossible Questions, Sayings, and Tasks," *Semeia* 17 (1980) 19–34; and *Samson*.

[181]Claudia V. Camp and Carol R. Fontaine, "The Words of the Wise and Their Riddles," *Text and Tradition: The Hebrew Bible and Folklore* (ed. Susan Niditch; SBLSS; Atlanta, GA: Scholars Press, 1990) 127.

must be sought . . . in behavioral situations." Although linguistic units carry potential values, these values are limited and controlled by the utterance context, so that "the effective meaning [of an utterance] depends upon the interaction of the two," language and social situation.[182] Hymes proceeds to describe a three–pronged analysis of speech behavior, which explores speech events, the constituent factors of speech events, and the social functions of speech. A thorough consideration of all three elements would contribute both to anthropology and linguistics by outlining the "ethnographic context of speech" for the language group under investigation.[183]

Hymes' perspective was quickly applied to folkloristics by Alan Dundes and E. Ojo Arewa in their 1964 article, "Proverbs and the Ethnography of Speaking Folklore." Proverb performance involves two domains of knowledge, memory of fixed traditional texts and the ability to apply these texts to relevant social situations. The study of proverbs must therefore include both the traditional texts and the social situations in which such texts may be applied.[184] Collection reports specify "the typical and appropriate contexts or situations for individual proverbs," including the "oral literary criticism" of informants on the meaning of a proverb in all its potential social contexts. Dundes and Arewa illustrate the ethnographic approach by analyzing twelve Yoruba proverbs in terms of hypothetical social situations in which they might be used.[185]

---

[182]Dell H. Hymes, "The Ethnography of Speaking," *Anthropology and Human Behavior* (ed. Thomas Gladwin and William C. Sturtevant; Washington, DC: The Anthropological Society of Washington, 1962), first quotation 16, second quotation 19.

[183]Hymes insists that language, as a social phenomenon, must be studied "on the ground" to determine when, where, how, and by whom particular patterns may be used. "In sum, the description of semantic habits depends upon contexts of use to define relevant frames, sets of items, and dimensions of contrast" ("Ethnography of Speaking" 20). Clarifying Jakobson, Hymes asserts that, while "all features of the speech event, including all features of the linguistic code, may participate in all the functions," the referential function must receive methodological priority (32–33).

[184]"Such texts" above includes both the genre and specific proverbs. Alan Dundes and E. Ojo Arewa, "Proverbs and the Ethnography of Speaking Folklore" (1964; rpt. in *Essays in Folkloristics* [Alan Dundes; New Delhi: Manohar Book Service, 1978]) 50–52, 63.

[185]Dundes and Arewa, "Proverbs" 55–62, quotation 53.

Building directly on Hymes' model and following the precedent of Dundes and Arewa, Peter Seitel outlined a sophisticated approach to proverb performance. Seitel's goal is thoroughly ethnographic, seeking to determine the social "rules" by which speakers and audiences determine whether a particular traditional proverb is appropriate to a situation. These "rules" of performance reveal a cognitive process which Seitel refers to as "metaphorical reasoning," "the application of an imaginary situation to a real situation through a process of correlation." As a genre, proverbs use analogy to alleviate perceived conflict in a social situation by offering a plan for resolving this conflict or by counseling the audience to accept it.[186] Much of Seitel's study was dedicated to explaining how speakers correlate proverb situations and real situations to strategically manage conflict.

Seitel suggests that proverb performance involves three contexts. The first is "the social context of proverb use," which concerns the social relations between the speaker and audience in the speech situation. The second and third contexts are united in a metaphorical relationship. Seitel refers to the second context as "the proverb situation," and to the third context as "the social situation to which the proverb is applied." He expresses the relationship between these three contexts in the following diagram:

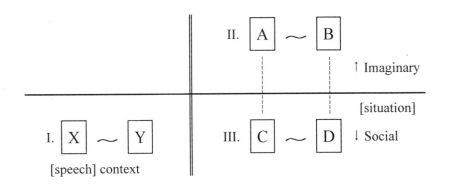

[186]Peter Seitel, "Proverbs: A Social Use of Metaphor" (1969; rpt. in *The Wisdom of Many: Essays on the Proverb* [ed. Wolfgang Mieder and Alan Dundes; New York, NY: Garland, 1981]) 122–124, 134.

Here X represents the proverb speaker, Y the audience, and ⁀ the social relationship between them. The symbol ⁀ in contexts II and III represents "a relationship which is seen by the speaker as obtaining between the objects (or people) in the social world C and D) and between the concepts in the imaginary proverb situation (A and B)." The dotted lines connecting situations II and III represent the suggested analogy, so that the total diagram expresses the statement, "X says to Y that A is to B as C is to D."[187]

Seitel describes the relationship between context I, the interaction situation, and context III, the social situation under discussion, in terms of "correlation." He suggests six types of correlation, following the six persons of grammar, first, second, or third person, singular or plural. First and second person correlations equate participants in the interaction situation (I) with participants in the social situation (III). Third person correlation equates parties outside the interaction situation with participants in the social situation. For example, a first–person singular correlation equates the speaker (X) with a person in the social situation (C); a third person plural correlation equates a plural third party, "they," with people in the social situation.[188] Change in person and number does not alter the surface text of the proverb, but does determine the proverb's meaning in the speech context by anchoring it to a particular referent. This demonstrates the need for an ethnographic approach, inasmuch as the situational nuances of proverb meaning depend on the correlation matrix of a particular performance.[189]

---

[187]Seitel, "Social Use," all quotations 127. Note that the visual representation of Seitel's diagram has been slightly modified here. Seitel stresses that both the relationship between speaker and audience (X⁀Y) and the values and relationship of the proverb terms (A⁀B) are culturally defined (136).

[188]Seitel, "Social Use" 129. Correlation may involve more than one person, as when the speaker uses a proverb to characterize the relationship between the audience and a third party, or the relationship between two third parties.

[189]Seitel urges that field reports should indicate the full range of meanings an individual proverb could take in different social situations and with different correlations. Such data could be obtained by observation or interrogation, but in either case "the aim [of collecting] is to construct usages of the same proverb in which a minimal difference in application signals a difference in meaning" ("Social Use" 133).

Camp and Fontaine's discussion of Samson's riddle builds directly on Seitel's study but is more sophisticated in its response to the peculiar problem of folk performances portrayed in narratives. Seitel's corpus included texts from African novels, treating fictive interaction situations as real performances with observable social configurations. His discussion, however, did not address the relationship between these units and other elements of the narrative.[190] Camp and Fontaine move beyond Seitel by combining folkloristic, linguistic, and narrative–critical models to make the narrative functions of embedded folk performances explicit. This creates a three–tiered reading of Judges 14. The first level is an examination of the riddle text as a linguistic unit. The second level of their reading uses folklore models to examine the interaction situation in the narrative world of Judges 14. At the third level, Camp and Fontaine use literary–critical tools to discuss the narrator's presentation strategy.[191] Camp and Fontaine's approach thus creates a hierarchy of readings for the narrative portrayal of folk performance: a linguistic reading encompassed by an ethnographic reading encompassed by a literary–critical reading.

Camp and Fontaine's discussion follows a modified version of Seitel's proverb paradigm, adapted to accommodate the linguistic and metaphorical ambiguities discussed by Pepicello and Green:

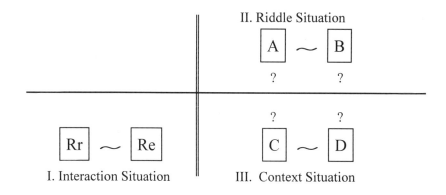

II. Riddle Situation

A ∽ B
?   ?

?   ?
Rr ∽ Re   C ∽ D
I. Interaction Situation   III. Context Situation

---

[190]Seitel, "Social Use" 125–126.
[191]Camp and Fontaine, "Words of the Wise" 128–130. In their discussion of Judges 14, literary–critical observations are interspersed throughout the other two levels of analysis.

"The Riddler (Rr) says to the Riddlee (Re) under the following circumstances (⁀), 'Guess (? ?) how A related to (⁀) B in this riddle is to be connected to C's relationship to (⁀) D in an unspecified context."[192] This approach allows them to discuss Judges 14:5–20 in terms of Seitel's three situations, considering the social dimension of the contest within the "interaction situation," the problem of linguistic ambiguity within the "riddle situation," and the problem of metaphorical ambiguity within the analogy (? ?) between the riddle situation and the context situation.

The "interaction situation" of Judges 14 concerns "the power relations between Samson and the Philistines before and after the riddle match," and the motives of each for participating in the contest.[193] Appealing to Burns' six interaction contexts, they suggest that Samson's challenge has characteristics of initiation, wedding, and leisure–time riddle performance. Outnumbered in a foreign land but possessed of "supreme and fearless self–confidence," Samson attempts to establish supremacy over the Philistines by proposing a non–violent verbal dual with an appropriate wager (the thirty garments). He signals the ludic nature of his discourse by stating his intention to initiate a riddling session at 14:12. In every sense, the interaction situation of Judges 14 follows "the typical rules of cross–cultural riddle performance."[194]

Camp and Fontaine's analysis of the "Riddle Situation" and the "Context Situation" follows Pepicello and Green's discussion of linguistic and metaphorical ambiguity. At the linguistic level, Samson's riddle is doubly ambiguous. Morphological ambiguity is generated by a play on the various parts of speech represented by the alliterated Hebrew morpheme מ.[195]

---

[192]Camp and Fontaine, "Words of Wise" 130.

[193]Camp and Fontaine, "Words of Wise" 130.

[194]Camp and Fontaine, "Words of the Wise" 133–136, first quotation 133, second quotation 135.

[195]Camp and Fontaine, "Words of the Wise" 138–139. Camp and Fontaine do not identify this as "morphological" ambiguity, but such is suggested by their emphasis on the dual uses of מ as a preposition ("from") and a comparative particle ("-er"). This follows Pepicello and Green's insistence that ambiguity can be present in the question or answer segments of the riddle, as Samson's question uses מ unambiguously as a preposition while the answer requires a shift to the comparative usage (139). Ambiguity is signaled to the Philistines by "the remarkable alliteration of the letter מ" in the question and the answer.

Syntactical ambiguity is generated through the use of poetic parallelism, which makes it unclear whether one or two answers are indicated. Metaphorical vagueness arises from the absence of a clear context to which the Philistines may relate the riddle text. Samson distracts his opponents by playing on the innuendo typical of wedding riddles. "The singular answer suggested by the wedding context . . . would presumably have something to do with love or, more likely, sex."[196]

Camp and Fontaine's approach to narrative riddles sets an important precedent for applying folklore models to written texts. As they indicate, such analysis requires a redefinition of "verisimilitude." Here one suspends judgements on "historicity" and evaluates the interactions described in the narrative according to the broader findings of folkloristics. Whether or not Samson ever entered into a verbal duel with thirty Philistines, Judges 14 accurately portrays cross–cultural patterns of riddle performance. This passage may therefore be analyzed as traditional folk performance in service of a broader literary–critical reading, making folkloristics a tool of Narrative Criticism.

Camp and Fontaine's approach clarifies the relationship between the immediate audience of a folk performance and secondary audiences. Riddles in narrative have two audiences: the riddlee, a character or group of characters within the text; and, the composer or narrator's audience, the audience of the narrative. When a narrative episode portrays riddle performance, it creates a dual interaction situation: [X⌣Y]⌣A. Within the story, the characters X

---

[196]Camp and Fontaine, "Words of the Wise" 141. This type of riddle normally suggests a double answer, here one answer explaining eater/strong and another eaten/sweet. Thus the "strong eater" might be the groom or the bride; the "sweet eaten" might be vomit from excessive drinking, semen, or the bride's pre–coital lubrication or post–natal milk. Camp and Fontaine's analysis thus rejects the popular notion that Samson's challenge is a "neck riddle," which cannot be solved without prior knowledge of his experience. Although the situation to which the riddle refers is unclear, the Philistines could discover the answer by focusing on the linguistic ambiguities utilized and by applying "a complex of culturally known associations" between love/marriage, lions, and honey (146). The cultural associations in question are evident in the Philistines' answer at 14:18, which may build on a traditional poetic conception that love is stronger than a lion and sweeter than honey (145). Samson's riddle is thus a well crafted text, "answerable, if exceedingly difficult" (148).

and Y are related in a fictional social setting, a relationship parallel to that obtaining between riddler and riddlee in a "real" performance. At the same time, however, the narrator relates the audience (A) to that performance as a non–participant observer. The narrator's audience takes a role similar to that of the "bystander" of a real performance, a person who may hear and ponder the proposed riddles but who is not the immediate audience of the riddler. In a narrative, both interaction contexts, X⁓Y and [X⁓Y]⁓ A, are strategically manipulated by the narrator. Because the oral narrator speaks aloud on behalf of both herself and the characters in the story, this phenomenon may be referred to as "dual vocalization." The discourse pattern of the dual vocalization of riddles in oral narrative is represented by the following table:

	Speaker	speaks as→	→speaks what→	→to whom
Real World	composer	narrator	the narrative	audience
Story World	narrator	riddler (character 1)	riddle	riddlee (character 2)

Narrative riddles thus operate at two rhetorical levels. This places them at once at two separate positions on Abrahams' "structure of context" spectrum. As noted above, Abrahams considers the riddle a type 1 play genre, a genre which involves direct conversation between participants who fulfill stereotypical roles in a play world. At this level, the riddling session directly involves both performer and audience in the production of the text. When a riddling session is portrayed in a narrative, however, it participates in a "fictive" genre. In these genres, the audience participates in the conflict only vicariously. Narrative riddling sessions thus operate at two levels: the characters in the story are involved in direct and unresolved verbal conflicts in which group norms are tested; at the narrative level, the performer represents both riddler and riddlee to the audience, directing riddles both to the characters in the story and to the audience at once, and then providing the audience with the responses of the riddlee. The narrative audience participates in the riddling session by hearing the riddles but is distanced from the unresolved conflict of the riddling session. In this way, narrative riddling sessions provide catharsis.

In contrast to their progressive treatment of literary–critical issues, Camp and Fontaine's emphasis on "solvability" represents a disappointing return to Taylor's "true" and "false" riddles. Their analysis also echoes Taylor's aesthetic prejudices by associating solvability with literary integrity, stressing that "Samson's riddle is a carefully crafted traditional form" rather than "a 'bad riddle' or [one] easily dismissible as a 'neck riddle.'" Beyond aesthetics, answerability is a generic prerequisite in their analysis: "If Samson's riddle is an answerable one, then the course of events described here [in Judges 14] is quite explicable in terms of folkloristic performance studies."[197] These sentiments indicate the degree to which Pepicello and Green, whose research is cited more than twenty times in Camp and Fontaine's study, have influenced their thinking. This has unfortunate consequences for their analysis, because Samson's riddle falls under Burns' wedding context, while Pepicello and Green's research is based exclusively on leisure–time riddles. Failure to recognize possible differences between these two interaction situations leads Camp and Fontaine to overemphasize the possibility of solution, and to overlook the explicit narrative connection between Samson's unique experience and the riddle text.

It has been difficult for Western scholars to overcome the "criterion of solvability." A corrective response to this overemphasis may begin with a theme developed by Archer Taylor himself. Taylor notes that oftentimes "the same [riddle] question or [true] riddle might with little or no elaboration have several answers."[198] This observation has been highlighted more recently by Edgar Slotkin. Slotkin argues that few riddles "are solvable on any rational ground. That is, few so–called 'true' riddles admit to logical solutions where one and only one answer satisfies the descriptive grid imposed on the riddle topic." When a riddle can arguably refer to more than one referent, how does one determine the "correct" answer? "[M]ost riddles depend for their solution on either inspired guessing or simply knowing the riddle—which is to say, knowing traditions." Indeed, "some riddles are solvable [only] in that they

---

[197]Camp and Fontaine, "Words of the Wise," both quotations 148. Note the similar concern of Crenshaw, *Samson* 114.

[198]Taylor, "Riddle" 131. This explains Taylor's belief that classification must be based solely on the riddle text itself, not the answer.

depend on general or sometimes arcane knowledge."[199] By linking "general" and "arcane" knowledge, Slotkin dissolves much of Taylor's distinction between "folk" riddles and literary or "learned" riddles.

Almost all of the theorists surveyed here specifically acknowledge that some riddles rely on "special" knowledge rather than logical deduction. The fact that Western riddling favors deduction has prompted a number of ingenious maneuvers to prefer logical riddles over a–logical riddles. Taylor refers to a–logical riddles as "false" riddles; Abrahams and Dundes speak of "reverse" riddles; Abrahams refers to these as "wisdom questions"; Maranda calls them "monk's questions"; Pepicello and Green refuse to call them "riddles" at all. Commenting on this unanimity, Slotkin concludes that "we tend to be ethnocentric in supposing that riddles and riddle contests cross–culturally are supposed to involve principles of deduction rather than memorization or some other mental ability."[200] Attacking Taylor's analysis, Pepicello and Green ironically level a devastating critique against themselves:

> If we wish to deal with riddles as traditional oral phenomena, then, we should be suspicious of the literary origin of the term 'true riddle.' Moreover, this notion seems burdened by unwarranted preconceptions and, therefore, incompatible with the dispassionate ideals of scholarly investigation.[201]

The tendency of Western folklorists to make "solvability" a defining feature of the riddle genre simply because Westerners prefer riddles which can be "figured out" is methodologically indefensible. This is especially true in cases where there are no apparent formal or functional differences between these texts and "real," logical riddles.

---

[199]Edgar Slotkin, "Response to Professors Fontaine and Camp," *Text and Tradition: The Hebrew Bible and Folklore* (ed. Susan Niditch; SBLSS; Atlanta, GA: Scholars Press, 1990), all quotations 154. See also Glazier and Glazier, who comment on one Mbeere riddle, "Once again we may be struck by the arbitrariness of the correct answer. The acceptable reply is dictated by the rules of riddling, not by a rule which admits any logical response" ("Ambiguity" 216). In a brief rebuttal to Slotkin, Camp and Fontaine admit that they may have overemphasized the riddle's answerability, but continue to insist that the Philistines could have solved it ("Words of the Wise" 129 n. 2).

[200]Slotkin, "Response to Fontaine and Camp" 154–155.

[201]Pepicello and Green, "Folk Riddle" 16.

The common distinction between "true" and "false" riddles has been facilitated by the lack of a clear definition of "special" knowledge. All knowledge, even "common" knowledge, is at best cultural knowledge, learned by participation in a group. For example, when Taylor observes that many "true" riddles compare their referent to a house or something in the vicinity of a house, whose house is in question? Since different cultures have different conceptions of living environments, this set of themes must be regarded as "special" knowledge, since it belongs to the knowledge of a particular group. On the other hand, a group of scholars from a variety of cultures and language groups may share academic knowledge which hints at the answer to a particular riddle; this, too, must be regarded as special knowledge. Further, it is important to stress that the patterns of logic and deduction cherished in Western riddling are themselves "special knowledge," learned and culturally determined, and therefore fall under the heading of cultural schematics which lie outside the riddle text. All riddles are "false" from the perspective of the person who is not a member of the riddler's knowledge group, however large or limited that group may be.

This point raises a related problem, the general failure of theorists to distinguish groups from subgroups when speaking of "esoteric" knowledge. For example, "monk's questions," puzzles which require the recall of special theological knowledge, are generally treated as "false" riddles because most members of the society may not have access to such knowledge. But while a riddle delivered by one monk to another monk in a monastery may involve knowledge unknown to persons outside the monastery, such knowledge may be universal *within* the monastery. Here the "esoteric" knowledge is common knowledge within the subgroup, making the riddle answerable to members of the subgroup. The scholars surveyed above seem to conceptualize a "group" as a total language or social group, so that any knowledge not possessed by the majority of group members is "arcane." Riddlers, however, do not perform for all members of the group, but for an immediate audience who may share "esoteric" or "secret" knowledge.

To conclude, riddle answers are not necessarily "logical," and are often arbitrary. Most riddle questions can reasonably support many possible answers, which Maranda refers to as "suitable alternatives."[202] What discriminates among these is not the "logic" of the riddle text but the authority of the riddler to dictate that only one possible referent is "correct" at that moment. This fact of riddle performance is obscured by Abrahams', Maranda's, and Pepicello and Green's insistence that the linguistic unit under analysis is a question–and–answer sequence. Maranda and Pepicello and Green can explain how a given answer is the "right" answer for that particular question, but they fail to explain what makes other answers *wrong*. Once the answer to a riddle is known, it becomes predictable; once the answer is known, the "logic" for arriving at that answer can be deduced. But from the perspective of the riddlee and any secondary audience in live riddle performance, terms such as "right" and "wrong" are unrelated to the riddle as a linguistic unit. A "right" answer is any answer the riddler wants, and any answer the riddler does not want is "wrong." Such is the "logic" of riddles.

CONCLUSION: THE RIDDLE AS SPEECH GENRE AND JOHN

Before offering a precise definition of the riddle, it will be helpful to highlight an important point on the nature of Folkloristics and Literary Criticism. No theory of literature or folk performance, or of any specific genre of performance, proceeds from a vacuum. Each theory is thus, to some degree, a description, even if that description encompasses only the theorist's own textual experience. Since every theory of the riddle begins with the observation of texts intuitively identified as "riddles," each study surveyed here is the sum of two variables: the specific corpus under investigation; and, trends in folklore methodology at the time of the investigation.

Both variables are, in their own way, heavily conditioned by situational factors. As outlined in Chapter 3, speech genres are thoroughly situational, dependent on recurring social factors which provide continuity from one performance to the next. As such, different cultures with different social structures may use texts as "riddles" which are formally or logically very different from another group's tradition. To the extent that such is the case, studies of the riddle genre come to divergent conclusions simply by nature of

---

[202]Maranda, "Theory and Practice" 55.

the data under observation. This diversity is magnified by the fact that folklorists, like researchers in any field, approach their data within specific methodological guidelines. It is not surprising, for example, if an anthropological approach to the riddle produces varying results from a linguistic analysis. When both variables are considered, and studies of the riddle apply different methods to different collections, one may expect the type of diversity which the above survey of recent theorists has documented.

Remaining consistent with the definition of speech genres developed in Chapter 3, the "riddle" may be defined as a discourse unit generated in a special performance context, the riddling session. This utterance context is widely distributed both geographically and historically, and riddles may be documented in ancient Judaism and the Greco–Roman world. The riddling session suspends normal conventions of discourse to facilitate the artistic blurring of referents. The speaker, who plays the role "riddler," must propose ambiguous utterances, which the audience, who plays the role "riddlee," may or may not be able to resolve. The participants in this exchange may be "persons to whom other institutionalized expression is denied."[203] The utterances delivered by participants in this speech environment may be spontaneous creations, but are often recompositions of memorized, "traditional" performances. The tone of the interactions is agonistic, and may involve explicit challenges to group beliefs and norms. For this reason, the riddling session serves a cathartic social function, providing entertainment, stress management, or controlled exploration of group values. Riddling sessions often operate within other socially defined interaction contexts, such as weddings, wakes, and initiations. The specific textual forms which arise in this speech environment will depend on the linguistic, social, and performance norms of the group in question.

While no universal surface "form" or "deep structure" may be associated with the riddling session, the approaches surveyed here suggest that this speech environment typically evokes a unique reference system. As text, the "riddle" may be defined as *a concise, interrogative unit of language that intentionally and at once conceals and reveals its referent with a single set of signs*. While "concise" is a relative term, riddles, particularly oral riddles, cannot be as

---

[203]Maranda, "Theory and Practice" 58.

lengthy as other genres because an overextension of confusion would make it impossible for the text to "reveal" its referent. The "interrogative" dimension of the riddle is not a formal feature of the text but an invitation to the audience to focus the blurred reference links. As Pepicello and Green stress, this "blurring," or concealing of the referent, must be intentional and artistic, and can be achieved either by the suggestion of multiple possible referents or by the failure to adequately specify any referent.

To focus this referential blurring, the audience must appeal to at least one of two types of special knowledge: knowledge of cultural items, which may include prior exposure to the riddle in question or to other texts; knowledge of ideological schematics, including group logic systems. The first type of knowledge involves the mental operations memory and recall, while the second type of knowledge involves deduction. The "group" or "culture" which possesses this knowledge may represent the total cultural or language group or a subgroup of which the riddler is a member. If the riddlee is not a member of this group or subgroup, and therefore does not have access to this prerequisite knowledge, she will not be able to answer the riddle.

Because riddles appeal to prerequisite group knowledge, riddle performance assists in the definition of the knowledge boundaries of the riddler's group or subgroup. "Insiders" will be equipped to understand the desired answer, whether or not they are capable of suggesting it. Once revealed, whether by themselves or by the riddler, the answer appears "reasonable" to group members. The "logic" of the answer may not, however, be apparent to "outsiders," who do not possess the knowledge necessary to propose an answer, and who could not understand the basis for determining the "correct" answer without further explanation. In this sense, "riddles establish worth or identity rather than native intelligence."[204] For example, a native Finn, acquainted with the double–bladed Finnish fork plough, would presumably understand why "plough" is a logical answer to Elli Köngäs Maranda's simple riddle, "One pig, two snouts." For sake of her international academic colleagues, who may not be acquainted with the fork plough, Maranda must explain the referent.[205] Here the cultural knowledge prerequisite

---

[204]Crenshaw, *Samson* 100.
[205]Maranda, "Logic" 198.

to understanding the answer serves as a distinguishing feature of the Finnish knowledge community.

It seems reasonable to suggest that the riddle might appeal to a marginalized, heterodox group such as FE's community. As an "antilanguage," riddle performance would help such a community establish ideological boundaries between themselves and "orthodox" Judaism by proposing linguistic puzzles which only "insiders" could solve. If FE uses riddles, they would presumably reiterate group beliefs to "insiders" while illustrating the "ignorance" of "outsiders," who do not share the group's peculiar perspective. But how can one test this hypothesis? As Camp and Fontaine suggest, riddling sessions may be portrayed in narratives such as FG. The fact that riddles are not definable at the surface level of the text, however, raises an obstacle to form–critical analysis. To identify riddles in FG, criteria must be established to determine which units of discourse are intended to represent the artistic concealment of their referent. Four such criteria will be utilized here.

First, the narrator may directly inform the audience in an aside that a particular character is using discourse with intentional referential blurring. John 10:6 is an obvious case, where FE indicates that Jesus has spoken a παροιμία which the crowds did not understand. Less explicitly, at John 2:19 Jesus urges the Jews to "destroy this temple," which he will raise in three days. Since Jesus is standing in the Temple courts, the Jews standing nearby assume that his words refer to the buildings of the Temple complex. FE, however, indicates a second referent at 2:21, the "temple" of Jesus' body.

The second and third criteria involve clues offered by characters within the narrative. A saying is a riddle when the speaking character signals that her words are intentionally ambiguous, either by stating so directly, by offering an "answer," or by providing a riddle performance frame. Samson's challenge, for example, opens with a direct riddling formula (Judg. 14:12) which signals to both the Philistines and the reader that his statement will involve a blurred referent. On the other hand, the riddlee's response may indicate that the referent of a particular remark is confusing and intentionally unclear. For example, at John 7:33 Jesus tells the Jews that he is going away to a place where they cannot come. The Jews' response indicates that this statement could refer to multiple referents, creating confusion (7:35–36).

As a fourth and final criterion, when a character's discourse seems inherently contradictory within the normal conventions of language, or which seems to intentionally challenge conventional logic, the saying may be a riddle. For example, the testimony of the Baptist at John 1:15 is not marked as ambiguous by the narrator or a character, but creates ambiguity by juxtaposing three verbs whose literal meanings are incompatible: Ὁ ὀπίσω μου ἐρχόμενος ἔμπροσθέν μου γέγονεν ὅτι πρῶτός μου ἦν ("the one coming behind me became ahead of me because he was before me"). The tension between the three spatial clauses cannot be immediately resolved at the surface level: if someone "was before" and "has become ahead" of John, how can that person be "coming behind" him? This ambiguity clues the narrator's audience to explore the three clauses in terms of FE's opinion about the relationship between John and Jesus. Since the text does not explicitly identify such language as ambiguous, however, this criterion should be applied with extreme caution.

Chapter 5
The Riddles of Jesus in John

As indicated in Chapter 4, the search for traditional riddles in the surface text of FG is facilitated by four criteria. First, a saying is a riddle if the narrator informs the audience that it is intentionally ambiguous, regardless of its surface form. Any culturally sensitive analysis of oral texts must accept the composer's understanding of the material he or she produces, even when that understanding disrupts neat analytic categories. Second, a speaking character may signal that his or her words are intentionally ambiguous, either by stating so directly or by delivering the message in a discourse context which would naturally suggest that riddles are being used. Third, the audience within the story may respond to a saying with confusion, or may indicate that the saying could reasonably take more than one referent. To assure that the reader lays blame for this confusion on the riddlee rather than the riddler, the narrator may highlight those aspects of the discourse situation which point away from the true answer. Finally, when a character uses vocabulary which seems inherently contradictory within the normal conventions of language or logic, the saying may be a riddle.

Applying these four criteria to FG, the sayings in Table 1 on the following pages may be identified as riddles. Discussion of the specific criteria relevant to each unit will appear in the detailed analysis in the next three chapters. The remainder of this chapter will explore the implications of the presence of these riddles to broader issues in Johannine studies.

Table 1: Riddles in FG

Verses	Text	Criteria	Riddler/ Riddlee
1:15, 30	"The one coming behind me became ahead of me because he was before me"	4	John/ Pharisees(?)
2:4b	"My hour has not yet come"	3	Jesus/Mary
2:16	"Do not make my father's house a house of merchandise"	1, 3	Jesus/ the Jews
2:19	"Destroy this temple and in three days I will raise it"	1, 3	Jesus/ the Jews
3:3, 5	"Unless you are born (ἄνωθεν/of water and spirit) you cannot see the Kingdom of God"	2, 3	Jesus/ Nicodemus
4:7, 10	"Give me a drink"	2, 3	Jesus/ Samaritan
4:20	"Our fathers worshiped on this mountain, and you [Jews] say that in Jerusalem is the place where it is necessary to worship"	4	Samaritan/ Jesus
4:32	"I have food to eat that you don't know about"	2, 3	Jesus/ the Disciples
6:5	"Where will we buy bread?"	1, 3	Jesus/Philip
6:32	"Moses did not give you the bread from heaven; rather, my father gave you the true bread from heaven"	2, 3	Jesus/ the Jews
6:51	"This bread I will give for the life of the world is my flesh"	2, 3, 4	Jesus/ the Jews

Verses	Text	Criteria	Riddler/ Riddlee
7:23	"If a man receives circumcision on Sabbath so that the Law of Moses would not be broken, are you angry with me because I made a whole man healthy on the Sabbath?"	4	Jesus/ the Jews
7:34, 8:21, 13:33	"Where I am going you cannot come"	3	Jesus/ the Jews; Jesus/ the Disciples
7:37–38	"If anyone is thirsty let her come to me, and let the one who believes in me drink"	1	Jesus/ ?
8:4–5	"We caught this woman in adultery, in the very act. In the Law of Moses it says to stone such a woman. What do you say?"	4	Pharisees/ Jesus
8:18	"I witness on behalf of myself and the father who sent me witnesses"	3	Jesus/ the Jews
8:24	"Unless you believe that I am, you will die in your sins"	3, 4	Jesus/ the Jews
8:26	"What I heard from the one who sent me I speak in the world"	1	Jesus/ the Jews
8:31–32	"If you abide in my word, you are truly my disciples, and [then] you will know the truth, and the truth will set you free"	2, 3	Jesus/ the Jews
8:38	"I speak what I have seen with the father, and you also should do what you heard with your father"	2, 3	Jesus/ the Jews

Verses	Text	Criteria	Riddler/ Riddlee
8:51	"Should anyone keep my word, they will not see death unto eternity"	3, 4	Jesus/ the Jews
8:56	"Abraham your father rejoiced to see my day, and he saw it and was glad"	2, 3, 4	Jesus/ the Jews
9:2	"Who sinned, this man or his parents, that he should be born blind?"	4	Jesus/ the Disciples
9:39	"For judgement I came into this world, so that those not seeing would see and those seeing would become blind"	2, 3, 4	Jesus/ the Pharisees
10:1–5	The Parable of the Shepherd and the Strangers	1, 2	Jesus/ the Jews
10:34–36	"Is it not written in your law, 'I said, "You are gods"'? If God said this to those to whom the word of God came, and the Scripture cannot be broken, how can you say to the one whom the father sanctified and sent into the world, 'You blaspheme,' because I said, 'I am son of God'?"	4	Jesus/ the Jews
11:11	"Our friend Lazarus is asleep"	1, 2, 3	Jesus/ the Disciples
11:23	"Your brother will rise again"	3	Jesus/Martha
11:25–26	"The one who believes in me will live even if they die, and anyone who lives and believes in me will not die unto eternity"	3, 4	Jesus/Martha
12:32	"Should I be lifted up from the earth, I will draw all people to myself"	1, 3	Jesus/ the crowd

Verses	Text	Criteria	Riddler/ Riddlee
13:10	"You are clean, but not all of you"	1	Jesus/ the Disciples
13:21	"One of you will betray me"	2, 3	Jesus/ the Disciples
14:4	"You know the way where I am going"	2, 3	Jesus/ the Disciples
14:7	"Now you know him [the father] and have seen him"	2, 3	Jesus/ the Disciples
14:19	"A little while and the world will no longer see me, but you will see me"	2, 3	Jesus/ the Disciples
16:16	"A little while and you will no longer see me, and again a little while and you will see me"	2, 3	Jesus/ the Disciples
21:18	"When you were younger you girded yourself and went about where you wished, but when you grow old you will stretch out your hands and another will dress you and lead you where you do not want to go"	1	Jesus/Peter
21:22	"Should I desire for him [the BD] to remain until I come, what is that to you?"	1	Jesus/Peter

As Table 1 indicates, these four criteria reveal 38 riddles in the present text of FG, three of which appear in more than one context. This list may not be exhaustive. Other large sections of FG in which Jesus speaks of his identity and mission, such as chapters 5 and 15, may include statements which FE understood to be riddles but which cannot be identified by these criteria.

A brief survey of Table 1 will reveal that many of FG's riddles appear in clusters. These clusters coincide with the Johannine dialogues, discussions between Jesus and characters who do not know Jesus' identity. The narrative structure of these dialogues indicates that they are "riddling sessions," controlled performance environments in which characters pose and answer riddles. FG's riddling sessions follow a consistent compositional pattern: 1) Jesus poses a riddle; 2) the riddlee or the narrator indicates confusion; 3) Jesus provides his own, often elaborate, answer; 4) the answer may introduce another riddle; 5) the new riddle again confuses the riddlee; 6) Jesus provides an answer to the new riddle. John 6:26–65, the Bread from Heaven dialogue, is a good illustration of this pattern. After the Jews request a sign that Jesus is truly Son of Man (6:26–31), Jesus engages them in a riddling session which goes through two cycles of the pattern described above.

Riddle 1: "Moses did not give you the bread from heaven; rather, my father gave you the true bread from heaven" (6:32)

    Confusion: "Lord, give us this bread [to eat] forever" (6:34)

    Answer: "I am the bread of life . . . I have come down from heaven" (6:35–40)

        Further Confusion: "Is this not Jesus, the son of Joseph . . .? How does he now say, 'I have come down from heaven?'"(6:41–42)

    Answer: "I am the bread of life . . . This is the bread that comes down from heaven . . ." (6:43–50)

Riddle 2: "The bread I will give for the life of the world is my flesh" (6:51)

    Confusion: "How can this man give us his flesh to eat?" (6:52)

    Answer: ". . . unless you eat the flesh and drink the blood of the Son of Man, you have no life in yourselves . . ." (6:52–58)

        Further Confusion: "This is a hard saying. Who can hear it?" (6:60)

    Answer: ". . . Some of you do not believe" (6:61–64)

The frequency and extent of this outline in FG, and the fact that the riddling session is a common cross–cultural oral performance environment, suggest that this narrative pattern was a key structural element in the Johannine oral archive.

    Chapters 6, 7, and 8 will offer a brief analysis of each riddle which appears on the table above. Before proceeding to exegesis, however, it is relevant to consider the broader implications of this study's conclusions. The recognition that riddles play a prominent role in FG's discourses has a significant impact on two major issues in Johannine scholarship: the nature of "misunderstanding" and irony in FG; and, the potential validity of the developmental and source–critical approaches to FG's dialogues and speeches.

RIDDLES AND "MISUNDERSTANDING"

Many scholars have recognized a pattern of "ambiguity, misunderstanding, and clarification" in the Johannine dialogues, where "a character misunderstands the meaning of Jesus' words, leading Jesus to communicate fuller and deeper truths about himself."[1] The conclusions of this study strongly affirm the notion that misunderstanding and irony are key devices in FG's narrative. In fact, it may be said that *FG's irony and misunderstandings are achieved primarily through the use of riddles and riddling sessions*. To elaborate this point, it will be necessary to explore the narrative strategies of FG's riddles and riddling sessions in more detail.

The riddles in FG generally do not take the form of questions. Their interrogative nature is indicated by the responses of the people to whom they are directed, and by FE's careful attempts to insure that the audience of FG understands the correct answers. Most of these interrogative declarations are "catch riddles." The "catch riddle" is a question in which

> it appears to be possible to guess the referent of the catch [question]. But, as with all catches, the ease of guessing is simply a device to get the other person to make a move that places [her or] him in a vulnerable and often embarrassing position. Catch–riddles . . . usually frustrate expectations by appearing to refer to one object when they actually refer to another.[2]

---

[1]First quotation E. Richard, "Expressions of Double Meaning and Their Function in the Gospel of John," *NTS* 31 (1985) 97–99; second quotation J. Bryan Born, "Literary Features in the Gospel of John (An Analysis of John 3:1–21)," *Directions 17* (1988) 5. For a concise introduction to Johannine misunderstanding see Herbert LeRoy, *Rätsel und Missverständnis* (Bonn: Peter Hanstein, 1968) 45–47, 53–67.

[2]Roger D. Abrahams and Alan Dundes, "Riddles," *Folklore and Folklife: An Introduction* (ed. Richard Dorson; Chicago, IL: University of Chicago Press, 1972) 140.

Catch riddles set their traps in a variety of ways. Two techniques for "catching" the victim are prominent in FG. In some cases, obvious features of the discourse situation prompt Jesus' riddlee to light on the wrong answer. The riddle at John 4:7, for example, confuses the Samaritan woman by playing on the term "water" in a performance environment which includes a well (4:6). The riddle at 8:38 "catches" the Jews by enticing them to assert that Abraham is their father after Jesus has explicitly stated, οἶδα ὅτι σπέρμα Ἀβραάμ ἐστέ ("I know that you are Abraham's seed"; 8:37). In other cases, confusion is generated because the obvious or "catch" answer is absurd (2:19; 3:4, 9; 6:7–10; 6:42, 52; 8:52–53, 57). For example, Jesus "catches" the Jews at 2:19 by standing in the Temple courts and suggesting that in three days he can rebuild "this Temple" (ὁ ναὸς οὗτος), which has been under construction for more than four decades. Similarly, at 8:57 the Jews are amazed that Jesus would claim to have seen Abraham. The classic victim of catch riddles is Nicodemus, who is so completely confused by Jesus that FE has him verbalize the ridiculous proposition that a grown man return to his mother's womb in order to be "born again" (3:4). Even the disciples, returning from their Samaritan shopping trip, fall victim to Jesus' reference to "food" at 4:33, and at 11:12 naturally assume that the "sleeping" Lazarus will wake up. FE does not, however, intend to represent Jesus as a poor riddler. The ease with which Jesus catches his unwitting victims in verbal traps simply magnifies Jesus' rhetorical prowess and their own lack of perception.

The Johannine pattern of "ambiguity, misunderstanding, clarification" is created by the use of catch riddles in Jesus' dialogues. The catch riddle allows the dialogue to move forward when the riddlee's incorrect answer provides Jesus or FE with an opportunity to elaborate on the true meaning of Jesus' words. It is important to note, however, that these "clarifications" do not operate at the level of the story world. Almost by definition, catch riddles do not meet the "criterion of solvability" so valued in western riddling. As a consequence, Jesus' riddles can only be answered by those who have access to the special Johannine interpretation of Jesus and salvation. Jesus' victims, however, are never given access to this information, which leaves their misunderstanding unresolved. For this reason, it seems in many cases that the answers to Jesus' riddles would be more confusing than the riddles themselves.

This phenomenon is illustrated by the encounter between Jesus and Nicodemus in John 3. Nicodemus' inability to explain the terms "born again" and "born of spirit" (3:3–5) leads Jesus, and then FE, into an elaborate discussion of Jesus' nature and Christian rebirth (3:11–21). One must ask, however, to whom this "communicat[ion] of fuller and deeper truths" is directed. Certainly not to Nicodemus, who could scarcely be expected to decode Jesus' highly nuanced language. A similar situation appears with the riddle of the Shepherd and the Stranger in John 10. If the Pharisees cannot answer Jesus' παροιμία ("proverb," "riddle") at 10:1–6, it is difficult to imagine how they could understand anything he offers as the answer to the riddle at 10:7–18. In such cases, the misunderstandings are left unresolved.

Jesus' tendency to further obfuscate matters when his dialogue partners are clearly confused is a key aspect of Johannine irony. FE's use of riddles to create irony is best understood from the perspective of dual vocalization. Within the interaction situation of the story world, Jesus plays the role "riddler" and his audience plays the role "riddlee." At this level, FE speaks as the character Jesus to other characters in the story. At the same time, the oral narrator's voice directs these verbal exchanges to the audience of FG. Thus, in presenting Jesus' *riddles*, the Johannine composer speaks "as Jesus" and "about Jesus" at the same time. In presenting Jesus' *answers*, however, FE does not maintain a solid boundary between these overlapping performance contexts. Jesus' "clarifications" ignore the other characters in the story and directly address the real world audience of FG as if that audience were immediately present to the riddling session. Thus, while Jesus' questions are directed to characters in the story, his answers are directed exclusively to FG's real world audience.

	Audience of FG	Characters in FG
Hear Jesus' Riddles	always	always
Hear Jesus' Answers	always	sometimes
Understand Jesus' Answers	always	never
Hear Narrator's Explanations	always	never

By blurring the two speech contexts into one voice, FE can increase the audience's catharsis by making them participants in the events portrayed in the riddling sessions, allowing them to hear the voice of Jesus more clearly. On the other hand, because the riddlees within the story do not realize that Jesus' words are meaningful at more than one level, they cannot identify the logic underlying his remarks, leaving their "misunderstanding" unresolved.

As several scholars have observed, Johannine irony is founded on this fraternity of special knowledge between FE and the audience of FG. Paul Duke has described FG's irony as an "irony of identity." "Irony of identity" occurs when "one character or group of characters fails to recognize the true identity of another . . . and consequently acts or speaks in ways either grossly inappropriate or accidentally appropriate."[3] Many of Jesus' statements and actions in FG can only be understood by those who know the information about Jesus revealed in the Prologue (John 1:1–18). Jesus' various dialogue partners, who are ignorant of this information, cannot answer his riddles because they respond to Jesus on the basis of erroneous assumptions. These characters serve as "foils for Jesus' revelation of that which is from above . . . blindly unaware of the higher plane," while FG's audience "is invited to the 'upper room' where he or she can share in the fellowship of the implied author."[4] While the characters remain in a world of confusion, FG's audience possesses the hermeneutical key to his riddles. This gives the real world audience an advantage over these characters and allows them to evaluate the character's incorrect responses. FE guides this evaluation through the use of intrusive commentary, reporting confusion when the riddlee makes no direct response (10:6, "they did not know of what he spoke"), offering answers for his audience when Jesus does not (2:21–22, "but he said this concerning the temple of his body"), and indicating who is winning the riddling contest (8:30, "as he said these things, many believed in him"). Jesus, FE, and FE's audience thereby "know" what the others do not.

The ironic tension between the knowledge possessed by Jesus' victims and the knowledge possessed by FG's audience is specifically highlighted from

---

[3]Paul Duke, *Irony in the Fourth Gospel* (Atlanta GA: John Knox, 1985) 100.

[4]R. Alan Culpepper, *Anatomy of the Fourth Gospel: A Study in Literary Design* (Philadelphia, PA: Fortress, 1983) 168.

time to time in the narrative. On several occasions Jesus directly informs his opponents that they do not understand his riddles because they lack essential information. Nicodemus, for example, cannot answer riddles which concern "heavenly things" because he is "earthly" (John 3:12), and at 8:23 Jesus frankly warns the Jews that they are doomed to lose the riddling contest because "you are from below, but I am from above; you are from this world, but I am not from this world." Because of this, although every interaction between Jesus and the "Jews" or "Pharisees" in FG involves riddle performance, the Jews are never able to comprehend his words. Throughout much of the narrative this special knowledge is also hidden from Jesus' followers, who serve as riddlee on twelve occasions but are generally no more successful at answering his riddles than his enemies. This places FG's audience in a consistently superior position, allowing them to judge things from the otherwordly perspective of the Johannine Jesus.

RIDDLES AND JOHANNINE SOURCE CRITICISM

As noted in earlier chapters, the basic premises of the present study challenge many of the established *methods* of Johannine Source Criticism. It may now be said that the conclusions of this study challenge many source–critical *conclusions* as well. Many of the aporias (apparent narrative or theological discrepancies) on which such studies depend are naturally resolved by their association with riddles or riddling sessions. The "difficulties and tensions" created by most of these aporias are actually carefully constructed to generate intentional ambiguity. This conclusion has significant implications for several major issues in Johannine studies, two of which will be explored in the remainder of this chapter: the developmental approach to FG's composition-history; and, the genre and compositional history of John 13–17.

RIDDLES AND FG'S "DEVELOPMENT"

The recognition that many of the Johannine dialogues are riddling sessions raises serious questions about the developmental approach, which sees the current text of FG as the product of a lengthy process of composition and revision. The developmental approach treats the aporias in FG as evidence of a series of revisions which adapted the text to the developing needs of the Johannine community.[5] The hermeneutical theory behind this method was established in J. Louis Martyn's 1968 *History and Theology in the Fourth Gospel*, which argues that John 9 must be read at two levels, the life of Jesus and the experience of FE's community. This episode is particularly important because it reflects a pivotal crisis in the community's experience, their expulsion from the synagogue, which shifted FE's theology toward a soteriological dualism ("children of God" vs. "the world") and consequently forced a significant revision of the Johannine Jesus tradition.[6]

Martyn's model has been further developed in several significant studies. Raymond Brown, whose *Anchor Bible Commentary* anticipated Martyn's conclusions, traces the development of the Johannine community from Palestine to the second century in *The Community of the Beloved Disciple*. Brown's discussion focuses on theological anomalies in FG: "high christology next to low christology, realized eschatology next to final eschatology, individualism next to stress on community." These tensions reveal FE's "synthetic" thinking and continual editing of the tradition in light of community experience.[7] John Painter also detects community history

---

[5]Proponents of this approach differ in their understanding of the base material at the earliest stage of this evolution. Raymond Brown sees this earliest layer as "a body of [oral] traditional material pertaining to the words and works of Jesus" which began to take written form shortly before the first edition of FG (AB 1.xxxiv–xxxv); *The Community of the Beloved Disciple: The Life, Loves, and Hates of an Individual Church in New Testament Times* [New York, NY: Paulist Press, 1979] 27–28). John Painter agrees with Brown, stressing that this underlying tradition cannot be reconstructed from the present text of FG (*The Quest for the Messiah: The History, Literature and Theology of the Johannine Community* [2nd ed.; Nashville, TN: Abingdon, 1993] 28). By contrast, Martyn, the doctoral advisor for Robert Fortna's *The Gospel of Signs*, argues that a distinct, apparently written signs source underlies all subsequent editions of FG (*The Gospel of John in Christian History: Essays for Interpreters* [New York, NY: Paulist Press, 1978] 28–32).

[6]J. Louis Martyn, *History and Theology in the Fourth Gospel* (2nd ed.; Nashville, TN: Abingdon, 1979) 30, 37–41; *Christian History* 102–107.

[7]Brown, *Community* discussion 51–54, quotation 51. For example, statements indicating a "high Christology" emerge from a period after "a group of Jews of anti–Temple views and their Samaritan converts" entered the community, while statements which espouse a "low Christology" illustrate the community's thinking before that time (43–45).

behind FG's aporias and uses this history as a key to compositional development. FG's dialogues evolved as FE "transformed the traditional [oral] stories into quest stories because he perceived the turmoil of human life as a quest and Jesus as the fulfillment of the quest." At each stage in the community's life the discourses were expanded to reflect FE's theological concerns.[8]

The present study calls for a careful reconsideration of the developmental approach to FG's discourses by indicating that these passages, as riddling sessions, evidence a high degree of structural unity. Many of the "narrative difficulties" which the developmental approach detects in these dialogues are actually intentional devices which create or sustain ambiguity. FG's dialogues are indeed difficult to outline in terms of conventional narrative logic, but such difficulties are resolved when the dialogues are outlined as Johannine riddling sessions. Further, the division of specific speeches into stages of composition on the basis of "theological anomalies" despite their overall structural unity seems dangerously subjective. Theological "discrepancies" in the speeches of FG may actually represent intentional challenges to ideological taxonomies, or may simply illustrate that FE's personal theology was less systematic and more open to ambiguity than modern western readers would prefer.

For illustration, the conclusions of the present study may be compared with Raymond Brown's analysis of the Light of the World discourse (John 8:12–58). Brown highlights the aporias in the passage, which seem to suggest several stages of revision. The staging remarks at John 8:21 ("again he said to them") and 8:31 ("then Jesus said to the Jews who had believed in him") provide natural breaks in the discourse, but the sequence within each section is "far from simple" and often involves "doublets of other discourses." Doublets and parallels with other speeches in the first subsection, 8:12–20,

---

[8]Painter, *Quest* 212. Painter largely follows Brown's reconstruction of the community's history and suggests three major stages in the development of FG: oral tradition; three written editions published by FE; final redaction (66–79). The first edition of FG was written sometime before 70 CE and "contains the traditions shaped in the period of open dialogue with the synagogue concerning the messiahship of Jesus." The second edition was written after the community's expulsion from the synagogue; the third edition "manifests issues bound up with a growing schism within the Johannine community" (66).

lead Brown to conclude that this passage "is a composite and must have had a complicated literary history before it took its present form." The same is the case with the second subsection, 8:21–30. Parallels between these verses and John 7 lead Brown to ask, "Can there be any doubt that John has preserved two different forms [chaps. 7 and 8] of the same scene?" The genitive absolute at 8:30 ("*as he said these things*, many believed in him") is rare in FG and Brown concludes that it must be "an editor's device." Once this verse was added to "break up the discourse" into "more tractable units," it became necessary to rename Jesus' audience before the speech continued. This was achieved by the composer of 8:31, who made the "believing Jews" of 8:30 the audience of Jesus' subsequent remarks. This person, perhaps "the final redactor" of FG, was apparently unaware that "believing Jews" are an oxymoron in FG. The same editor may be responsible for the insertion of v. 35, "a once independent saying from the Johannine tradition," into Jesus' discussion of slavery in the third section of the Light discourse.[9] In Brown's view, then, John 8:12–58 is rife with structural problems which indicate a complex compositional history.

The problems Brown highlights disappear when the Light Discourse is understood as a Johannine riddling session. The first subsection which Brown identifies, John 8:12–20, opens with Jesus' claim to be "the light of the world" (8:12) and a brief defense of the validity of this claim. Jesus then begins a riddling session which occupies the rest of this subsection and the entirety of the next subsection, 8:21–30. This reading provides a clear and coherent outline which accommodates the problematic features of the text:

Riddle 1: "I witness on behalf of myself and the father who sent me witnesses" (8:18)
Confusion: "Who is your father?" (8:19)
Answer: "You do not know me nor my Father . . ." (8:19)
Riddle 2: "Where I am going you cannot come" (8:21)
Confusion: "He will not kill himself, will he?" (8:22)
Answer: "You are from below, I am from above . . ." (8:23)

---

[9]Raymond Brown, *The Gospel According to John* (AB; New York, NY: Doubleday, 1966), all quotations 1.342-355.

Riddle 3: **"Unless you believe that I am, you will die in your sins"** (8:24)
Confusion: "Who are you?" (8:25)
Answer: "What have I said from the beginning?" (8:25)
Riddle 4: **"What I heard from the one who sent me I speak in the world"** (8:26)
Confusion: Narrator—they did not know he spoke about the Father (8:27)
Answer: "when you have lifted up the Son of Man, then you will know that I am . . ." (8:28–29)

Verse 30 concludes the episode with a narrative aside which indicates Jesus' victory over the Pharisees (8:13): "As he said these things, many believed in him." The repetition of themes which Brown detects within the subsections of the dialogue are due to the fact that all four riddles explore related facets of Jesus' heavenly identity. Whether John 8:12–58 was taken from a written source or an oral tradition, there is no reason to conclude that this passage is the product of a complex redactional process.

THE COMPOSITION AND GENRE OF JOHN 13–17

FE closes Jesus' public ministry with the grim admission that "even though he had done so many signs before them they still were not believing him" (John 12:37). The next five chapters, John 13–17, show Jesus' last–ditch effort to insure that at least the disciples recognize his true identity. Jesus does not reveal himself to the disciples with more signs, but through a long discourse which explores his identity and the mission which the disciples will continue after his death. Most scholars today believe that these chapters, or at least portions of them, are patterned after a widely attested ancient genre, the "farewell address." John 13–17 is therefore generally referred to as "the Farewell."

Among the discourse sections of FG, the Farewell has probably received the most concentrated attention from source–critical scholarship. John 13–17 is filled with the sort of literary problems and theological tensions which facilitate source reconstruction on the basis of aporias. These issues have generated a vast literature which cannot be surveyed here. For convenience, the present study will review the methods and conclusions of Fernando Segovia, who produced a series of key studies on the Farewell between 1981 and 1991. Segovia's research is typical of many recent studies of the Farewell, and is notable for its thorough interaction with other scholarship. His work will therefore serve as a representative foil for the present study. It will be important here to consider both the method espoused in Segovia's work and his overall conclusions about the genre of John 13–17.[10] The present study will challenge some facets of Segovia's research and positively build on others.

Segovia's earlier studies of the Johannine Farewell utilize the tools of Redaction Criticism. This is an ambitious project, for Redaction Criticism inherently depends on the comparative analysis of written texts, but very few parallels exist between John 13–17 and other extant gospels. Segovia's source separation therefore focuses on "the many difficulties and unevennesses" in the present text of FG as keys to its compositional history.[11] The aporias with which Segovia is concerned fall into two categories, narrative difficulties and theological tensions.

Segovia frequently highlights the narrative difficulties in the current text of John 13–17. The most significant problem is John 14:31c, "Arise, let us go from here." This is, in Segovia's view, a "clearly concluding statement" which should be followed by 18:1–2 "sequentially and contextually." In the present text of FG, however, the verse inexplicably introduces "a new discourse."[12] John 15–17 must therefore be explained as a redactional addition to the original Farewell, which encompassed only John 13:31–14:31. Further, it is obvious that chapters 15–17 are not a single coherent unit, for "there are too many abrupt and unexpected transitions to warrant a single author." Indeed, one must suggest that several interpolations were added to the original

---

[10]Segovia does not discuss John 17 in any of the works cited here, and at times distinguishes this chapter from the Farewell Address. His most exhaustive study, *The Farewell of the Word: The Johannine Call to Abide* (Minneapolis, MN: Fortress, 1991), states that "John 13:31–16:33 functions as a self–contained and coherent prelude to the prayer," implying that the prayer itself is not an aspect of the genre (283, n. 1). In the Preface to the same volume he anticipates a "subsequent literary–rhetorical reading of John 17" which will "engage the text at the level of intercultural criticism" (ix, see 57, 283, 283 n. 1).

[11]Fernando Segovia, *Love Relationships in the Johannine Tradition: Agapē/Agapan in I John and the Fourth Gospel* (SBLDS; Chico, CA: Scholars Press, 1982) 1.

[12]Fernando Segovia, "The Theology and Provenance of John 15:1–17" (*JBL* 101 [1982] 115; see *LRJT* 82.

Farewell at various points. These smaller units may also be identified on the basis of aporias. John 15:1–17, for example, opens with the figure of the Vine, which is "totally unexpected after the concluding command of 14:31c." This interpolation must end at 15:17, for the love command, which figures so prominently in this section, disappears after that verse, and the theme of the world's hatred, which is taken up at 15:18–16:4a, "is not anticipated at all in the preceding verses."[13] These literary aporias provide evidence that later discourses were interpolated into the original Farewell to serve the developing theological needs of the Johannine community.

Segovia undergirds these conclusions by highlighting the theological aporias in John 13–17. Noting the heavy emphasis on relationships in these chapters (Jesus—God; Jesus—the world; Jesus—disciples; God—disciples; disciples—world; etc.), Segovia proposes to analyze the Johannine view of "love relationships." Such a study reveals "theologically different" notions of love relationships in FG and 1 John. Under "the presupposition that 1 John was written later than the [Fourth] Gospel and that it comes from a different hand," these theological differences suggest an evolving perspective on love in the Johannine community. One may therefore speculate that those portions of the Farewell which express the view of love adopted in 1 John were added to FG by a contemporary of the author of 1 John.[14] Following this premise, Segovia concludes that John 13:34–35 and 15:1–17 are interpolations into an earlier document. The ethical and doctrinal concerns raised in 15:1–17 are parallel to those expressed in 1 John, and 13:34–35 is so similar in content to 15:1–17 that it "either stands or falls" with the larger unit.[15] On the other hand, these two passages seem to advocate a doctrine of love which is inconsistent with that of other sections of FG.[16] Combining theological and literary aporias,

---

[13]Segovia, "John 15:1–17" 117–118, quotations 118; see also *LRJT* 97, 100. Segovia identifies 15:18–16:4a as another "originally independent discourse" on the subject of the world's hatred but does not associate this passage with the author of John 15:1–17 ("John 15:1–17" 118 n. 11).

[14]Segovia, *LRJT*, first quotation 23, second quotation 22..

[15]Segovia, *LRJT* 97–125.

[16]Segovia, *LRJT* 134–135. Segovia analyzes four types of love relationship: the disciples' love for Jesus; the Father's love for the disciples; Jesus' love for the disciples; and, Jesus' love for the Father. A comparison of the presentation of these relationships in

Segovia concludes that John 13–17 as a composite text which can be separated into distinct literary strata.[17]

Segovia's most recent and most significant study of John 13–17, *The Farewell of the Word*, adopts a somewhat different strategy, integrating the tools of Redaction Criticism with those of Genre Criticism to accommodate both the diachronic and synchronic dimensions of the text.[18] While many studies have attempted to demonstrate that John 13–17 is patterned as an ancient farewell address, Segovia's analysis is the most sophisticated to date. His conclusions depend on what he calls a "maximalist approach" to genre. In Genre Criticism, the terms "maximalist approach" and "minimalist approach"

13:34–35 and 15:1–17 with the rest of FG reveals major thematic differences. In respect to Category 1, elsewhere in FG "the [disciples'] love of Jesus is nothing other than faith in Jesus." This is quite different from the presentation of John 13:34–35, 15:1–17, which focus instead on the ethical expression of one's love for Jesus in the love one shows to other believers. FE addresses Categories 2 and 3 (the Father's love and Jesus' love for the disciples) exclusively in terms of the sending of the Paraclete, a "post–resurrectional activity." But in John 13:34–35 and 15:1–17 the love of God is expressed exclusively in terms of a past historical event, Jesus' death. The presentation of Category 4, Jesus' love for the Father, elsewhere in FG is also quite different from the presentation of that theme in the disputed passages. John 14:31 presents Jesus' love for the Father in terms of his obedience to the Father's command that he die. John 15:1–17, however, stresses that Jesus' love for and obedience to God should be the foundation for love in the community, a theme which FG does not address (*LRJT* 156–160).

[17]More recently, Segovia has highlighted the overall unity of the text ("The Tradition History of the Fourth Gospel," *Exploring the Gospel of John*, Ed. R. Alan Culpepper and C. Clifton Black [Louisville, KY: Westminster John Knox, 1996]). There Segovia states that "by and large I find that the proposed aporias [in the Farewell] can be readily explained in other—and, I would add, simpler—ways" (185–186, quotation 186, see also 186 n. 12). While he still recognizes the presence of "contradictions . . . tensions . . . dissenting voices in the text," "I regard such other 'aporias' as neither dismantling the overall unity and coherence of the text—whether at the literary, rhetorical, or ideological level—nor requiring the introduction of constitutive literary layers, but rather as points of tension in the construct" (186).

[18]In terms of the synchronic dimension, one must analyze the present text as a coherent literary unit with specific rhetorical objectives; in terms of the diachronic dimension, one must speculate on the "process of accretion and expansion" which produced the present text and which explains its many aporias (*FOW* 49).

represent two theories about how texts should be categorized. A "minimalist approach" to genre would insist that every one of a small number of typical motifs must appear in a work before that work can be considered a member of a particular genre. For example, the minimalist approach might identify only five characteristic features of ancient farewell discourses, but would insist that all five must appear in John 13–17 before that passage can be considered a farewell. A "maximalist approach," on the other hand, would offer a longer list of typical motifs but would not insist that all must appear in every member of the genre. For example, the maximalist approach might identify fifteen characteristic features of ancient farewell discourses, but would consider John 13–17 a farewell even if only seven or eight of these features appear in that text. The maximalist approach, then, allows for more variation among the individual members of a genre.

Following the maximalist approach, Segovia identifies nine typical features of ancient farewell discourses and observes that "six appear prominently in John 13:31–16:33," making that passage a farewell. These six features are: 1) the announcement of the hero's approaching death; 2) parenentic exhortations to those who will outlive the dying hero; 3) prophecies or predictions of what will occur after the hero's death; 4) reflection on major events from the hero's life; 5) establishment of the hero's heirs or successors; and, 6) final instructions for the hero's family or followers.[19] The presence of these features in John 13–17 suggests that FE has combined and revised several earlier texts to produce a typical farewell address.

The present study will attempt to answer two questions in light of Segovia's research. First, is it possible to conceive of John 13–17 as a unified composition? In other words, is it necessary to conclude that the apparent aporias in the text represent redactional seams? Second, what is the genre of this passage, and how do the narrative strategies of the text relate to this genre? In answer to the first question, it will be shown that the current text of John 13–17, or at least of John 13–16, is a unified riddling session which does not include a sufficient number of aporias to support a separation of sources. The

---

[19]Segovia, *FOW* 308–316, quotation 308. Segovia appeals to both Jewish and Greco–Roman texts to establish these nine constituent motifs. For Segovia's specific understanding of the "maximalist approach" see 18–20, 309.

"aporias" which have been highlighted by Segovia and others are essential features of this riddling session, and are the key means by which ambiguity and tension are generated in the narrative. In answer to the second question, it will be shown that the words of Jesus in John 13–17 operate at two narrative levels, and that the passage is a "farewell" at only one of these levels. The discrepancy between these two narrative levels generates the notable ambiguity, misunderstanding, and irony in the passage.

Putting aside for a moment the farewell motifs in John 13–17, the text presents a series of seven riddles and their answers (13:10, 13:21, 13:33, 14:4, 14:7, 14:19, 16:16). These riddles are held together in the typical pattern for Johannine riddling sessions. In each case, Jesus makes an ambiguous statement which confuses the disciples. He then responds to their confusion with an obtuse answer, followed by another riddle.

The Footwashing (13:5–12)

Riddle 1: "You (pl., ὑμεῖς) are clean, but not all of you" (13:10)

Confusion: Narrator—"For already he knew the one betraying him" (13:11)

Answer: "Do you know what I have done for you . . .?" (13:12–20)

Riddle 2: "One of you will betray me" (13:21)

Confusion: Narrator—"The disciples were looking at each other, wondering about whom he spoke" (13:22); Peter—"Who might it be of whom he speaks?" (13:24)

Answer: "The one for whom I dip the morsel and give it to him. . . . Now is the Son of Man glorified . . ." (13:26–32)

Riddle 3: "Where I am going you cannot come" (13:33)

Confusion: Peter—"Where are you going? Why can't I follow you now?" (13:36, 37)

Answer: "you will deny my three times. . . should I go and prepare a place for you, I will come back and return you to myself" (13:38–14:3)

Riddle 4: "You know the way where I am going" (14:4)

Confusion: Thomas—"Lord, we do not know where you are going; how can we know the way?" (14:5)

Answer: "I am the way, the truth, and the life . . ." (14:6)

Riddle 5: "Now you know him [the father] and have seen him" (14:7)

Confusion: Philip—"Lord, show us the father, and that will be enough for us" (14:8)

> *Answer: "The one who has seen me has seen the father. . . . I will not leave you orphans. I will come to you."* (14:9–18)

Riddle 6: "A little while and the world will no longer see me, but you will see me" (14:19)

Confusion: Judas (not Iscariot)—"Lord, what has happened that you are going to reveal yourself to us but no longer to the world?" (14:22)

> *Answer:* "If anyone loves me they will keep my word. The one who does not love me does not keep my words. . . . Everything the father has is mine; because of this I said that he takes from me and proclaims it to you." (14:23–16:15)

Riddle 7: "A little while and you will no longer see me, and again a little while and you will see me" (16:16)

Confusion: Disciples—"What is this that he says to us? . . . We do not know what he is saying" (16:17–18)

> *Answer:* "You now have sorrow, but you will see me again and your heart will rejoice. . . . I have spoken these things to you in riddles (ἐν παροιμίαις) . . . I came from the father and entered the world. Again I am leaving the world and going to the father" (16:19–28)

Understanding: Disciples—"Now you are speaking openly (ἐν παρρησίᾳ) and you speak riddles (παροιμίαν) no longer. . . . We believe that you have come from God"(16:29–30)

Prayer for the Believing Disciples (17:1–26)

Throughout this final riddling session, Jesus builds tension by answering the riddles only partially and by refusing to reveal critical information about his identity and proposed departure. Ambiguity arises because his statements about his heavenly origin, of which the disciples are unaware, are cloaked in language which could also be interpreted in reference to his earthly identity. After the hermeneutical key to all the riddles in FG is revealed directly at 16:28, Jesus closes the session with a long prayer for the disciples, now true believers.

The understanding that John 13–17 is an extended riddling session sheds light on the enigmatic John 14:31c, "Arise, let us go from here." The verse is admittedly awkward, for the command to depart seems inconsistent with the fact that Jesus continues to speak for three more chapters. Segovia highlights this inconsistency, referring to 14:31c as a "clearly concluding statement" and noting that the sudden appearance of the "Vine and Branches" parable is "abrupt" in its present context.[20] Even D. A. Carson calls John 14:31c "the major structural challenge of the entire [farewell] discourse."[21] Aside from the suggestion that Jesus and the disciples left the room and continued their discussion on the road, is there any way in which John 14:31c could fit a unified model of the compositional structure of the Farewell? Specifically, does this verse play a natural role in the larger riddling session?

The recognition that John 13–17 is a unified riddling session suggests that John 14:31c does, indeed, serve a specific narrative function which is consistent with the movement of the Farewell. Despite all appearances, the verse is not a stage direction, for FG's narrator, notably intrusive elsewhere, does not indicate that Jesus and the disciples have actually left the room before 18:1. It is also difficult to understand how this statement could be, as Segovia suggests, the conclusion of the original Farewell, for it does not report Jesus' death and in fact implies that he will remain active. In the context of a riddling session, however, John 14:31c clearly functions to further confuse the disciples. The preceding verse, 14:30, summarizes everything Jesus has said up to this point: "I will not speak much more with you for the ruler of this world is coming" (14:30). The disciples could not be surprised at this, for the entire discussion (from their perspective) has elaborated the theme of Jesus' betrayal and escape. But 14:31c suddenly contradicts everything Jesus has said: after stressing that he is about to abandon them, Jesus now tells them to come with him! At the very least, this creates further uncertainty about the time frame of Jesus' departure. The disciples' confusion would be heightened by the "Vine and Branches" parable which immediately follows (15:1–17), for this passage urges them to "remain" (μένω) in Jesus and suggests that their

---

[20]Segovia, "John 15:1–17" 115, quotation here; *FOW* 24–25.

[21]D. A. Carson, *The Gospel According to John* (Grand Rapids, MI: Eerdmans, 1991) 477.

bond of friendship with him will continue. From the disciples' perspective, then, John 14:31c–15:17 is abrupt and inconsistent with Jesus' previous remarks. Rather than suggesting a literary seam, this abrupt transition reinforces the ambiguity which has been building throughout the riddling session, leaving the disciples bewildered about the true nature of Jesus' departure.

It may be reasonably argued, then, that John 13–17 follows the typical outline for a Johannine riddling session and therefore evidences a high degree of rhetorical unity. The literary and theological tensions which appears in these chapters seem be used in an intentional way to generate and sustain ambiguity, as the disciples attempt to discover Jesus' true origins and impending departure. In order to highlight the specific means by which this ambiguity is achieved in the narrative, it will be necessary to turn to the second problem mentioned above, the genre of John 13–17.

While John 13–17 is structured as a riddling session, it also bears a strong resemblance to ancient farewell addresses. As noted, Segovia associates John 13–17 with other ancient farewells on the basis of a "maximalist approach" to genre. The view of text production and speech genres advocated in this study would combine elements of the maximalist and minimalist approaches. In support of Segovia, the maximalist approach more accurately reflects the creative process by which human beings produce texts, even in cases where an author is explicitly attempting to write in a certain genre. Genre Criticism is descriptive rather than prescriptive, and for this reason it is rare for any text to evidence every constituent feature of its genre. At the same time, however, Roman Jakobson's discussion of the "dominant" must be taken into account. While no text will evidence every feature of a given genre, certain generic motifs will tend to dominate the development of texts in that genre. These dominant motifs will therefore be more important than secondary motifs for purposes of categorization and analysis. For example, one might observe that a certain genre includes fifteen typical features. The maximalist approach would suggest that only seven or eight of these features need to appear in a text before it can be considered a member of that genre. But one or two of these fifteen features may be dominant, making them critical elements which *must* appear in *every* member of the genre. For this reason, it may be necessary to prioritize the constituent motifs one would expect to find in texts of that genre.

Under the guise of a maximalist approach, Segovia does not discuss which farewell motifs are most important to the farewell genre and which are optional. He seems to suggest that all are optional, and that a sufficient number of any combination of farewell motifs would make John 13–17 a farewell discourse. But at least one of the generic features which Segovia identifies in ancient farewell speeches must be considered a dominant motif: the announcement of the hero's approaching death. The death announcement provides the overriding theme of departure and postures the audience to interpret the speech which follows as the hero's last words.[22] In fact, all of the other motifs which Segovia associates with the farewell genre depend on the death announcement: parenentic exhortations are given because the hero knows that his successors must continue without his guidance; prophecies speak explicitly of what will happen after the hero is gone; events of the past find closure in the hero's present death; heirs or successors must be chosen to continue the hero's work or heritage; final instructions frequently address the hero's unfinished business or burial plans.[23] One could reasonably say that the death announcement is the lynchpin of a farewell address.

Considering the crucial role of the death announcement in ancient farewells, one is surprised to discover that the death announcement in John 13–17 is, in Segovia's words, "implicit and indirect," being "presented in largely metaphorical terms . . . (for example, glorification and departure)." It is hard to see why the author of these chapters, who obviously desired to cloak the last words of Jesus in the familiar language of a farewell, does not have Jesus make an explicit statement near the beginning of the speech that he is about to die. Segovia attempts to explain this by identifying a number of "explicit references" to Jesus' death throughout the discourse, namely,

---

[22]See Genesis 48:21–49:2; Joshua 23:2, 14; 1 Kings 2:2; Josephus, *AJ* 4.315–331, 7.383–391; *Test. 12 Patr.* 1; *As. Mos.* 1.

[23]The same may be said of the three farewell motifs which Segovia does not find in John 13–16: the hero's *prayer* generally relates to the needs of the successors; *burial instructions* are necessary in light of the hero's impending death; and the "*promises and vows requested of the gathering*" insure that the hero's instructions will be observed (*FOW* 309).

13:31–32, 33a–b; 14:2–3a, 19a, 25–30; 16:4b–5a, 7a–b, 16–20, 28.²⁴ But a
cursory review will reveal that these texts refer to Jesus' death "explicitly" only
when viewed from one particular perspective, the post–resurrection perspective
of FE's audience. From the perspective of the disciples, none of these verses
would even indirectly suggest that Jesus is about to die.

At John 13:31–32, Jesus declares, "Now the son of man is glorified and
God is glorified in him." While the reader might associate this glorification
with Jesus' return to his heavenly abode, the disciples do not even know the
identity of Jesus' father, much less that this "glorification" must involve Jesus'
death. In fact, since their faith is, as Segovia notes, "correct but incomplete"
at this point, it is difficult to imagine what the term "glorification" could
possibly mean to them. The second text Segovia cites, 13:33 ("where I am
going you cannot come"), simply repeats a riddle that Jesus has offered on two
previous occasions. Even though the Jews had earlier interpreted this as a
possible reference to Jesus' suicide (8:21–22), the disciples clearly do not see
it as a death announcement, for Peter interrupts Jesus to ask, "Lord, where are
you going? Why can't I follow you now?" (13:36–37). The closest thing to
a death announcement in the early stages of the Farewell appears in the
discussion about the traitor at 13:18–30. But strangely, the disciples do not
view even the direct predictions of betrayal or Judas' sudden departure as
signals for Jesus' impending demise.

The same may be said of the texts Segovia mentions in chapters 14 and
16. John 14:2–3 ("I am going to prepare a place for you") builds on the
thought of 13:33 by suggesting that Jesus will take the disciples with him to
dwell in his father's house. They clearly do not understand this as a reference
to his upcoming death, for Thomas asks him for directions to this place so they
can meet him there (14:5). It is unclear how the disciples could understand
14:19a ("a little while and the world will no longer see me, but you will see
me; because I live you will also live") as a reference to Jesus' death, since that
saying plainly states that both he and they will continue living. The closest
thing to an "explicit" death announcement in 14:25–30 is the cryptic statement
that Jesus is going away to see his father, a remark which could not be very
significant to those who do not know who Jesus' father is and therefore would

---

²⁴Segovia, *FOW* 309–310, both quotations 309.

not understand the implication of such a visit. The same is true of 16:4–5, where Jesus says he is going to see the one who "sent him." In light of several earlier comments (5:37–38; 8:18, 26), the disciples could only see this as parallel to 14:25–30 and at best would understand both statements to mean that Jesus intends to go home and withdraw from public life. Hence, at 16:7, "It is better for you that I go away" would suggest to them that Jesus intends to go back home to his father, wherever that may be. Finally, Jesus' statement at 16:16, "A little while and you will no longer see me, and again a little while and you will see me," which appears almost at the end of the Farewell rather than the beginning, is clearly not understood as a death announcement. At this point the disciples explicitly complain that they cannot understand what Jesus is talking about (16:17–18).

All of these verses are "explicit" references to Jesus' death only for those who already expect Jesus to leave the world and return to God. While there are a number of death announcements in John 13–17, all of them are directed exclusively to the second rhetorical level of the narrative, the audience of FG, rather than the first rhetorical level of the narrative, the disciples in the story. Jesus does not explicitly announce his upcoming death to the disciples until the very end of the speech, when he reveals to them what the audience of FG already knows: "I came from the Father and entered into the world; again I am leaving the world and going to the Father" (16:28). This statement clearly represents a breakthrough, for the disciples now finally understand "that you came from God" (16:30).

Segovia notes that narrative rhetoric works indirectly, touching its real world audience only as that audience observes characters in the story. In the case of John 13–17, the character Jesus speaks words of comfort and instruction to other characters, the disciples, but these words are always overheard by the real world audience of FG.[25] Segovia does not, however, address the relationship between this dual vocalization of Jesus' words and the generic features of John 13–17. A closer look at this relationship will reveal that the author of this passage is using two different rhetorical strategies at once, one strategy to guide Jesus' discussion with the disciples and another strategy to guide the real world audience's observation of that discussion. At

---

[25]Segovia, *FOW* 300.

"the extraliterary level of the author and intended audience [of FG]," Jesus' words follow the familiar pattern of a farewell discourse, in which Jesus' statements about departure and sudden demands for loyalty and love are perfectly coherent.[26] But unlike most of the other farewells in ancient literature, nothing before John 16:28 indicates to the characters in the story, the disciples, that Jesus has only a few hours left to live. They therefore do not suspect that these are his last words until the speech is almost over.

As a result of this dual vocalization, John 13–17 is both a riddling session and a farewell at the same time. This tension creates the irony of identity which characterizes the passage, for Jesus' remarks make perfect sense in the context of a farewell but remain ambiguous outside that context. To guide the audience of FG, FE rehearses the most significant points of the Prologue at 13:1–3, just before the Farewell begins. Unlike this audience, the disciples do not know a) where Jesus comes from, b) the identity of Jesus' true father, or c) that Jesus must die in order to return to the one who sent him. This explains why the disciples cannot understand any of Jesus' remarks before 16:28—they have not been given the special information which one must possess in order to comprehend Jesus' words and answer his riddles.

This understanding of John 13–17 clarifies the relationship between the Farewell and the Book of Signs (John 2–12). The Book of Signs is a story of Jesus' self–revelation. The object of this revelation is the world, and the means of this revelation are miraculous deeds which indicate Jesus' true identity. This story is a tragedy, gradually spiraling downward from the testimony of the Baptist and the faith of the first disciples through a series of incredible works and hostile dialogues to FE's grim admission that "though he had done so many signs, they were not believing him" (12:37). John 13–17 is another story of Jesus' self–revelation. The object of this revelation is the disciples, and the means of this revelation is a long dialogue in which Jesus attempts to teach the disciples his true identity. This story is a comedy, moving upward from predictions of betrayal through the disciples' incomprehension to a final revelation of Jesus' heavenly identity and, at last, preliminary faith (16:29–30). The Farewell thus redeems the Book of Signs as a symbolic account of the journey from unbelief to true faith in Jesus.

---

[26]Both quotations Segovia, *FOW* 55.

The riddles in the Farewell warn that the journey of faith is no easier for the disciples than it is for the world. The Farewell riddles parallel the signs: they reveal who Jesus is to those who already know who he is; to those who don't, they only make his real identity more obscure. The relationship between the Book of Signs and the Farewell is therefore thematic rather than chronological, for the Farewell simply highlights a story which has been developing within the disciples all along. In this story, faith conquers ambiguity.

TYPES OF RIDDLES IN JOHN

Before proceeding to analyze the specific passages of FG which include riddles, it will be helpful to separate the texts into a broad taxonomy. Consistent with the theory of speech genres adopted in this study, such a taxonomy must utilize compatible categories, and these categories should highlight the functional dimension of the texts in question. The riddles in FG divide naturally into four categories on the basis of their narrative function:

1) "Dramatic Riddles"—riddles which build dramatic or ironic tension in an episode, or which develop a deeper profile of characters in the story. FE uses these riddles to build suspense and to secure the audience's interest by increasing the entertainment value of the narrative. Seven riddles in FG fall into this category: John 6:5; 11:11; 11:23; 13:10; 13:21; 21:18; 21:22.

2) "Neck Riddles"—riddles in which Jesus poses or answers a difficult puzzle to save himself from a dangerous situation. In most cases, a threat is posed to Jesus' reputation as a sage, placing him in a situation where he might suffer public shame. FE uses these riddles to demonstrate Jesus' wit and to prove his mental superiority over his dialogue partners. Five riddles in FG fall under into this category: John 4:20; 7:23; 8:4–5; 9:2; 10:34–36.

3) "Mission Riddles"—riddles which play on the Johannine understanding of Jesus' identity and mission. These riddles assume a particular view of Jesus and can only be answered from that perspective. FE uses these riddles to explore the revelation of God through Jesus' signs and death, and to highlight the failure of the world to receive that revelation. Seventeen riddles in FG fall into this category: John 2:4b; 2:16; 2:19; 4:32;

8:18; 8:24; 8:26; 8:31–32; 8:38; 8:51; 8:56; 9:39; 10:1–5; 12:32; 13:33 (///7:34; 8:21); 14:4; 14:7.

4) "Salvation Riddles"—riddles which play on the Johannine understanding of the relationship between believers and God. Many of these riddles utilize biological metaphors (birth, drinking, seeing, dying) which signify spiritual realities. FE uses these riddles to develop the unique relationship between God and true believers, a relationship which the world does not enjoy and cannot comprehend. Eight riddles in FG fall into this category: John 3:3–5; 4:7–10; 6:32; 6:51; 7:37–38; 11:25–26; 14:19; 16:16.

It should be stressed that these categories are presented for their heuristic value, not as an absolute, form–critical taxonomy. FE probably did not think of specific riddle units in terms of these categories, but they do seem to reflect several of his major concerns in producing FG. Several of the riddles could reasonably fit into more than one category. When this is the case, the unit has been categorized on the basis of its apparent primary function in the present text of FG. Where two or more riddles of the same category appear in close proximity in the narrative, the analysis which follows will discuss them together. For example, Jesus' Light of the World discourse in John 8 includes seven riddles, all of which relate to Jesus' mission. For sake of convenience, the analysis which follows will address the entire riddling session rather than isolating each unit.

The analysis of each riddle in the next three chapters will attempt to answer two questions. First, what makes this saying a "riddle"? How does the narrative indicate that the language used is intentionally ambiguous? Second, what are the exegetical implications of reading this saying as a riddle, and, where relevant, of reading the larger dialogue in which it appears as a riddling session? This question will be addressed by offering commentary on each passage. Because the riddles under consideration are currently accessible only through a written narrative, the commentary will utilize features of Historical, Narrative, Rhetorical, Sociological, and Reader–Response Criticism, adapting all these methods to the unique problems of orally produced texts.

Chapter 6
Dramatic Riddles and
Neck Riddles in John

FG's "dramatic riddles" and "neck riddles" will be treated together in this chapter. Both categories represent widely recognized uses of the riddle in cross–cultural folk performance, and neither is used in FG to explore the more peculiar aspects of Johannine theology. As a practical consideration, these riddles are fewer in number and require a less detailed analysis.

DRAMATIC RIDDLES IN JOHN

Seven of the riddles delivered by Jesus in FG cast an aura of suspense around specific characters or situations. All seven are delivered to disciples, and all are resolved immediately by Jesus or the narrator. These riddles seem to have two narrative functions. First and primarily, in their immediate narrative contexts these riddles create or sustain the drama of an episode by highlighting a problem or introducing a topic in an interesting way. More generally, the dramatic riddles go along with the other riddles in FG to support FE's broad characterization of Jesus as a riddler. Jesus does not limit his ambiguous statements to casual observers or enemies, and his riddles do not always address deep theological principles. The specific dramatic effect created by each of these riddles will be briefly noted here.

JOHN 6:5—*"Where will we buy bread?"*
FG's first dramatic riddle appears in the story of the Miraculous Feeding (John 6:1–15). Noting the size of the crowd and the late hour, Jesus asks Philip, "Where will we buy bread so that these may eat?" (6:5). Taken aback,

Philip can only stress the impossibility of this suggestion: two hundred denarii worth of bread would not buy enough for everyone to receive a morsel (6:6–7). A similar episode appears in the Synoptics. In the Markan feeding story, the disciples recognize that the hour is late and advise Jesus to send the people away to buy food. Jesus responds, "You give them something to eat" (δότε αὐτοῖς ὑμεῖς φαγεῖν). The Markan disciples offer the same response as Philip, sarcastically asking where they will get 200 denarii to buy food for the crowd (Mark 6:37).

In both the Markan and Johannine stories, Jesus' statement that the disciples should purchase food for the crowd is a dramatic riddle. The point of ambiguity in each case concerns the problem of securing sufficient supplies. The disciples take Jesus literally and state the obvious fact that it would not be possible to buy this much food. The correct answer is that Jesus doesn't buy food, he makes food. FE highlights the ambiguity of Jesus' statement in an aside at John 6:6, explaining that Jesus said this to "test" (πειράζω) Philip because "he knew what he was about to do." For this reason, in FG it is Jesus who initiates the discussion rather than the disciples, implying that the remark is calculated to be obtuse in light of the discourse context. Both Mark and FE suggest that Jesus introduced the miraculous feeding with an enigmatic statement, but FE more clearly marks this statement as a riddle.

JOHN 11:11; 11:23—*"Our friend Lazarus is asleep"*;
  "Your brother will rise again"

Two dramatic riddle appears in the story of Lazarus. Similar to John 6:5, at 11:11 Jesus uses a riddle to introduce his intention to perform a sign. Jesus learns of Lazarus' illness but waits two days before going to him, telling his disciples, "Our friend Lazarus is asleep, but I am going [there] to wake him up" (11:11). Ambiguity is generated by the terms "asleep" and "awake." Jesus has already informed the disciples that Lazarus' sickness "is not unto death" (11:4), and just before delivering the riddle stresses the need for one to go about during the day rather than the night (11:9–10). The disciples therefore conclude that "sleep" is used in the conventional sense, something a sick person would do at night to recuperate. They assure Jesus that there is no need to return to Jerusalem, because Lazarus' sleep will assist his recovery (11:12).

The disciples' response is followed by two clear indications that Jesus has used ambiguous language. First, the narrator carefully specifies that, although Jesus was referring to Lazarus' death, the disciples thought he meant literal sleep (John 11:13). Second, Jesus himself directly states the correct answer at 11:14 (Λάζαρος ἀπέθανεν). This exchange provides a dramatic introduction to Jesus' final return to Jerusalem. Since the resurrection of Lazarus is the climax of Jesus' public ministry in FG, taking the place of the Temple Incident as the source of the plot against his life (11:45–57), it is appropriate that FE dramatizes the introduction to this episode.

The second dramatic riddle in the Lazarus story appears in Jesus' brief discussion with Martha. After Martha affirms her continuing faith in Jesus despite Lazarus' death, Jesus tells her, "Your brother will rise again" (John 11:23). From FE's perspective this statement is not a riddle but a forecast of what Jesus intends to do. His words are literally fulfilled later in the story when Lazarus is called forth from the tomb. In normal language, however, and in the context of a funeral, ἀναστήσεται ("he will rise") would only be used in a spiritual or symbolic sense. Martha, who sees Jesus primarily as a gifted healer, therefore assumes that Jesus is consoling her by referring to Jewish eschatological hopes: "I know that he will rise in the resurrection on the last day" (11:24). It is not surprising that a disciple such as Martha would come to this conclusion, for the Johannine Jesus subscribes to the Pharisaic view of physical resurrection (5:25–29). The ambiguity of Jesus' language and Martha's confused response contribute to the aura of mystery surrounding Jesus' trip to Lazarus and build suspense about what Jesus will do.

JOHN 13:10; 13:21—*"You are clean, but not all of you";*
"One of you will betray me"

The first two riddles in John 13–17 occur in the transition from farewell setting to farewell speech. During the footwashing, Jesus tells the disciples that not all of them are "clean" (καθαρός). The narrator immediately informs the audience of FG that "not clean" is synonymous with "betraying him," a revelation which is not surprising in light of 13:1 (cf. 6:71, 12:4). Presumably, the disciples are "clean" in the sense that they are innocent of any treason. The point of ambiguity in the episode relates to the status of the disciples as clean.

Modern commentators have devoted considerable attention to the theological implications of "cleanness" and "innocence." Segovia, for example, believes that "the [foot]washing can be understood correctly only if regarded as a symbol" of Jesus' death and glorification, which will bring salvation to the disciples.[1] While this conclusion accurately reflects FE's theological interests, all such symbolism would be lost on the disciples, who at this point do not even realize that Jesus will be betrayed, much less that he is soon to die. The difference between the characters' perspective and FE's perspective is indicated by Brown's comment that "the disciples could have understood Jesus to mean that they had been clean but not entirely (their feet were dusty), while he really meant [for the audience of FG to see] that . . . one was a sinner."[2]

Brown's observation is highlighted when a sharp distinction is made between FE's rhetorical objectives and the rhetorical objectives of the character Jesus. In the context of a footwashing, especially one conducted before a sacred meal, the statement "you (pl.) are clean, but not all of you (pl.)" would seem to refer to ritual cleansing. The disciples would therefore conclude that one who is "not clean" has simply failed to take a bath ("The one who has bathed has need only to wash his/her feet, but is wholly clean"; John 13:9), which would suggest insufficient preparation for the Passover meal. At best, the disciples might take Jesus' words as a symbolic reference to repentance and moral purity. This reading is consistent with the fact that the disciples do not suspect treachery at this point. They are shocked when Jesus says a traitor is among them at 13:18–21, and they apparently never identify Judas as the "unclean" person (13:22, 29). From their perspective, Jesus is exhorting them to make proper preparation, ritually and perhaps morally, for the Passover.

The dual meaning of the term "clean" lays the foundation for the ambiguity underlying the second riddle, "one of you will betray me" (John

---

[1]Fernando Segovia,"John 13 1–20: The Footwashing in the Johannine Tradition" (*ZNW* 73 [1982]) 42–45, 48–50, quotation 43. Carson takes a similar view (*The Gospel According to John* [Grand Rapids, MI: Eerdmans, 1991] 464–466, quotation 465).

[2]Raymond Brown, *The Gospel According to John* (AB; Garden City, NY: Doubleday, 1970) 2.552, 565–568, quotation 552.

13:21). For the audience of FG, who have just been reminded of Jesus' betrayal (13:11), "one of you is unclean" (13:10) and "one of you will betray me" (13:21) are parallel statements. Further, since this audience knows that the "unclean one" is Judas, there is little surprise when Judas receives the morsel and leaves the feast (13:26–27, 30). From the disciples' perspective, however, 13:21 is no less confusing than the previous riddle, and they are unable to identify the traitor (13:22). The participle ἀπορούμενοι highlights their misunderstanding, suggesting that they are "disturbed" or "at a loss" to understand what Jesus is talking about. Neither riddle is answered to the disciples' satisfaction, leaving them unable to say what it means to be "clean" or which of them will betray Jesus.

The dual vocalization of John 13:10 and 13:21 creates a major narrative difficulty. At 13:26–29 Jesus tells the Beloved Disciple that the one to whom he gives a dipped morsel is the traitor; he then immediately dips a morsel and gives it to Judas, telling him to do what he must do quickly; Judas receives the morsel and leaves; the disciples wonder why Judas is leaving and speculate that he is going to give alms or buy supplies. How can the disciples fail to identify Judas as the traitor?

This problem arises from the tension between FE's rhetorical objectives and the demands of the narrative. In order to preserve the notion that Jesus has complete control over his own death (10:17–18), FE must assure his audience that Jesus knows the identity of the traitor. Within the story world, however, the disciples must remain ignorant of the traitor's identity so that they will not prevent Judas from leaving the feast.[3] FE must, then, conceal and reveal Judas' intentions at once. The riddles at 13:10 and 13:21 partially satisfy this requirement, and FE attempts to undergird them by recourse to the uniquely Johannine presentation of Judas as the group treasurer (13:29; cf. 12:6). This information about Judas creates a plausible explanation for his departure, which prevents the disciples from connecting "uncleanness" with treachery. FE has not, however, woven his web of ambiguity very tightly, leaving the real

---

[3]Brown suggests that John 13:28–29 means that no–one except BD and Peter knew that Judas was leaving to betray Jesus (AB 2.575). It is hard to imagine, however, that the Peter of FG would allow Judas to leave unhindered if such treachery were suspected, especially in light of his violent attempt to save Jesus from arrest later in the story (18:10).

world audience of FG at a loss to explain the disciples' incomprehension. The riddles succeed, however, in heightening the dramatic tension of the narrative.

JOHN 21:18; 21:22— *"When you were younger you girded yourself and went about where you wished, but when you grow old you will stretch out your hands and another will dress you and lead you where you do not want to go";* *"Should I desire for him [the BD] to remain until I come, what is that to you?"*

The last two dramatic riddles in FG appear at 21:18 and 21:22. Both are proleptic references to the fate of major characters, and both are clearly aimed at the audience of FG, for in this case the characters seem to know the answers before the audience. Jesus challenges Peter's dedication as the two walk beside the sea after the meal of fish. Peter professes his love for Jesus three times and is told to "follow" Jesus by "feeding my sheep/lambs." Jesus then makes an oblique prediction about Peter's fate: "when you were younger, you girded yourself and went about where you wished, but when you grow old you will stretch out your hands and another will dress you and lead where you do not want to go" (John 21:18). Since Peter is young and free at this point in the story, Jesus' saying is ambiguous. In order to assist the audience of FG, the author explains that Jesus was "signifying" (εἶπεν σημαίνων) the manner of Peter's death (21:19). The ambiguity in this riddle is generated by a play on the terms "dress you" and "stretch out your hands," which seem to allude to the tradition that Peter died by crucifixion. This riddle dramatizes the story of Peter's restoration by adding an air of mystery to his fate as a "shepherd" of Jesus' people.

The narrative dynamic of the first riddle is somewhat unusual, for while the audience of FG needs to be told that Jesus is referring to Peter's death, Peter seems to realize this on his own. He therefore inquires about the fate of the Beloved Disciple, who seems to be following them along the beach. Jesus is unwilling to answer, but instead offers another riddle: "Should I desire for him to remain until I come, what is that to you?" (21:22). Peter apparently understands this saying as well, but it seems to have been ambiguous to some members of the Johannine community. Some believe that Jesus would return before BD's death, and the author of this passage wants to correct that notion. The narrator therefore clarifies that the emphasis in Jesus' statement is not on the BD's "remaining until I come," but on the sovereignty of Jesus' "desire" over the fate of his disciples. This riddle, then, heightens the mystique of BD, but may have a secondary, apologetic purpose as well.

NECK RIDDLES IN JOHN

The "neck riddle" is a widely attested folk genre which generally appears in the plot of a larger story. Neck riddles occur at crisis points in the narrative where the protagonist must use her wits to escape from danger or "save her neck." To effect this escape, the protagonist must either "pose a riddle that cannot be solved, or unravel one given him on penalty of death should he fail."[4] The villain, following the logic of oral narrative, generally admits defeat and sets the hero free.[5] The neck riddles in FG usually appear in contexts where Jesus' public reputation as a sage is in jeopardy. Neck riddles highlight the importance of public debate in oral cultures, where ability to pose and resolve difficult problems is considered a mark of wisdom.

JOHN 4:20—*"Our fathers worshiped on this mountain, and you people say that in Jerusalem is the place where it is necessary to worship"*
The first of FG's neck riddles appears in Jesus' discussion with the Samaritan woman just after the exchange on "living water." The woman calls Jesus a "prophet" after he reveals her sordid past (John 4:19). Scholars are divided on the meaning of this acclamation. Brown, noting the role of Deut. 18:15–18 (the "Prophet like Moses") in Samaritan eschatology, sees here a fledgling belief in Jesus as the Messiah who would "settle legal questions." Schnackenburg, however, thinks that "prophet" should be understood in the "general sense" here of "a man of God at work." In either case, the woman's

---

[4]James L. Crenshaw, "Riddle," *The Interpreter's Dictionary of the Bible Supplemental Volume* (ed. Keith Crim; Nashville, TN: Abingdon, 1976) 749, quotation here; *Samson: A Secret Betrayed, A Vow Ignored* (Atlanta, GA: John Knox, 1978) 113–114.

[5]A familiar example from western folklore is the tale of Rumpelstiltskin, in which the heroine must guess the name of the fairy Rumpelstiltskin before he will break the curse over her child. Samson's challenge to the Philistines at Judges 14:5–14 is another neck riddle. Though the stakes in this contest are not so high as one's "neck," the Philistines stand to lose a bet and suffer shame if they cannot unlock Samson's puzzle about the lion and the honey.

question about worship at 4:20 is an attempt to test Jesus, for if he is a true prophet he will surely be able to unlock a simple theological puzzle.[6] The riddle she offers highlights a contrast between "our fathers" and "you (Jews)": "Our fathers (οἱ πατέρες ἡμῶν) worshiped on this mountain, and you people say (ὑμεῖς λέγετε) that Jerusalem is the place where one must worship" (John 4:20). Because the woman has already sharply distinguished Samaritans from Jews at 4:9, this statement is generally taken to mean, "*We Samaritans* worship here but *you Jews* say we should worship there; which is correct?"[7] It seems strange, however, that the woman, whose posture toward Jesus has been hostile up to this point, would suddenly ask a genuine question which invites him to condemn her entire faith system. Further, her final response at 4:24, "I suppose that when Messiah comes he will pronounce all things to us," suggests that she remains suspicious of Jesus even after his elaborate answer (4:21–23). These difficulties in the narrative are resolved if the term "our (ἡμῶν) fathers" at 4:20 is inclusive of Jesus. From this perspective, the woman's question is a test of his prophetic competence: if our ancestors (those of the Jews and Samaritans) worshiped on this mountain (Gerizim), how can you Jews now justify worshiping somewhere else (Jerusalem)? The proposed dilemma is based on the Samaritan understanding that Abraham, Moses, and Joshua had established Gerizim (Shechem) as the

---

[6]Brown, AB 1.171; Rudolf Schnackenburg, *The Gospel According to St. John* (trans. Kevin Smith; HTKNT; New York, NY: Herder and Herder, 1968) 1.433–434. With Brown, O'Day sees the reference as FE's indication that the woman's faith is taking "a step in the right direction" (Gail R. O'Day, *Revelation in the Fourth Gospel: Narrative Mode and Theological Claim* [Philadelphia, PA: Fortress, 1986]) 67, 132 n. 50). Schnackenburg's position is also adopted by Carson, who argues that the term may not even imply the belief that Jesus is "a full–orbed Old Testament prophet" (*John* 221). Lindars offers a compromise, concluding that the woman believes Jesus is "*a* prophet" and wants to determine if he is "*the* prophet" by testing his teaching (*The Gospel of John* [NCBC; Grand Rapids, MI: Eerdmans, 1972] 187).

[7]Rudolf Bultmann, *The Gospel of John: A Commentary* (trans. G. R. Beasley–Murray, R. W. N. Hoare and J. K. Riches; Philadelphia, PA: Westminster, 1971) 189; Schnackenburg, HTKNT 1.434–435; Lindars, NCBC 187–188; O'Day, *Revelation* 68; Carson, *John* 221–222.

sole place of worship long before the Jerusalem cult came into existence.[8] The woman's question therefore does not contrast "our fathers" with "your fathers," but rather contrasts "our fathers" with current Jewish custom, implying that Jewish custom is somehow innovative. If Jesus is a true prophet, how can he, as a "Jew," sanction such innovative worship?

Jesus' wisdom is demonstrated by his ability to surmount this apparent difficulty. Without denying the inconsistency suggested in the woman's riddle, he moves the discussion to a level in which the proposed paradox is irrelevant. "True" worship does not occur on Gerizim or Zion, but rather "in spirit" and "in truth," a point which would seem self–evident because "God is a spirit" (John 4:21–24). The woman's casual response at 4:25 ("I know that when Messiah comes he will tell us everything") indicates that her riddle was a trap rather than a request for genuine information. Once the trap is sprung she attempts to nullify the consequences of Jesus' victory by suggesting that his answer is insufficient, but is unable to offer a specific critique of its deficiencies. Jesus has won the contest.

JOHN 7:23—*"If a man receives circumcision on Sabbath so that the Law of Moses would not be broken, are you angry with me because I made a whole man healthy on the Sabbath?"*

This riddle is delivered during the Feast of Tabernacles shortly after the Bread of Life discourse. FE stresses throughout the episode that Jesus is in grave danger. He at first refuses to go to the Feast because the Jews seek to kill him (John 7:1, 7), and when he finally decides to make the journey he must do so secretly (7:9). In Jerusalem, the masses cannot speak about him publicly for fear of the authorities (7:13). Defying their threats, Jesus begins to teach in the Temple and specifically discusses the plot against his life (7:19); the crowds feign ignorance but later confirm his suspicion (7:20, 25). After escaping arrest, Jesus reappears on the last day of the Feast, at which time the "chief priests and Pharisees" send officers for his arrest (7:37–45). This atmosphere of danger makes 7:23 a classic "neck riddle," an attempt by Jesus to escape harm through a verbal puzzle.

---

[8]See discussion in Carson, *John* 222; Brown, AB 1.171–172; Schnackenburg, HTKNT 1.434–435.

The Jews' hostility toward Jesus seems to derive from lingering tensions over the healing at Bethesda (John 5:1–9). In defense of his actions, Jesus asks them, "If a man receives circumcision on Sabbath so that the Law of Moses would not be broken, are you angry with me because I made a whole man healthy on the Sabbath?" Although Jesus offers no direct answer and the crowd does not express confusion, this statement may be identified as a neck riddle by Criterion 4. Jesus is in danger because his actions have violated the popular understanding of Sabbath law, and he attempts to escape the consequences of this violation by highlighting an apparent inconsistency in the Jews' thinking. If the laws protecting Sabbath are rigorously applied, it would not be possible to circumcise a child on the eighth day if the eight day fell on a Sabbath. Since popular theology says that circumcision of the penis is not a violation of the Sabbath, how can anyone suggest that Jesus has violated the Sabbath by healing "the whole man" (ὅλον ἄνθρωπον)? The riddle successfully saves Jesus' neck, for the Jews, rather than seizing him, begin to debate whether he might be the Christ (7:25).

JOHN 8:4–5—*"In the Law of Moses it says to stone such a woman"*
The next neck riddle appears in the story of the woman caught in adultery, John 7:53–8:11. This pericope is generally excluded from monographs on FG for text–critical reasons. The strongest witness in favor of the passage is D, a fifth–century manuscript notorious for apparent interpolations, against the unanimous voice of ℵ, B, and the Church Fathers. For this reason, and because the language and narrative style of the episode resemble the Synoptics, most scholars conclude that the passage is a later interpolation. At the same time, John 7:53–8:11 is generally seen as an ancient tradition, perhaps a fragment from a lost gospel and possibly representative of Jesus' actual activity.[9] Debate over these issues, alongside the raw dramatic power of the presentation, has distracted researchers from the fact that the story is replete with features of an oral world. If not Johannine, the passage will be relevant to the present study as further evidence that the Johannine riddles are related to a broader narrative motif in early Jesus traditions.

---

[9]See Brown, AB 1.335; Schnackenburg, HTKNT 2.162, 168–171; Lindars, NCBC 305–306; Carson, *John* 333.

To highlight the oral features of this narrative and to explain the role of the riddle at John 8:4–5, the discussion here will focus on three aspects of the story which have received considerable attention: the nature of the "test" put to Jesus and the implication of his response (8:4–7); the emphasis on Jesus' "writing on the ground" (8:6, 8); and, the note that the "older men" among the woman's accusers leave the scene first (8:9).

The author of this pericope clarifies the nature of the encounter between Jesus and the scribes at John 8:6. The Jewish authorities are "testing" (πειράζω) Jesus in order to establish some charge against him. As Brown notes, similar language appears at John 6:6 in an aside which indicates that Jesus was "testing" Philip by asking him where to buy bread for the crowd.[10] The scribes' trap takes the form of an "alternative" riddle. The "alternative" presents the riddlee with two options and asks for a choice, where the less attractive choice generally represents the "correct" answer. In some cases neither answer is attractive and the riddlee must choose between the lesser of two evil. A well known example is the English joke, "Do you still beat your wife?", which both the answers "yes" and "no" force the riddlee to admit to a scandalous activity.[11]

One of Jesus' undesirable alternatives is stated directly in the scribes' riddle: "in the Law Moses tells us to stone such a woman" (John 8:5). Jesus can choose to enforce this Law or to forgo the Law and allow the woman to live. The latter choice, forgiveness, is unattractive because it might be perceived as a public abrogation of the Law or a lax stance on morality. Scholars are divided on the specific dangers associated with the choice to enforce the Law. Some suggest that the choice for stoning would represent an anti–Roman sentiment, since the Roman government had removed the right of execution from the Jewish authorities.[12] Others appeal to the Synoptic presentation of Jesus as the "friend of sinners" and conclude that strict adherence to the letter of the Law would ruin his reputation for compassion.

---

[10]Brown, AB 1.333.
[11]See Archer Taylor, "The Riddle," *California Folklore Quarterly* [*WF*] 2 (1943) 145–146; "The Varieties of Riddles," *Philologica: The Malone Anniversary Studies* (ed. Thomas A. Kirby and Henry Bosley Wolf; Baltimore, MD: Johns Hopkins Press, 1949) 8.
[12]Brown, AB 1.337.

These possibilities are not mutually exclusive and both may be intended; either would make this "a critical political question" for Jesus.[13] Jesus' response at 8:7 cleverly combines the two alternatives, supporting the Law but with a condition which neutralizes the potential danger of this option. Stones must be cast, but mercy demands that the first should be thrown by a person who is without guilt (8:7).

Considerable speculation has been given to the relationship between this response and Jesus' "writing on the ground" at John 8:6, 8. Carson suggests that this was a "delaying action" which gave Jesus time to think about his answer, and Lindars sees the writing as an indication that Jesus "did not wish to be involved in the matter."[14] Schnackenburg and others take the more complicated position that Jesus' writing is an allusion to Jeremiah 17:13, "All those who forsake Thee will be put to shame. Those who turn away on earth will be written down" (NASV). From this perspective, Jesus is supporting his answer by referring to a text which indicates that all are sinners and that judgement should therefore be left to God.[15]

A less complicated conclusion may be reached by recognizing that the story is written from the perspective of an oral culture. As Lindars notes, "the point [of the story] is the skill with which Jesus maintains his own position without falling into the trap of publicly repudiating the Law."[16] Jesus' writing functions to underline his skill at riddling. In a culture which was 90% illiterate, Jesus' ability to write would be a further indication of his sagacity.[17] Jesus' accusers in this episode are "scribes," persons whose knowledge of Scripture is based on their ability to write. By writing, Jesus demonstrates that he is capable of debate at their level.

Jesus' shrewd answer and his writing signal complete victory over his opponents, who can only slink away in disgrace, leaving the woman with Jesus

---

[13]Schnackenburg, HTKNT 2.164–165; Lindars, NCBC 310; Carson, *John* 335.
[14]Carson, *John* 336; Lindars, NCBC 310.
[15]Schnackenburg, HTKNT 2.166–167.
[16]Lindars, NCBC 308.
[17]On ancient literacy rates and the ancient Jewish view of writing see William V. Harris, *Ancient Literacy* (Cambridge, MA: Harvard University Press, 1989) 17–24; Tom Thatcher "Literacy, Textual Communities, and Josephus' *Jewish War*," *JSJ* 29 (1998) 127–133.

(John 8:9). Overemphasis on the devotional value of the passage has confused the note that the "older men" among the accusers left first. Lindars, for example, concludes that "it is psychologically sound that the more experienced senior men would be likely the first to acknowledge the falsity of their position." Schnackenburg whimsically reminds us that "old age is very ready to condemn the passions of youth, and needs to bear in mind the accumulation of its own sins over a long life."[18] Without limiting the value of the episode for modern preaching, the note about the older men is geared to the logic of an oral audience. The rigid conventions of public debate and riddling sessions in oral societies, particularly patriarchal societies such as ancient Judaism, would scarcely permit the younger men to propose further questions or leave without the permission of the elders. Realizing that Jesus has sprung their best trap, the senior scribes depart to regroup, followed by their academic inferiors. Jesus has won the day.

JOHN 9:2—"Who sinned, this man or his parents?"

The next neck in FG appears at 9:2. As Jesus walks with his disciples he sees a man "blind from birth" (John 9:1). The disciples question him about the cause of the man's condition: "Rabbi, who sinned, this man or his parents, that he should be born blind?" While the tone of this riddle is considerably less hostile than the previous examples, Jesus is again forced to demonstrate his wisdom publicly by unlocking a difficult theological problem.

The disciples' question, like John 8:4–5, is an alternative riddle, and again both alternatives are undesirable.[19] Exodus 20:5 states that children may suffer the consequences of their parents' sin to the third and fourth generation. Perhaps God has punished this man for a sin his parents committed; is such a punishment just? Or perhaps God punishes infants who commit sin in the womb, for the man is "blind from birth"? Both possibilities were discussed in ancient Judaism,[20] and both would require Jesus to endorse a causal connection between sin and suffering. Jesus cleverly avoids this conclusion by moving

---

[18]Lindars, NCBC 311; Schnackenburg, HTKNT 2.167.

[19]Without referring to the scholarship cited here, Bultmann notes that the disciples' question poses "an impossible alternative" (John 330 n. 8, 331).

[20]See discussion in Brown, AB 1.371; Carson, John 361–362.

from abstract generalities to the specific case of the blind man and then shifting the problem from the cause of the man's suffering to its purpose. The man was not born blind because of anyone's sin, but so that the works of God could be manifested in him (9:3–4). Remarkably, this answer contradicts Jesus' warning to the healed cripple at Bethesda that further sin will cause further suffering (5:14), another indication that FE wishes to demonstrate Jesus' brilliance rather than present a coherent doctrine of human suffering. Just as the cripple allowed Jesus to reveal his divine power, the blind man gives Jesus a chance to reveal his wit.

JOHN 10:34–36—*"Is it not written in your Law, 'I said, "You are gods"'?"*

Like John 7:23, 10:34–36 presents another situation in which Jesus escapes from danger by offering a riddle which his audience cannot resolve: "Is it not written in your Law, 'I said, "You are gods"'? If God said this to those to whom the word of God came, and the Scripture cannot be broken, how can you say to the one whom the father sanctified and sent into the world, 'You blaspheme,' because I said, 'I am son of God'?" Unfortunately, many commentators have taken an aesthetic approach to this passage, criticizing Jesus' logic as fallacious and pedantic.[21] One scholar who has carefully avoided this trap is Jerome Neyrey. Neyrey's sensitivity to the logic of the passage follows from his conclusion that Jesus' use of Psalm 82:6 appeals to a broader midrashic interpretation. The present study will critique and expand Neyrey's reading to discuss the narrative development of the episode.

---

[21]See Bultmann: "This sort of intellectual subtlety always picks out what suits its own case and can easily be defeated at its game," despite the fact that the Jews in the story cannot refute Jesus' words (*John* 389). Lindars thinks Jesus' logic is "fallacious" because the fact that some people have been addressed as gods is irrelevant to Jesus' special relationship with God, the point under discussion. The argument was developed in FE's debate with the synagogue, and FE either has not realized that it is inappropriate for Jesus to use it or means to suggest that Jesus "may have had no greater equipment to see the fallacy than his opponents" (NCBC 373). Some commentators ironically highlight the apparent "fallacy" of the argument even while trying to defend its validity. Brown stresses that Jesus is using rabbinic hermeneutics "which were often different from modern attitudes" so that "to a Western mind this argument seems to be a deceptive fallacy" (AB 409–410). Carson suggests that Jesus may not subscribe to the logic of his own statement, but insists that, in any case, "although the argument is *ad hominem* . . . it is not for that reason silly" (*John* 399).

The major interpretive issue associated with John 10:34–35 concerns the intended subject of the second person plural verb ἐστε ("you are") in Psalm 82:6: "I say, '*You are* gods, children of the Most High, all of you'" (NRSV). Four major views have been offered on the identity of the "gods" here: angels; Melchizedek; Israel's judges; and, the Israelites on Mt. Sinai.[22] The author of the Psalm probably intended to refer to Israel's unjust judges, who would "fall" and "die like men" (Ps. 82:7) for their wickedness. A first–century CE audience, however, would most likely see this as a reference to the Sinai event, as is evident from several rabbinic midrashim on the passage.[23] The rabbis believed that the Law sanctified the Israelites at Sinai and made them immortal, a quality reserved for "gods." This status was revoked, however, after the sin of the golden calf, and the demoted Israelites were once again doomed to die as humans. Thus, "when Psalm 82 is cited in Jewish midrash, writers generally understand that Israel is called *god* because of its holiness and/or deathlessness."[24]

This background explains, for Neyrey, why Jesus quotes Psalm 82:6 in this particular context. John 10 depicts two "forensic proceedings" against Jesus. Both include a claim by Jesus, the judgement of the people against Jesus, and Jesus' apology. In the first forensic proceeding, Jesus' claim to be the "Good Shepherd" (10:1–18) creates a hung jury (10:19–24), leading Jesus to proclaim that his judges cannot accept his evidence because "you are not my sheep" (10:25–27). The second forensic proceeding opens with the claim that Jesus "gives life" to the sheep because he is "one" with the Father (10:28–30). "Ultimate power over death" is, in the view of the Jews, an exclusively divine prerogative. Jesus' claim is therefore "blasphemy" because he "makes himself [equal to] God" even though he is "a man" (10:33).

The unit under investigation here, John 10:34–36, opens Jesus' apology against this charge. Neyrey understands the logic of Jesus' citation of Psalm 82:6 this way: "If Israel, who became holy, may be called *god*, then it is not blasphemy if Jesus, whom God consecrated and sent as his apostle to the world

---

[22]Jerome Neyrey, "'I Said: You are Gods': Psalm 82:6 and John 10," *JBL* 108 (1989) 647–649; Carson, *John* 397–398.

[23]Neyrey, "You are Gods" 654–658.

[24]Neyrey, "You are Gods" 656–658, quotation 658.

[10:36], is called *god.*" Neyrey stresses that the citation of the Psalm does not establish Jesus' equality with God, but does rebut the Jews' claim that "you, being a man, make yourself God." "Jesus' judges judged wrongly when they accused him of *making himself* god . . . because God Himself *makes Jesus* Son of God, just as God *made Israel* 'god' by delivering the Torah."[25]

Neyrey's reading is insightful and will be followed in most points here. Recognition that John 10:34–35 is a neck riddle, however, requires a reevaluation of the function of this unit in the broader narrative. Neyrey's basic outline of the two "forensic proceedings" in John 10 does not adequately describe the dynamics of the discourse. Neyrey suggests that each proceeding follows the pattern, "claim (by Jesus)," "judgement (by the Jews)," "apology/defense (by Jesus)." His own analysis, however, suggests that the actual pattern underlying these proceedings is "claim—judgement—counter–judgement." In the first proceeding, Jesus' claim to be the "Good Shepherd" is so elaborate that the Jews cannot make any judgement at all. Neyrey realizes this, and further notes that Jesus' "apology" at 10:25–27 "contains no new material which proves its [the claim's] truth, but is itself a judgement on his judges."[26] Jesus' counter–judgement explains the Jews' confusion in ontological terms: they cannot accept the clear testimony of his works because they are not his "sheep."

The same pattern repeats at John 10:28–39. Jesus now claims that he can protect his sheep and give them eternal life because he is "one with the Father" (10:28–30). The Jews finally unite on the sentence of execution for blasphemy (10:33). Jesus' second countercharge at 10:34–39 opens with the riddle "you are gods," implying that the Jews do not understand Scripture, and proceeds to reiterate that they do not understand the implication of his works. He concludes by restating the claim to unity with the Father (10:38), which

---

[25]Neyrey, "You are Gods," first quotation 659, second quotation 660. Similarly, Brown believes this passage is informed by the Jewish concept of the *šālîah* or "deputy." The commissioned deputy bears the full authority of the one he or she represents. In the case of Jesus, this includes the authority to do the sender's "good work" of granting life (John 10:28, 32, 37; AB 1.411; see also Schnackenburg, HTKNT 312).

[26]Neyrey, "You are Gods" 650. In a footnote Neyrey notes that this illustrates a general pattern in FG: "It is vintage Johannine argument to turn a judgement against Jesus into a judgment against his accusers" (650 n. 23).

again provokes the Jews to violence. Rather than an "apology," then, 10:34–35 may be seen as Jesus' counter–charge that the Jews are ignorant of Scripture and therefore not qualified to serve as judges in a blasphemy case.

To identify this counter–charge as a riddle, it is necessary to highlight two features of John 10:34–35 which are notably absent from Neyrey's discussion. First, Neyrey does not discuss Jesus' sidenote that "Scripture cannot be broken" (10:35). This statement apparently refers to the Psalm Jesus is citing, with the assumption that this Psalm refers to the Sinai episode. If this statement "cannot be broken," a premise the Jews of FG would accept, then one of the terms of the riddle is apparently inviolable and must be accepted as a "given."[27] Jesus thereby grounds the riddle in the Jews' own ideological taxonomy. This taxonomy is then challenged via the second feature of the text which Neyrey overlooks. Although Neyrey is primarily concerned to show connections between these verses and rabbinic midrash, he fails to mention that 10:34–35 follows one of Hillel's "Seven Ways," *qal wahomer* ("the lesser to the greater").[28] Accepting Neyrey's conclusion on the identity of the "gods," the logic of Jesus' statement may be paraphrased, "If those who received the Law at Sinai were sanctified and called 'gods,' *how much more* should the one whom God sanctified and sent as his emissary be called 'god'?" Since the Jews accept both the Scriptures and the *qal wahomer* method of interpreting them, they are forced into an undesirable alternative. Either the Scripture can be broken, or they must reject standard methods of interpreting Scripture, or Jesus is, indeed, worthy of the title "god." Any of these three choices would violate the Jews' ideological taxonomy. Frustrated by Jesus' superior wisdom, they can only resort to violence once again (10:39).

---

[27]Carson, *John* 399.
[28]See discussion in Bultmann, *John* 389; Brown, AB 1.410; Schnackenburg, HTKNT 2.311–312.

Chapter 7
Mission Riddles in John

The "mission riddles" in FG explore facets of Jesus' divine identity and mission, and highlight the inability of human wisdom to comprehend him. They derive their ambiguity from the fact that Jesus' words of self–revelation always function at two levels. At the level of FG's audience, they engender faith by revealing Jesus as "the Christ, the Son of God" (John 20:30–31). At the level of the characters in the story, however, the mission riddles seem to be unusual or grotesque comments about everyday things. The tension between these two levels of meaning generates irony in those episodes where Jesus discusses his identity and mission with other characters.

JOHN 2:4B—*"My Hour Has Not Yet Come"*

This saying may be classified as a riddle on the basis of criterion three: when characters in the story are confused by a saying, or indicate that a saying could reasonably take more than one referent, that saying is a riddle. Neither Jesus nor the narrator indicate that John 2:4b is a "riddle," but Mary's request and subsequent response suggest that Jesus' words are ambiguous. Further, Jesus' "hour" is a uniquely Johannine way of referring to his death, which the disciples could not predict at this point. It is therefore impossible for Mary to identify the true referent of Jesus' words, making this the first riddle of Jesus in FG.

Unfortunately, Mary's sudden appearance at John 2:1 has distracted commentators from the irony in the passage. While John 2:1–11 is certainly relevant to theological discussions of Mary's role as intermediary and Jesus' sinlessness, the Cana story is not about Mary or a wedding or wine. FE presents this as the first "sign" of Jesus' heavenly identity and the climax of FG's "call of the disciples" (1:35–2:11).[1] Mary is apparently associated with this group, for she appears in the midst of their story without introduction and later travels with them to Capernaum (2:12). As such, she presumably shares the disciples' ignorance of Jesus' true identity. The statement, "They have no wine" (2:3), should be understood in this light. Many scholars have suggested that Mary hoped for a miraculous resolution to the problem,[2] but at this point in the story she and the disciples do not know enough about Jesus to formulate such a hope. Mary thinks Jesus can alleviate the shortage through some natural means, unaware of the resources at his disposal.[3]

Jesus' response to this apparently innocent request, τί ἐμοὶ καὶ σοί γύναι ("What to me and to you, woman?"; John 2:4a), is notoriously difficult. Many commentators would accept Brown's translation, "What has this concern of yours to do with me?," and would also, perhaps for apologetic reasons, accept Brown's conclusion that Jesus wants only to maintain a "simple disengagement" from the wine problem.[4] Others detect a more hostile tone in Jesus' words, expressing indignation that Mary would ask him to get involved. Almost all would agree that Jesus' reply represents "his utter freedom from any kind of human advice, agenda or manipulation"; indeed, "human ties and obligations in no way influence Jesus' action."[5]

Being free from human influences, Jesus refers to his mother as γύναι, "woman." This unusual designation is highlighted by the fact that the narrator refers to Mary as "the mother of Jesus" in vv. 3 and 5. While commentators

---

[1]Rudolf Schnackenburg, *The Gospel According to St. John* (trans. Kevin Smith; HTKNT; New York, NY: Herder and Herder, 1968) 1.323; Barnabas Lindars, *The Gospel of John* (NCBC; London: Marshall, Morgan & Scott, 1972) 123.

[2]See Schnackenburg, HTKNT 1.327; Robert T. Fortna, *The Fourth Gospel and Its Predecessor: From Narrative Source to Present Gospel* (Philadelphia, PA: Fortress, 1988) 55; Painter, *Quest* 190–191.

[3]Lindars, NCBC 129; see also Carson, *John* 169–170; Brown, AB 98, 102–103. Mary's ignorance of Jesus' true identity is also a recurrent theme in the Synoptics (Mark 3:20–21, 31–35; 6:1–3; Luke 2:19, 33–35, 50–51).

[4]Brown, AB 1.99. See also Schnackenburg, HTKNT 1.328; Lindars, NCBC 129.

[5]Carson, *John* 171, first quotation here; Rudolf Bultmann, *The Gospel of John: A Commentary* (trans. G. R. Beasley–Murray, R. W. N. Hoare and J. K. Riches; Philadelphia, PA: Westminster, 1971) 117, second quotation here.

have been struck with the possible impropriety of Jesus' term,[6] the narrator's usage is actually more surprising, for FE clearly does not think of Mary as Jesus' "mother." FE's Jesus has no "mother," having "come down from heaven" (John 6:33; 16:28). Elsewhere in FG, it is the Jews who believe that Mary is Jesus' "mother," proof that they do not know where he came from (6:41–42). The designation "the Mother of Jesus" at 2:1–5 must therefore represent Mary's, and the disciples', understanding of Jesus' identity. By addressing Mary in a way which varies from the disciples' understanding, Jesus signals that his discourse is moving to a set of referents which depend on his true identity. The riddle, "My hour has not yet come," explores the issue of Jesus' identity with a person who does not know who he really is.

As an answer to Mary's request, "My hour has not yet come" is inconsistent with the flow of the narrative, for Jesus almost immediately turns the water into wine. When understood as a riddle, however, the saying becomes a challenge which explores her understanding of Jesus: What is "my hour"? Since Jesus' "hour" elsewhere in FG refers to the culmination of his earthly ministry (John 12:23–25; 13:1), the question actually relates to Mary's understanding of Jesus' mission. From this perspective, the riddle at John 2:4b might be paraphrased in less esoteric terms as, "What would I care about the wine, anyway, and how would that achieve my purposes?" Since Mary does not yet realize these purposes, she is not able to respond to Jesus' riddle. The "sign" of plenteous wine which follows answers the riddle by resolving the questions of identity and mission in a preliminary way, generating "belief" in the disciples (2:11). In light of the Prologue, the answer to 2:4b is, "Jesus' 'hour comes' when he reveals the Father."

---

[6]The value of the term "woman" as a form of address in Jesus' vocabulary is difficult to determine. The majority of usages occur in FG, with only two real synoptic parallels. Brown, citing Matt. 15:28 and Luke 13:12, insists that "woman" "is not a rebuke, nor an impolite term, nor an indication of a lack of affection" (AB 1.99). The former of these passages, however, is the story of the Syrophonecian woman, whom Jesus also refers to as "dog," and in any case these parallels do not adequately explain Jesus' application of the term to his own mother in John 2.

JOHN 2:16; 2:19—
"Do not make my father's house a house of business";
"Destroy this temple and in three days I will raise it"

These two sayings appear in a riddling session during Jesus' first encounter with the Jews at the Temple. Both are signaled as riddles by the confusion of the characters in the story and by FE's direct revelation of their meaning to the reader. Indeed, FE seems unusually concerned that the audience of FG understand this episode. Jesus' actions are connected with Scripture twice in six verses, are interpreted in light of his upcoming resurrection, and, like the immediately preceding wine miracle, effect "belief" in the disciples. The characters in the story could not make these connections because, as FE freely admits, the Temple Incident is comprehensible only in light of Jesus' death (John 2:20–21). To fully appreciate the irony generated by this hidden information, it will be necessary to speculate on what Jesus' words *could have meant* to the characters in the story. Specifically, one must ask how Jesus' actions in the Temple might have been interpreted by the Jerusalem Jews, and then evaluate this interpretation in light of the special information which the audience of FG receives.

FE's version of the Temple Incident opens with the brief explanation that Jesus, having previously moved from Cana to Capernaum (John 2:12), is now going to observe the Passover in Jerusalem. Although he has never visited that city, Jesus has apparently formed some definite opinions about the Temple cult. There is something very wrong, in his view, with the presence of animal vendors and moneychangers in the Temple courts, and he takes violent steps to correct the problem. The first saying under consideration explains the motive behind this action: "Do not make my father's house a house of business" (2:16). The ambiguity in this riddle depends on the aside at 2:17 ("His disciples remembered that it had been written, 'Zeal for your house will consume me'"). In light of 2:22 ("After he had risen from the dead, his disciples remembered that he said this"), 2:17 could simply mean that the disciples did not realize Jesus' actions fulfilled Psalm 69:9 until after his death.[7] Painter, however, suggests that the disciples connected Jesus' outrage with this text as they watched him driving out the moneychangers.[8] In support of this reading, Jesus' actions would be perfectly comprehensible to the characters in the story against the backdrop of OT prophetic passages which bemoan violations of the Temple.[9] Nothing about the disciples' observation at 2:17 depends on knowledge of Jesus' true identity. The abandon with which Jesus pursues his agenda, and the prophetic tone of his remarks, could certainly bring to mind a passage concerning "zeal." But because they do not know Jesus' true identity, the disciples fail to see that Jesus' zealous actions are much less significant than his claim that the Temple is "my father's house." Not realizing the full implication of this claim, they cannot identify the real reason for Jesus' indignation.

If the disciples do not fully understanding what Jesus is doing, the situation of the Jews is much less hopeful. The Jews have had no experience in dealing with Jesus up to this point and are therefore unprepared to analyze his enigmatic discourse. As Carson notes, in normal language "reference to God as one's Father, though perhaps strange, was not itself tantamount to making oneself equal to God."[10] It is widely accepted in contemporary scholarship that the historical Jesus encouraged his disciples to address God as "father" in this broad sense.[11] Nothing about Jesus' reference to the Temple as "my father's house" would require the Jews to seek a deeper level of significance. Their failure to go beyond the most obvious referent makes the question, "What sign do you give us that you do these things?" (John 2:18), heavily ironic. In the Jews' vocabulary and in the context of Jesus' protest, the

---

[7]The citation of Ps. 69:9 at John 2:17 shifts from the aorist "consumed me" of the LXX to the future "will consume me" to highlight the theme of fulfilled prophecy.

[8]Painter, *Quest* 193. Note that Painter is speaking of the disciples as characters in the story, not as actual human beings who may have gained such an impression from the actions of the historical Jesus.

[9]This possibility is strengthened if, as Brown and Carson suggest, Jesus' words at 2:16 are an allusion to Zech. 14:21 (Brown, AB 1.121–122; Carson, *John* 149).

[10]Carson, *John* 179–180.

[11]See discussion in Robert Funk, Roy Hoover and the Jesus Seminar, *The Five Gospels: The Search for the Authentic Words of Jesus* (New York, NY: MacMillan, 1993) 148–149, 326–327.

word "sign" refers to the prophetic or academic credentials prerequisite to such a dramatic critique of established custom. In FE's vocabulary, however, "signs" are things Jesus does to reveal his heavenly identity (2:11). The request of the Jews is redundant, for Jesus has already revealed his identity through his claim that the owner of the Temple, God, is "my father." It must be stressed that the Jews' request for a sign is redundant only within the context of FE's special language for speaking about Jesus. At the level of the narrative in John 2, it is a perfectly reasonable response to Jesus' statement. As Petersen notes, the Jews "understood what Jesus was saying but not what he meant."[12]

Rather than resolving this ironic tension, FE prolongs it by introducing a second riddle, "Destroy this temple and in three days I will raise it" (John 2:19). It was earlier noted that a riddle intentionally reveals and conceals its referent with a single set of signs. The terms in the saying at 2:19 could logically refer to at least two, and perhaps three, distinct sets of referents, only one of which is "correct." Further, the linguistic elements of the saying serve as both clues to, and distractions from, the correct set of referents. Although the Jews have used the term "sign" incorrectly, Jesus' challenge is, at the most basic level, a sensible response to their demand: the ability to rebuild the Temple in three days would be a sufficient "sign" that one is authorized to critique the cult. Remaining within this set of referents, the Jews can only point out the absurdity of Jesus' proposal (2:20), which is obviously too extreme to be tested.

The Jews' inability to move beyond the most obvious meaning of Jesus' words is highlighted by several clues that something more weighty is under consideration. The absurdity of his offer to rebuild the Temple in three days is one such clue. The Jewish prophetic tradition would offer further clues. Bultmann notes that the Jews might have understood Jesus' words against the backdrop of OT passages about a purified eschatological Temple and the

---

[12]Petersen makes this statement of 2:19 but it applies equally to 2:16 (*The Gospel of John and the Sociology of Light: Language and Characterization in the Fourth Gospel* [Valley Forge, PA: Trinity Press, 1993] 38–39). If the Jews' use of "sign" reflects real world vocabulary, either from the life of Jesus or from FE's subsequent debates with the Jewish authorities, the play between the two meanings of the term here would be a case of Johannine antilanguage (5, 89).

similar protests of other first–century C.E. prophets.[13] This possibility should have occurred to the Jews, since they apparently understand Jesus' actions as a prophetic claim. Further reflection could have led them see the Temple as Jesus' metaphor for a "new eschatological community of salvation."[14] It seems, however, that the Jews were overwhelmed by the immediate presence of the Temple buildings and therefore saw no need to move beyond them, regardless of how absurd Jesus' claims might sound. Jesus in fact encourages them to look in this direction by urging them to destroy ὁ ναὸς οὗτος, "*this* Temple*," a seemingly obvious statement when made in the Temple courts.

More subtle clues point the audience of FG to the deepest level of Jesus' words. The first clue is Jesus' use of the term ναός for "Temple." Following Brown, a number of scholars have suggested that ναός may refer only to the actual Temple building or sanctuary, in distinction from ἱερόν, the term used by the narrator at John 2:14–15 to refer to the whole complex including "the outer court of the Temple, the Court of the Gentiles."[15] Whether or not such a distinction is implied in John 2, in Jesus' vocabulary ναός refers to neither of these, but rather, as FE indicates, to his own body (2:21). As at 2:3–5, this special vocabulary is signaled by Jesus' shift from the narrator's term, ἱερόν, to ναός, a shift which is especially notable since 2:19–21 is the only occurrence of ναός in FG.[16] The Jews, lacking the advantage of FE's special knowledge about Jesus, do not catch the clue, and their response to Jesus highlights this lack of perception (2:20). They restate Jesus' challenge word for word, indicating that they have heard him clearly, but continue to interpret his remarks in reference to the Temple buildings.

The Jews' response at John 2:20 shows that ναός is not the only clue they have missed. The verb in Jesus' riddle, ἐγείρω ("raise up"), can also be understood in more than one way. In the dictionary of the Jews, where ναός is a type of building, ἐγείρω is synonymous with οἰκοδομέω, the usual term

---

[13]Bultmann, *John* 126 n. 1, 128.

[14]Schnackenburg, HTKNT 1.352.

[15]Brown, AB 1.115. See also Lindars, NCBC 138, 141; Francis J. Moloney, "Reading John 2:13–22: The Purification of the Temple," *RB* 97 (1990) 444.

[16]Moloney sees this distinction as particularly significant to the interpretation of the passage ("Reading John 2" 446). Fortna recognizes the shift in terminology as an intentional "wordplay" but does not comment on its significance (*FGIP* 122).

for "construction" which describes what has been happening to the Temple "for forty–six years." This definition is, in their language, supported by proximity to the pronoun οὗτος ("*this* Temple"), which points specifically to the Temple buildings which form the backdrop of their discussion with Jesus. Perhaps realizing the subtlety of Jesus' remarks, FE intrudes at this point to clarify that, in Jesus' vocabulary, ναός is synonymous with σῶμα ("body") rather than ἱερόν, and that ἐγείρω is what happens when someone who is dead comes back to life (2:21–22). If this seems unusual, FE freely admits that such language can be translated only by those who possess not only the special knowledge about Jesus revealed in the Prologue but also specific facts about his impending death and resurrection.

JOHN 4:32—"*I have food to eat that you don't know about*"

Early in the story of the Samaritan Woman, FE indicates that the disciples had gone into the city to buy food (John 4:8). They reappear as the Woman leaves the scene, wondering why Jesus has been speaking with her (4:27). Having secured the items for the meal, they urge him to eat (4:31). Jesus replies, "I have food to eat that you do not know about" (4:32). The ambiguity of this statement is indicated by the disciples' confusion: Where did Jesus get something to eat? Since it is mealtime (4:6), and since the disciples have just returned from the market, the terms "food" (βρῶσις) and "eat" (φάγω) would apparently refer to the noon meal.

Jesus clarifies that the word "food" refers to his commission to do the work of the one who sent him. He has thus been "eating" the whole time the disciples were gone by revealing himself to the Samaritan woman. Jesus then extends the food metaphor to speak of his revelatory mission as a "harvest," one the disciples are about to reap as the Samaritans come out to meet him (John 4:39–42). While the images "food" and "eat" also appear in the consumption riddles discussed in the next chapter, in this context Jesus uses them to grab the disciples' attention so that he may instruct them on his missional objective.

THE LIGHT OF THE WORLD

John 8:12–58, the Light of the World discourse, is an extended riddling session between Jesus and a group of Jews. All seven riddles in this session explore aspects of Jesus' identity. The ambiguity in this episode is sustained by the Jew's ignorance that Jesus' "father," the "one who sent me," is actually God rather than a human being. Based on this ignorance, Jesus renounces them as children of the devil.

As is often the case in the Book of Signs, the riddles in John 8 are delivered in a highly symbolic context. The Light of the World dialogue apparently takes place during the same Feast of Tabernacles described in chapter 7. On the first night of this festival four huge lamps on golden stands were lit in the Court of Women, illuminating the Temple. These lamps may have reminded the Jews of the pillar of fire which led the Israelites through the Wilderness. FE's staging of the dialogue plays on this broad symbolism, as the "treasury" where Jesus proclaims himself "the light of the world" (John 8:12) was near the area were the lamps were erected. Beyond this immediate backdrop, "light" was a powerful metaphor in ancient Judaism, variously representing the Torah, the Temple, Jerusalem, Israel, God, and the great Jewish sages.[17]

The discourse context of John 8 would thus provide the Jews of FG with many possible reference points for Jesus' words. To obtain a correct understanding, however, one must know that in FE's special language "light" symbolizes Jesus' revelatory entrance into a dark world (John 1:4–5). Jesus hints at this special meaning at 8:12b by proclaiming that anyone who follows him will not walk in darkness but instead will have "the light of life." The Pharisees challenge this proposition. Apparently thinking that Jesus is claiming to be a great sage, and knowing that he has no proper rabbinic training (7:15), they demand that he produce witnesses to validate his credentials. The riddling session which follows is based on the Pharisees' confusion over the witnesses Jesus offers, himself and his "father."

---

[17]See Brown, AB 1.343–344; Schnackenburg, HTKNT 2.189–190.

JOHN 8:18—"*I witness on behalf of myself and the father who sent me witnesses*"

The audience of FG may not immediately realize that this statement is ambiguous, because FE has made it very clear that Jesus' "father" who "sent him" is God. For different reasons, the Pharisees in the story do not realize that it is ambiguous, either. The Galilean Jews know that Jesus is the son of Joseph (John 6:41–42), and while the Jerusalem Pharisees may not possess this biographical information, they have no reason to suspect that Jesus' father is not a human being like himself. The saying may be identified as a riddle by the confusion it generates. Apparently willing to allow Jesus to testify on his own behalf, the Pharisees ask him to produce his father so they can question that person about his credentials (8:19).

The Pharisees would view Jesus' answer to the riddle as a statement of the obvious: "You do not know me or my father. If you knew me, you would also know my father" (John 8:19). The Pharisees could reasonably reply that they have just said as much themselves. The latter part of Jesus' statement, however, is a hermeneutical key to all the riddles in John 8. As the Prologue indicates, only Jesus has seen God and therefore only Jesus can reveal God (1:18). As a converse principle, failure to understand Jesus' relationship to God makes it impossible to comprehend Jesus' revelation of God. Because the Pharisees judge things "by the flesh" (8:14–15), meaning that they do not speak FE's special language, they have little hope of answering Jesus' riddles correctly. The remaining riddles in the session move the discussion of Jesus' identity away from physical considerations and toward a revelation of his heavenly origin.

JOHN 8:21—"*Where I am going you cannot come*"

This riddle about Jesus' departure has already appeared at John 7:34 and will reemerge at 13:33, where Jesus will offer the disciples a final and definitive answer. Since this answer is yet to be revealed, the Jews can only guess that Jesus intends to kill himself (8:21). Schnackenburg feels their suggestion is "evil and malicious" because many Jews believed that suicide made one ineligible for participation in the age to come. He therefore paraphrases 8:22 as, "[the Jews said,] he wants to go to hell—we can't and won't follow him."[18] It is by no means clear, however, that such a hostile tone is implied. The Jews are genuinely confused over Jesus' ambiguous use of the term ὅπου, "where." In proximity to ὑπάγω ("go away") and ἐλθεῖν ("come"), ὅπου implies that Jesus will travel from one place to another. Following this logic, the Jews concluded at 7:35 that Jesus intended to flee to the diaspora and "teach the Greeks." The failure of that answer leads them to seek a symbolic meaning when Jesus restates the riddle in chapter 8. Taking their cue from Jesus' prefatory remark that they will die in their sins (8:21a), the Jews conclude that Jesus means he will die and go to heaven while they will not.

In one sense, this answer is ironically correct. Jesus' "going away" will, in fact, involve his voluntary death (10:17–18). A clue to the fuller implication of this death is offered in the answer to the riddle at 8:24, "You are from below (ἐκ τῶν κάτω), I am from above (ἐκ τῶν ἄνω)." Jesus' heavenly origin was explained to Nicodemus in chapter 3, but because the Pharisees are, like Nicodemus, "from below," they cannot understand that his "going away" represents a return to God. They are partially correct in that physical death would obviously be an aspect of this journey.

JOHN 8:24; 8:26—*"Unless you believe that I am, you will die in your sins"; "What I heard from the one who sent me I speak in the world"*

Having answered the previous riddle to his own satisfaction, Jesus immediately offers a new one which elaborates the benefits of accepting his mysterious claims. To go where Jesus is going, one must "believe that I am"; those who do not will "die in your sins." This riddle creates ambiguity by both revealing and concealing what the Jews must believe. Since ἐγώ εἰμι ("I am") is unpredicated, it is best to understand this usage as Jesus' appropriation of the divine name.[19] The Jews, however, do not recognize this. Since Jesus opened the discussion with the statement, "I am the Light" (ἐγώ εἰμι τὸ φῶς; 8:12), and since he has yet to clarify his credentials, they expect him to complete the sentence and tell them who he "is." Jesus proceeds to do this in verses 25b–29, but it is hard to imagine that the Jews in the story could comprehend what he

---

[18]Schnackenburg, HTKNT 2.198.
[19]Brown, AB 1.348–350; Schnackenburg, HTKNT 2.199–200.

is talking about. FE states that they do not understand in an intrusive aside, telling the audience of FG that the Jews still do not realize that Jesus has been sent by God (8:27). In fact, they would have no way to know this, since Jesus' identity as ἐγώ εἰμι will not be revealed until he has been "lifted up" (8:28), a phrase parallel to "go away" in the first riddle in this session. Whatever it means for Jesus to be "I am" will be clear only after his death.

JOHN 8:31-32; 8:38—*"If you abide in my word, you are truly my disciples, and [then] you will know the truth, and the truth will set you free"; "I speak what I have seen with the father, and you also [should] do what you heard with your father"*

The riddle about "truth" depends on an ambiguous use of the verb ἐλευθερόω, "to manumit" or "set free." Jesus says the Jews can experience freedom if they receive the liberating truth which comes from "remaining in my word." This is ambiguous because, as the Jews point out, they are not slaves in the first place (John 8:33). The popular notion that the Jews are hypocritically overlooking their enslavements to Egypt, Babylon, and Rome has homiletic value but misses the point of the exchange. Even when dominated by other nations, the Jews would think of themselves as servants of God alone, and would see their political fortunes as God's blessing or punishment.[20] Their objection reflects the accurate perception that Jesus is questioning their status as God's people, the issue FE wishes to explore in vv. 31–47. As Abraham's seed, the Jews see themselves as the beneficiaries of the patriarch's spiritual estate and status. They therefore do not understand how Jesus' offer of truth and freedom applies to their situation.

Jesus' answer to the riddle at John 8:34–38 specifies the type of "freedom" he has in mind. Allowing that the Jews are descendants of Abraham, Jesus says they are still slaves of sin. While any Jew would accept this thesis in the context of moral exhortation, Jesus clearly has much more than ethics in mind. Sin has in some way jeopardized the elect status of the Jews, for "the slave does not remain in the house forever" (8:35). As a true son, Jesus has power to free the Jews from this slavery and give them a share in Abraham's estate (8:36).

---

[20]Schnackenburg, HTKNT 2.207; Brown, AB 1.355.

The specific sin which has enslaved the Jews is explored with the new riddle at John 8:38, "I speak what I have seen with the father, and you also [should] do what you heard with your father." This translation follows Brown's contention that ποιεῖτε at vv. 38, 41 should be taken as an imperative ("*you should do* the works of your father").[21] Jesus does what he has learned from his father and urges the Jews to do what their father, Abraham, would do. Abraham never threatened to kill someone simply because she told him the truth, yet the Jews seek to kill Jesus for this very reason. Presumably, Abraham would accept the truth Jesus is offering and be freed from sin. The charge that the Jews are not acting like their ancestor casts doubt on their spiritual lineage.

The Jews apparently realize that the discussion is moving from Jesus' credentials to their own spiritual status and affirm their heritage at John 8:41: "We were not born from adultery. We have one father, God." While this claim may echo later Jewish–Christian debate over Jesus' legitimacy, in the storyworld of FG it is clearly a defense of the Jews' own faithfulness. Since Abraham was considered the father of true religion, Jesus' suggestion that the Jews are not acting like Abraham casts doubt on their spiritual integrity. Their insistence that they are not "born of adultery" reflects the OT motif that Israel's idolatry is a form of marital unfaithfulness.[22] Jesus counters that the Jews cannot be God's children for the same reason that they cannot be Abraham's children. If they were children of Abraham, they would not reject Jesus as a messenger of truth; if they were God's children, they would love Jesus because he came from God (8:42).

The Jews' true lineage is deduced from the principle that the child acts like the parent. The Jews act like liars by rejecting Jesus, the truth, and will soon act like murderers by trying to kill him (John 8:59). Since lying and killing are typical behaviors of Satan, Jesus concludes that the Jews are children of the devil. The modern reader, like the Jews in the story, might protest that this line of reasoning begs the question: in a debate over Jesus' identity, the Jews' rejection of Jesus' claims cannot be used to prove that the Jews are children of the devil. But since riddles and riddling sessions operate

---

[21]Brown, AB 1.356.
[22]Schnackenburg, HTKNT 2.212.

on group logic, and since FE's audience presupposes that Jesus is the Truth sent from God, Jesus has no need to defend this line of argument.

FE's deduction that the Jews are children of the devil also demonizes the normal language which they speak. This perspective is evident in the ambiguous use of the terms "truth," "slavery," and "sin" in this dialogue. The "truth" that Jesus urges the Jews to accept is apparently "the eschatological revelation of salvation which Jesus, as God's messenger, has brought."[23] "Knowing the truth" would thus mean accepting Jesus' revelatory proclamation. Since this knowledge provides freedom, the sin which has enslaved the Jews is not moral failure but disbelief in Jesus. It is this very disbelief, however, which makes it impossible for them to understand Jesus' revelatory language in the first place. From this perspective, any normal discourse which does not utilize the unique Johannine vocabulary is inherently false, and anyone who speaks this normal language is a liar. FE can therefore insist that the Jews do not believe Jesus *because* he speaks the truth (8:45); "truth," as FE understands it, is simply not in their devilish vocabulary. Unfortunately for the Jews, only those who are fluent in the special dialect of the Johannine Jesus can have life.

Earlier in this episode FE indicated that Jesus' riddles had a positive effect on some members of the crowd. A number of Jews were moved by his words and believed in him (πολλοὶ ἐπίστευσαν εἰς αὐτόν; John 8:30). These believing Jews revise their opinion after being told that they are children of the devil. It is Jesus, not they, who is of the devil and a "Samaritan" (8:48). Aside from the obvious racial implication, "Samaritan" suggests that Jesus is a blasphemous heretic. This returns the discussion to Jesus' defense of his identity, which is explored in the last two riddles in this session, 8:51 and 8:56.

JOHN 8:51; 8:56—*"Should anyone keep my word, they will not see death unto eternity"; "Abraham your father rejoiced to see my day, and he saw it and was glad"*

Jesus' next riddle makes a bold claim about the effect of his teaching. Anyone who keeps his word "will not see death unto eternity" (θάνατον οὐ μὴ θεωρήσῃ εἰς τὸν αἰῶνα). In normal language the words "never" and

---

[23]Schnackenburg, HTKNT 2.205.

"death" cannot appear together because all people, even Abraham and the prophets, must die (John 8:52). It is also apparently unusual to speak of "seeing" death, for when the Jews repeat Jesus' riddle they change θεωρέω to γεύομαι ("taste"). This unusual use of θεωρέω is actually a valuable clue that Jesus is not using "death" in the normal sense of the term. Although the Jews do not realize this, they have a sufficient grasp of Jesus' meaning to question his orthodoxy. The rhetorical question, "You are not greater than our father Abraham, are you?" parallels the sarcasm of the Samaritan Woman (4:12) and insinuates that Jesus' claims are inappropriate. No teacher can make such exclusive soteriological claims about his or her message. The Jews therefore demand that he stop speaking about himself in such a veiled fashion: "Who do you make yourself?" (8:53).[24]

The Jews' suspicion shows the widening gap between their thinking and the logic of Jesus. From their perspective, the fact that Abraham and the prophets "tasted death" utterly disarms Jesus' claim. The Jews are utilizing an ideological taxonomy which places Jesus in the category of divine emissaries. If even God's greatest messengers (Abraham and the prophets) died, how can Jesus give a teaching which will eternally preserve the lives of people who are not even messengers themselves? Jesus can only point out that his unique paternal relationship with God challenges the Jews' taxonomy (John 8:54–55). He cannot explain this relationship in terms they would understand because he cannot speak lies, the language of those who do not know God (8:55). He therefore continues to explain himself in a way which is necessarily oblique to them, offering a final riddle at 8:56: "Abraham you father rejoiced to see my day, and he saw it and was glad."

The riddle at John 8:56 highlights the categorical difference between Jesus and the Jews. Throughout this dialogue the Jews have insisted that they are Abraham's children. Jesus now suggests that this claim is insignificant because even Abraham recognized that Jesus was greater than himself.[25] In normal language such a contention is absurd, for Jesus is "not fifty years old" (8:57). While this is obviously not what Jesus meant, modern commentators are divided on exactly what Jesus does mean when he says that "Abraham saw

---

[24]Schnackenburg, HTKNT 2.220.
[25]Schnackenburg, HTKNT 2.221.

his day." Some, like Bultmann and Carson, see a general association between Abraham and Jesus in the overall plan of salvation–history. "Abraham knew that he was not himself the fulfillment of the saving will of God" and therefore "looked forward to the fulfillment in the Messiah, and welcomed the day when he himself would be judged by one greater than himself."[26] Others, like Schnackenburg and Brown, feel that Jesus is alluding to the ancient rabbinic tradition that Abraham had a visionary revelation of the coming Messiah.[27] Lindars agrees that Jesus is alluding to a rabbinic tradition in the earlier part of the riddle but insists that "Abraham saw and rejoiced" "must mean that Abraham is alive and in Paradise at the time" of Jesus' proclamation.[28] Whether or not any of these solutions accurately represent FE's thinking, the intended rhetorical effect of the riddle is clear. Returning to his earlier logic, Jesus suggests that if the Jews were truly Abraham's children they would, like Abraham, recognize that God's covenant promises are being confirmed before their eyes.[29]

Jesus ends the riddling session by providing the hermeneutical key to all the riddles in John 8: "Before Abraham became, I am" (8:58). Brown and others have suggested that the unpredicated ἐγὼ εἰμί is an "implication of deity."[30] From this perspective, the Jews attempt to stone Jesus because he makes himself equal to God (cf. 5:18, 10:33). While FE would certainly understand ἐγὼ εἰμί in this way, it seems doubtful that the Jews of FG have reached this conclusion. Throughout the riddling session the Jews have been unable to understand Jesus' revelation of his identity. In light of this incomprehension, their attempt to stone Jesus is probably motivated simply by his use of the divine name "I Am." In the broader irony of FG, the Jews defy the divine revelation by attempting to protect God's name.

---

[26]Bultmann, *John* 326; Carson, *John* 356–357.

[27]Schnackenburg, HTKNT 2.221–223; Brown, AB 1.359–360.

[28]Lindars, NCBC 334–335. Brown refutes Lindars' position (AB 1.359–360).

[29]Schnackenburg, HTKNT 2.224.

[30]Brown, AB 1.367. See also Schnackenburg, HTKNT 2.223–224; Carson, *John* 358; Painter, *Quest* 302.

JOHN 9:39; 10:1–5—*"For judgement I came into this world,*
so that those not seeing would see and those seeing would become blind";
THE PARABLE OF THE SHEPHERD AND THE STRANGERS

The story of the healing of the blind man opens with a neck riddle delivered to Jesus by the disciples (John 9:2) and ends with a mission riddle from Jesus to the Pharisees (9:39). The brief exchange which follows the second riddle introduces the parable of the Shepherd and the Strangers. Both 9:39 and 10:1–5 explore the problem of belief in Jesus. The first riddle is delivered on the heels of the blind man's worship of Jesus as the Son of Man and in the face of the Pharisees' disbelief (9:35–40). The second riddle leads the Jews to debate whether Jesus is legitimate or demon–possessed (10:21).

The blind man whom Jesus encounters in John 9 is a tragic figure. Aside from the fact that he cannot see, he must live with the popular notion that his handicap is a divine punishment for someone's sin (9:2). Jesus removes the blindness but leaves him a sinner by forcing him to travel and wash his eyes on the Sabbath (9:6–7, 14). This makes him an unfortunate pawn in the ongoing power struggle between Jesus and the Pharisees, and the man's refusal to condemn Jesus ultimately leads to his excommunication (9:34). Jesus encounters him again after his trial and leads him to faith in the Son of Man (9:35–38). Reflecting on the irony that a blind man perceives his divine identity while the Pharisees do not, Jesus offers a riddle: "For judgment I came into this world, so that those not seeing would see and those seeing would become blind" (9:39).

John 9:39 may be considered a riddle under criterion number four: when a character uses language that seems intentionally incongruous by normal patterns of language, and when such incongruity blurs the links between language and referent, such discourse may represent a riddle. The incongruity of Jesus' words is highlighted in FE's presentation. Earlier in chapter 9, and again immediately after the riddle is delivered, FE uses the term τυφλός to refer to blindness (ἄνθρωπον τυφλὸν ἐκ γενετῆς, 9:1; οἱ βλέποντες τυφλοὶ γένωνται, 9:40). The riddle, however, refers to this condition as μὴ βλέποντες to highlight the paradox that "those not seeing" can "see": ἵνα οἱ μὴ βλέποντες βλέπωσιν. The juxtaposition of μὴ βλέποντες and βλέπωσιν challenges the Pharisees to explain how one can "see" and "be blind" at the same time. At least one of these terms must be an ambiguous reference to something other than physical sight.

The Pharisees' answer ("We are not also blind, are we?") may or may not indicate that they realize the true answer to Jesus' riddle. "Blindness" was a popular metaphor for spiritual imperception in ancient Judaism,[31] and against this background the Pharisees may see Jesus' words as a thinly veiled criticism of their refusal to accept his claims. If this is the case, these individuals are among the larger group of Pharisees who are responsible for the blind man's excommunication (John 9:13, 22, 24–34). Carson takes this position, commenting that "some Pharisees who were listening in on this [Jesus'] assessment understood little of it, and, utterly self–centered, they wanted only to find out whether Jesus thought his statements . . . applied to them."[32] If this is the case, the Pharisees understand Jesus' statement but reject its application to themselves.

On the other hand, it is possible that the Pharisees are genuinely confused by the riddle and desire more information. These characters appear suddenly in the narrative and are introduced as "the Pharisees who were with him [Jesus]" (John 9:40). "With him" may mean that these Pharisees are sympathetic to Jesus, and perhaps therefore opposed to the blind man's excommunication. This would place them in the same category as Nicodemus, and would make their response a genuine attempt to apply Jesus' riddle to their situation, parallel Nicodemus' response at 3:4. If this is the case, the Pharisees' question is an attempt to understand what it means to be "blind" and why it is that Jesus considers them "blind" despite their sympathy with his cause.

In either case, the correct answer to the riddle is that those who "see" will worship Jesus as the Son of Man (John 9:35–38), while those who do not worship him are "blind" to his true identity. "Son of Man" is Jesus' most common self–designation in the Synoptics, but the title is rare in FG and apparently highlights his deity (1:51, 3:13, 8:24). As in chapter 8, failure to recognize this secret identity is sin (8:24). Jesus' rebuttal at 9:41 stresses the consequence of the Pharisees' incomprehension: "If you were blind you would

---

[31]Schnackenburg, HTKNT 2.256.
[32]Carson, *John* 378. See also Lindars, NCBC 352.

have no sin. But since you say, 'We see,' your sin remains." Thus, if the Pharisees were physically blind they would not necessarily be sinners (contra 9:2), but claiming to possess spiritual sight while denying Jesus is tantamount to lying. This sin remains as long as they refuse to accept him.

Jesus follows this statement with a lengthy discourse on various facets of the livestock industry (John 10:1–5). These remarks are so far removed from the preceding discussion that the Pharisees cannot comprehend what he is talking about, and FE explains to the audience of FG that Jesus has spoken a παροιμία (10:6). As Carson notes, παροιμία (Hebrew מָשָׁל, *mashal*) "can refer to an extraordinarily wide variety of literary forms, including proverbs, parables, maxims, similes, allegories, fables, riddles, narratives embodying certain truths, taunts and more."[33] Most scholars have concluded that παροιμία means "parable" in this context and have attempted to interpret John 10:1–5 in conjunction with the Synoptic parables. J. A. T. Robinson's 1955 article "The Parable of John 10:1–5" was a landmark study in this area, the conclusions of which were developed and popularized by C. H. Dodd. According to Dodd, FE's preference for the term παροιμία over παραβολή is insignificant to form–critical analysis of the passage, revealing "not a distinction of *genres*, but one more indication that John sometimes reaches back to the primitive Aramaic tradition by way of a different Greek translation." John 10:1–5 is thus "the one *pericopé* in this gospel [FG] which is offered explicitly as a parable."[34] Bultmann's influential commentary on FG

---

[33]Carson, *John* 383. See also Friedrich Hauck, "Παροιμία," *TDNT* (ed. Gerhard Friedrich; trans. Geoffrey W. Bromiley; Grand Rapids, MI: Eerdmans, 1967) 5.854–855.

[34]C. H. Dodd, *Historical Tradition in the Fourth Gospel* (Cambridge: Cambridge University Press, 1963) 383; John A. T. Robinson, "The Parable of John 10:1–5," *ZNW* 46 (1955) 233, 233 n. 2. Both Robinson and Dodd believe that John 10:1–5 was produced through the fusion of two traditional parables. The first, 10:1–3a, compares the one who enters the sheepfold by the gate with the one who steals in over the wall, concluding that only the former is the true shepherd. The second parable, 10:3b–5, compares this true shepherd with a stranger. The sheep will only follow the shepherd because they do not recognize the stranger's voice (Robinson, "Parable" 235; Dodd, *HTFG* 383). Although these two traditional parables have "no exact formal parallel," "it is clear that the broad elements of structure" are similar to several Synoptic parables. The characters in FG's parable are also familiar from the Synoptic parables and function in similar ways in the story. Dodd therefore concludes that "there is good reason to believe that the material [John 10:1–5] was drawn

promoted a similar conclusion. Bultmann agrees that John 10:1–5 is "a genuine parable which may not be allegorized." This parable was taken from a pre–Johannine source, where the parable ended at 10:4 and focused exclusively on the relationship between the shepherd and the thieves. Verse 5 "is clearly the Evangelist's own explanatory addition," and v. 6 was added to focus attention on the inability of unbelievers to understand Jesus' revelation. The theme of unbelief is developed in the allegorical expansion at 10:8ff.[35]

Many subsequent commentators have followed Dodd and Bultmann's conclusion that the παροιμία at John 10:1–5 is a traditional parable with a Synoptic flavor. Brown, for example, says that 10:6a should be translated "'[he] spoke this parable.'" He proceeds to cite many OT passages which may have provided the pastoral imagery for this parable and compares the Johannine use of these images to the Synoptic presentation.[36] From the developmental perspective, Painter also relates John 10:1–5 to the Synoptic parables and allegories. At an earlier stage in the tradition, the shepherd in the parable represented Jesus, the gatekeeper represented John the Baptist, and the overall point of the pericope was "to judge the Jewish leaders by their attitude to Jesus." FE allegorized this parable in Christological terms by adding vv.

---

from the same reservoir of tradition as the Synoptic parables" (Dodd, *HTFG* 385). Going further, Robinson argues that both of these pre–Johannine parables were authentic to Jesus (Robinson, "Parable" 236, 239). The first parable, 10:1–3a, probably arose "out of the claims of Jesus for his own teaching, when his authority is challenged by the Scribes and Pharisees" (235). The second parable, 10:3b–5, was delivered in "the closing stages of Jesus' ministry, when he is concerned to warn the Jews, and particularly their leaders, of the urgency of the eschatological situation in which they are living and of the short time left before the final crisis comes upon them" (237). Lindars, who supports Robinson's hypothesis, also believes that 10:1–21"has sufficient links with the Synoptic tradition to ensure that it has its basis in authentic memories of Jesus' teaching" (NCBC 352–353).

[35]Bultmann, *John* 371–373, first quotation 371 n. 3, second quotation 373 n. 3.

[36]Following Robinson, Brown sees two parables at John 10:1–5. The first stresses that authentic spiritual leaders "enter by the gate," while the second highlights Jesus' pastoral care for his followers. Also with Robinson, Brown concludes that both parables are authentic, and further speculates that the allegorical expansion of the parables at 10:7–18 includes "traces of an explanation that may very well stem from Jesus himself" (AB 1.391–393, quotation 391).

7–10.[37] As is evident from the readings of Robinson, Dodd, Bultmann, Brown, and Painter, the view that the παροιμία at John 10:1–5 is a "parable" can have significant implications for one's understanding of the passage.

While these commentators have much to say about the form and tradition–history of John 10:1–5, the recognition that this unit is a "parable" does not adequately explain its function in the current text of FG. Brown's commentary provides a convenient illustration. Following the Synoptic model, Brown defines a "parable" as "a simple illustration or illustrative story having a single point." Whereas "[John] xvi 25 indicates that in Johannine thought Jesus' parables were not easily understood, the present passage [10:1–5] leaves no doubt that Jesus spoke this way to make himself understood."[38] It is hard to see how this could be the case. In the first place, 10:1–5 is directly preceded by Jesus' pronouncement that the Pharisees are "blind" to his true identity and immediately followed by FE's explanation that "they did not know what he said to them" (10:6). Further, the "explanation" of this discourse at 10:7–18, which includes two "I am" sayings and a reference to prospective converts in FE's own day (10:16),[39] is obviously aimed at FE's audience rather than Jesus' audience in the story world. Brown recognizes this but concludes that the Pharisees' "failure to understand [the parable] is not surprising, for similar lack of comprehension greets the parables *in the Synoptic tradition*."[40]

---

[37]Painter, *Quest* 345–353, quotation 348. FE directed the earliest version of this episode to "waverers in the synagogue," who were admonished to suffer excommunication and enter the Johannine community in order to receive life (352). After the Johannine Christians were excommunicated, FE added 10:11–18 to address "an internal Jewish Christian conflict concerning leadership in the [Johannine] community. The evangelist argued that no leader [=the "hireling," 10:12–13] in the community replaced Jesus" (353). The "hireling" represents leaders who failed to resolve a serious doctrinal division created by "wolves" (10:13), heretical teachers (354–355).

[38]Brown, AB, first quotation 1.390, second quotation 1.386.

[39]These potential converts are variously understood to be Gentile prospects (Bultmann, *John* 383–384; Schnackenburg, HTKNT 2.299–300; Lindars, NCBC 363; Carson, *John* 388) or non–Johannine Christians (J. Louis Martyn, *The Gospel of John in Christian History* [New York, NY: Paulist Press, 1978] 15; Raymond *Brown, The Community of the Beloved Disciple: The Life, Loves, and Hates of an Individual Church in New Testament Times* [New York, NY: Paulist Press, 1979] 78, 90; Painter, *Quest* 357).

[40]Brown, AB 1.393, emphasis added.

A more accurate appraisal of John 10:1–5 appears in Hauck's article on παροιμία in *TDNT*. Outside the NT this term normally refers to proverbs or gnomic maxims, but in FG it refers to Jesus' "'hidden, obscure speech' which stands in need of interpretation." The use of παροιμία at 10:6 "retrospectively calls the allegory of the shepherd a concealing speech."[41] Language which creates confusion by intentionally concealing its referent falls into the riddle genre, irrespective of its surface form. The riddle at John 10:1–5 takes the surface form of a parable but still functions to generate ambiguity in the present text of FG. As such, it is better to follow Schnackenburg's understanding that John 10:1–5 "is a real riddle" which "sets out to illustrate in a figurative manner facts which comprised part of Jesus' self–revelation but which were made known [only to FE's audience] as background material."[42]

John 9:39 and 10:1–5 represent, then, two riddles. The larger unit in which they are situated, 9:35–10:18, is a typical Johannine riddling session: riddle (9:39); confusion (9:40); answer (9:41); new riddle (10:1–5); confusion (10:6); new answer (10:7–18); confusion (10:19–21). The entire session is a commentary on the events of chapter 9. Some people, like the blind man and others who recognize Jesus' identity, are sheep. Others, like the Pharisees, are thieves and bandits who seek to oppress the faithful. Jesus is the shepherd who cares for the sheep and acts in their best interest. The true sheep, recognizing this posture of self–sacrifice, will follow Jesus and not the thieving Pharisees.

JOHN 12:32—*"Should I be lifted up
from the earth, I will draw all people to myself"*

This statement may be categorized as a riddle on the basis of two criteria. First, FE intrudes at John 12:33 to explain that ἐὰν ὑψωθῶ ("should I be lifted up") "signifies" (σημαίνω) the manner of Jesus' death. Second, Jesus' words are incompatible with conventional messianic beliefs and

---

[41]Hauck, "Παροιμία" 5.856. Bultmann recognizes that παροιμία can be translated as "both proverb and riddle," and that John 10:6 focuses on "the hearers' inability to understand this 'riddle'" (*John* 375, 375 n. 4).

[42]Schnackenburg, HTKNT 2.284–286, quotation 2.285.

therefore confuse his audience (12:34). The riddle thus explores two related themes, Jesus' messianic identity and the significance of his impending death. The audience of FG should have no difficulty deciphering this riddle. John 12:32 is the third "lifted up" saying in the Book of Signs. The first of these sayings appears in the dialogue with Nicodemus at 3:15, where Jesus says that the Son of Man, like Moses' bronze serpent, will be lifted up to give life. The second "lifted up" saying appears at 8:28 in the Light of the World dialogue, where Jesus tells the Jews that they will know who his father is after they have lifted up the Son of Man. All three "lifted up" sayings seem to build on Isaiah 52:13, "See, my servant shall prosper; he shall be exalted and lifted up, and shall be very high" (NRSV). This text provides the hermeneutical key for the dual meaning of ὑψόω in FG. As FE notes at 12:33, "lifted up" is a euphemism for "hung on a cross," but the term also encompasses Jesus' resurrection and return to the Father, "one continuous action of ascent" and exaltation.[43] Both meanings are clearly in view in chapter 3, where Nicodemus is told that only the one who came down from heaven can ascend into heaven (3:13), and in chapter 8, where the Jews cannot understand Jesus because "you are from below, I am from above" (8:23). These earlier usages should prepare the audience of FG to understand the final "lifted up" saying at 12:32.

The notion that "lifted up" is a dual reference to Jesus' crucifixion and ascension is also reenforced for FE's audience by the narrative context of John 12:32. The resurrection of Lazarus, Jesus' last sign, has aroused the interest of the Passover crowd, who openly discuss Jesus' identity in the Temple (11:45, 55–56). Before appearing publicly in Jerusalem, Jesus is anointed by Mary at Bethany, an act which he describes as preparation for his burial (12:7). The Triumphal Entry follows, during which the crowds proclaim Jesus "King of Israel" (12:12–18). Jesus' growing popularity frustrates the Jewish leaders, who resolve to terminate him (11:46–53, 57; 12:19). At this point a group of Greeks (ἕλληνές) suddenly appear at the festival and seek an audience with Jesus (12:20–21). Their arrival coincides with, and perhaps inaugurates, Jesus' hour of glorification as the Son of Man. As the parable of the grain indicates, this hour must end in Jesus' death, for a seed cannot reproduce until it dies

[43]Brown, AB 1.146, quotation here. See also Schnackenburg, HTKNT 2.393; Carson, *John* 444.

(12:23–24). Reflecting on this prospect, Jesus reaffirms his commitment to the Father's glory (12:28–30). John 12:31–36 is a commentary on this larger sequence of events, explaining how Jesus' death will fulfill, rather than end, his mission.

With such strong connections to the larger narrative, John 12:32 should be relatively easy to decipher. But the present text of FG, whether an oral composition or a product of redaction, has not been carefully constructed. This has created three glaring inconsistencies in the narrative. First, the specific point of ambiguity at 12:32 is unclear. Second, the crowd's discussion at v. 34 is obviously prompted by Jesus' riddle but does not seem related to the problem raised by the riddle. Third, Jesus' answer at 12:35–36 does not seem to address the point of ambiguity which the crowd has identified. The present study will explore these inconsistencies and attempt to demonstrate that they can be resolved when 12:32 is understood to be a riddle.

FE's dual understanding of ὑψόω makes the term particularly ripe for Jesus' ambiguous discourse. According to FG's typical narrative pattern, the characters in the story should light on the most obvious meaning of the riddle in the immediate context. The Jews of John 12 should therefore interpret "lifted up" in the literal sense as a reference to crucifixion and, following 7:20, should proceed to protest that they are not seeking to kill Jesus. Since they are unaware of Jesus' heavenly origin, they should not realize that Jesus is actually referring to his impending ascent to the Father. Verses 33–34, however, suggest that Jesus has used "lifted up" literally (crucifixion) while the Jews have interpreted the term figuratively (ascent). FE's explanatory comment, "he said this signifying what kind of death (σημαίνων ποίῳ θανάτῳ) he was about to die," indicates that Jesus is using "lifted up" in the more obvious sense. The Jews, however, are thinking at a deeper level. They have come to understand Jesus as a messianic figure, and in their view it is necessary for the Messiah to "remain forever" (12:34). They therefore conclude that Jesus is making a distinction between the Christ and the Son of Man and ask, "Who is this 'Son of Man'?" This suggests that the ambiguity in the riddle does not derive from the dual meanings of ὑψόω in FG, but rather from a conflict between Jesus' statement and conventional messianic expectations.

The second problem in the present text of FG builds on the first. When the Jews request clarification, their restatement of the riddle is quite different from what Jesus actually said: "We have heard from the Law that *the Christ* must remain forever, and how do you say, '*It is necessary* (δεῖ) that *the Son of Man* be lifted up?'" (John 12:34). Jesus has not referred to himself as "the Christ" anywhere in this context, and his last mention of "the Son of Man" appeared as a circumlocution at 12:23.[44] To further complicate matters, the Jews' paraphrase implies a distinction between "Christ" and "Son of Man" which clearly reflects FE's own Christology. In FG, "Son of Man" is a higher Christological title than "Christ," expressing Jesus' unique incarnational identity (1:51; 3:13; 6:27, 53, 62; 8:28; 9:35–39). The Jews in the story should not be privy to this special usage. The Jews have also changed the tone of "lifted up," shifting from Jesus' subjunctive ("should I be lifted up") to a δεῖ + infinitive construction ("it is necessary to be lifted up") which implies that Jesus has threatened to depart. On the surface, this response is similar to their earlier confusion over the riddle, "Where I am going you cannot come" (7:33; 8:21). Reflecting on that riddle, the crowd speculated that Jesus would flee to the diaspora or kill himself. But the implication at 12:34 that Jesus "*must* be lifted up" also betrays a distinctly Johannine perspective, for in FE's view Jesus must ascend from the earth to complete his salvific mission and return to his pre–existent state (3:14–15; 6:62–63; 7:33–34; 8:23–24, 28; 10:11–18; 14:1–3, 28; 16:5–7, 28). The Jews in this episode thus seem to possess special information about Jesus which has not been revealed to any character in the story up to this point.

The final problem in the passage under consideration involves the relationship between Jesus' riddle and its answer (John 12:35–36). Rather than alleviating the crowd's confusion, Jesus warns the Jews that the light will be with them for only a short time (ἔτι μικρὸν χρόνον) and that they must act quickly to become "sons of light" before the darkness overcomes them. This answer is problematic for two reasons. First, it seems to focus on the imminence of Jesus' departure and the subsequent urgency of the appeal to respond. As noted above, this theme is not present in the actual riddle ("should I be lifted up"), but is introduced by the Jews' paraphrase ("*must* be lifted up").

---

[44]From the Jews' perspective, the statement, "The hour has come for the Son of Man to be glorified," would presumably be equivalent to, "The hour has come for me to be glorified."

In fact, the theme of urgency may only be *implied* from this paraphrase, for the Jews seem concerned with the basic possibility of Jesus' departure, not its timing. Jesus does suggest at 12:31 that judgement has come upon the world "now" (νῦν), but this claim is more closely connected to the thunderous voice from heaven (12:28–30) than to the "lifted up" saying. Second, as is often the case in FG's riddling sessions, Jesus' answer is not directed to the concern the Jews have raised. They have asked Jesus how he understands the term "Son of Man." His answer sidesteps that issue and actually addresses FE's interpretation of the riddle at v. 33: the Jews must accept Jesus quicky because he is soon to die. This answer would only sustain the Jews' confusion by confirming their belief that Jesus will not remain with them.

All three problems are easily resolved within the model of dual vocalization discussed in Chapter 5. Commentators agree that the encounter between Jesus and the Jews in John 12 reflects issues from the Christian–Jewish controversy of the late first–century.[45] The riddle at 12:32 is directed to the question: how can Christians claim that Jesus is the Christ when he died on a cross (v. 34)? FE could have addressed this question directly by making the riddle at 12:32 read, "If *the Son of Man* be lifted up he will draw all people to himself." The Jews' remarks at 12:34 are in fact a response to this version of the riddle, where ambiguity is generated by the juxtaposition of the terms "Son of Man" and "lifted up." In conventional thinking, "Son of Man" and "Christ" are synonymous terms, and it is impossible for the Christ to "be lifted up" and go away rather than remaining with his people. Why, then, has FE obfuscated his presentation by changing "Son of Man" to "I" in the present text of FG? As an oral composer, FE speaks not only to his own audience but also as Jesus to the Jews in the story. Consistent with the story setting, FE's "Son of Man" becomes "I" on the lips of Jesus. But this simple accommodation to the narrative setting has disrupted the flow of the text by eliminating the ambiguous term from the riddle.

While the present text of FG suggests that Jesus is playing on the dual meanings of ὑψόω, FE is actually concerned with the tension which the Jews of his own day would see between Jesus' death and his claim to be Son of Man. The Jews in the story therefore respond in the words of FE's

---

[45]Schnackenburg, HTKNT 2.395; Brown, AB 1.479; Carson, *John* 446.

contemporaries, "Who is this Son of Man?" Their question is answered at John 12:35–36—the Son of Man is the light which has come into the world to make people children of light. While this answer would not be satisfactory to the Jews in the story world or the real Jews in FE's world, it would support the later Christian understanding of Jesus' death and resurrection.

JOHN 13:33 (//7:34; 8:21)—*"Where I am going you cannot come"*

Judas' departure sets the events of Jesus' "hour" in motion; the audience of FG realizes that Jesus does not have much time left. But rather than revealing himself to the disciples directly, Jesus states that the Son of Man will soon be glorified and that God will be glorified in him (John 13:31). This statement would be puzzling enough, but Jesus further obfuscates matters by repeating a riddle he has delivered to the Jews on two earlier occasions. At 7:34, after many from the crowd believe, Jesus tells the Jews that they will not be able to come where he is going. This riddle reappears at 8:21 in the Light of the World discourse. It will be helpful to review these earlier occurrences before discussing the function of this riddle in the Farewell.

John 7 explores two dimensions of "seeking Jesus" (ζητέω). On one hand, some seek Jesus out of genuine desire to determine his identity. As the dialogue unfolds, members of the crowd attempt to situate Jesus in conventional categories: is Jesus a "good person" or a "deceiver"? (7:12); how can he teach when he has no formal education? (7:15); is he the Christ? (7:26); how could he be the Christ, since his origins are known while no one will know the origins of the Christ? (7:27); could even the Christ do more miracles than Jesus has done? (7:31); perhaps Jesus is the Prophet? (7:40); how can Jesus be the Christ when he comes from Galilee rather than Bethlehem? (7:41–42, 52). Jesus does not respond to any of these speculations and, perhaps to avoid them, simply reiterates the claim that his teaching will be self–validating for those who sincerely desire to serve God (7:16–17, 24, 28–29). After closing the discussion with the riddle of living water (7:37–38), Jesus disappears from the scene, leaving the crowd to make their own decision about his identity.

Alongside this story, John 7 tells another story of the Jewish authorities "seeking Jesus" in order to arrest him and silence his message. The chapter opens with Jesus in Galilee because the Jews of Judea seek to kill him (7:1). Jesus tells his brothers that he cannot go up to the Feast for this reason, and when he does go up he must do so in secret (7:6–10). Those who seek to know his identity must conduct their search behind closed doors, for "no one spoke openly about him for fear of the Jews" (7:13). Jesus confronts this persecution in a public forum at 7:19, asking why they seek to kill him. The crowd's attempt to deny this accusation cannot be genuine, for they themselves later identify Jesus as "the man whom they seek to kill" (7:20, 25). Jesus' suspicion is confirmed at 7:30 as some from the crowd seek to apprehend him, and again at 7:32 as the Pharisees and Chief Priests send officers for his arrest.

The riddle at John 7:33 plays on these two dimensions of seeking Jesus: "You will seek me and you will not find me, and where I am you are not able to come." The statement which precedes the riddle offers a clue to the audience of FG: "A little while I am with you and I go away to the one who sent me." In light of the Prologue, this audience knows that "the one who sent" Jesus is God, and that Jesus, as God, is indeed to be on earth only for a short while. Because they do not know this, the Jews seek Jesus in the first sense, attempting to know his identity by placing him in conventional categories. Their pursuit will be fruitless because Jesus violates all categories, and the Jews will be left unable to identify Jesus and therefore unable to go where he is going, heaven. But the characters in the story do not have enough information to come to this conclusion, and must look for clues in the immediate discourse context. Since Jesus' life is in danger, it is logical that he would flee in order to avoid arrest. The Jews are confused only by the last phrase, for they cannot identify a hiding place where they could not go. Repeating the riddle amongst themselves, they speculate that Jesus will become a wandering sage, teaching Greeks in the Diaspora (7:35–36).

The second appearance of this riddle at John 8:21 also involves a debate over Jesus' identity. After proclaiming himself the "light of the world" and insisting that his father witnesses for him, Jesus says, "I am going away, and you will seek me, and you will die in your sins. Where I am going you are not able to come." Having learned from previous experience that Jesus is not leaving for the Diaspora (as his continued presence in Jerusalem indicates), the crowd wonders whether this means that Jesus will kill himself (8:22). For the audience of FG this conclusion is ironic, for Jesus' departure will indeed involve his voluntary death. The Jews will certainly die as well, but because of their "sin" they will not be able to go where Jesus is going, back to God.

In both John 7:34 and 8:21, the Jews' confusion arises from their inability to identify a place where they could not go. For those who know that Jesus has come from God and is returning to God, it is obvious why human beings cannot follow him. But because the Jews are not privy to the information revealed in the Prologue, even those who believe his signs cannot answer his riddle.

These earlier occurrences of the departure riddle explain the interaction between Jesus and Peter at John 13:36–38. Like the Jews, Peter cannot identify a place where only Jesus could go. He therefore concludes, like the Jews, that Jesus is planning a distant journey and insists that he is willing to travel anywhere to remain with Jesus. Apparently believing that Jesus is ordering him to stay behind because of the dangers of the trip, he assures his teacher that he would even lay down his life in order to stay with him (13:37). This would seem to be an ideal occasion for Jesus to reveal his heavenly identity to the disciples, telling them that they cannot come with him because he is going to die and return to his special place with God. Instead, to prolong their confusion, he simply restates the riddle at 13:36: "Where I go you are not able to follow me now, but you will follow later" (13:36). This statement is apparently intended to comfort Peter, but it fails to alleviate his confusion because it does not address the ambiguous term ὅπου ("where"). Jesus still has not indicated "where" (ὅπου) he is going, and in fact aggravates Peter further by replacing "not able to come (ἐλθεῖν)" with "not able to follow (ἀκολουθῆσαι)." Peter has already been "following" Jesus for quite some time, and can only question why he cannot continue to do so now (13:37).

It is clear throughout this exchange that Peter, lacking the special knowledge of the Prologue, believes with the Jews at John 7:34 that Jesus will travel to some other city or town. In Peter's vocabulary, "come" and "follow" mean "travel with me," which Peter is willing to do even at cost of his life. The true answer to the riddle, however, is closer to that offered by the Jews at 8:22, for in Jesus' vocabulary "where I am going" refers to his death and subsequent return to the Father. This is something Jesus must do now but which Peter can experience only "later" (ὕστερον). Ironically, Peter will do this, as he suggests, by laying down his own life (cf. 21:18–19).

In the narrative world of John 13, Peter functions to distract the disciples from the real answer to Jesus' departure riddles by suggesting a more obvious solution which does not require special information about Jesus' identity. While washing Peter's feet, Jesus says that one of them is "unclean"; shortly after this Jesus says that one of them will betray him; after Judas leaves, Jesus tells Peter that he cannot follow him, and then says that Peter will deny him three times before the cock crows (13:38). The disciples would thereby be led to believe that Peter is the unclean one who will betray Jesus and that Jesus must flee to escape Peter's treachery. This would adequately explain Jesus' statement that one of those at the table would hand him over (13:18), and also Jesus' reasons for not permitting Peter to follow him. By using Peter as a distraction, the Johannine Jesus can sustain the disciples' ignorance of the true reason for his departure throughout the rest of the teaching section.

JOHN 14:4; 14:7— *"You know the way where I am going";*
"Now you know the Father and have seen him"

After silencing Peter through incrimination, Jesus proceeds to discuss the details of his departure and return. He plans to visit his "father" and make preparations for the disciples to go to his father's house with him (John 14:1–3). For the audience of FG, who know that Jesus' father is God and that he is about to return to God (13:1–3), this is a logical extension of his earlier remarks, for Jesus' betrayal and death would necessarily initiate his return to God's abode. At the same time, Jesus' words at 14:2–3 would reinforce the disciples' misconceptions. Peter has asked where Jesus is going, and the disciples are now told that he is going to his father's house; Peter has asked why he cannot follow Jesus, and the disciples are now told that they must wait because Jesus has not prepared a place for them yet.[46] These remarks are followed by a new riddle which opens with an undefined ὅπου: "You know the way *where* I am going." Since the disciples still do not know the identity of Jesus' father, much less where his father lives, Thomas can only states the obvious: "Lord, we don't know where you are going; how could we know the way?" (14:5).

---

[46]Segovia, *FOW* 82–83.

Jesus' response to Thomas' question is directed only to the audience of FG and not to the disciples. The faithful know "the way" to Jesus' father because Jesus himself is "the way, and the truth, and the life"; for this reason, "no one comes to the father except through me" (John 14:6). The audience of FG recognizes that the latter statement is the answer to the riddle at 14:4: the disciples know the way to God because they know Jesus, who is God. This exclusive Christological statement is lost, however, on the disciples, for apart from the Prologue and scattered asides (5:18; 8:27) there is no way to know that Jesus' father is God and that Jesus, as the revelation of God, is himself the way to God. Thomas has asked Jesus to draw a map from Jerusalem to somewhere in Galilee, and from the perspective of this expectation Jesus' words remain ambiguous and confusing.

The disciples' sustained ignorance of the identity of Jesus' father also explains the enigmatic John 14:8. After being told that he knows Jesus' father, has seen Jesus' father, and knows the way to the house of Jesus' father, Philip says, "Lord, show us the father, and it is enough for us." Commentators have generally failed to recognize the dual rhetorical levels of Jesus' words in the Farewell and have consequently assumed that Philip is speaking from the perspective of FG's audience. Hence Segovia's conclusion that "Philip's request for Jesus to show them the Father . . . represents a request to see God, whom Jesus claims as his Father—that is, a request for a theophany." Carson similarly muses that Philip "joins the queue of human beings through the ages who have rightly understood that there can be no higher experience, no greater good, than seeing God as he is." At the same time, most commentators acknowledge that Philip is still ignorant of Jesus' true identity. In Segovia's words, "the disciples remain at a complete loss with regard to the nature and implications of Jesus' mission."[47] But if Philip does not yet understand Jesus' mission and identity, it is hard to understand his statement as a request for a theophany. What does he mean, then, when he asks Jesus to show them the father?

This problem may be resolved by recognizing that Philip, as a character in the story, does not know what the audience of FG knows about Jesus. For

---

[47]First quotation Segovia, *FOW* 88 n. 55; second quotation Carson, *John*, 494; third quotation Segovia, *FOW* 88. See also Brown, AB 2.631–632.

the audience of FG, Philip's request is ironic and even comical. Philip has seen God many times, and is looking at God even as he speaks to Jesus. Commentators who read Philip's remark from the audience's perspective can only conclude that Philip is requesting a deeper and perhaps more mystical experience of God. But at the story level, in the context of a Johannine riddling session, Philip's request is much more modest and follows the same logic as the Jews' question at John 8:19 ("Where is your father?"). Confused by Jesus' riddles and thinking that Jesus' father is a person from Galilee, Philip simply asks Jesus to tell them who his father is before explaining how to get to the man's house. Jesus' answer would only exacerbate Philip further: "the one who has seen me has seen the father" (14:9). In any normal language register, a person cannot be his own father. Not so in the special language of the Johannine Jesus.

Chapter 8
Salvation Riddles in John

The eight "salvation riddles" in FG explore aspects of the Christian experience. FE uses these riddles to describe the unique relationship between believers and God, a relationship which is incomprehensible to the world. Ambiguity arises from the fact that Jesus speaks of this spiritual relationship in terms of biological functions. Two of the salvation riddles play on the biological metaphors "birth" and "life," and four more play on the metaphors "eating" and "drinking." In John's vocabulary, these biological functions refer to spiritual realities, but the characters in the story cannot understand Jesus' words because the discourse context seems to point to a more literal meaning.

BIRTH/LIFE RIDDLES

"Life" (ζωή) is perhaps the most common Johannine metaphor for salvation, appearing 36 times in FG and 13 times in 1–2–3 John. The Father and Son possess "life" (John 1:4, 5:25, 11:25, 14:6, 17:2) and bestow this quality on those who "know God," i.e., those who accept Jesus as the one whom God has sent (17:3). To receive this new life, believers must undergo a radical transformation which FE frequently describes with cognates of γεννάω ("give birth"; John 1:12–13; 1 John 2:29; 3:9; 4:7–8; 5:1; 5:18). Both terms, "[eternal] life" and "rebirth," are common in contemporary Christian discourse, so that modern readers of FG readily recognize them as metaphors for deeper spiritual realities. At the same time, "birth" and "life" are entirely comprehensible outside these special Johannine usages as references to biological processes. The coexistence of these two usages, literal and spiritual,

263

makes both terms ripe for ambiguity. Such is the case in the riddles at John 3:3, 5 and 11:25–26.

JOHN 3:3, 5—*"Unless you are born (ἄνωθεν/of water and spirit) you cannot see the Kingdom of God"*
     The conversation between Jesus and Nicodemus contains two of the best known verses in the Bible. Almost anyone who has been exposed to Christian thought is aware that "God so loved the world that he gave his only Son" (3:16), and millions of Christians refer to themselves as "born again" on the basis of John 3:3. Banners bearing reference to one of these two texts are perennial fixtures at sporting events around the world. Unfortunately, this sense of familiarity distracts from the very complex textures of this episode. The interpretation offered here will loosely follow F. P. Cottrell's article "The Nicodemus Conversation," which applies the tools of discourse analysis to John 3:1–15. Cottrell's article concisely introduces several issues which have dominated discussion of this passage. Before proceeding, it will be helpful to summarize these issues, supplementing Cottrell's remarks as necessary to map out the contours of previous research.
     Cottrell begins his discussion of John 3 by establishing the role of Nicodemus in the larger narrative. It is almost universally accepted that Nicodemus is a representative character, and many would agree with Cottrell's view that Nicodemus speaks for those at John 2:23–25 to whom Jesus did not entrust himself because their faith was based on "signs."[1] Others would narrow the field somewhat to make Nicodemus a spokesman only for the leaders of "official Judaism," the "doctors of the Law" with whom he is associated at 3:1.[2] In either case, the conversation between Jesus and Nicodemus is typical

---

[1]F. P. Cottrell, "The Nicodemus Conversation," *ExpT* 96 (1985) 237–238. See also G. R. Beasley–Murray, "John 3:3, 5. Baptism, Spirit and the Kingdom," *ExpT* 97 (1986) 16; J. Bryan Born, who states that FE does this to "cast doubt on the character [Nicodemus] he is about to introduce" ("Literary Features in the Gospel of John [An Analysis of John 3:1–21]," *Directions* 17 [1988] 7).

[2]Rudolf Schnackenburg, *The Gospel According to St. John* (trans. Kevin Smith; HTKNT; New York, NY: Herder and Herder New York, 1968) 1.364; Raymond Brown, *The Gospel According to John* (AB; New York, NY: Doubleday, 1966) 1.135; Barnabas Lindars, *The Gospel of John* (NCBC; Grand Rapids, MI: Eerdmans, 1972) 144.

of how Jesus would respond to an entire group of people whose belief is inadequate. Why, then, does the Johannine Jesus, who is elsewhere generally impatient with those who do not believe in him, attempt to initiate Nicodemus into the deeper mysteries of his identity? Cottrell believes that Nicodemus' three appearances in FG (3:1–12; 7:45–52; 19:38–41) are a subplot representing the faith pilgrimage of the larger group he represents.[3] Jesus apparently accepts such people as candidates for discipleship, and is therefore willing to engage Nicodemus in discussion.

Cottrell's further analysis is guided by the premise that John 3 can be analyzed in terms of the "presuppositions lying behind all discourse." These presuppositions include "the principle of co–operation (that all participants [in the discussion] will genuinely attempt to further the discourse)" by minimizing ambiguity; "the principle of comprehensibility, the expectation that all words and word strings will be employed in the conventional manner"; and "contextual appropriateness," the principle that participants in the discussion will follow the socio–linguistic conventions relevant to the context of the discourse.[4] In applying these principles, Cottrell makes the important assumption that the Nicodemus dialogue can be analyzed under the conventions of "normal language." This approach runs against the grain of recent literary–critical studies, which see 3:1–10 as a classic case of Johannine irony and therefore presume that Nicodemus is not intended to comprehend Jesus' words on any level.[5] While such studies have forcefully highlighted the rhetorical effect of irony on the reader of FG, they generally do not explore the

---

[3]Cottrell, "Nicodemus" 238; Brown, AB 129; Schnackenburg, HTKNT 1.365; Lindars, NCBC 133, 149. Culpepper agrees that the Nicodemus story is a representative subplot but concludes that Nicodemus "remains outside" the kingdom of God at the end (*Anatomy* 134–136).

[4]Cottrell, "Nicodemus" 237.

[5]See R. Alan Culpepper, *Anatomy of the Fourth Gospel: A Study of Literary Design* (Philadeplphia, PA: Fortress, 1983) 152–155; Born, "Literary Features" 8–10; Norman Petersen, *The Gospel of John and the Sociology of Light: Language and Characterization in the Fourth Gospel* (Valley Forge, PA: Trinity Press, 1993) 41–47; Paul D. Duke, *Irony in the Fourth Gospel* (Atlanta, GA: John Knox, 1985) 45–46, 108; Gail R. O'Day, *Revelation in the Fourth Gospel: Narrative Mode and Theological Claim* (Philadelphia, PA: Fortress, 1986) 46–47, 61–62.

internal logic of the discussion within the context of the story world of John 3. This internal logic indicates that Nicodemus could have come to some legitimate, though inaccurate, conclusions about the meaning of Jesus' words.

Proceeding under this premise, Cottrell considers the significance of the note that Nicodemus came to Jesus "by night" (John 3:2). Some see this as an expression of Johannine dualism, where "light" and "dark" are symbols for the realm of God and the world.[6] A similar note at 13:30 indicates that Judas left the Supper to betray Jesus "at night." The rhetorical effect of such symbolism would, however, operate outside the story world and therefore cannot be seen as a conscious motive for the character Nicodemus. Recognizing this, others argue that Nicodemus has come under cover of darkness due to the dangers of associating with Jesus. FE's Jewish audience could certainly sympathize, for in their own world association with Jesus can result in expulsion from the synagogue (9:22; 16:2).[7] But it is by no means clear that association with Jesus would be dangerous for Nicodemus at this point in the narrative. Although FE has introduced conflict between Jesus and some Jews in the Temple Incident, it seems that those opposed to Jesus are still in the minority (2:23). In fact, Nicodemus presents himself as the spokesman for a larger group of Jews who presumably share his curiosity about Jesus (hence the plurals at 3:2).

A third, and more likely, explanation of Nicodemus' motive for coming after dark is offered by Cottrell, Schnackenburg, and Brown. These scholars suggest that John 3:1ff is patterned after first–century rabbinic debates, which were typically conducted at night.[8] Nicodemus indicates that this is true reason he has come by night when he addresses Jesus as a wonder–working "rabbi."[9] This social setting would offer specific procedural guidelines for the content and flow of the dialogue, and the irony in John 3 is generated by Jesus'

---

[6]Lindars, NCBC 149; Culpepper, *Anatomy* 135, 192; Born, "Literary Features" 7; D. A. Carson, *The Gospel According to John* (Grand Rapids, MA: Eerdmans, 1991) 186.

[7]This possibility is mentioned in most studies but seldom sanctioned; for an apparent exception see John Painter, *The Quest for the Messiah: The History, Literature and Theology of the Johannine Community* (2nd ed.; Nashville, TN: Abingdon, 1993) 197.

[8]Cottrell, "Nicodemus" 238; Brown, AB 1.130.

[9]The rabbinic literature verifies a later belief that God performed miracles to sanction the teachings of great sages (Schnackenburg, HTKNT 1.366; Brown, AB p. 1.137).

systematic violation of these guidelines.[10] Jesus outdoes Nicodemus through the use of riddles which *could* be meaningful in the context of a nocturnal rabbinic debate, but which are *ultimately* comprehensible only in terms of FE's special knowledge about Jesus.

Jesus opens the debate by informing Nicodemus that he "cannot see the kingdom of God" unless he is "born ἄνωθεν" (John 3:3; KJV/NASB/NIV "born again"). Because ἄνωθεν can mean "again," "from the beginning," or "from above," the term is potentially ambiguous, especially since Jesus has not yet established a context which would center its value. The intended effect of this ambiguity will be discussed below, but for now it should be noted that "Nicodemus could intelligently have furthered the dialogue." Against the backdrop of broad Jewish notions of a higher world and eschatological hopes of a divine kingdom, he "could have understood that Jesus was speaking of an event [rebirth] brought about by God's grace."[11] From this perspective, Nicodemus' response at 3:4 ("how can a man be born when he is old?"), which highlights the paradoxical absurdity of Jesus' statement, can be interpreted in several ways, not necessarily exclusive of one another. Nicodemus may be genuinely confused and unable to determine any referent for Jesus' remark. Or perhaps he is embarrassed by his inability to counter Jesus' opening repartee and is attempting to buy time by moving the argument in a different direction. In the context of an academic discussion, he may wish to test Jesus' competence as a sage by challenging him to untwist a hyperliteral interpretation of his own words. In any case, it is important to note that, at this point in the dialogue, Nicodemus *could* understand Jesus' words to mean *something* within the broader context of Jewish beliefs and the specific setting of a rabbinic debate. Jesus' language, then, is directed both to FE's audience in the real world and to Nicodemus in the story world, and is potentially meaningful in both contexts.

The same may be said of Jesus' next statement that only those "born of water and πνεῦμα" (John 3:5; KJV "Spirit") can enter the kingdom. Many scholars have taken a sacramental approach to this saying, insisting that "every

---

[10]Cottrell, "Nicodemus" 239.

[11]Cottrell, "Nicodemus" 240, first quotation here; Schnackenburg, HTKNT 1.368, second quotation here; Brown, AB 1.139; Beasley–Murray, "John 3:3, 5" 167–168.

Christian hearer or reader of the [Fourth] Gospel must have thought at once of [Christian] baptism."[12] Whether or not this is the case, such considerations explicitly move beyond the interaction between Jesus and Nicodemus. What could the terms "water and spirit" mean to a Jew in the story world of FG? Cottrell suggests that "water" does refer to some sort of baptism but not Christian baptism. Nicodemus could see Jesus' words as a reference to proselyte baptism or, more likely in the context of FG, to John the Baptist's baptism or Jesus' own baptizing activity (3:26).[13] "Born of spirit" might also carry specifically Christian connotations to FE's audience, but this term, too, should have been comprehensible to a "teacher of Israel." Nicodemus could see in this concept a reference to familiar prophetic passages which describe an outpouring of God's spirit in the last days. Thus, while he might not pick up the Johannine nuances of Jesus' language, "at least Jesus' words should have meant for him [Nicodemus] that the eschatological outpouring was at hand."[14]

Other aspects of John 3:1–10 suggest that Jesus intended to lead Nicodemus to a reasonable, though inaccurate, interpretation of his words. Several of these aspects are noted by Schnackenburg. "Do not be amazed," the introduction to the wind proverb at 3:7, was a familiar appeal in Jewish and Hellenistic rhetoric that evidence not be discounted. The "evidence" in question here, the wind proverb, adopts a metaphor "already at use in Judaism to depict the incomprehensibility of God's providence." Jesus' final retort to Nicodemus at 3:10 ("You are the teacher of Israel . . .?") is appropriate in a rabbinic debate as a criticism of Nicodemus' inability to identify the Scriptural texts and themes to which Jesus alludes. In light of these considerations, Cottrell concludes that Nicodemus' reactions to Jesus in the story betray a

---

[12]Schnackenburg, HTKNT 1.369; Brown, AB 1.141; Lindars, NCBC 152; Beasley–Murray, "John 3:3, 5" 168; Rudolf Bultmann, *The Gospel of John: A Commentary* (trans. G. R. Beasley–Murray, R. W. N. Hoare, and J. K. Riches; Philadelphia, PA: Fortress, 1971) 138 n. 3. Carson concludes that there is no reference to baptism of any sort in the passage (*John* 191–196); see also Klyne Snodgrass, "That Which is Born from *Pneuma* is *Pneuma*: Rebirth and Spirit in John 3:5–6," *Covenant Quarterly* 49 (1991) 17.

[13]Cottrell, "Nicodemus" 240–241.

[14]Brown, AB 140–141, quotation here. See also Cottrell, "Nicodemus" 241; Schnackenburg, HTKNT 1.370–371.

"woodenly uncooperative" posture rather than complete inability to understand.[15]

It may be said, then, that Nicodemus could have gathered some meaning from Jesus' words even without the special knowledge offered in the Prologue. The irony in the episode develops from the fact that Jesus' language is comprehensible at more than one level, and that Nicodemus does not have access to the level at which it becomes truly meaningful to FE. The first indication of this appears at John 3:6 in the differentiation between "flesh" and "spirit." Within the context of Johannine dualism these terms represent cosmological polarities, "two different orders of being."[16] They also represent two registers of discourse. These two registers are identified at 3:12, where Jesus indicates that he can speak of "earthly" things (ἐπίγειος) and "heavenly" things (ἐπουράνιος). Through the use of riddles, he speaks of both heavenly and earthly things at the same time.

The first riddle (John 3:3) turns on the dual meaning of the phrase "γεννηθῇ ἄνωθεν," "born again" (KJV). Nicodemus, whether genuinely confused or simply trying to defuse Jesus' argument (neither of which are acceptable responses in FG), takes the phrase in the "earthly" sense. Within the earthly language system which Nicodemus uses, γεννηθῇ ἄνωθεν is impossible for a person who is γέρων, a grown man, because "old" and "newborn" are logical opposites (3:4). Within the "heavenly" language system of Jesus, however, an "old" person can be "born again" because a) ἄνωθεν means "from above" rather than "again" (cp. 3:31, 19:11); and, b) irrespective of the meaning of ἄνωθεν, γεννάω does not refer to physical birth. From the ἐπουράνιος perspective there is no contradiction in Jesus' words, which simply indicate that those who wish to enter the kingdom of Jesus must become like Jesus, the one who came down "from above."

Unfortunately for Nicodemus, Jesus does not directly indicate that his words are more than ἐπίγειος, the language of rabbinic discussion. But before the Pharisee can come to this conclusion on his own, Jesus further obfuscates matters with a "clarification" of the saying. Since Nicodemus has chosen to focus on the "birth" problem rather than ἄνωθεν, Jesus restates his

---

[15]Schnackenburg, HTKNT 1.370–371; Cottrell, "Nicodemus" 240.
[16]Schnackenburg, HTKNT 1.371.

riddle with terms which are, in the ἐπουράνιος language system, apparently synonymous with ἄνωθεν. Now Nicodemus must be "born of water and spirit" to enter the kingdom. While "water" may remind FE's audience of Christian baptism, Nicodemus cannot detect reference to *any* form of baptism here. Such is the case because Jesus' repetition of γεννάω at John 3:5 implies that the discussion will remain in the realm of "earthly" language. "Born of water" would appear to be a crude reference to normal human birth, apparently in contrast to a "spiritual" experience. This contrast actually offers a clue that Jesus is operating in a different register of language, but before Nicodemus can take advantage of this clue Jesus pushes him further off the track by expounding on πνεῦμα, a term which is particularly ripe for the type of ambiguity employed in Jesus' riddles.

From Nicodemus' "earthly" perspective, πνεῦμα can refer either to a physical element, "wind," or to a non–physical element, "spirit." The contrast of πνεῦμα with ὕδωρ ("water") at John 3:5 and σάρξ ("flesh") at 3:6, and the repetition of "born ἄνωθεν" at 3:7, would direct Nicodemus toward the spiritual meaning: water and flesh are physical elements, spirit is not because it is "from above." But Jesus, in apparent contradiction to this implication, follows these clues with a proverb (3:8) in which πνεῦμα clearly refers to physical wind by association with the verb πνέω, "blow." Within the "earthly" language register, Jesus appears to be saying, "The wind blows where it wills and you hear its voice but do not know where it comes from or where it goes" (3:8). The clarity of this proverb, however, would only make the riddle more confusing for Nicodemus, and would also suggest to him that 3:8c should mean, "so it is with everyone born of the wind." Unable to unlock the riddles as "earthly" language, Nicodemus can only suggest that Jesus' challenge cannot be met: "How can these things be?" (3:9).

Having demonstrated his superiority as a sage (John 3:10), Jesus explains why Nicodemus could not answer the riddles. The shift to the plural at 3:11 indicates that such puzzles are comprehensible only to "we" who "know" and "have seen" who Jesus really is, whereas "you" (Nicodemus and the group he represents) "do not know" what Jesus is talking about because "you" "have not seen" the truth. What "we know" is summarized at vv. 12–15: since the Son of Man has come down from heaven and is going back to heaven (3:13), he speaks both the ἐπίγειος language of this world and the ἐπουράνιος language of that world. From Nicodemus' perspective, γεννάω means physical birth, ἄνωθεν indicates repetition, and πνεῦμα is an element of nature. But each of these terms has an alternate meaning in Johannine antilanguage, where γεννάω is spiritual transformation (cp. 1:12–13), ἄνωθεν means "from above" (a synonym for "like Jesus"), and πνεῦμα is a Comforter whom God sends to help Jesus' disciples (7:39).

Term	Normal Lanaguage: ἐπίγειος reference system	Johannine Lexicon: ἐπουράνιος reference system
γεννάω	physical birth	spiritual transformation
ἄνωθεν	again/a second time	from above/from heaven
πνεῦμα	wind	Spirit/the Paraclete

It is the fact that such terms are meaningful within both registers of discourse that generates Nicodemus' confusion.[17] For this reason, John 3:3 and 3:5 are classic expressions of the "riddle" genre, and form the basis of the irony in this episode.

JOHN 11:25–26—*"The one who believes in me will live even if he dies, and anyone who lives and believes in me will not die unto eternity"*

John 11:25–26 is the third riddle in the Lazarus story. The first two riddles, 11:11 and 11:23, both function to heighten the mystery of Jesus' intentions in Bethany and have already been discussed as dramatic riddles. This final riddle explores the problem of Jesus' identity by expanding his claim, "I Am the Resurrection and the Life" (11:25a). Both the I Am saying and the riddle appear in an exchange between Jesus and Martha. A brief survey of the source–critical treatment of this passage will provide a backdrop for the present analysis of 11:25–26.

---

[17]Richards' compromise that ἄνωθεν can be read as "born again from above" fails to recognize this distinction in language registers; in FE's view, "born again" is the wrong answer. ("Expressions of Double Meaning and Their Function in the Gospel of John," *NTS* 31 [1985] 102–103).

Bultmann's discussion of John 11 set the parameters for recent source–critical analysis of the Lazarus story. Bultmann detects four layers of composition in this passage. The first layer is "an old narrative," possibly an oral tradition, in which Jesus brings a dead person back to life. This narrative was absorbed into the written Signs Source which underlies many of the Johannine narratives. In the Signs Source version, Jesus hears of Lazarus' illness and goes to "wake him up" with the reluctant disciples. Upon arriving in Bethany they discover that Lazarus has already died. Jesus goes to the tomb, orders it opened, and calls Lazarus forth.[18] FE then expanded and elaborated the Signs Source version. Sayings from the *Offenbarungsreden* were incorporated at John 11:9–10 and 11:25–27 to highlight the Christological significance of the episode, along with several of FE's own editorial notes. At the fourth and final stage of development, an ecclesiastical redactor added 11:2, creating the present text of FG.[19]

Bultmann interprets the exchange between Martha and Jesus (John 11:21–27) in light of this source–critical model. FE used this discussion to illustrate ideal faith in Jesus the Revealer. Martha's opening remark at 11:21–22 ("If you had been here my brother would not have died, but even now I know that whatever you ask of God he will give you") indicates not only her faith in Jesus as a healer but "is [also] an indirect request to raise her brother." This faith in Jesus' power over life and death leads her to confess him as "the Christ, the Son of God" (11:27). In Bultmann's view, this confession illustrates "the genuine attitude of faith" which recognizes in Jesus's presence "the eschatological invasion of God into the world." Why, then, does Martha object when Jesus asks that the stone be removed from

---

[18]Bultmann, *John* 395 n. 4. Bultmann does not attempt to reconstruct the story. The paraphrase above is inferred from his view that the Signs Source included John 11:1, 3, 5–6, 11–12, 14–15, 17–19, 33–39, 43–44.

[19]Bultmann, *John* 395 n. 4, 402 n. 3. In the *Offenbarungsreden*, the discussion between Jesus and Martha, which includes the riddle under consideration here, was connected to the speech which formed the basis of John 5:19–47. Bultmann notes that this differs from FE's normal practice of following miracles from the Signs Source with discourses which explain their revelatory significance. FE's "editorial notes" include 11:13 and the phrase "the one who believes in me" at 11:25 The ecclesiastical redactor's hand is evident from the term κύριος at 11:2.

Lazarus' tomb (11:39)? Bultmann sees this as a remnant from the Signs Source, which FE has retained to sustain Jesus' anger and dismay over the Jews' disbelief.[20] In Bultmann's view, FE has introduced 11:21–27 into an older miracle story in order to present Martha as a model of true faith in Jesus as the giver of life.

A similar approach is taken by Robert Fortna in *FGIP*. Fortna admits that "separation of source and redaction in [John] chapter 11 is more difficult than in any of the other miracle stories" in FG.[21] Nevertheless, he proceeds to isolate several stages in the story's compositional history. The earliest layer was "a highly derived form of the parable . . . of the Rich Man and Lazarus (Luke 16:19–31)." This story was developed and incorporated into the Signs Gospel, where it was the first in a series of three Judean miracles. Consistent with the interests of that document, in SG the Lazarus story demonstrated Jesus' messianic identity. Like Bultmann, Fortna believes the SG version of the story was much simpler than that in the present text of FG. After hearing of Lazarus' illness Jesus journeys to Bethany, where he learns that his friend has been dead for four days. Mary greets him and says Lazarus would have lived if Jesus had arrived sooner. After the resurrection of Lazarus, the SG story ended with the statement, "those who saw what he did believed in him [i.e., believed he was the Christ]." FE turned this simple miracle story into the "climactic theological development" of FG, moving it to the end of Jesus' public ministry and expanding the narrative with speech materials which made the event a preview of Jesus' own death and glorification.[22]

Fortna sees John 11:21–27, the passage which includes the riddle under consideration here, as "a self–contained theological dialogue" and the "chief means" by which FE adapted the Lazarus story to his own purposes.[23] In SG, only Mary spoke briefly with Jesus. FE seems to have learned from a broader tradition that Mary had a sister, Martha, and made her the leading lady in the new version of the story. Martha's initial statement (John 11:21–22) expresses

---

[20]Bultmann, *John*, 401–407, first quotation 401, second quotation 404.

[21]Robert Fortna, *The Fourth Gospel and Its Predecessor: From Narrative Source to Present Gospel* (Philadelphia, PA: Fortress, 1988) 104.

[22]Fortna, *FGIP* 93–98, quotation 96.

[23]Fortna, *FGIP* 105, 99.

confidence in Jesus' healing power and insinuates that he should use that power to raise her brother from the dead. Jesus affirms this "expectant trust" by assuring her that Lazarus will rise again, but Martha "takes Jesus' promise literally as a reference to the general resurrection at the end of the age."[24] Jesus then reveals himself as "the Resurrection and the Life" with a Johannine "I Am" saying. Martha responds to this revelation by confessing Jesus as "the Christ, the Son of God who comes into the world" (11:27). This confession, "so singularly christological," would seem to be a remnant from SG, but Fortna takes it as FE's indication that "Martha's initial faith in Jesus' signs has matured into both an understanding of his saving work on earth and a commitment to it."[25]

Delbert Burkett's 1994 article "Two Accounts of Lazarus' Resurrection" is perhaps the most detailed source–critical reading of John 11 to date. Burkett's careful analysis of the many aporias in the Lazarus story leads him to conclude that the present text "resulted not from the redaction of a single source [contra Fortna] but from the combination of two distinct accounts."[26] One of these accounts, "Account B," was originally part of Fortna's Signs Gospel.[27] The SG version may be distinguished from the other account,

---

[24]Fortna, *FGIP* 101. Fortna suggests that every reference to Martha in John 11 may originate with FE and that the dialogue between Martha and Jesus seems to have been created as a doublet to the exchange between Jesus and Mary in SG (105 n. 233, 106).

[25]Fortna, *FGIP* 102. Urban von Wahlde's brief remarks on John 11 seem consistent with Fortna's presentation. von Wahlde asserts that FE's extensive additions to the source move the miracle from the level of physical life to Jesus' ability to give spiritual life. He argues that verses 21–27 were added to the source by FE on the basis that a) the current text is "awkward," with 11:21–27 simply repeating the meeting with Mary at 11:30–32; b) 11:21–27 are clearly motivated by FE's desire to apply the themes of resurrection and life to eschatology and Christology; c) Martha's confession that Jesus is "the Son of God who comes into the world" is clearly a Johannine perspective (*The Earliest Version of John's Gospel: Recovering the Gospel of Signs* [Wilmington, DE: Michael Glazier, 1989] 118–121).

[26]Delbert Burkett, "Two Accounts of Lazarus' Resurrection in John 11," *NovT* 36 (1994) 210.

[27]Burkett, "Two Accounts" 228–229. SG provided verses 5–6a, 7b–10, 16–17a, 19, 20b–22, 28–29, 31, 33b, 35–37, 41b–44; verse 11a is FE's composition, and v. 17 is FE's fusion of parallel materials from the two accounts (226).

"Account A," on the basis of "recurrent motifs." "Account A," for example, focused on the divine determination of Jesus' actions as revelations of God's glory, while "Account B" (SG) highlighted Jesus' love for Lazarus and the Jews' witness of the miracle. In this connection, in "Account B" (SG) Jesus returned to Judea solely out of concern for Lazarus, whereas in "Account A" he intentionally delayed his return until Lazarus died so that he could reveal his glory by raising him.[28] Going beyond Fortna, Burkett believes FE created the present text in FG through a cut and paste process, omitting some materials from each account but not altering the retained material in any significant way.[29]

The exchange between Jesus and Martha (John 11:21–27), which includes the riddle under consideration here, plays a key role in Burkett's analysis. These verses "present two inconsistent pictures of Martha's faith." Verses 21–22 suggest a "strong faith" which expects that Jesus can still help her brother. At vv. 23–27, however, Martha "exhibits weak faith," concluding that Jesus is speaking of Lazarus' resurrection only in a futuristic sense. "This hesitation ill fits with her confident assertion just two verses earlier . . . that Jesus could raise Lazarus 'even now.'" In Burkett's view, this is the sort of aporia which is significant to source–critical analysis. "We can thus conclude that the portrayal of Martha as confident in the power of Jesus . . . belongs to account B [SG], while the portrayal of Martha as weak in faith belongs to account A."[30] Burkett does not see any other way to resolve this apparent discrepancy. It is impossible to imagine that a single author could miss this glaring inconsistency, unless that person "was either senile, incompetent, or unable to finish the work."[31]

Whether or not such inconsistencies represent valid criteria for source–critical analysis cannot be discussed here. At present it is sufficient to note that the tensions which Fortna and Burkett see in John 11:21–27 do not

---

[28]Burkett, "Two Accounts" 215, 217–218, 225.

[29]Burkett, "Two Accounts" 226–227.

[30]Burkett, "Two Accounts," first quotation 219, second quotation 219–220, third quotation 220. Burkett believes Account A was generally more favorable to Mary, whereas SG was more favorable to Martha (225).

[31]Burkett, "Two Sources" 230. Burkett fails to mention that, if his conclusions are correct, the same judgement must be passed on the editor of the present text of FG.

necessarily exist. This is particularly the case when one recognizes that this passage contains two riddles and that Martha cannot answer either of them. It is by no means certain that Martha's statement, "even now I know that whatever you ask from God will give you" (11:22), "indicates confident assertion . . . that Jesus could raise Lazarus 'even now.'"[32] Nothing in the story up to this point would lead Martha to expect, or even hope for, Lazarus' resurrection. Jesus' earlier riddle about "waking Lazarus up" (11:11) was not uttered in Martha's presence and was incomprehensible to the disciples. Her first words to Jesus only absolve him of blame for arriving too late. John 11:21–22 might be paraphrased, "Lord, if you had been here my brother would not have died, but I still trust that your power comes from God." This response is not substantially different from that of the grieving Jews, who testify that Jesus could have healed Lazarus had he arrived in time (11:37). Martha does not even realize that Jesus intends to heal Lazarus when he states directly, "Your brother will rise again" (11:23). She seems to think that Jesus is offering her pastoral consolation that Lazarus is at peace with the Lord: "I know that he will rise again in the resurrection on the last day" (11:24). For this reason, she concludes that Jesus wishes to view the tomb so that he can mourn over his lost friend, and is appalled at his suggestion that the stone be removed (11:39).

Jesus complicates matters for Martha with the second riddle in this sequence, "The one who believes in me will live even if they die, and anyone who lives and believes in me will not die unto eternity" (John 11:25–26). This saying is a riddle under criterion number 4: its language is incongruous, because it is impossible for a person to experience death and life at the same time in any normal language system. It is also nonsense to say that someone οὐ μὴ ἀποθάνῃ εἰς τὸν αἰῶνα ("will not die unto eternity"), as the Jews have pointed out at 8:52. At least one of the terms in the riddle, "live" or "die," must be ambiguous, and Jesus complicates matters by switching the ambiguous term in the two parts of the riddle. In the first part, "live" is figurative while "dies" refers to physical death: any person who dies physically will continue to live spiritually if they believe in Jesus. In the second clause, however, "lives" is physical life and "dies" refers to a lost relationship with God: any

---

[32]Burkett, "Two Accounts" 219–220.

person who believes in Jesus while physically alive will never experience spiritual death.

The ambiguity in both sections of the riddle hinges on the peculiar Johannine meaning of "life" (ζωή). In the context of a wake and in proximity to the term ἀνάστασις ("resurrection"), ζωή would seem to refer to physical life. This implication is supported by Jesus' apparent endorsement of the Pharisaic view of physical resurrection (John 5:25, 29). The question, "Do you believe this?" which follows the riddle (11:26c) is actually a challenge to Martha to explain what "life" means in Jesus' vocabulary. At first glance, Martha's response seems to be the correct answer. Her confession, "You are the Christ, the Son of God who comes into the world" (11:27) includes several key terms in Johannine Christology. But Martha's answer is only accidentally correct, for she is using this Johannine language in a nonJohannine sense. First, although she affirms her respect for Jesus' power, she carefully avoids the challenge Jesus has presented and does not comment on the word "life." Second, whatever the terms "Christ" and "Son of God" mean to FE, it is plain throughout this episode that Martha thinks of Jesus primarily as a healer. She identifies him as such at the beginning of the discussion, and later asks him not to open Lazarus' tomb because it is beyond his power to heal a dead man. Martha's confidence in Jesus' power is sincere, but she does not understand his identity and subsequently cannot explain what "life" and "death" mean in Jesus' vocabulary.

The interaction between this riddle and its context is particularly complex, pushing Jesus' convoluted chain of reference almost to the breaking point. The "I Am" statement (John 11:25a) which precedes the riddle is a clue to the answer: to "have life" means to believe in Jesus and to enjoy the soteriological benefits of that belief, a condition which is unaffected by physical death. It is therefore not entirely wrong for Martha to associate ζωή with the experience Lazarus will have on "the last day." As the story continues, however, Jesus proceeds to grant Lazarus *physical* life *now*, which would direct Martha back towards the more conventional meanings of ἀνάστασις and ζωή. By itself, the riddle focuses on the mystery of spiritual life and death; in the present context FE makes it refer also to literal, physical resurrection. The entire Lazarus episode illustrates Jesus' claim to be "resurrection and life," and the riddle extends the implication of the physical miracle into the spiritual realm.

CONSUMPTION RIDDLES

Four of FG's salvation riddles describe the believer's experience of God in terms of eating and drinking. These riddles appear at John 4:7, 6:32, 6:51, and 7:37–38.

JOHN 4:7, 10—*"Give me a drink"*

Jesus' encounter with the Woman at the Well is a classic case of Johannine irony. The entire conversation at John 4:7–15 clearly operates on two levels of discourse. Jesus speaks words which are meaningful in an ἐπουράνιος or "heavenly" sense, while the Woman consistently interprets them in an ἐπίγειος or "earthly" sense. The resultant dialogue is almost comical, highlighting the subtlety of Jesus' language and the necessity of knowing his identity before one can understand him.

Jesus opens the exchange with a short riddle, "Give me a drink" (δός μοι πεῖν; John 4:7). Nothing in this context would lead the Woman to suspect that Jesus is using ambiguous language. FE carefully notes at 4:6 that Jesus is sitting by a well at midday, and follows the riddle by revealing that Jesus is alone because the disciples have gone to buy food (4:8). In this setting, Jesus' words seem to mean that he can quench his thirst only with the aid of the Samaritan Woman. His apparently simple request depends, however, on a special understanding of two of its three terms. First, one must know that the "me" (μοι) who asks for a drink is, in fact, the "Christ" (4:26, 29). Second, one must know that "drinking" does not mean putting liquid into one's mouth but refers instead to a special experience of "me." The correct answer to the riddle, in light of this special vocabulary, is offered at 4:10. Those who know Jesus and the "gift of God" will answer his request by demanding that he give them "living water," which John will identify as the Spirit at 7:39. If the Woman realized this, "she would recognize that she herself was the thirsty one."[33]

---

[33]O'Day, *Revelation* 58–60, quotation 60.

The two responses that the Woman offers to the riddle (John 4:9, 11–12) indicate that she knows neither "the gift of God" nor "who it is who asks" her for a drink. Indeed, she seems to be unaware that Jesus has asked a question. Her initial retort, "How is it that you, being a Jew, ask to drink from me (παρ' ἐμοῦ πεῖν αἰτεῖς), being a Samaritan?" is doubly ironic. First, Jesus is certainly not a "Jew" in the sense that FE uses that term; the Jews are, in fact, his constant opponents in FG. Second, as 4:32 and 7:37–39 indicate, Jesus does not take water from anyone; rather, others come to him and drink. The generous clues offered with the restatement of the riddle at 4:10 do little to alleviate the Woman's misconception. Her new response challenges Jesus' ability to give the "gift" of living water. Since he has no bucket, Jesus' offer would apparently require a miracle similar to "our father Jacob's" ability to supply himself, his family, and his cattle from one well (4:12).[34] Assuming that Jesus is not in the category of Jacob, she demands to know "from where do you have the living water?" (4:11). FE's audience will soon discover that Jesus stores the living water in his κοιλία and therefore needs no bucket to obtain it (7:37–39).

Jesus, however, is not ready to give the answer to his riddle just yet, and instead offers another clue which points the Woman beyond literal drinking water. The three qualities of "living water" which he identifies—that it quenches forever, becomes a spring in the consumer, and gives eternal life (John 4:14)—suggest that the referent for his words is not in the same category as Jacob's well.[35] At the same time, however, Jesus further complicates the issue by comparing his living water to "this water," the water in the well (4:13). This comparison allows the Woman to conclude that Jesus is speaking of literal drinking water with remarkable medicinal qualities, perhaps from a flowing spring or stream. Jesus' clues thus push the Woman both toward and away from the correct answer to the riddle. This mixture of legitimate clues and false leads explains the Woman's final remark at 4:15: "Lord, give me this [living] water so that I would not thirst nor ever come to draw [from this well] again." The depth of this statement's irony is remarkable. As O'Day notes, even FE would have to admit that the first part of 4:15 is "an appropriate

[34]O'Day, *Revelation* 62.
[35]O'Day, *Revelation* 63; Schnackenburg, HTKNT 1.430.

response to Jesus' words."[36] In light of 4:10, the statement "give me this water so that I would not thirst" is the correct answer to the riddle "give me a drink." The Johannine Christian who heard this narrative might suspect that it would end as a conversion story, were it not for the last part of the Woman's statement. The hope that drinking Jesus' living water" will lessen her chore of "coming to draw water" shows that her ironically insightful answer is anchored in the mundane, ἐπίγειος register of those who cannot understand Jesus.

JOHN 6:32; 6:51—"*Moses did not give you the bread from heaven, rather, my father gave you the true bread from heaven*"; "*The bread I will give for the life of the world is my flesh*"

These two statements form the backbone of the "Bread of Life" discourse, a complete riddling session (John 6:22–58). This discourse is prompted by, and draws its themes from, the miraculous feeding described at 6:1–15. Foiled in their attempt to make Jesus king, the crowd locates him on the other side of the lake the following day (6:22–25). Jesus' remarks are uncomplimentary and ambiguous, indicating at that the outset that he intends to speak to the Jews in his special, ἐπουράνιος dialect.

Jesus opens the discussion by challenging the Jews' motive. They seek him not because they "saw signs" (σημεῖα) but because they "ate from the bread" (ἐφάγετε ἐκ τῶν ἄρτων) (John 6:26). The difference between "seeing signs" and "eating bread" is not readily apparent, since Jesus' miraculous provision of bread led the crowd to conclude that he was "the Prophet" (6:15).[37] Instead of clarifying this point, Jesus urges the Jews to stop working (ἐργάζεσθε μὴ) for perishable food (τὴν βρῶσιν τὴν ἀπολλυμένην) and work instead for the "food which remains to eternal life" (τὴν βρῶσιν τὴν μένουσαν εἰς ζωὴν αἰώνιον) which the Son of Man "will give" (δώσει) (6:27). This statement would appear to be self–contradictory at any level: if the Jews must "work" for the imperishable food, how can it be a gift "given" by the Son of Man (6:27)? The exact nature of this "food" is also ambiguous. In proximity to the feeding miracle and by contrast with the

[36]O'Day, *Revelation* 64.
[37]Brown, AB 1.263–264. Brown offers a concise introduction to the relationship between "signs" and "faith" in FG in Appendix 3 of the same volume (AB 1.525–532).

"food that perishes" (6:26–27), the Jews could only assume that "food which remains to eternal life" refers to some sort of bread which will not grow stale or moldy. Faced with these uncertainties, the crowd determines that Jesus is warning them about spiritual sloth and invites him to explain how they can "work the works of God" (6:28).

Since the Jews have chosen to focus on the "work" idea, Jesus leaves the true nature of the "food" he has in mind hidden. The only "work" they need to do is to believe "the One Whom God Sent" (John 6:29). The Jews do not directly challenge Jesus' claim to this status but instead demand a sign for verification, shifting to what work *he* can do to prove his qualifications (τί ἐργάζῃ; 6:30–31). Their willingness to continue the dialogue, however, is a product of their misunderstanding of the term "sent" (ἀποστέλλω). Up to this point in the chapter the Jews have recognized Jesus as "Prophet" and "Rabbi" (6:15, 25). Since "Son of Man" is a higher Christological title than these in FG, the Jews' request for another miracle is reasonable: Jesus has proven himself to be "Prophet" with the miraculous feeding, but more evidence is required before they accept him as the Son of Man "sent" by God. Even if they did accept this claim, however, it would only mean to them that Jesus is an emissary of God, perhaps quantitatively, but not qualitatively, different from a prophet.[38] But the Johannine Jesus has not been "sent" by God in the same way that other prophets or messianic figures might be, and it is this point which he seeks to establish as the dialogue unfolds.

Even before the first riddle is offered at John 6:32, then, Jesus has introduced language which is intentionally ambiguous. This ambiguity occurs not only at the level of vocabulary but also at a deeper ideological level. The Jews' remarks in this episode reveal an ideological taxonomy with includes three distinct categories: God (6:28); emissaries sent by God; gifts of God, which are mediated through these emissaries but which one can obtain by work (6:27).[39]

---

[38]Maarten J. J. Menken, "Some Remarks on the Course of the Dialogue: John 6, 25–34," *Bijdragen* 48 (1987) 145. See also Painter, *Quest* 270–273.

[39]The term "emissary" is borrowed from Painter (see *Quest* 271–276), but its use here does not indicate acceptance of his developmental reading.

Category 1: God [*sui generis*]	Category 2: Emissaries [sent by God]	Category 3: Gifts [earned by work]
	Prophet (6:15)	bread (ἄρτος)
	King (6:15)	food (βρῶσις)
	Rabbi (6:25)	manna
	Moses (6:31)	
	Son of Man	
	Jesus	

Jesus has already made a minor adjustment to this taxonomy by pointing out that anything in Category 3 (the gifts of God) which is truly worth having cannot be obtained by "work" but must instead received as a gift (John 6:27). His further remarks highlight a more serious flaw in the Jews' thinking. Throughout chapter 6, the Jews have assumed that Jesus belongs in Category 2 as a divine emissary. Jesus, however, collapses the entire matrix by participating simultaneously in all three categories at once, a possibility the Jews are not equipped to understand. Jesus explores their need for a new paradigm by offering the Jews riddles, clues, and answers which challenge not only their view of Jesus but their entire ideological paradigm.

Jesus' first riddle at John 6:32 openly challenges the Jews' categories but remains within the bounds of orthodoxy: "Moses did not give you the bread from heaven, rather, my father gave you the true bread from heaven." From the Jews' perspective this would only highlight the fact that God, not the human emissaries in Category 2, is the true source of any gift. Jesus' audience could not be very surprised by this statement. They would also see 6:33 as a further elaboration of this point: even the bread which Moses gave—the manna that sustained the "life" of God's people in the wilderness—"came down from heaven," indicating that God was its true source. This would represent, again, only a minor adjustment to the Jews' way of thinking, quite consistent with typical rabbinic exhortations.

Jesus' apparently innocent observations, however, are undergirded by a radically different taxonomy, which manifests itself in the surface text of the riddle as the distinction between the "bread from heaven" given through Moses and the "*true* bread from heaven" (τὸν ἄρτον ἐκ τοῦ οὐρανοῦ τὸν ἀληθινον). While the Jews' conceptual categories would lead them to see this as a contrast between Moses the emissary and God the source, Jesus is actually suggesting a qualitative difference between the type of gift given by a person in Moses' category, the type that "perishes" (John 6:27), and the type of gift given by God himself. From this perspective, the gift which God gives is qualitatively better because it "gives life (ζωή) to the world" (6:33). Unbeknownst to the Jews, Jesus is not only the emissary of this gift but also the gift itself which "came down from heaven."

Concluding that Jesus is speaking of a new and better gift, a "bread" which gives life, the Jews ask Jesus the emissary to give them this bread forever (John 6:34). Their request parallels the response of the Samaritan woman at 4:15 in several important ways. First, it shows that the Jews, like the Woman, have not been able to move from the normal meaning of the terms "food" and "bread" to a language system in which these terms refer to an experience of Jesus. Second, like the Woman, this inability leads them to conclude that Jesus is speaking about something in the category of literal "food" which would possess extraordinary qualities. Water from a well water is nice, but it would be even better to have "living water" so that fetching water would no longer be necessary. Manna and the bread Jesus gave by the sea are good, but it would be even better to enjoy a lifetime supply of life–giving bread. In both cases, Jesus' words are taken to indicate only a differentiation of quantity (more water/food) within a conceptual category, whereas Jesus intends to mark a qualitative difference between conceptual categories (living water vs. well water; true bread vs. manna). Not realizing this and remaining within the ἐπίγειος mindset, the Jews can only repeat their earlier request, "Lord, give us this bread forever." The wording of this request offers a final parallel to the Samaritan Woman. As at 4:15, the Jews actually verbalize the correct response to Jesus' riddle at 6:32. From FE's perspective, when Jesus offers "true bread from heaven" one should respond by accepting the offer. Like the Woman at the Well, the Jews ironically say the right words but with the wrong meaning.

Jesus continues the riddling session by directly revealing the answer to his first riddle. The "true bread from heaven" is not the manna given by Moses nor anything in the gift category. Jesus himself is both emissary and "bread of life" (John 6:35). He then restates the benefits of coming to him and believing in terms of the consumption motif: those who accept his gift will never hunger nor, as he promised the Samaritan woman, thirst again (6:35). Unaware that the consumption motif refers to a mystical experience of Jesus, the Jews cannot understand Jesus' riddle even after he has revealed the answer. Their second response at 6:41 (How can this man say, "I am the bread which came down from heaven"?) highlights two points of ambiguity in Jesus' words. The first point of ambiguity concerns the claim that Jesus "came down from heaven" when he is clearly the son of Joseph (6:42), while the second concerns the claim that Jesus can give himself as food (6:52). These two problems form an outline for the rest of the Bread Discourse. Verses 42–51 explore the possibility that Jesus "came down from heaven." Jesus' further elaboration of this point ignores the problem of his origins and instead reiterates that he is the "bread of life" (6:47–50). The second claim is explored through a second riddle offered at 6:51, "The bread I will give for the life of the world is my flesh," and Jesus' answer at 6:53–58.

The debate over whether John 6:51–58 is an allegorical discussion of the Eucharist, symbolized by Jesus' emphasis on eating his flesh and drinking his blood, has generated an enormous literature which cannot be surveyed here.[40]

---

[40]For a convenient summary of the parameters of the Eucharist debate, see Maarten J. J. Menken, "John 6,51c–58: Eucharist or Christology?" *Biblica* 74 (1993) 1–6. While the issue cannot be argued in detail here, it suffices to note that John 6:51–58 does not bear a sufficient number of literary or theological aporias to justify source separation. On the stylistic aporias, Menken has demonstrated that there are no clear discrepancies between John 6:51–58 and the rest of chapter 6 ("Eucharist or Christology?" 9–24). On the theological aporias, the evidence points to the conclusion that John 6:51–58 is *not* an allusion to the Eucharist. The passage is better understood as an extension of the christological claims raised in the previous section. If this is the case, "flesh and blood" are simply intensified references to Jesus' person. John 6:26–58 refers to Jesus as the one who "came from heaven" eight times (vv. 32, 33, 38, 41, 42, 50, 51, 58), focusing on his incarnation. The connection between the bread metaphor and the human Jesus is highlighted by the three I Am sayings at 6:35, 48, 51, all of which suggest that Jesus can feed his people. At 6:35 Jesus reveals himself to be the "bread of life" (ὁ ἄρτος τῆς ζωῆς), apparently an attributive genitive reaffirming the claim at 6:33 that the bread of God "gives life." FE adjusts this claim at 6:51 to introduce the discussion of Jesus' identity: "I am the living bread" (ἐγώ εἰμι ὁ ἄρτος ὁ ζῶν). The riddle which immediately follows equates this "bread" with

One aspect of this debate, however, is important to the present study. Many scholars who take the view that this section refers to the Eucharist also assert that these verses did not appear in the original FG. Bultmann, for example, concludes that 6:51–58 was added by "an ecclesiastical editor" who wished to ground the Christian sacraments in the life of Jesus.[41] Brown agrees that a redactor added these verses but believes they represent materials from the Johannine repertoire which FE chose not to utilize when writing FG.[42] Painter believes that 6:51–58 were added to FG in a subsequent revision by FE himself.[43] The present study will support Schnackenburg's suggestion that the links between 6:51–58 and the preceding discourse are "easier to account for if the whole section is the work of one author."[44]

The Jews' confusion over Jesus' riddle at John 6:51 is not generated by the terms "bread," "flesh," or "blood," but by Jesus' ambiguous use of "eat"

Jesus' "flesh," apparently a more graphic term for his incarnate self. As a final consideration, it is relevant to note that FE never explicitly mentions the Eucharist, baptism, or any other Christian sacrament (except possibly footwashing) despite the very intrusive posture of FG's narrator. The attempt to identify sacraments in FG seems to arise more from a desire to discover a uniform Jesus tradition than from analysis of the text itself. It is therefore best to read 6:51–58 in continuity with the preceding discussion as a more graphic illustration of the need to believe in Jesus as the bread of life. Any Eucharistic overtones are secondary to the main thrust of the passage.

[41]Bultmann, *John* 218–220, 234. According to Bultmann, this same editor is responsible for the veiled references to Christian baptism in John 3 (138 n. 3, 220).

[42]Brown, AB 1.xxxiv–xxxviii. Brown summarizes this stage of FG's composition by stating that after FE's death "a disciple made a final redaction of the Gospel, incorporating other material that the evangelist had preached and taught, and even some of the material of the evangelist's co–workers" (1.xxxix).

[43]According to Painter, the first edition of the story, 6:1–35, was created during the period of "dialogue between the Johannine Christians and those Jews who . . . were open to the appeal of Jesus." FE's failure to convert such Jews led to increasing conflict between himself and the synagogue, and verses 36–59 were added to the story to reflect this conflict. At this stage FE demanded not only that the Jews accept Jesus as emissary, but also that they believe "in the saving efficacy of his death." This revised Christology alienated a number of FE's Christian–Jewish constituency, creating a schism. John 6:60–66 were added to the story at this stage (Painter, *Quest* 267–282). It must be stressed that Painter believes the passage refers primarily to faith in Jesus.

[44]Schnackenburg, HTKNT 2.56–59, 65, quotation 65.

and "drink." As noted earlier, in Johannine language Jesus' claim to be/give food and water actually refers to a mystical experience. The Jews, having eaten their fill of physical bread the previous day, interpret Jesus' words from the ἐπίγειος perspective as some form of cannibalism. The ambiguity is heightened by Jesus' comparison of eating the bread of life with the fathers' consumption of manna (6:49–50). The term δίδωμι ("the bread *I will give* is my flesh) is also used in a special way here. The Jews associate Jesus' "giving" of his flesh with physical "eating" and conclude that "giving" refers to the preparation of a grotesque meal. Their reply highlights this association: "How is this man able *to give* us his flesh *to eat*?" (6:52). In Jesus' vocabulary, however, "giving flesh" is not synonymous with preparing a meal, but describes instead his "coming down from heaven." FE has already described Jesus' advent as God's "giving" of the son at 3:16. As Menken suggests, this "giving" may also allude to Jesus' impending death on behalf of the world.[45] The answer to the riddle at 6:51c ("The bread I will give for the life of the world is my flesh") would be that Jesus comes into the world to give life to those who believe in him.

The soteriological implications of this riddle are explored at John 6:53–58. Those who "eat and drink" Jesus "have life," and will be "resurrected on the last day." To sustain the ambiguity of his claims even while expounding the answer to the riddle, Jesus refers again to the bread eaten by the fathers in the wilderness. "This is the bread which came down from heaven, not like [the bread] the fathers ate and died. The one who eats this bread will live forever" (6:58). While the Jews would again focus on the analogy between Jesus' flesh and the manna, FE is concerned to distinguish two types of "eating." The type of eating the Jews have in mind, the consumption of bread into the body, cannot prevent death. The type of eating FE has in mind, belief in and union with Jesus, leads to life.

The Jews' final response is an attempt to end the riddling session, parallel to the remarks of Nicodemus at John 3:9 and the Samaritan Woman at 4:25. Unable to answer Jesus' riddles or even to comprehend his answers, the Jews suggest that Jesus is a poor riddler: "This is a hard saying. Who is able

---

[45]Menken, "Eucharist or Christology?" 10–11. See also Carson, *John* 296–298; Painter, *Quest* 280–281.

to hear him?" (6:60). FE, however, has a different view of the situation. The problem is not that Jesus tells bad riddles, but rather that "some of you do not believe" (6:64). Jesus' words are in fact "spirit and life," but they can be comprehended only by those whom God has "given" to Jesus (6:63, 65). Since many of Jesus' riddles relate to his identity, those who do not believe cannot possibly understand him.

JOHN 7:37–38— *"Should anyone thirst, let her come to me, and let the one who believes in me drink"*

Jesus delivers this riddle on the last day of the Feast of Tabernacles, a week filled with controversy over his identity (John 7:10–36). He closes the debates with a simple invitation to "come and drink" (7:37–38). This invitation is notoriously difficult to translate. If the phrase ὁ πιστεύν εἰς ἐμέ ("the one who believes in me") at 7:38a belongs with verse 37, Jesus seems to be speaking in chiasm: "(A) should anyone thirst/(B) let them come to me//(-B) and let the one who believes in me/(-A) drink." According to this translation, the "Scripture" Jesus cites at v. 38 demonstrates that *he* is the source of "living water." On the other hand, it may be that FE sees ὁ πιστεύν εἰς ἐμέ as the subject of v. 38. According to this translation, those who believe in Jesus may "come to me and drink," which will secure the Scriptural promise of a "river of water" springing up within the believer. In this case, *the believer* becomes a source of water through contact with Jesus. There is no easy answer to this problem, for the grammar of the verses allows for either translation and the theological implications of both are supported elsewhere in FG.[46] While 7:37–38 would be a riddle in either case, the means by which ambiguity is generated in this saying supports the view that Jesus refers to himself as the source of living water at v. 38. This preference is reflected in the translation of the riddle offered above.

FE indicates that the saying is a riddle by directly revealing that Jesus' remarks on "living water" actually refer to the Spirit, something the characters in the story could not suspect because the Spirit has not yet been given (John

---

[46]That Jesus is the source of the Spirit is plain from John 14:26, 16:7–15, and 20:22 (and 19:34?), while at 4:13–14 Jesus uses language similar to 7:38 to promise the Samaritan woman that whoever drinks the water he gives will have a spring welling up within them.

7:39). Even if the Spirit had been given at this point, however, it is doubtful that the Jews would identify this as the true subject of Jesus' ambiguous remarks. The Feast of Tabernacles included a daily procession from the pool of Siloam with a libation of water which was poured on the altar. The water ritual on the "last, great day of the feast" (7:37) was particularly solemn, involving a large number of Temple personnel and crowds of worshipers. FE may envision Jesus making his proclamation during this ritual.[47] This discourse context would lead Jesus' audience to assume that his words refer to an eternal supply of literal water (cf. John 4:15). It is possible, however, that some Jews would detect a deeper symbolism. Water was a popular metaphor in Jewish thought, variously representing Wisdom, cleansing, the Torah, healing, God's Spirit, God himself as a source of life, and "the final state of salvation."[48] Many OT texts promise abundance of water in the eschatological age, and the water libation at Tabernacles may have been associated with such expectation. In light of the preceding debate over whether Jesus is "the Christ" (7:25–27, 31), some members of Jesus' audience might interpret his riddle to mean that this eschatological age is about to dawn through him.[49] That some do come to this conclusion is evident in the renewal of the argument over Jesus's identity at 7:40–41. The Feast of Tabernacles and OT prophecies about abundance of water would therefore offer the Jews two obvious answers to Jesus' riddle, literal water and the dawn of the last days, neither of which is correct.

The Jews' ignorance of the connection between the Spirit's advent and Jesus' death is not, however, the only reason they cannot answer his riddle. The water libation and the potential symbolic value of water would suggest to the Jews that Jesus is playing on the meaning of the term "water" in the "Scripture" he cites at John 7:38: "from his belly there will flow rivers of living water." This suspicion would be confirmed by the references to "thirsting" and "drinking" in the riddle itself. But this "citation" is actually a

---

[47]Schnackenburg, HTKNT 2.152; Bultmann, *John* 305; Carson, *John* 321–322.

[48]Dale Allison, "The Living Water," *St. Vladimir's Theological Quarterly* 30 (1986) 144–145. See also Schnackenburg, HTKNT 2.154–155; Brown, AB 1.320–321.

[49]Allison, "Living Water" 146–147; Bultmann, *John* 305.

distraction. Aside from the fact that no such "Scripture" exists,[50] the riddle is not about "water" at all, but about "drinking" (πίνω) from Jesus: "should anyone *thirst*, let them come to me; and let the one who believes in me *drink*." The Jews are challenged to answer the question, What does it mean to "drink from Jesus"? FE refers his own audience to Jesus' dictionary for the answer, where "water" refers to "the Spirit" and "drinking from Jesus" means "receiving" (λαμβάνω) the Spirit (7:39). The same special vocabulary is key to the "born again" riddle at 3:3, 5. There Jesus explicitly associates "water and spirit" with the process of Christian "birth." Confusion over the nature of this "birth from above" (γεννηθῇ ἄνωθεν) leads Nicodemus to ask whether a grown man can "enter into the womb (κοιλία) of his mother a second time." At John 7:38, *Jesus'* "womb" (κοιλία) is the source from which the living water proceeds. FE has thus shifted from the motif of "rebirth" to the motif of drinking/consuming Jesus to describe the process of Christian transformation. The key element in both motifs is πνεῦμα. Christian rebirth is ἐξ πνεύματος (3:5), and the water which flows forth from Jesus to quench the believer is the Spirit given after Jesus' glorification (7:39). Combining the motifs, Johannine believers come forth from the Spirit and also absorb Jesus into themselves through consumption of the Spirit which he gives. There is, then, much more to "drinking" (7:37) than meets the eye.

Any interpretation of FG's consumption riddles is complicated by the fact that metaphors of this sort are unfamiliar to most modern readers. While contemporary Christian discourse has popularized the Johannine symbols "life" and "born again," the image of drinking water from Jesus' belly seems almost grotesque. Such metaphors were, however, widely distributed in the ancient church, and would be familiar to the original audience of FG. An obvious parallel appears in the words of Jesus at the institution of the Eucharist. The earliest account of this event, 1 Cor. 11:23–26, uses πίνω to describe the consumption of the wine, which Jesus refers to as the new covenant "in my blood." Paul proceeds to shame the Corinthians on the basis of the consumption motif, warning them to consider how they behave toward the Lord's "body" (σῶμα). Like Paul, Matthew locates Jesus' teaching

[50]Numerous speculations have been offered about the texts FE has in mind; see Schnackenburg, HTKNT 2.155–156; Brown, AB 1.321–323; Carson, *John* 325–327.

concerning his "body and blood" on the last night of his life, and includes his graphic command to eat (φάγω) his body and drink (πίνω) his blood (Matt. 26:26–28).

Paul and Matthew limit "eating and drinking Jesus" to the Eucharist, a sacrament which is not mentioned explicitly in the Johannine literature. Outside the NT, however, the consumption motifs in the Gospel of Thomas closely parallel the Johannine concept. FE's association of drinking from Jesus, receiving the Spirit, and experiencing rebirth follows the logic that "you are what you eat." Ingesting Jesus and the Spirit makes one "spiritual" by nature, "born from above" or "born of God" (John 1:12–13, 3:3). The notion that one takes on the characteristics of a thing by consuming it may also be found in the Gospel of Thomas. At Gos. Thom. 108 Jesus says, "Whoever drinks from my mouth will become like me; I myself shall become that person, and the hidden things will be revealed to him."[51] Here as in John 7, drinking from Jesus unites one with him and makes one "like him." In an ethical vein, Gos. Thom. 7 offers the beatitude, "Lucky is the lion that the human will eat, so that the lion becomes human. And foul is the human that the lion will eat, and the lion still will become human." Here, consumption transfers the nature of one thing (human) to something else (lion). If Funk is correct that the lion symbolizes human passions here, this saying warns against the dangers of being consumed by one's passions and thereby losing one's humanity.[52] The reverse image of fasting appears at Gos. Thom. 27:1, "If you do not fast from the world, you will not find the [Father's] domain." Since Thomas understands "the world" to represent material wealth and power (see 81:2; 85:1), "fasting" suggests abstinence from worldliness. The presumed opposite of this would be "eating the world," filling oneself with worldliness and thus jeopardizing one's spiritual estate.

It is clear, then, that FE's suggestion that one can achieve union with Jesus by eating or drinking from him touches on a broad motif in early Jesus traditions. Presumably, the original audience of FG would have no difficult resolving the ambiguity in the riddles which utilize these metaphors.

---

[51]Robert J. Miller, ed., *The Complete Gospels* (Sonoma, CA: Polebridge, 1994).

[52]Robert Funk, Roy Hoover and the Jesus Seminar, *The Five Gospels: The Search for the Authentic Words of Jesus* (New York, NY: MacMillan, 1993) 477.

SALVATION RIDDLES IN THE FAREWELL

The last two salvation riddles in FG appear in the Farewell discourse (John 13–17), as Jesus gradually reveals his identity to the disciples and describes the special relationship they enjoy with him.

JOHN 14:19—*"A little while and the world will no longer see me, but you will see me"; "A little while and you will no longer see me, and again a little while and you will see me"*

The last two salvation riddles in FG appear in the Farewell, an extended riddling session (see discussion in Chapter 5). Jesus has been playing on the disciples' ignorance of his "father" and their misconceptions about his impending departure. The disciples seem to think that Jesus plans to withdraw from public life for a short while by retreating to his father's home in Galilee. In the midst of this discussion, Jesus informs them that he will send a helper to assist them while he is away. If the disciples do not clearly understand who this paraclete might be, they need not worry in any case because Jesus himself will soon come to them again (John 14:18).[53]

The riddle at 14:19 suggests Jesus will return with a new philosophy of ministry, focusing his attention exclusively on the disciples. Since Jesus' entire career to this point has been a public affair, the disciples do not understand this change in policy. Judas' (not Iscariot) inability to answer the riddle reflects their confusion about this issue: "Lord, what then has happened that you are going to disclose yourself to us, and not to the world?" (14:22; NASV). Jesus' answer suggests that he is tired of the Jews and wants to focus his energies on those who love him, for only those who love him keep his word. As an added bonus, when Jesus returns from hiding he will bring his father with him to give the true disciples further instruction (14:23–24). In the meanwhile, the unnamed helper (paraclete) will give them peace and keep them mindful of Jesus' teaching (14:25–28). Of course, the audience of FG knows that the relationship between Jesus and this Paraclete is much closer

---

[53]The designation of the Paraclete as the "spirit of truth" (John 14:17) would not necessarily indicate that Jesus' father is God, for in Johannine vocabulary "spirit" can refer to human teachers (see 1 John 4:1–6).

than the disciples realize (7:39), and also understands that Jesus' "departure" is more than a friendly visit to his family (13:1–3).

JOHN 16:16—*"A little while and you will no longer see me, and again a little while and you will see me"*
The last riddle in the Farewell, John 16:16, follows a long discussion of the disciples' fate after Jesus' departure (15:18–16:15). Any hope of the continued intimacy suggested by 14:31c and the Vine parable is put to rest by a new riddle which resumes the theme of 13:33 and 14:19: "A little while and you will no longer see me, and again a little while and you will see me" (16:16). It now appears that the disciples will not remain with Jesus after all. He will indeed abandon them for a time, but will soon return to them. Having no better luck with Jesus' riddles than the Jews, the disciples no longer attempt to answer: "we do not know what he is saying" (16:18). Jesus ignores their protest and, without explaining why they will be separated from him, promises that their grief will be turned to joy when they see him again (16:19–22).

At this point, perhaps because the disciples have admitted defeat, Jesus suddenly brings the riddling session to a close and promises to elevate them to a level of special knowledge. "These things I have spoken to you in riddles (ταῦτα ἐν παροιμίαις λελάληκα ὑμῖν), but an hour is coming when I will no longer speak to you in riddles (οὐκέτι ἐν παροιμίαις λαλήσω ὑμῖν), but rather in plain speech (παρρησίᾳ) I will tell you about the father" (John 16:25). The terms παροιμία and παρρησία represent opposing language registers in FG. "Παροιμία" refers to Jesus' riddling discourse, ambiguous language which hides its true meaning (10:6). "Παρρησία" is used in specific contrast to this ambiguous language on two occasions in the Book of Signs. After Jesus' long exposition of the παροιμία of the Shepherd (10:1–6), the Jews demand, "If you are the Christ, tell us *plainly* (εἰπὲ ἡμῖν παρρησίᾳ; 10:24)." In chapter 11, after the disciples are unable to answer the riddle "Lazarus is asleep" (11:11), FE indicates that "Jesus [then] said to them *plainly*, 'Lazarus is dead'" (11:14). To act or speak παρρησίᾳ in FG is to openly reveal one's meaning and intention.[54] Jesus' use of this term at 16:25

---

[54]The term carries the same implication at 1 John 3:21 and 4:17, where John indicates that true believers may be confident on the day of judgement because they have nothing to

indicates that he is finally prepared to speak clearly to the disciples about his identity. Like the Jews, the disciples would have no hope of obtaining this information on their own. They are privileged to receive it because of their love for Jesus and their faith (16:26–27).

The substance of Jesus "plain" revelation appears at John 16:28: "I left the father and came into the world; again I am leaving the world and going to the father." For the audience of FG this is a digest of the Prologue and appears to be yet another riddle, for Jesus still has not directly identified himself as God. But the hint that Jesus "came into the world" and is "leaving the world" is a sufficient clue for the disciples that Jesus' father is not a human being. John 16:28 is a turning point in both the Farewell and the larger narrative of FG, for the disciples' sudden knowledge of the hermeneutical key to Jesus' riddles moves them from the story world to FE's world. In their own words, Jesus has finally spoken to them "plainly" (παρρησίᾳ), the way he speaks to FG's audience, "and you speak riddles to us no longer" (καὶ παροιμίαν οὐδεμίαν λέγεις; 16:29). By 16:30 they have come to a basic understanding of the mystery of Jesus' person: πιστεύομεν ὅτι ἀπὸ θεοῦ ἐξῆλθες ("we believe that you have come from God").[55] Belief in this revelation obviously distinguishes the disciples, those who know that Jesus has come from God, from the "Jews," who cannot understand Jesus' riddles because they do not recognize his identity.

The boundary created by John 16:30 between Jew and disciple extends beyond the story world. The audience of FG differs from the Jews in that they

---

hide from God and may therefore speak plainly. When παρρησία is used of actions rather than words in FG it characterizes these actions as "public." At John 7:4 Jesus' brothers chastise him for not going to the feast, saying that "no one acts in secret who seeks to be known publicly" (ζητεῖ αὐτὸς ἐν παρρησίᾳ εἶναι). Later in the same episode, after describing the popular debates over Jesus' identity, FE indicates that no–one would speak "openly" (παρρησίᾳ) about Jesus for fear of arrest. During his trial before Annas, Jesus insists that his teaching was always παρρησίᾳ, delivered "in the synagogue and in the Temple, where all the Jews come together" (18:20).

[55] As Jesus indicates, their understanding is still not entirely sufficient because Jesus' hour has not been fulfilled (John 16:31–33). John 16:29–30 thus indicates the disciples' preliminary move toward a faith which can be fully realized only after Jesus' ascension (see also John 2:17, 22; 7:39).

possess the hermeneutical key to all of Jesus' riddles, his descent and ascent. Like the disciples, this audience also receives this key at the end of a faith drama, a struggle to accept Jesus as the revelation of God. His words are therefore always παρρησία ("plain") to FG's audience, a later community that recognizes Jesus as the Son of the Prologue. Those not possessing this hermeneutical key, unbelievers, remain locked in the Book of Signs, forever unable to understand Jesus' self–revelatory riddles and damned by their ignorance (1:10–12).

As a social device, knowledge of the correct answers to Jesus' riddles separates FG's audience from the vanquished riddlees within the story and places them in a privileged position. Groups often use riddles in this way to distinguish members by what they "know," even when the acquisition of such knowledge relies on group membership rather than individual skill or intelligence. The various riddlees of FG are confused because they seek to comprehend Jesus' words through conventional channels of logic. The logic of Jesus' discourse, however, is a special group logic. The correct referents depend on group knowledge about Jesus' identity; the whole affair remains a mystery to "the Jews."

Bibliography

Johannine Studies

Allison, Dale. "The Living Water." *St. Vladimir's Theological Quarterly* 30 (1986) 143–157.

Bacon, Benjamin Wisner. *The Fourth Gospel in Research and Debate.* New York, NY: Moffat and Yard, 1910.

Barrett, C. K. *The Gospel According to St. John.* 2nd ed. Philadelphia, PA: Westminster, 1978.

———. "John and the Synoptic Gospels." *ExpT* 85 (1973–1974) 228–233.

Beasley–Murray, G. R. *John.* WBC 36. Waco, TX: Word Books, 1987.

———. "John 3:3, 5: Baptism, Spirit and the Kingdom." *ExpT* 97 (1986) 167–170.

Boismard, M. E. "Un procédé rédactionnel dans le quartrième évangile: la Wiederaufnahme." *L'Èvangile de Jean: Sources, Rédaction, Théologie.* Ed. Marinus de Jonge. BETL 44. Leuven: Leuven University Press, 1977.

Borgen, Peder. "John and the Synoptics: Can Paul Offer Help?" *Tradition and Interpretation in the New Testament: Essays in Honor of E. Earle Ellis for His 60th Birthday.* Ed. Gerald F. Hawthorne and Otto Betz. Grand Rapids, MI: Eerdmans, 1987.

———. "John and the Synoptics: A Reply [to Frans Neirynck]." *The Interrelations of the Gospels.* Ed. David L. Dungan. BETL 95. Leuven: Leuven University Press, 1990.

Born, J. Bryan. "Literary Features in the Gospel of John (An Analysis of John 3:1–21)." *Direction* 17 (Fall 1988) 3–17.

Brodie, Thomas L. *The Quest for the Origin of John's Gospel: A Source–Oriented Approach.* New York, NY: Oxford University Press, 1993.

Brown, Raymond. *The Community of the Beloved Disciple: The Life, Loves, and Hates of an Individual Church in New Testament Times.* New York, NY: Paulist Press, 1979.

———. *The Gospel According to John.* AB. New York, NY: Doubleday, 1966.

Bultmann, Rudolf. *The Gospel of John: A Commentary.* Trans. G. R. Beasley–Murray, R. W. N. Hoare, and J. K. Riches. Philadelphia, PA: Fortress, 1971.

———. *Jesus and the Word.* Trans. Louise Pettibone Smith and Erminie Huntress Lantero. New York, NY: Charles Scribner's Sons, 1958.

Burkett, Delbert. "Two Accounts of Lazarus' Resurrection in John 11." NovT 36 (1994) 209–232.

Carson, D. A. "Current Source Criticism of the Fourth Gospel: Some Methodological Questions." *JBL* 97 (1978) 411–429.

———. *The Gospel According to John.* Grand Rapids, MA: Eerdmans, 1991.

Coppens, J. "Les logia johanniques du fils de l'homme." *L'Évangile de Jean: Sources, Rédaction, Théologie.* Ed. Marinus de Jonge. BETL 44. Leuven: Leuven University Press, 1977.

Cottrell, F. P. "The Nicodemus Conversation." *ExpT* 96 (1985) 237–242.

Cullmann, Oscar. *The Johannine Circle.* Trans. John Bowden. Philadelphia, PA: Westminster, 1975.

Culpepper, R. Alan. *Anatomy of the Fourth Gospel: A Study in Literary Design.* Philadelphia, PA: Fortress, 1983.

Dodd, C. H. *Historical Tradition in the Fourth Gospel.* Cambridge: Cambridge University Press, 1963.

———. *The Interpretation of the Fourth Gospel.* Cambridge: Cambridge University Press, 1968.

———. "The Portrait of Jesus in John and in the Synoptics." *Christian History and Interpretation.* Ed. W. R. Farmer, C. F. D. Moule, and R. R. Niebuhr. Cambridge: Cambridge University Press, 1967.

Duke, Paul D. *Irony in the Fourth Gospel.* Atlanta, GA: John Knox, 1985.

Dunn, James D. G. "John and the Oral Gospel Tradition." *Jesus and the Oral Gospel Tradition.* Ed. Henry Wansbrough. JSNTSup 64. Sheffield: JSOT, 1991.

Fortna, Robert T. "Christology in the Fourth Gospel: Redaction–Critical Perspectives." *NTS* 21 (1974–1975) 489–504.

———. *The Fourth Gospel and Its Predecessor: From Narrative Source to Present Gospel.* Philadelphia, PA: Fortress, 1988.

———. *The Gospel of Signs: A Reconstruction of the Narrative Source Underlying the Fourth Gospel.* SNTSMS 11. Cambridge: Cambridge University Press, 1970.

———. "Source and Redaction in the Fourth Gospel's Portrayal of Jesus' Signs." *JBL* 89 (1970) 151–166.

Freed, Edwin D., and R. B. Hunt. "Fortna's Signs–Source in John." *JBL* 94 (1975) 563–579.

Funk, Robert W., Roy W. Hoover, and the Jesus Seminar. *The Five Gospels: The Search for the Authentic Words of Jesus.* New York, NY: Polebridge, 1993.

Gardner–Smith, P. *St. John and the Synoptic Gospels.* Cambridge: Cambridge University Press, 1938.

Jesus Seminar. "Voting Record: The Passion Narratives." *Forum* n. s. 1 (1998) 227–233.

Koester, Helmut. *Ancient Christian Gospels: Their History and Development.* Philadelphia, PA: Trinity Press, 1990.

Kümmel, Werner Georg. *Introduction to the New Testament*. Trans. Howard Clark Kee. Nashville, TN: Abingdon, 1975.

Kysar, Robert. *The Fourth Evangelist and His Gospel: An Examination of Contemporary Scholarship*. Minneapolis, MN: Augsburg, 1975.

Lindars, Barnabas. *Behind the Fourth Gospel*. London: SPCK, 1971.

———. *The Gospel of John*. NCBC. Grand Rapids, MI: Eerdmans, 1972.

———. "Traditions Behind the Fourth Gospel." *L'Évangile de Jean: Sources, Rédaction, Théologie*. Ed. Marinus de Jonge. BETL 44. Leuven: Leuven University Press, 1977.

Martyn, J. Louis. *The Gospel of John in Christian History: Essays for Interpreters*. New York, NY: Paulist Press, 1978.

———. *History and Theology in the Fourth Gospel*. 2nd ed. Nashville, TN: Abingdon, 1979.

Menken, Maarten J. J. "John 6,51c–58: Eucharist or Christology?" *Biblica* 74 (1993) 1–26.

———. "Some Remarks on the Course of the Dialogue: John 6,25–34." *Bijdragen* 48 (1987) 139–149.

Miller, Robert J., ed. *The Complete Gospels*. Sonoma, CA: Polebridge, 1994.

Moloney, Francis J. *The Johannine Son of Man*. Biblioteca Di Scienze Religiose 14. Rome: Libreria Ateneo Salesiano, 1976.

———. "Reading John 2:13–22: The Purification of the Temple." *RB* 97 (1990) 432–452.

Neirynck, Frans. "L'Epanalepsis et la critique littéraire. À propos de l'Évangile de Jean." *ETL* 56 (1980) 303–338.

———. "John and the Synoptics." *L'Évangile de Jean: Sources, Rédaction, Théologie*. Ed. Marinus de Jonge. BETL 44. Leuven: Leuven University Press, 1977.

———. "John and the Synoptics: 1975–1990." *John and the Synoptics*. Ed. Adelbert Denaux. BETL 101. Leuven: Leuven University Press, 1992.

———. "John and the Synoptics: The Empty Tomb Stories." *NTS* 30 (1984) 161–187.

———. "John and the Synoptics: Response to Peder Borgen." *The Interrelations of the Gospels*. Ed. David L. Dungan. BETL 95. Leuven: Leuven University Press, 1990.

Neyrey, Jerome. "'I Said: You are Gods': Psalm 82:6 and John 10." *JBL* 108 (1989) 647–663.

Nichol, W. *The Sēmeia in the Fourth Gospel: Tradition and Redaction*. NovTSup 32. Leiden: Brill, 1972.

O'Day, Gail R. *Revelation in the Fourth Gospel: Narrative Mode and Theological Claim*. Philadelphia, PA: Fortress, 1986.

Painter, John. *The Quest for the Messiah: The History, Literature and Theology of the Johannine Community*. 2nd ed. Nashville, TN: Abingdon, 1993.

Perrin, Norman, and Dennis C. Duling. *The New Testament, An Introduction: Proclamation and Parenesis, Myth and History*. 2nd ed. New York, NY: Harcourt, Brace, Jovanovich, 1982.

Petersen, Norman R. *The Gospel of John and the Sociology of Light: Language and Characterization in the Fourth Gospel.* Valley Forge, PA: Trinity Press, 1993.

Richard, E. "Expressions of Double Meaning and Their Function in the Gospel of John." *NTS* 31 (1985) 96–112.

Robinson, John A. T. "The New Look on the Fourth Gospel." 1959. Rpt. in *Twelve New Testament Studies.* London: SCM, 1962.

———. "The Parable of John 10:1–5." *ZNW* 46 (1955) 233–240.

———. *The Priority of John.* Ed. J. F. Coakley. Oak Park, IL: Meyer–Stone, 1985.

Ruckstuhl, E. *Die literarische Einheit des Johannesevangeliums, der gegenwärtige Stand der einschlägigen Erforschung.* Studia Friburgensia new ser. 3. Freiburg: Paulus–Verlag, 1958.

Sabbe, Maurits. "The Arrest of Jesus in Jn 18,1–11 and Its Relation to the Synoptic Gospels: A Critical Evaluation of A. Dauer's Hypothesis." *L'Èvangile de Jean: Sources, Rédaction, Théologie.* Ed. Marinus de Jonge. BETL 44. Leuven: Leuven University Press, 1977.

Schnackenburg, Rudolf. *The Gospel According to St. John.* Trans. Kevin Smith. HTKNT. New York, NY: Herder and Herder New York, 1968.

Schweizer, Eduard. *Ego Eimi, die religionsgechichtliche Herkunft und theologische Bedeutung der johanneischen Bildreden, zugleich ein Beitrag zur Quellenfrage des vierten Evangeliums.* Ed. Rudolf Bultmann. FRLANT 56. Göttingen: Vanderhoeck and Ruprecht, 1939.

Segovia, Fernando F. "John 13 1–20: The Footwashing in the Johannine Tradition." *ZNW* 73 (1982) 31–51.

———. *Love Relationships in the Johannine Tradition: Agapē/Agapan in I John and the Fourth Gospel.* SBLDS. Chico, CA: Scholars Press, 1982.

———. *The Farewell of the Word: The Johannine Call to Abide.* Minneapolis, MN: Fortress, 1991.

———. "The Theology and Provenance of John 15:1–17." *JBL* 101 (1982) 115–128.

———. "The Tradition History of the Fourth Gospel." *Exploring the Gospel of John.* Ed. R. Alan Culpepper and C. Clifton Black. Louisville, KY: Westminster John Knox Press, 1996.

Smith, Dwight Moody. *The Composition and Order of the Fourth Gospel: Bultmann's Literary Theory.* New Haven, CT: Yale University Press, 1965.

———. "Johannine Christianity: Some Reflections on Its Character and Delineation." 1974–1975. Rpt. in *Johannine Christianity: Essays on Its Setting, Sources, and Theology.* Columbia, SC: University of South Carolina Press, 1984.

———. "John 12:12ff. and the Question of John's Use of the Synoptics." 1965. Rpt. in *Johannine Christianity: Essays on Its Setting, Sources, and Theology.* Columbia, SC: University of South Carolina Press, 1984.

————. *John Among the Gospels: The Relationship in Twentieth–Century Research.* Minneapolis, MN: Augsburg–Fortress, 1992.

————. "John and the Synoptics: Some Dimensions of the Problem." 1980. Rpt. in *Johannine Christianity: Essays on Its Setting, Sources, and Theology.* Columbia, SC: University of South Carolina Press, 1984.

————. "The Milieu of the Johannine Miracle Source: A Proposal." 1976. Rpt. in *Johannine Christianity: Essays on Its Setting, Sources, and Theology.* Columbia, SC: University of South Carolina Press, 1984.

————. "The Setting and Shape of a Johannine Narrative Source." 1976. Rpt. in *Johannine Christianity: Essays on Its Setting, Sources, and Theology.* Columbia, SC: University of South Carolina Press, 1984.

Snodgrass, Klyne. "That Which is Born from *Pneuma* is *Pneuma*: Rebirth and Spirit in John 3:5–6." *Covenant Quarterly* 49 (1991) 13–29.

Streeter, B. H. *The Four Gospels: A Study of Origins.* Rev. ed. London: MacMillan, 1964.

Temple, Sydney. *The Core of the Fourth Gospel.* London: Mowbrays, 1975.

————. "A Key to the Composition of the Fourth Gospel." *JBL* 80 (1961) 220–232.

von Wahlde, Urban C. *The Earliest Version of John's Gospel: Recovering the Gospel of Signs.* Wilmington, DE: Michael Glazier, 1989.

————. "A Redactional Technique in the Fourth Gospel." *CBQ* 38 (1973) 520–533.

————. "The Terms for Religious Authorities in the Fourth Gospel: A Key to Literary Strata?" *JBL* 98 (1979) 231–253.

————. "*Wiederaufnahme* as a Marker of Redaction in Jn 6,51–58." *Bib* 64 (1983) 542–549.

Riddles and Speech Genres

Aarne, Antti. *The Types of the Folktale: A Classification and Bibliography.* 2nd revision and translation by Stith Thompson. FFC 184. Helsinki: Suomalainen Tiedeakatemia Academia Scientiarum Fenniga, 1961.

Abrahams, Roger D. *Between the Living and the Dead: Riddles Which Tell Stories.* FFC 225. Helsinki: Suomalainen Tiedeakatemia, 1980.

————. "The Complex Relations of Simple Forms." 1969. Rpt. in *Folklore Genres.* Ed. Dan Ben–Amos. Austin, TX: University of Texas Press, 1976.

————. "Introductory Remarks to a Rhetorical Theory of Folklore." *JAF* 81 (1968) 143–158.

————, and Alan Dundes. "Riddles." *Folklore and Folklife: An Introduction.* Ed. Richard Dorson. Chicago, IL: University of Chicago Press, 1972.

Aristotle. *The Poetics.* Trans. W. Hamilton Fyfe. LCL. Cambridge, MA: Harvard University Press, 1982.

Athenaeus of Naucratis. *The Deipnosophists.* Trans. Charles Burton Gulick. LCL. Cambridge, MA: Harvard University Press, 1927.

Aune, David E. *The New Testament in Its Literary Environment.* Library of Early Christianity. Philadelphia, PA: Westminster, 1987.

Bakhtin, Mikhail Mikhailovitch. "The Problem of Speech Genres." 1952–1953. Rpt. in *Speech Genres and Other Late Essays.* Ed. Caryl Emerson and Michael Holquist. Trans. Vern W. McGee. Austin, TX: University of Texas Press, 1986.

———. "The Problem of the Text in Linguistics, Philology, and the Human Sciences: An Experiment in Philosophical Analysis." 1959–1961. Ed. V. Kozhinova. Rpt. in *Speech Genres and Other Late Essays.* Ed. Caryl Emerson and Michael Holquist. Trans. Vern W. McGee. Austin, TX: University of Texas Press, 1986.

Ben–Amos, Dan. "Solutions to Riddles." *JAF* 89 (1976) 249–254.

Bitzer, Lloyd. "The Rhetorical Situation." *Philosophy and Rhetoric* 1 (1968) 1–14.

Blomberg, Craig L. "Form Criticism." *Dictionary of Jesus and the Gospels.* Ed. Joel B. Green, Scot McKnight, and I. Howard Marshall. Downers Grove, IL: IVP, 1992.

Bryant, Mark. *Riddles Ancient and Modern.* New York, NY: Peter Bedrick Books, 1983.

Bultmann, Rudolf. *The History of the Synoptic Tradition.* Rev. ed. Trans. John Marsh. New York, NY: Harper & Row, 1963.

———. "The Study of the Synoptic Gospels." 1932. Rpt. in *Form Criticism: Two Essays on New Testament Research.* Ed. and trans. Frederick C. Grant. New York, NY: Harper and Brothers, 1962.

Burns, Thomas A. "Riddling: Occasion to Act." *JAF* 89 (1976) 139–165.

Camp, Claudia V., and Carol R. Fontaine. "The Words of the Wise and Their Riddles." *Text and Tradition: The Hebrew Bible and Folklore.* Ed. Susan Niditch. SBLSS. Atlanta, GA: Scholars Press, 1990.

Crenshaw, James L. "Impossible Questions, Sayings, and Tasks." *Semeia* 17 (1980) 19–34.

———. "Riddle." *The Interpreter's Dictionary of the Bible Supplemental Volume.* Ed. Keith Crim. Nashville, TN: Abingdon, 1976.

———. *Samson: A Secret Betrayed, A Vow Ignored.* Atlanta: John Knox, 1978.

———. "Wisdom." *Old Testament Form Criticism.* Ed. John H. Hayes. San Antonio, TX: Trinity University Press, 1974.

Dibelius, Martin. *From Tradition to Gospel.* Trans. Bertram Lee Wolf. Greenwood, SC: Attic Press, 1971.

Dundes, Alan. "The Study of Folklore in Literature and Culture: Identification and Interpretation." 1965. Rpt. in *Analytic Essays in Folklore.* Alan Dundes. The Hague: Mouton, 1975.

———. "Texture, Text, and Context." 1964. Rpt. in *Interpreting Folklore.* Alan Dundes. Bloomington, IN: Indiana University Press, 1980.

————, and E. Ojo Arewa. "Proverbs and the Ethnography of Speaking Folklore." 1964. Rpt in *Essays in Folkloristics*. Alan Dundes. New Delhi: Manohar Book Service, 1978.

————, and Robert A. Georges. "Toward a Structural Definition of the Riddle." *JAF* 76 (1963) 111–118.

Edwards, Viv, and Thomas J. Sienkewicz. *Oral Cultures Past and Present: Rappin' and Homer*. Cambridge, MA: Basil Blackwell, 1990.

Finnegan, Ruth. *Oral Poetry: Its Nature, Significance, and Social Context*. Bloomington, IN: Indiana University Press, 1992.

Foley, John Miles. *The Theory of Oral Composition: History and Methodology*. Bloomington, IN: Indiana University Press, 1988.

Friedreich, J. B. *Geschichte des Rätsels*. Dresden: Rudolf Kuntze, 1860.

Glazier, Jack, and Phyllis Gorfain Glazier. "Ambiguity and Exchange: The Double Dimension of Mbeere Riddles." *JAF* 89 (1976) 189–238.

Greenstein, Edward L. "The Riddle of Samson." *Prooftexts* 1 (1981) 237–260.

Hain, Mathilde. *Rätsel*. Stuttgart: J. B. Metzler, 1966.

Hamnet, Ian. "Ambiguity, Classification and Change: The Function of Riddles." *Man* n. s. 2 (1967) 379–392.

Hamp, V. "חידה *chîdhāh*." *Theological Dictionary of the Old Testament*, vol. 4. Ed. G. Johannes Botterweck and Helmer Ringgren. Trans. David E. Green. Grand Rapids, MI: Eerdmans, 1980.

Harris, William V. *Ancient Literacy*. Cambridge, MA: Harvard University Press, 1989.

Hart, Donn V. *Riddles in Filipino Folklore: An Anthropological Analysis*. Syracuse, NY: Syracuse University Press, 1964.

Hasan–Rock, Galit. "Riddle and Proverb: Their Relationship Exemplified by an Aramaic Proverb." *Proverbium* 24 (1974) 936–940.

Hauck, Friedrich. "Παροιμία." *Theological Dictionary of the New Testament*, vol. 5. Ed. Gerhard Friedrich. Trans. Geoffrey W. Bromiley. Grand Rapids, MI: Eerdmans, 1967.

Hellholm, David. "The Problem of Apocalyptic Genre and the Apocalypse of John." SBLSP 1982. Ed. Kent Harold Richards. Chico, CA: Scholars Press, 1982.

Hymes, Dell H. "The Ethnography of Speaking." *Anthropology and Human Behavior*. Ed. Thomas Gladwin and William C. Sturtevant. Washington, DC: The Anthropological Society of Washington, 1962.

Jacobs, Joseph. "Riddle." *The Jewish Encyclopedia*, vol. 10. Ed. Isidore Singer. New York, NY: Funk and Wagnalls, 1905.

Jakobson, Roman. "The Dominant." 1935. Trans. Herbert Eagle. Rpt. in *Language in Literature*. Ed. Krystyna Pomorska and Stephen Rudy. Cambridge, MA: The Belknap Press of Harvard University Press, 1987.

————. "Langue and Parole: Code and Message." 1942. In *On Language*. Ed. Linda R. Waugh and Monique Monville–Burston. Cambridge, MA: Harvard University Press, 1990.

————. "Linguistics and Poetics." 1958. Rpt. in *Language in Literature*. Ed. Krystyna Pomorska and Stephen Rudy. Cambridge, MA: The Belknap Press of Harvard University Press, 1987.

————. "Parts and Wholes in Language." 1960. Rpt. in *On Language*. Ed. Linda R. Waugh and Monique Monville–Burston. Cambridge, MA: Harvard University Press, 1990.

————. "Patterns in Linguistics (Contribution to Debates with Anthropologists)." 1952. Rpt. in *Selected Writings*, vol. 2. The Hague: Mouton, 1971.

————. "Two Aspects of Language and Two Types of Aphasic Disturbances." 1956. Rpt. in *Language in Literature*. Ed. Krystyna Pomorska and Stephen Rudy. Cambridge, MA: The Belknap Press of Harvard University Press, 1987.

Josephus. *Antiquities of the Jews*. Trans. H. St. J. Thackeray. LCL. Cambridge, MA: Harvard University Press, 1966.

Kallen, Jeffrey L. *Linguistics and Oral Tradition: The Structural Study of the Riddle*. Dublin: Trinity College, 1981.

Kegler, Jürgen. "Simsson—Widerstandskampfer und Volksheld." *Communio Viatorum* 28 (1985) 97–117.

Kennedy, George. *New Testament Interpretation Through Rhetorical Criticism*. Chapel Hill, NC: University of North Carolina Press, 1984.

LeRoy, Herbert. *Rätsel und Missverständnis: Ein Beitrag zur Formgeschichte des Johannesevangeliums*. BBB 30. Bonn: Peter Hanstein, 1968.

Lohr, Charles H. "Oral Techniques in the Gospel of Matthew." *CBQ* 23 (1961) 403–435.

Lord, Albert B. "The Gospels as Oral Traditional Literature." *The Relationships Among the Gospels: An Interdisciplinary Dialogue*. Ed. William O. Walker, Jr. San Antonio, TX: Trinity University Press, 1978.

————. *The Singer of Tales*. Cambridge, MA: Harvard University Press, 1960.

Maranda, Elli Köngäs. "The Logic of Riddles." *Structural Analysis of Oral Tradition*. Ed. Pierre Maranda and Elli Köngäs Maranda. Philadelphia, PA: University of Pennsylvania Press, 1971.

————. "Riddles and Riddling: An Introduction." *JAF* 89 (1976) 127–138.

————. "Theory and Practice of Riddle Analysis." *JAF* 84 (1971) 51–61.

————. "A Tree Grows: Transformations of a Riddle Metaphor." *Structural Models in Folklore and Transformational Essays*. Pierre Maranda and Elli Köngäs Maranda. The Hague: Mouton, 1971.

————, and Pierre Maranda. "Introduction." *Structural Analysis of Oral Tradition*. Ed. Pierre Maranda and Elli Köngäs Maranda. Philadelphia, PA: University of Pennsylvania Press, 1971.

Margalith, Othniel. "Samson's Riddle and Samson's Magic Locks." *VT* 36 (1986) 225–234.

McKnight, Edgar V. *What Is Form Criticism?* GBSNTS. Philadelphia, PA: Fortress, 1969.

Müller, Hans Peter. "Der Begriff Rätsel im Alten Testament." *VT* 20 (1970) 465–489.

Nel, Philip. "The Riddle of Samson." *Bib* 66 (1985) 534–545.

Ohl, Raymond Theodore, trans. and ed. *The Enigmas of Symphosius.* Philadelphia, PA: University of Pennsylvania, 1928.

Ohlert, Konrad. *Rätsel und Rätselspiele der alten Griechen.* 2nd ed. 1912. Rpt. New York, NY: Olms, 1979.

Ong, Walter J. *Orality and Literacy: The Technologizing of the Word.* New York, NY: Routledge, 1982.

Parks, Ward. "Orality and Poetics: Synchrony, Diachrony, and the Axes of Narrative Transmission." *Comparative Research on Oral Traditions: A Memoriae for Milman Parry.* Ed. John Miles Foley. Columbus, OH: Slavica, 1987.

———. "The Textualization of Orality in Literary Criticism." *Vox Intexta: Orality and Textuality in the Middle Ages.* Ed. A. N. Doane and Carol Braun Pasternack. Madison, WI: The University of Wisconsin Press, 1991.

Parry, Milman. *L'Épithète traditionnelle dans Homère: Essai sur problème de style homérique.* 1928. Rpt. in *The Making of Homeric Verse: The Collected Papers of Milman Parry.* Ed. Adam Parry. Oxford: Clarendon Press, 1971.

Pepicello, W. J. "Linguistic Strategies in Riddling." *WF* 39 (1980) 1–16.

———, and Thomas A. Green. "The Folk Riddle: A Redefinition of Terms." *WF* 38 (1979) 3–20.

———, and Thomas A. Green. *The Language of Riddles: New Perspectives.* Columbus, OH: Ohio State University Press, 1984.

———, and Thomas A. Green. "The Riddle Process." *JAF* 97 (1984) 189–203.

———, and Thomas A. Green. "Sight and Spelling Riddles." *JAF* 93 (1980) 23–34.

———, and Thomas A. Green. "Wit in Riddling: A Linguistic Perspective." *Genre* 11 (1978) 1–13.

Petersen, Norman R. *Literary Criticism for New Testament Critics.* GBSNTS. Philadelphia, PA: Fortress, 1978.

Post, Robert C. "A Theory of Genre: Romance, Realism, and Moral Reality." *American Quarterly* 33 (1981) 367–390.

de Saussure, Ferdinand. *Course in General Linguistics.* Trans. Roy Harris. La Salle, IL: Open Court, 1986.

Schmidt, Karl Ludwig. *Der Rahmen der Geschichte Jesu. Literarkritische Untersuchungen zur ältesten Jesusüberlieferung.* Berlin: Trowitzsch, 1919.

Schrecter, Solomon. "The Riddles of Solomon in Rabbinic Literature." *Folklore* 1 (1890) 349–358.

Scott, Charles T. *Persian and Arabic Riddles: A Language–Centered Approach to Genre Definition.* Bloomington, IN: Indiana University Press, 1965.

Seitel, Peter. "Proverbs: A Social Use of Metaphor." 1969. Rpt. in *The Wisdom of Many: Essays on the Proverb*. Ed. Wolfgang Mieder and Alan Dundes. New York, NY: Garland, 1981. Also rpt. in *Folklore Genres*. Ed. Dan Ben–Amos. Austin, TX: University of Texas Press, 1976.

Slotkin, Edgar. "Response to Professors Fontaine and Camp." *Text and Tradition: The Hebrew Bible and Folklore*. Ed. Susan Niditch. SBLSS. Atlanta, GA: Scholars Press, 1990.

Stern, David. *Parables in Midrash: Narrative and Exegesis in Rabbinic Literature*. Cambridge, MA: Harvard University Press, 1991.

Taylor, Archer. *A Bibliography of Riddles*. FFC 126. Helsinki: Suomalainen Tiedeakatemia Academia Scientiarum Fenniga, 1939.

———. *The Literary Riddle Before 1600*. 1948. Rpt. Westport, CT: Greenwood Press, 1976.

———. "The Riddle." *California Folklore Quarterly [WF]* 2 (1943) 129–147.

———. "Riddles in Dialogue." *Proceedings of the American Philosophical Society* 97 (1953) 61–68.

———. "The Varieties of Riddles." *Philologica: The Malone Anniversary Studies*. Ed. Thomas A. Kirby and Henry Bosley Wolf. Baltimore, MD: Johns Hopkins Press, 1949.

Thatcher, Tom. "Literacy, Textual Communities, and Josephus' *Jewish War*." *JSJ* 29 (1998) 123–142.

Thompson, John M. *The Form and Function of Proverbs in Ancient Israel*. The Hague: Mouton, 1974.

Todorov, Tzvetan. *The Fantastic: A Structuralist Approach to a Literary Genre*. Trans. Richard Howard. Ithaca, NY: Cornell University Press, 1975.

———. *Genres in Discourse*. Trans. Catherine Porter. Cambridge: Cambridge University Press, 1990.

———. *Introduction to Poetics*. Trans. Peter Brooks. Minneapolis, MN: University of Minnesota Press, 1981.

———. *Symbolism and Interpretation*. Trans. Catherine Porter. Ithaca, NY: Cornell University Press, 1982.

Torcyzner, Harry. "The Riddle in the Bible." *HUCA* 1 (1924) 125–150.

Zug, Charles G., III. "The Nonrational Riddle: The Zen Koan." *JAF* 80 (1967) 81–88.

Index of Modern Authors